Informing the People

LONGMAN SERIES IN PUBLIC COMMUNICATION
Series Editor: **RAY ELDON HIEBERT**

A Public Affairs Handbook

Informing
the
People

Edited by

Lewis M. Helm
Ray Eldon Hiebert
Michael R. Naver
Kenneth Rabin

Longman
New York & London

INFORMING THE PEOPLE
A Public Affairs Handbook

Longman Inc.; 19 West 44th Street; New York, N.Y. 10036
Associated companies, branches, and representatives
throughout the world.

Developmental Editor: Gordon T. R. Anderson
Editorial and Design Supervisor: Joan Matthews
Interior and Cover Design: Dan Serrano
Manufacturing and Production Supervisor: Maria Chiarino
Composition: A & S Graphics, Inc.
Printing: Crest Litho
Binding: American Book-Stratford Press

Library of Congress Cataloging in Publication Data
Main entry under title:

Informing the people.

   (Longman series in public communication)
   Bibliography: p.
   1. Government publicity—United States.   2. Govern-
ment information—United States.   I. Helm, Lewis M.
II. Series.
JK849.A3153   353.0081'9   80-18390
ISBN 0-582-28200-4

Manufactured in the United States of America

9 8 7 6 5 4 3 2 1

Contents

Preface

In planning this public information handbook, the editors saw the need for a useful, up-to-date guidebook for the practitioner. The most recent and most useful book in the field prior to this one was *The Voice of Government*, edited by Ray Eldon Hiebert and Carlton E. Spitzer (New York: John Wiley & Sons, 1968). We saw a need for a new book that would bring public information practice up to the post-Vietnam, post-Watergate period of the 1980s and reflect the large growth of government programs since the mid-sixties.

This book has been planned to be useful not only to government information personnel, but also to line managers and program specialists who work with information on a day-to-day basis. Often, it's these executives in program areas who have the greatest need for realistic insights into public information practices, and the public information specialist spends a good deal of his or her time trying to educate those executives.

But this book is not limited to the executive branch information field. It is also aimed at legislative staff personnel who have information jobs or who work with executive branch representatives. Nor is this book limited to federal-level government information. It should be of use to information people in executive and legislative branches at the state and local levels as well. And of course it should be useful to the student of public communication, public relations, public administration, and political science.

We have not mentioned the judicial branch of government because, traditionally, the court system has not been concerned with publicity, and, in fact, has eschewed public expression outside the courtroom as an act that could unbalance the objective scales of justice. But even the judicial branch of government must communicate, and while it does not yet have the extensive apparatus for communication that exists in the executive and legislative branches, there are increased efforts by the courts to provide the public with certain kinds of needed information. And so the judicial branch is represented in this handbook with a chapter by the information officer of the Supreme Court.

The authors represented in this book were chosen because of their experiences in their fields and their ability to provide thoughtful insights into their areas of expertise. They include government public information executives, journalists who cover various aspects of government on a regular basis, private industry communicators who have dealt extensively with government, and academic experts in public communication. As a result of this variety of backgrounds, readers will discover a mix of viewpoints toward the public information profession. In general, however, the book emphasizes the practical approach to public information work, as the title implies, rather than the theoretical, critical, or analytical.

However, this is not simply a how-to-do-it book. A great variety of issues are touched upon here that will continue to be of concern to all who are involved in the government communication process. Many of those issues lie below the surface of the subjects dealt with by the authors of the chapters that follow. And so it might be useful to point them out here at the outset, since there is no one chapter that deals with all these issues separately. They include such questions as:

• Who makes, and who should make, government information policy—the executive or legislative branch?

• Is advocacy of government programs good or bad? Either way, should Congress or the legislative branch hold hearings to attempt to define the role of public information in government?

• Is advertising of government programs in commercial media appropriate? If so, under what conditions?

• Should the public information function in government be centralized and put into sharp relief by establishing a ministry of information, as many other countries have done?

• Who is the client of government public information—the legislative branch? the news media? special interest groups? the public at large? And what happens when there are competing interests?

Anyone familiar with the field will recognize that these are just a few of the important questions for which there are as yet no final answers. But they should be kept in mind as one reads this book. It is hoped that as a result of providing a better definition for the profession, its purposes, and its techniques, society will in the future get better answers to these issues.

Finally, the editors want to note that this book is not a government publication. It was written and edited by people acting in their private capacities, and the opinions they express are not necessarily those of their agencies. No official support or endorsement by any department or agency of the U.S. government is intended or should be inferred.

Washington, D.C.   *The Editors*
1980

OVERVIEW

The manner in which the government of the United States communicates has been a source of concern and controversy since the founding fathers first sought to codify in the Constitution the limits of government in a democracy. During the last two centuries, the media's role, privileges, and responsibilities in the government communication scenario have been repeatedly defined and redefined. However, little clarity has been given to the role government itself should play in this process.

Ray Eldon Hiebert points out in Chapter 1, "A Model of the Government Information Process," that many believe that the executive branch has "no authority to communicate, to persuade, or to lead." Others are equally adamant that unless the executive branch fulfills its responsibilities in these areas, the public is denied its rightful access to information that is essential to informed participation in the democratic process. After raising this issue, Dr. Hiebert describes how the communication process works and what techniques are available for use by government.

Dr. Hiebert has served as a public affairs consultant to a number of government agencies. He was educated at Stanford University and the Columbia University Graduate School of Journalism. He was founding director of the Washington Journalism Center, chairman and then dean of journalism at the University of Maryland from 1968 to 1979, and is now a full professor on the faculty there. He has edited and authored numerous books and articles in the communications field, including *The Press in Washington* (Dodd, Mead, 1965), *The Voice of Government* (Wiley, 1968), *The Political Image Merchants* (Acropolis, 1971, 1976), *Mass Media* (McKay, 1974), and *Mass Media II* (Longman, 1979).

The evolution of government communication, especially during the 65 years following the establishment of a World War I propaganda office headed by George Creel, is traced by Dr. David Herold in Chapter 2 of this section, "Historical Perspectives." It is Dr. Herold's contention that many of the techniques developed by the Creel group to gain public support for the war effort formed the basis for broader present-day government information practices. Dr. Herold holds a Ph.D. in American Studies from the University of Minnesota and has specialized in the historical aspects of public relations and government public information while assistant professor in the public relations graduate program at The American University.

In Chapter 3, Scott Cutlip explains how the growth of government public information has been a part of the growth of government and the profession of public relations, producing an interlocking public information system. He shows that while the press and government have continued their traditional adversary relationship, the press is not really able to cover government adequately and has increasingly grown to depend upon the public relations function of government. Thus, he says, both press and government have a new responsibility toward each other and toward the public to do the very best possible job in communicating what the people need to know in order to govern themselves. Cutlip is dean of the Henry W. Grady School of Journalism at the University of Georgia and was for many years a professor of public relations at the University of Wisconsin. He is coauthor of the leading textbook in the field, *Effective Public Relations* (Prentice-Hall, 1980), now in its sixth edition.

While Cutlip argues that persuasion is the basis of power, and that to communicate is to advocate a position and point of view, Edward Cowan concludes our overview by pointing out some of the problems in government advocacy. Hiebert and Cutlip argue that government information personnel must be involved in program and policy formulation, but Cowan argues from a journalist's point of view that certain types of information, especially statistical data, should be free from political advocacy. He shows that administrations have been guilty of manipulating facts and information for political purposes. He concludes that there are limits to what government can and should advocate. Cowan's view is based on his 23 years as a newspaper reporter, including 18 with the *New York Times*, most of them spent covering government in Washington. During this period, Mr. Cowan, who holds an M.A. in economics, has covered government economics under five presidents and has gained insight into government information practices.

CHAPTER 1

A Model of the Government Communication Process

Ray Eldon Hiebert

The government of the United States, unlike most other governments of the world, has a particular communication problem. Like all governments everywhere, it has a need to communicate with all citizens in order to exercise effective leadership. But unlike many other countries, in the United States we have a long-standing tradition that governments at every level—federal, state, and local—should not engage too overtly or directly in communicating with the people.

If the government does so, it is "propagandizing," interfering with the free thinking of people and preventing the public from making up its own mind. So in the United States, the government owns no daily newspapers or radio or television stations; none of its publications can be easily purchased at the local newsstand or bookstore; and information it produces for foreign audiences cannot by law be published or broadcast within the United States. As a diverse and pluralistic society, the United States has a government which does not speak with one voice. Unlike many other countries of the world, the United States does not have a ministry of information to coordinate its communications efforts. There are literally thousands of governments within governments, at the local, state, and national levels, competing with each other to be heard.

Indeed, the legal tradition in the United States has been to interpret the Constitution to mean that laws affecting the communication process are more restrictive of government itself than of the mass media. The government cannot censor the press, but the press can censor the government. The government has to divulge certain public information; the press doesn't have to divulge anything. The government has to protect its own security and the privacy of individuals. The press takes much less risk in violating security and privacy.

It is, without a doubt, much more difficult for the government to govern in our kind of society than in more authoritarian or totalitarian societies in which governments can command or control the communication process. However, that does not mean that authoritarian or totalitarian governments are more effective in communicating with their citizens. In fact, it would be rather easy to document the fact that when authoritarian or totalitarian governments over-control the communication process, they lose credibility and impact with their own citizens.

The extraordinary thing about the democratic process—the prime vision of our founding fathers—is that by having a free and independent press to serve as a watchdog of government, that government achieves more credibility. The people have faith that they are not being propagandized by government, that they can get a free and independent version of the facts and make up their own minds about the truth. Sometimes, however, this philosophy has been interpreted to mean that government has no authority to communicate, to persuade, or to lead. The legislative branch has often taken this point of view. Congress says it has the right to communicate with the people in order to make laws that are responsive to public needs. The executive branch, Congress would say, exists merely to carry out those laws. Its role is only to dispense information derived from the actions and programs approved by the legislative branch. The politician needs to communicate with the people in order to win public office and represent constituencies. The bureaucrat, says the politician, exists to carry out the will of the public's elected representatives.

Thus, the executive branch of government in America has traditionally been given a narrowly defined role. It is only supposed to pass out information, through highly restricted channels, making no attempt to lead or persuade, and forbidden from overt efforts to assess public attitudes or measure public response. But that narrow definition of the executive branch's role does not properly represent the reality of the communication process nor the necessity for leadership in government.

The basic premise of this book is that the government—in all its branches and at all levels—owes its citizens effective leadership, and that leadership derives from effective communication. We need not elaborate further about the first half of that premise—we can leave that to the political scientists and public administration scholars. However, this book is about the second half of that premise. And so we need to develop an idea of just what constitutes effective communication, and how governments can use it.

First of all, communication is a process; it is not a singular act. By sending out a message, we are performing an act, not necessarily communicating. A message that reaches no audience and causes no response is mere sound without value.

Communication is a process that can be broken down into component parts. We can label those parts in many different ways. One way is depicted in Figure 1. Harold Lasswell, a pioneer scholar of political communication, defined the communication process as shown in Figure 2. Applying these definitions to government communication, we can easily arrange the parts as shown in Figure 3. Viewed in these ways, the communication process is circular, not linear. It is a continuous process, with each component connected: the response affects the sender as much as the sender affects the response; the reactions affect the officials as much as the officials affect the reactions. Communication is not a one-shot action, nor is it one-way. Communication is *dialogue*, not *monologue*.

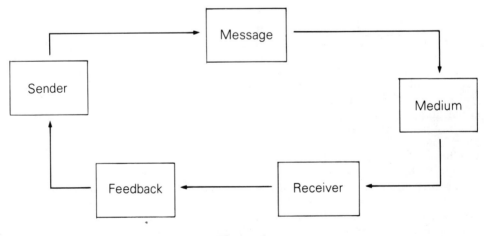

Figure 1

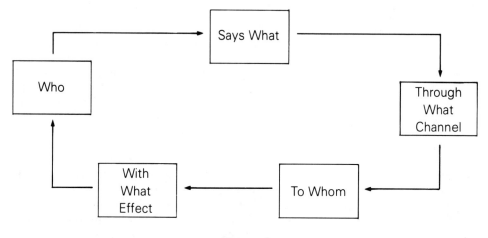

Figure 2

Yet, governments in the United States have too often failed to interpret their communication role in this way. The government official is merely supposed to send messages to the masses. The competition between elected official and appointed official, politician and bureaucrat, is perhaps one explanation for this interpretation that government should inform, not communicate. And perhaps we have misinterpreted the founding fathers concerning the separation between government and communications. Even Thomas Jefferson, the most outspoken of our founding fathers in advocating a press completely free of government, did himself arrange to have a newspaper published in Washington—the *National Intelligencer*—which would carry his views. And certainly since the New Deal we have reinterpreted the whole role of government in our society: now we accept the idea that government is needed to deal broadly with social, economic, environmental, and defense issues, among others, and that it must now exercise leadership in informing the people and persuading them about those issues.

Now, 200 years after America's nativity, and approaching the end of the twen-

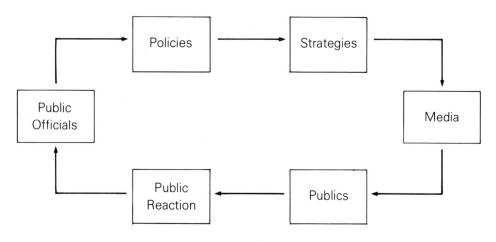

Figure 3

tieth century, the American government, in all branches and at all levels, is in the business of communicating and persuading, our traditions notwithstanding. Indeed, the American people lose nothing by keeping up the tradition of a free press, even while the government has to accept the challenge of having to communicate with the public through media it does not own or control. A free press keeps the government on its toes; forces the government to tell the truth; and makes the government work hard to develop acceptable programs and policies in the free and open marketplace of ideas. The free press is the fire that burns off the dross, the forge that tempers the steel of a democratic government and makes it strong.

In this kind of situation, the government needs expert help. It needs an organized and systematic effort in the field of communication if it is going to be effective. The American government has been slower in accepting the need for professional public relations advice and efforts than other components of American life such as business, education, and even religion. But today, public relations is an integral part of American government and politics, even though it may not always be called that.

What is public relations? The most complete definition was developed by Dr. Rex F. Harlow after a lengthy study:

> Public relations is a distinctive management function which helps establish and maintain mutual lines of communication, understanding, acceptance and cooperation between an organization and its publics; involves the management of problems or issues; helps management to keep informed on and responsive to public opinion; defines and emphasizes the responsibility of management to serve the public interest; helps management keep abreast of and effectively use change, serving as an early warning system to help anticipate trends; and uses research and sound and ethical communication techniques as its principal tools.[1]

There is nothing in Dr. Harlow's definition that cannot be applied to the work that needs to be done by public information officers for governmental activities at all levels.

Like communication, public relations is also a process. We can take Dr. Harlow's comprehensive definition and reduce it to a more simple model that diagrams the process, as we diagrammed communication. The process can be modeled to include five parts. (See Figure 4.) The public relations process, like communication, is circular. Evaluating the results affects the stating of the goals as much as the goals affect the results.

Stating goals, or policies, is, of course, a function of management, but these goals and policies will be worthless in a democratic society if they do not meet the needs of the people. To determine proper goals and policies, management needs public relations counsel to help understand public attitudes, opinions, and interests. Too many government agencies do not involve their public information officers sufficiently at the policy-making levels where their services are most essential to the entire communications process. Again, it has probably been the competition between the politician and the bureaucrat, and the misinterpretation of our traditions, that have kept the information officer out of the policy-formation process; and that failure is a serious one.

If public information officers are to help with stating goals and policies, they must be able to research the publics. They have to know the variety of publics that are affected and the differences between publics. They have to be able to research or otherwise find answers to such questions as: Who are our publics? What do they think? What will they accept?

Only after they know the goals and understand the public can they play a creative role in shaping ideas that will increase understanding. The creative role

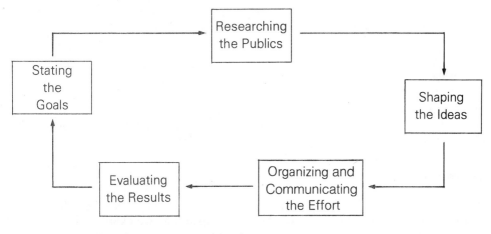

Figure 4

not only involves the shaping of ideas and sharpening of the message; it also involves deciding which medium, or media, should best carry the message. For the medium itself shapes the message, or, as Marshall McLuhan says, the medium *is* the message. If the president decides to use a press conference as the vehicle for sending out a message about boycotting the Olympics, the message will get shaped much differently than it would if he sent out a press release.

How does a press conference make a message different from the same message relayed in a press release? How does staging an event affect a message as opposed to using a public service announcement to say the same thing? What are the advantages and disadvantages of using government media as opposed to using the news media? What are the pitfalls of leaking information, and how does a leak affect a message? When can information be withheld legally, and when should it be withheld strategically?

These questions, and many others like them, are the concern of public relations experts. They are needed in government just as much as in business or in any other sphere of life in a democratic society. Public relations exists only in democratic societies. It is a legitimate function only in those societies where every person has a right freely and openly to express his or her point of view. In American society, government has that right just as much as business or education or the media or anyone else. Indeed, government has to compete with all the other spheres of influence for public attention through the media; it has no special legal status that allows it to command attention peremptorily or arbitrarily. Government not only has the right to public expression, it has the *obligation*, unless it wants to abdicate leadership.

The answers that the public relations expert should provide must increasingly be developed in an organized, objective, and systematic fashion. In an age of computers and cost analysis, it is essential for public relations to grow into a systematic and objective science. The process of public relations *is* rapidly becoming systematized; practitioners are learning how to quantify and measure the different results of different solutions to public relations problems.

In the past, public relations, particularly in government, has been least systematic in organizing and communicating the effort. But here too we can help by breaking that part of the process down into components to see how they fit together. Then we can decide how to orchestrate the parts and test the combinations to maximize effectiveness.

In organizing and communicating the effort, many different decisions must be made. First, one must decide upon one or more of four different strategies:

1. Withholding
2. Releasing
3. Staging
4. Persuading

In each of these strategies, a variety of techniques can be used, each to a different effect. If we put the process of organizing and communicating the effort into a model, we can see how the parts fit together. (See Figure 5.)

Withholding

Withholding information is often a legitimate strategy. There are both legal and strategic reasons for it. On a personal level, for example, we exercise this strategy continually: we put on clothes to cover up those parts of our anatomy we don't want to show to the world; we don't reveal to everyone every detail about our past; we underplay our defects and mistakes as much as possible. We put our best foot forward, as the saying goes.

Governments, too, have to protect themselves in order to lead. Of course, governments which hide fraud and corruption run serious risks of backfiring and losing their credibility. Secrecy is anathema in a free and open society; the American people abhor secret police and secret societies and secret governments. Decisions that are not arrived at openly are going to be suspect; they usually will arouse the insatiable curiosity of the press, and may ultimately cause far greater public scrutiny. So, withholding information as a strategy has great risks and is usually not the most effective way to communicate, although there are times when those risks have to be taken.

Legal exemptions from the Freedom of Information Act, as we shall see later in this book, provide nine areas where the government can, and often must, legally withhold information. To protect national security, to protect individual privacy, to protect certain business interests, for example, the government must withhold information. In other words, while the government cannot censor the press, it can censor itself. It can constitutionally require its employees, as does the CIA, to sign a contract stating that they will not reveal certain kinds of information. It can fire or punish an employee for unauthorized leaks of information.

Policy considerations also come into play. We have to recognize that there are times when, even though the government has no legal obligation to withhold, it might have to exercise common sense, practical wisdom, and experienced judgment to determine what should and should not be released, and *when* it should be released. These considerations are important in diplomatic negotiations, information that might affect the stock market, and in many other areas of public concern.

Off-the-record sessions can give the government some options in dealing with information in difficult circumstances. Information can be withheld by giving it to reporters on the condition that they do not use it. If one's reasons for withholding are legitimate, and if one can persuade reporters of that legitimacy, then an off-the-record session with the press can be helpful. If can help diffuse curiosity or anger over not getting the full story. It can provide reporters with background materials and explanations, enabling them to do a better job of interpreting a situation.

But off-the-record sessions have been misused, and many reporters are wary of them; some news organizations will not allow their reporters to participate in these encounters. Most frequently, reporters feel off-the-record sessions are used

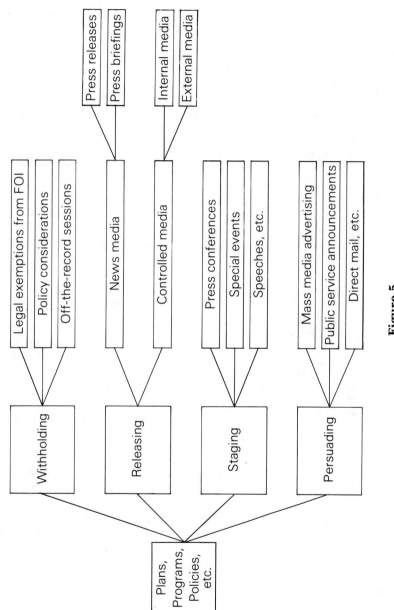

Figure 5

to float "trial balloons," allowing the official to duck responsibility if the public shoots down an idea on "probation." So the risks in off-the-record sessions require careful consideration. Reporters may decide not to attend; they may not agree to the ground rules, and even if they agree, they have only a *moral* obligation, not a legal obligation, to abide by the rules.

Releasing

Releasing information is a far more effective communication strategy than withholding. By taking the initiative in getting information out, the initiator gains an edge over the competition. The Catholic Church has long recognized that principle by seeking to propagate the faith in the child more than the man ("Give us a child until he is seven, and the Church will keep him forever"). Joseph Goebbels, the fascist master propagandist, said, "Whoever says the first word to the world is always right." Social scientists have proved empirically that human beings are far more apt to believe and be persuaded by the first version of anything they hear than by a subsequent version. The way in which information is released, however, greatly affects the message that is received. Careful consideration has to be given to releasing techniques. The first decision to make is whether to release information to and through the news media, or through government's own media.

The news media, of course, are neither owned nor controlled by the government. The newspapers, news associations, syndicates, magazines, book publishers, movie industry, networks, and broadcasting operations are all privately owned, and their owners are fiercely independent and zealous in guarding their rights and freedoms from government as guaranteed by the First Amendment to the Constitution. The news media, as we have shown elsewhere in this book, do not usually regard themselves as advocates of government. They are much more apt to think of themselves as representatives of their readers, listeners, and viewers; they see themselves as ombudsmen for the people, as watchdogs keeping the intruding government at bay.

Thus, the government in our society cannot exercise much control over the news media, and to release information to the news media is to lose control over the message. The reporters, producers, directors, and editors all have a perfect right to alter the message, to give it a big headline or a small one, to cut and paste and edit to fit their own needs, not the needs of government.

But while the government loses control of the message by releasing it to the news media, it gains credibility and circulation. When the news media publish or broadcast information, they give it third-party endorsement. It is no longer just a public official making a statement; now it is Walter Cronkite or CBS or the *Washington Post* or David Broder saying that the government official did indeed make the statement and that it must be important. The news media, of course, also provide a far better circulation system than anything the government can offer. The news media reach millions of people each day, and with superior penetration than government resources. The loss of control may well be worth the added credibility and distribution.

Press releases have been the traditional way of getting government information to the news media. Government agencies and offices crank them off mimeograph machines by the hundreds each day. A Washington reporter might get a stack of releases a foot high every day. Most of them end in the circular file, but that does not mean they are not useful in the right circumstances for the appropriate situation.

Press briefings are probably more useful. The major government newsmakers—White House, State Department, Defense Department—use this technique daily. It gives the reporter more control over the message, allowing him to ask his questions and influence the flow of information, but it gets more media attention because the reporter favors it, thus getting more information into the stream of communication. It also carries greater credibility than the press release. Such briefings can be handled individually as well as in groups. The placing of stories with individual reporters is a growing technique in getting information into the news media.

Press briefings can be conducted on several levels of background, giving the government more control over the release of information. The ground rules that can be used to govern these briefings could never be codified into law; they will always remain a gentleman's agreement between government official and reporter. The rules vary, of course, from situation to situation, but the ones that are usually applied are the so-called Lindley rules, named for the late Ernest K. Lindley, a long-time Washington correspondent who assigned background briefings to three categories:

1. *Background*, where the information can be used but attributed only to an unnamed source, such as a "high government official";
2. *Deep background*, where the information can be used but not quoted directly and not attributed to any source, merely the reporter's speculation;
3. *Deep deep background*, where the information may not be used at all.

Such briefings require a lot of mutual trust. Some background briefings are also known as leaks, and, as we shall see later, when mutual trust breaks down at any level inside government or between government and media, the leaks can cause floods that can wash back and drown the perpetrators.

Controlled media are those publications or productions which the government owns. The government is producing far more of them today than it did in the past, but there are still fewer of them than there are news media.

Internal media have become essential to organizational communication in government, in industry, in education, and in all other areas where groups of people work together. The government's employee newsletters and magazines are, of course, limited in their impact on the mass public, but employees are important publics and cannot be forgotten.

External media can also be used to supplement the information released to the news media, but they could never replace it. The government today uses its own published books and magazines to fill in areas of information often ignored by the private media. These can be used occasionally to target information at a specific audience. For example, by publishing in book form the Surgeon General's report on the hazards of cigarette smoking, the government could communicate a much larger amount of facts and figures than the news media could tolerate, and it could distribute this to a target group of key scientists. But much that government produces as its own media for public consumption languishes in government warehouses because the government can only sell these books or magazines in the few Government Printing Office bookstores or by direct mail from congressmen.

Staging

Staging events is perhaps the best way to get a message into the news media, in an age when so many different interest groups are competing for a limited amount of time and space in the media. But it is also the most difficult. Simply put, staging means arranging a situation in such a way that it attracts the attention of the news media and gets news coverage. Much of what happens in government and politics today involves the jockeying of political factions or interest groups for public attention by staging events. For example, as the "undeclared" war in Vietnam grew to a fever pitch in 1967, Senator Fulbright, a "dove," used his chairmanship of the Senate Foreign Relations committee to call for a congressional hearing to investigate the administration's pursuit of the war. A congressional hearing is often a staged event; it leads to no legal action; it may result in legislation; but usually its purpose is to get the spotlight of publicity on a particular problem.

President Johnson, no amateur in political publicity wars, "upstaged" Senator Fulbright's hearings. Just before the hearings were to start, LBJ announced that he was leaving for a two-week fact-finding tour of Southeast Asia. Of course, the cream of the Washington press corps left on press planes to follow the president, and they reported front-page stories of him dancing with Madam Marcos in Manila and shaking hands with GIs on the battlefront. The second-stringers were left in Washington to cover Fulbright's hearings; their stories were relegated to the inside pages; and the heat was taken out of Fulbright's fire. Staging, more than most other techniques, requires skill, intelligence, imagination, thorough preparation, and good timing. And it cannot be overused.

Press conferences are certainly staged events. They differ from press briefings in that briefings are usually handled by the information staff while conferences are conducted by the official—the president, the senator. By putting himself or herself on the firing line, the official can win news attention. But he or she must be carefully rehearsed and thoroughly prepared or the event could backfire. A president cannot afford to make a fool of himself in a nationally televised press conference before 50 million people. His information staff must brief him thoroughly beforehand on possible questions, and he must know the answers. He can perhaps get away with a "planted" or at least "suggested" question to a sympathetic reporter, but not very often. If he conducts the press conference properly, he can make it his medium for getting his message to the people. But it is a sword that cuts both ways.

Special events of all kinds can be staged to get news coverage. The military has done a good job of staging Armed Forces Day to get a special kind of publicity once a year. Anniversaries, even bicentennials, open houses, conferences, caucuses, conventions, and hundreds of other special situations can be exploited by the government.

Speeches are one of the commonest ways of staging an event to get publicity. The president's State of the Union message has become an enormously successful media event; now the party out of power is pressing for equal time.

The idea of the party out of power seeking to use the media to communicate raises an important issue. The president and his administration can use his publicity-generating powers to overwhelm the other branches of government and the party out of power. Increasingly, those on the outside have learned that they have to stage bigger and better events to capture the spotlight of the media away from the White House. During the 1960s, as the television era came into full flower, the outsiders discovered that they could get publicity by staging sit-ins, confrontations, marches on Washington, and street wars—the more violent the action, the more certain the TV coverage. By the 1980s, the media have learned how not to be so easily exploited. But the principle remains.

Persuading

Persuading is the fourth communication strategy that government can use. Persuasion is legitimate and often necessary. Facts and information may not always be sufficient to lead the people. There are times when we have to persuade the citizen to enlist in the military, to save energy, to stop litter, to be cautious about smoking, to prevent forest fires. Of course the politician has to persuade the people to vote for him or her in the first place, so he or she can get elected to office and set up the government to keep the people informed.

There is, of course, a lot of persuasion in most information. We normally communicate because we have some purpose in mind; we want people to do things or to change things or to think in a certain way. But news and information are supposed to be as free as possible from persuasion. Certainly when the government uses the news media, it must deal in facts that have intrinsic value, not just material serving government's purposes.

Advertising allows government to state its case for its own purposes by buying its own time or space in the mass media. As we shall see later, the government is doing more advertising, and there are guidelines for its use.

Public service announcements also allow the government to package its own persuasive messages, and, because of the requirement that radio and television must use some air time for public service, the government can often get free advertising for these announcement packages.

Direct mail has been used very effectively by political campaigners and by congressmen, but relatively sparsely by the executive branch. However, the combination of direct mail, demographic data, and the computer has brought about a revolution in targeting communication, allowing the communicator to get a specific message to a specific group with maximum accuracy and minimum cost, and this technique will be used more in the future.

Finally, it should be pointed out that there are both legitimate and sinister ways to persuade. One can legitimately persuade by using logical arguments and valid appeals. But one can also persuade through friendship, intimidation, or bribery. John F. Kennedy used his warm friendship with members of the press corps to persuade. Richard M. Nixon tried to persuade the *Washington Post* to back away from the Watergate story by intimidating them on the license renewal of a television station. Bribery probably starts with free lunches and goes on from there. But these, of course, are not techniques for effective communication. "Dirty tricks" are almost certain to backfire, to create more problems for the communicator than they solve, in any free and open society with a competent and watchful press. So this book does not and should not concern itself with devious and deceitful tactics. The purposes of government can ultimately be achieved only through open and valid strategies and legitimate and tested techniques.

This book is about those strategies and techniques, as they exist in theory and as they have been practiced in all aspects of government. By attempting to model the process, we can see how it all fits together, how one part relates to the other, and we can place the whole into an understandable context. By looking at communication as a process, we can remember that it has many parts. Communication is not just sending out messages. All the parts of the process affect those messages, including the media by which they are carried, the publics that receive them, and the reactions and responses they cause. If we ignore any element in the process, we can ruin the results. Too often, we have ignored the systematic evaluation of the responses to our messages, just as we have ignored the systematic analysis of the entire process. But we cannot do that in the future if government is to govern effectively in a democratic society. To that end, this book has been written.

Notes

1. Rex F. Harlow, "Public Relations Definitions Through the Years," *Public Relations Review* 2 (1976):36.

CHAPTER 2

Historical Perspectives on Government Communication

David Herold

The first amendment to the United States Constitution, guaranteeing freedom of speech and extending constitutional protection to the press, reflected the view of our early national leaders that citizens could be adequately informed about their government through an unhampered press. In this preadvertising, prepublicity era, presidents and agency heads did not employ press secretaries, but rather private secretaries. The presidential secretary who represents the transitional stage from private to press aide was Amos Kendall, who served President Andrew Jackson as a press advisor, public opinion analyst, speechwriter, and publicity expert during the 1830s.

Even during the Jacksonian era, however, the concept of mass media and mass publicity outlets was hardly well developed in this country. The role of newspapers was not that which the "fourth estate" was eventually to assume when the rise of advertising from department stores and other merchandisers freed metropolitan newspapers from their economic thralldom to political parties. Between 1800 and 1860, the period of the "partisan press," newspapers dependent on government printing contracts and party subsidies served a semiofficial capacity, communicating administration, or party, news and viewpoints. For the most part, public officials wrote their own speeches—one recollects the image of Lincoln scribbling the Gettysburg Address on an old envelope.

The Department of Agriculture in the nineteenth century gives a good example of the minimal extent to which the executive branch developed information policies or programs. Though the act creating the Department of Agriculture enjoined it "to acquire and diffuse among the people of the United States information on subjects connected with Agriculture . . .," for decades the primary means by which the department did this was its annual report, a publication containing information on new plants, statistics, lectures, and news of farm inventions such as barbed wire and the windmill. Letters of inquiry numbering 40,000 in a ten-month period directed to the secretary of agriculture led to the creation of plainly written farmer's bulletins, and in 1890, a Division of Records and Editing, and a Division of Illustration were created. Later with the invention of film and radio, these divisions were added.[1]

The Mondell Amendment

The publicity activities of the Department of Agriculture were the first in government to awaken the criticism of Congress. This occurred during Theodore Roosevelt's administration, the same period (1902–1908) in which public relations was emerging as a business technique. Gifford Pinchot, a Yale-educated forester, as chief of the division of forestry in the Department of Agriculture, set up a press relations bureau to assist him under the general theme of "conservation" in awakening interest in the relation of forestry to the public welfare. The problem facing the Forest Service was not "discovering facts and making them known to specialists, but of working into the everyday thought and everyday practice of great masses of men what the Forester already knows." To reach the general public it was "necessary to convert scientific information into common knowledge," he determined, and in his opinion "the periodical press of the country affords the best means of accomplishing this, since everyone who reads at all reads newspapers."[2]

However, in the view of Representative Franklin Mondell, speaking for western commercial interests which were thwarted in their attempts to utilize timber from forests set aside in the name of conservation, the Forest Service was "scandalously extravagant" in sending out thousands of self-laudatory bulletins at a cost of $87,000. Although the Forest Service was undoubtedly manufacturing public opinion, as one congressman charged, government propaganda as an issue was not the focus of the brief debate on March 30, 1908, when an amendment was passed by 51 votes to 27, providing that no part of the appropriation granted to the Department of Agriculture "shall be paid or used for the purpose of paying for in whole or in part the preparation of any newspaper or magazine articles." Congress had the opportunity to, but did not, consider comprehensively how the public should be informed, by whom, and for what purposes. The briefly worded amendment had no apparent effect on the information practices of the Department of Agriculture, a situation which was observed five years later when again the House of Representatives was discussing appropriations for Agriculture.

The Gillette Amendment

In September, 1913, Representative Frederick Gillette of Massachusetts learned of an announcement for an examination for a "publicity expert, for men only," in Agriculture's Office of Public Roads to prepare news matter and "secure the publication of such items in various periodicals and newspapers, particularly country newspapers." The congressman objected to the idea of the government employing a person simply as a "press agent to advertise the work and doings" of a department, and he proposed the following amendment:

> No money appropriations by this or any other act shall be used for the compensation of any publicity expert unless specifically appropriated for that purpose.[3]

Once again, after a brief debate, which considered among other things whether or not a government worker needed to be an expert to reach the mind of the average reader, or whether any competent worker ought to be able to communicate in plain, ordinary English, an ineffectual amendment was passed into law and stands today in a slightly altered wording as Section 3107, Title 5 of the United States Code.

With this shadow of illegitimacy placed on "publicity experts," agencies proceeded in time to carry out the same functions but with the funding and naming of such operations generally obscured from congressional review. Throughout the twentieth century, Congress from time to time has taken one agency or another to task for its publicity activities. In 1919, Congress added the prohibition that agencies could not use appropriations to pay for personal services to pressure Congress on pending legislation. Still later, in 1948, Representative Havenner of California complained to the attorney general (with the effect that no action was taken) that the War Department engaged in propaganda in support of universal military training. The much-lauded Hoover Commission on government reorganization took up the subject of self-serving agency propaganda in the following year, but was unable to effectively address the issue. Until the sustained campaign by Representative John Moss in the 1950s and 1960s, which resulted in the Freedom of Information Act, the attention of Congress in its overseeing of administration information programs was sporadic and ineffectual.

The Committee on Public Information

America's entry into World War I was a turning point in the development of government information practices. George Creel, a Progressive newspaper editor from Colorado who had supported Woodrow Wilson in his campaign for the presidency, convinced the president shortly after war was declared on Germany that the best way to create widespread sympathy for the war effort was to avoid undue censorship and instead flood the nation with positive publicity on behalf of the war effort. On April 13, 1917, President Wilson created the Committee on Public Information, and with George Creel as its head, it quickly moved in directions that would utilize every medium of communication available.

Two speakers' bureaus were formed. One was a group of distinguished notables who spoke across the country, but particularly in the West where support of the war was as unenthusiastic as it was with German and Irish groups. Four-Minute Men, conceived by Creel, were a volunteer corps of amateur speakers nationwide who delivered short, patriotic messages which had been prepared in Washington to almost any forum available—school assemblies, movie theatre audiences, or church congregations. They numbered 75,000 near the close of the war, and it is estimated that President Wilson's July Fourth message of 1918, which the Four-Minute Men read verbatim, came as close to approximating a presidential radio speech as was possible before network radio.

Under the leadership of the University of Minnesota historian Guy Stanton Ford, a group of the nation's historians were brought together to write pamphlets and books. Illustrators produced 1438 patriotic works, including the memorable Howard Chandler Christy's *Victory Liberty Loan* and James Montgomery Flagg's Uncle Sam with the pointing finger and the caption, "I Want You for U.S. Army." The Committee on Public Information went into the motion picture business as producer and distributor with such features as *Pershing's Crusaders* and *America's Answer*, grossing over $850,000. War expositions in Chicago and 20 other cities showing captured war items, a replica army camp, and staged sham battles grossed nearly $1.5 million. An *Official Bulletin*, reporting on government activities, was briefly published in Washington, and a news service distributed items to the national press. A foreign section placed information in the press of allied and neutral countries, while the organizations of foreign nationals in this country (Czechoslovakians, Hungarians, Yugoslavians, and Italians) were organized to support their homelands through support of the war. In short, the "Creel Committee," as this rapidly expanding ad hoc committee came to be called, vigorously propagandized foreign and domestic audiences alike. The budget, under $5 million, was extremely small.

The Committee on Public Information came to an end on a note of controversy, and the legacy of the committee and its activities has been keenly debated up to the present time.[4] After the armistice, and shortly before the peace treaty was to be negotiated in Paris, the Republican-controlled Congress cancelled the appropriations of the committee. To Republicans, the Creel Committee was too much the publicity agency of a Democratic president, an opinion which one political scientist confirmed years later, finding that a permanent byproduct of the Committee on Public Information was "a vastly enhanced image of the presidential office".[5]

The historian Samuel Eliot Morison has charged that the distortions and xenophobia generated by the Creel Committee helped bring on the "Red Scare" of the 1920s. At the very least, distinguished historians on the committee during the war—Guy Stanton Ford, Carl Becker, and James Shotwell—spent the rest of their academic careers justifying the role they had played and were subjected to the criticism that has followed H. L. Mencken's characterization of them as "star spangled men" who should receive an annual pension as compensation for having prostituted their professional ethics.

Other unintended byproducts of Creel's work were the development of a new awareness of propaganda and an acquaintance on the part of the American public with mass solicitation, such as characterized the war bond drives and United War Charities campaigns which led to today's United Way campaigns. The desirability of separating censorship functions from publicity functions (Creel officially had both but gave emphasis only to the latter) was learned from the reaction of wary newspaper editors to Committee on Public Information materials and suggestions, and in World War II these functions were separated.

Out of the ranks of the Committee on Public Information came two men—Carl Byoir and Edward L. Bernays—who used the experience to build careers as independent public relations practitioners. The activities of the committee, it has been suggested, introduced to the business world the value of public relations, but more recent scholarship has held that the utilities, particularly, practiced public relations techniques before the war and resumed them afterwards.[6] It can be claimed, however, that the Committee on Public Information taught government the value of public relations.

On the eve of World War II, Guy Stanton Ford, who had frequently written about the significance of the Committee on Public Information, was asked to compare the situation of the United States with that before its entry into the First World War. He noted among other differences that during the intervening years "almost every governmental division and department in Washington has set up its own information unit and has a public relations officer with many assistants."[7]

Growth of Government Public Relations Between Wars

In government, as in the business world, the 1920s and 1930s saw managers expand their information activities, with public relations increasingly becoming an established management function. Following defeat in the 1928 elections, the Democratic party established its first permanent publicity bureau, with Charles Michelson at its head. The Republicans soon followed this example, and the place of public relations in political campaigning assumed a significance which continues to change and grow. In these years a new form of lobbying by special interests, employing professional press agents and conducting grass-roots propaganda campaigns, came into being. The California firm of Whitaker and Baxter, conducting surreptitious campaigns on behalf of political candidates and, later, massive educational programs for the American Medical Association exemplified these new developments.[8]

With the election of Franklin D. Roosevelt and his administration's New Deal came a rapid expansion of government publicity activity. The creation of New Deal agencies brought jobs for advertising agencies and newspapermen, popularizing, for example, the blue eagle symbol of the National Recovery Act, explaining the aims of the Tennessee Valley Authority, recruiting young men for the Civilian Conservation Corps, and photographing newly settled farm families for the Farm Security Administration. In Washington, more newspapermen were hired for these activities than were employed by the newspapers.

Pare Lorentz, fired as a syndicated columnist by the Hearst publishing empire for his praise of the New Deal farm programs, brought Hollywood talent to government film production. Since 1908 the Department of Agriculture had been making films, but it had never used film to reach wide audiences. Lorentz's first film, *The Plow That Broke the Plains* (1936), utilizing stock footage from Hollywood, an original film score by the American composer Virgil Thomson, and scenes shot in the wake of the dust storms which had created desert land of the farms in the West, was shown in 3000 theatres, initiating a brief but distinguished chapter in the film history of government propaganda films. The prize-winning film *The River*, presenting such New Deal issues as flood control, soil conservation, and hydroelectric power, followed in 1937. It so impressed President Franklin Roosevelt that it gave rise to the creation of a U.S. Film Service, which made films for various agencies until 1940.[9]

During the first administration of Roosevelt's New Deal, a committee of the 75th Congress attempted one of the first head counts of government publicity workers. They came up with 146 full-time employees and 124 whose time was spent partially in this area. By the time the United States entered into the conflict of World War II, this figure was but a benchmark from which to measure growth, and no accounting was attempted again until the 1950s. Assuming that the writing of textbooks in a subject area indicates a field's current and potential growth, it is notable that the first book in this field, written by J. L. McCamy, was published in 1939. Private-sector public relations had been codified in a textbook and college course by Edward Bernays in the late 1920s.

The Office of War Information

During World War II the United States did not repeat the experience of the Committee on Public Information. President Roosevelt denied George Creel a position in his war-time administration when Creel volunteered to head an information effort similar to that which he created during World War I. Sensitive to potential political liabilities, Roosevelt wanted to convince a watchful press and Congress that his wartime publicity agency would not be manufacturing partisan propaganda. Several information units were formed as America entered the conflict—the Office of Facts and Figures, the Office of Strategic Services, and several agencies to promote hemispheric solidarity and cultural exchange.

In 1942 the Office of War Information, combining most of the wartime information functions, was formed with Elmer Davis, a widely respected news broadcaster, as its head. Reflecting a lesson learned from World War I, separate from this office, whose functions were information, publicity, and propaganda, was a censorship board. The Office of War Information directed its messages at domestic and foreign audiences using every available medium but without drawing the stigma of a propaganda machine. In fact, criticism of the Office of War Information was that it received too little authority and was too removed from policy-making to function as a genuinely reliable news source. The most celebrated production of film by the wartime government was done by the armed forces, the "Why We Fight" series directed by Frank Capra. The overseas branch of the Office of War Information produced a distinguished group of films targeted for foreign audiences, while domestic audiences were flooded with patriotic war movies from the Hollywood studios.

Establishing Post-War Information Programs

The year 1945 saw the State Department engage in a massive campaign to generate support for the United States' ratification of the United Nations treaty. As the war neared its end, a Division of International Information was formed, giving the United States a permanent commitment to disseminating its policies and views to other nations of the world. After several reorganizations, the peacetime overseas information programs were formally articulated with the Smith-Mundt Act of 1948, from which the United States Information Agency developed, up to the time of its most recent reorganization into the International Communication Agency. Viewed by some as an agency generally to promote understanding of America and its culture, and viewed by others as an arm of State Department policy abroad, its credibility and its ties with the State Department and the Voice of America have been redefined by nearly every presidential administration.

Another significant institution to develop out of the war years was the Advertising Council, named originally the National War Advertising Council. As a response to criticism of the advertising industry, the Association of National Advertisers and the American Association of Advertising Agencies had placed the advertising industry at the service of the nation weeks after Pearl Harbor to sell bonds and promote morale, victory gardens, the salvaging of vital materials, and the recruitment of military personnel. Since the war, the Advertising Council has continued to support national educational and promotional campaigns, producing public service advertising for nonprofit and government agencies such as the National Red Cross and the Departments of Transportation and Health and Human Services.

Factors Shaping Today's Government Information Function

The growth of information personnel employed by government agencies received occasional observation and challenge in the post-war years. The Veteran's Administration prior to World War II had only one or two public information positions, but with the mass demobilization following the war, this number swelled to some 300, with the result that Congress in a deficiency appropriation in 1947 established a limit of 100 employees to be engaged in public relations. This restriction was retained each year with the ceiling being lowered to 22 public information specialists, until 1973, when the number was allowed to increase once again. In the early 1950s, Senator Harry F. Byrd, supported by a Brookings Institution study, campaigned for government-wide cutting of expenditures for publicity, but the effort narrowly missed passage into law.

On the eve of the Bicentennial, officials of the Civil Service Commission estimated there were over 19,000 federal "public relations" people. The cost of this activity was put at over $400 million. Precise numbers have never been available. The Department of Agriculture, which in 1977 reported a public affairs budget of $24.7 million and 763 staff members, claimed that it did not "indulge in public relations."[10] Nevertheless, the Department of Agriculture and other agencies with greater or smaller budgets, without formally acknowledging their reliance on public relations, have come to rely on media and public affairs specialists, speechwriters, news summary editors, writer-editors, photographers, and others with less specific titles, such as special project assistants, who handle political and congressional liaison.

Freedom of Information as a Spur to Increased Public Information Activity

However, it was the attack on post-war government secrecy, under the broader issue of "freedom of information," which resulted in "significant legislative determination of government information practices." In 1946 the Congress, in an Administrative Procedure Act, denied the right of agencies to withhold information unless it was in the public interest, but the burden of proof lay with individual citizens, not the agencies, to demonstrate that release of information was in the public interest. The long campaign to shift this burden to government officials, requiring them to demonstrate a legal basis for information withheld, was initiated by Representative John E. Moss in 1955, becoming law on July 4, 1966, as an amendment to the Administrative Procedure Act of 1946. The Freedom of Information Act had far-reaching consequences, for as a records act, it affected all agencies of government, and, in its amended form (1974), its exemptions and the agency procedures which it required became the model after which the Privacy Act of 1974 and the Government in the Sunshine Act (1975) were patterned. The effect of this legislation has been an increase in the number of government information employees, but also a mandated commitment to an open government administration which has assisted agency information specialists in resisting on behalf of the public and the media the tendency toward bureaucratic secrecy. Nevertheless, the wartime secrecy system of classification, which was implemented through a series of executive orders by Presidents Truman, Eisenhower, Kennedy, and Nixon, remains virtually unchallenged by the legislative branch.

The growth and influence of the Department of Defense's public information and public affairs activities received national attention during four days in 1970 when Senator William Fulbright made speeches from the Senate floor against the information activities of the army, navy, air force, and marines. His book *The Pentagon Propaganda Machine*, and a CBS television report in March of 1971, drew attention to the fact that the public affairs apparatus of the Department of Defense had grown twice as large as the United States' official propaganda agency, the United States Information Agency, and was largely uncircumscribed in its activities. In 1971 the Congress imposed a $28 million limitation on Department of Defense public affairs activities. The number of public affairs personnel claimed by the military has declined to less than half of the 4450 claimed in a partial accounting in 1970.

Although the Congress has never established an effective system to regulate the output of government publicity, it has frequently recognized the necessity for and given authorization to programs as government agencies were created or given new missions. For instance, the Space Act of 1958 charged the administration with providing the "widest possible and appropriate dissemination of information concerning its activities and the results thereof." The Forest Service of today, with nearly 50 Washington-based information employees and over 200 in field units, has 13 acts, memoranda, and executive orders authorizing its information programs, including the Smokey Bear Act of 1952 to promote a nationwide forest fire prevention campaign. The Forest Service press bureau, which Gifford Pinchot created and which was never eliminated by the Mondell Amendment of 1908, eventually received its legitimacy from Congress.

Piecemeal, with specific goals and programs, or abuses, in mind, Congress has given its attention to the development of public relations as a function of government. What the government chooses to publicize, as well as what information it tries to withhold, are concerns of reasonable critics of the executive branch, as are the effectiveness and size of the government information shops and the degree to which they are centralized under White House direction. At the same time, information programs and publicity campaigns have come to be recognized as necessary tools of modern government. With recognition of information programs and personnel as a necessity of effective government has come growth in professionalism within the field and general acceptance—even by its critics in Congress and the media—of its essential utility.

Notes

1. Swann Harding, "Genesis of One 'Government Propaganda Mill,'" *Public Opinion Quarterly*, 11 (Summer 1947), pp. 227–232.
2. Letter to Congressman Charles H. Scott, March 30, 1908, *Congressional Record*, 60th Congress, 2nd Session, p. 4137.
3. *Congressional Record*, 63rd Congress, 1st Session, p. 4409.
4. See George T. Blakely, *Historians on the Homefront: American Propaganda for the Great War* (Lexington: University of Kentucky Press, 1970); and Carol Gruber, *Mars and Minerva: World War I and the Higher Learning in America* (Baton Rouge: Louisiana State University Press, 1975).
5. Elmer E. Cornwell, Jr., *Presidential Leadership and Public Opinion* (Bloomington: Indiana University Press, 1965), p. 60.
6. See Alan R. Raucher, *Public Relations and Business: 1900–1929* (Baltimore: Johns Hopkins Press, 1968).
7. Letter to Mrs. L. D. Coffman, December 2, 1941, University of Minnesota Archives, Minneapolis, Minnesota.
8. Stanley Kelley, *Public Relations and Political Power* (Baltimore: Johns Hopkins Press, 1956), pp. 39–65.
9. Eric Barnoun, *Documentary: A History of the Non-Fiction Film* (London: Oxford University Press, 1977). Lorentz's work is described in further detail on pp. 121–23.
10. Claude W. Gifford, Director of Communications, Memo to Agency Information Directors, August 1, 1977.

CHAPTER 3

Government and the Public Information System

Scott M. Cutlip

Since public relations emerged early in this century as an identifiable vocation, the public relations practitioner and the journalist have functioned in a mutually dependent relationship, sometimes as adversaries, sometimes as colleagues cooperating in mutual self-interest. Not as frequently, but sometimes, the news media become the captives of the public relations practitioner who often has not only superior manpower resources but also news control. The artillery of the press is often muffled or diverted to decoy targets by skillful public relations. Yet, equally often practitioners are frustrated in getting useful information to the public by the inadequacies and the frozen patterns of the media. Day to day the advantages and antagonisms in this relationship alternate from side to side, varying from situation to situation. Consequently, this relationship is a stormy one—a relationship that sometimes serves the public interest, sometimes defeats the public interest. In reporting today's news one party can't effectively function without the other, however much this might be desired by one or both parties.

This recurring adversary struggle between the news reporter or news editor and the public relations practitioner would not merit discussion if it were only a matter of individual skirmishes between individuals on opposite sides of the news fence. The relationship has an important public significance, a significance too little noted.

The reporter views himself or herself as the guardian of the public interest and the seeker of news, news that will be of maximum value in building an audience which advertisers will pay to reach. Thus the emphasis of the reporter is on news that emphasizes the aberrational, not the normal; the destructive, not the constructive; and on newsworthy personalities rather than on issues. Such stories are journalists' stock in trade. In the candid words of Washington reporter Martin Nolan: "The reporter has a vested interest in chaos."

The practitioner is employed to advance the interest of the employer by spotlighting the institution's favorable news and softening or suppressing what would be unfavorable to the employer if it became known. This is mostly a matter of emphasis and obfuscation. No practitioner tells untruths and survives any length of time. However, some skirt perilously close to the brink of falsehood. The practitioner has another objective—one made necessary by the news media's lack of adequate manpower and outmoded news values. It must be readily acknowledged that lack of reportorial and editorial manpower and the limits of news space or airtime are governed to some extent by the hard facts of economics, particularly in the print media. Journalism's outmoded news values could be more

Reprinted from the *Public Relations Review*, Vol. 2, No. 2, Summer 1976, by permission of the *Public Relations Review*.

easily modified. We must also acknowledge that the reader or viewer has a limited amount of time to pay attention to public affairs. This limitation on time on the part of the citizen greatly complicates the adequacy and perhaps even the integrity of the information process.

The public relations objective is to inform the public of constructive, complex subject matter which the media have neither the news space nor expert manpower to report in sufficient depth—nuclear power, for example. Public relations practitioners contribute much useful information to the public dialogue that would otherwise go unknown.

Since the Publicity Bureau was founded in Boston in 1900 to publicize Harvard University, railroads, and other clients, the practice of public relations has grown into a major force in this nation. The some 75,000 to 90,000 public relations practitioners—there is no accurate count—employed in government, in schools and colleges, in corporations, in voluntary agencies, and in churches have come to constitute an *influential and integral component of the nation's public information system*—the system upon which our citizens must depend to make their political judgments and their daily decisions. These practitioners have inserted themselves into this vital public information system with little public notice and operate off stage. It is proper when they are put under the spotlight of public scrutiny that they focus on their employers or clients when it suits their purpose. This is a joint responsibility of scholars and journalists.

Scholars, newsmen and newswomen, practitioners, and citizens alike have appeared to be unaware of the increasing role the public relations source has in making, shaping, and managing the day's news—news that determines our public agenda and thus strongly influences our nation's decisions. Harry S. Ashmore, former newspaper editor, now with the Center for Study of Democratic Institutions, has been more perceptive than most. Five years ago he observed:

> The proportionate weight of those functioning within the total communications system who are presumably beholden only to their readers, listeners or viewers has long since shifted in favor of those who dispense information and undertake persuasion in the acknowledged interest of public agencies or private employers. . . . The media as presently constituted could not function without the array of skills and resources provided them without cost in the name of public relations; and this consideration is compounded by their further reliance on advertising or political favors derived from the same sources.
>
> . . . This does not mean that the new condition is necessarily fatal to democracy, but it does mean that we are not going to find the solution to the new problem it poses . . . by succumbing to the seductive notion that we can somehow dispense with these new forms and structures altogether.[1]

One Interlocking System

To best understand and to assess the workings of a democratic nation's public information system, it is essential to see it as *one interlocking system*. This is a prerequisite to making the system more responsive to late twentieth-century needs. Such an overview is germane to the serious question posed by the late Walter Lippmann: "How will we be able to create a capacity to govern this enormously complicated and very rapidly changing environment?" He gloomily suggested "there is no answer" to this problem. That we may not achieve adequate, truthful two-way communication between citizen and government does not excuse those of us concerned with the problem from trying. We are obligated to try.

Most of the scholarly research in the related disciplines of political science and journalism over the past 30 years has been limited to a study of segments of the public information system, for example, studies of the relationship of government and the press or studies of the role of public relations in political parties and election campaigns, or on behalf of special interest groups. No comprehensive effort to put all parts of the public information machine together as one unified interlocking mechanism has been made.[2] Studies to date have generally neglected the linkage and interaction of all elements in the public information system. I think it would be useful to get this concept of a public information system and its role in governing today's complex society on the . . . agenda. . . .

Public Information System Defined

A democratic nation's public information system may be defined as consisting of all those elements and channels of communication through which a citizen learns of the activities of his government and conveys to government his views and his needs. This public information system embraces a nation's government, staffed by political leaders, bureaucrats, and information officers; its political parties, manned by agents, active workers, and public relations experts; the political pressure group staffed by executives and public relations personnel; and the media, manned by reporters and news gatekeepers.

Each of these elements performs an important, integral function in the democratic process of the public's being able to arrive at a consensus after disagreements are debated. What emerges as the public's picture of such a political system is the result of the interweaving, overlapping, and interacting of all these key informational elements. One element works in relation to other elements, thus all may be lumped together under the rubric of "public information system."

In this chapter we can focus on only one aspect of the many interrelationships of the above elements in the public information system. Thus, we will momentarily narrow our discussion to the relationship of the news media and the government public relations apparatus with the hope that the significance of this specific relationship will suggest the dimensions of a larger significance of this interlocking public information system. In a time when public confidence in government is dangerously low, I think it useful to raise questions about this public information system as it serves or fails to serve democratic government.

The conflict between the public relations practitioner and the news media is particularly acute in the reporting of government at the local, state, and federal levels. In government the public relations experts go under camouflaged titles of "information officer," "public affairs officer," "education officer," or some such sanitized euphemism. This is because these government practitioners are under steady assault from legislators, the media, the party out of power, and vested interests opposed to particular government programs. Hostility to the government public relations function keeps it in a twilight of shadowy legitimacy, and thus keeps it from being efficient in the discharge of its obligation to inform citizens about their government and to facilitate citizen feedback to government.[3]

Douglass Cater has written: "News is a fundamental force in the struggle to govern." He who shapes and manages the news in the public forum is most likely to carry the day. This struggle to shape and manage has escalated in intensity as the media's power and political stakes have increased. As the great Judge Learned Hand observed:

> The day has clearly gone forever of a society small enough for its members to have a personal acquaintance with one another. . . . Publicity is an evil substitute, and the art of publicity a black art. But it has come to stay. Every year adds to the potency, to the finality of its judgments.[4]

The public relations official's input into the public information system becomes more influential with each passing year. A comparison of the rather loose but straightforward public information practices of the Truman administration, whose leader was little concerned with "image" or with the elaborate, expensive, and often deceptive public relations practices of the Nixon administration, suggests the dimension and dangers of this increased role of public relations in government. The Nixon administration's public relations effort in its first four years was seemingly successful, yet, in the end, proved fatally flawed by Nixon's ill-conceived public relations concept that could not distinguish between ethics and success, between truth and untruth. No presidential administration in U.S. history put more effort and more expenditure into public relations than did that of Richard Nixon.[5]

Similarly, as political campaign costs mount and the skills of persuasion become more specialized, the practitioner is playing an ever more important role in the political campaigns which determine leadership and shape issues. Political publicity is one of the oldest phases of public relations, but it never had the scope, shape, and reach that it has today in the era of "The New Politics." Stanley Kelley, Jr., a political scientist, was among the first to observe the increased influence of public relations in politics. Noting that the public dialogue begins with the political campaign, Kelley observed:

> The public relations man is occupied with directing the course of public discussion as it relates to the selection of government officials and the settlement of controversial issues of public policy.[6]

The role of public relations in political campaigns and in government—the two are inextricably interrelated—is expanding. Public relations impact on democracy should come under sharper scrutiny. In recent years, it has. Epstein took note of the increased criticism of public relations' role in "The New Politics":

> Much of the criticism of the newer techniques is centered about the enterprise of public relations as such. The idea of selling candidates like soap is offensive to all those who . . . believe in the capacity of voters to absorb information and make reasoned decisions.[7]

The government's public information machinery and the political candidate's promotional efforts seek to utilize the growing sweep and power of the mass media to accomplish their missions. In the process of making and managing the news, the public relations official makes the reporter more and more dependent upon the news sources for her information and for her "angle." The White House reporter's dependence on the some 50 public relations professionals serving President Ford was unwittingly revealed in the passage of a National Press Club Committee appraisal: ". . . a press secretary must probe within the White House to learn what is going on and we are not persuaded that Nessen has done all that he could in this regard."[8] As the *Washington Post* editorialized: "Somewhere along the line, the idea seems to have taken hold, in some reporters' minds, that the press office is a service for them like transportation or hotel accommodations, to be complained about when found lacking as one would lodge a protest with the night manager."

In the growth of the imperial presidency under Kennedy, Johnson, and Nixon, old-fashioned reportorial exercise somehow got lost, digging muscles flabby. For example, when the White House press corps at Camp David was told by Nixon's public relations spokesman that Richard Danner, ex-FBI agent and then a Howard Hughes emissary, visited President Nixon for only a "ten-minute courtesy call," the news media dutifully reported that Mr. Danner visited with President Nixon at Camp David for a "ten-minute courtesy call," nothing more.[9] We now know this same Danner was the agent who passed the $100,000 Hughes payoff to Bebe Rebozo for Nixon's use—the transaction that ultimately triggered the Watergate break-in which led to Nixon's downfall.[10] Little wonder that one of Lyndon Johnson's press secretaries, Bill Moyers, once chided the White House press corps for being "the highest paid stenographers in Washington."

Persuasion Is Basis of Power

We constantly need to remind ourselves that the basis of power in a democracy is persuasion. In his illuminating study of presidential leadership, political scientist Elmer E. Cornwell, Jr., concluded that the president's "link with the public is his key relationship." He wrote: "The leverage the President has acquired in the law-making process has been indirect, based on the use of the arts of persuasion, and ultimately grounded in the popular support he can claim or mobilize." President Harry Truman, the most democratic of contemporary U.S. presidents, put it plainly in a letter to his sister, Mary, written November 14, 1947:

> The people can never understand why the president does not use his supposedly great power to make 'em behave. Well, all the president is, is a glorified public relations man who spends his time flattering, kissing and kicking people to get them to do what they are supposed to do anyway.[11]

Beginning with Theodore Roosevelt, who sensed the power of the burgeoning news media and the nation's first nationwide wire service, strong United States presidents have utilized the expertise of public relations to exploit the mounting power of the news media to mobilize public support for their policies. Roosevelt sensed the power inherent in the presidency and the necessity for mobilizing public opinion in order to use it. He created press offices in the White House, met regularly with reporters, developed the "leak" and "media event" techniques, and was the first to use the presidential junket as a calculated way of generating public support for his programs. He shrewdly saw the White House as a "bully pulpit."

His public relations-minded successors—Woodrow Wilson, Herbert Hoover, Franklin D. Roosevelt, Harry Truman, Dwight Eisenhower, John F. Kennedy, Lyndon B. Johnson, and Richard Nixon—greatly increased the power of the presidency and to the same degree diminished the power of the Congress. These presidents, utilizing the expertise of public relations and the enormous power of the news media, changed our government from one of balanced, separated powers to one of presidential government. By 1973 there was wide debate and concern in the United States about the "crisis of the Constitution." This impact of the growth of public relations on our political life has been too little noted and too little studied.[12]

Thus, the public relations official serving a government department, a political leader, a political party, an interest group, or any other cause, is an important and integral part of the nation's public information system. Walter Lippmann saw practitioners inserting themselves into the news system shortly after World War I. Then the numbers were few, the methods fairly straightforward. Today their numbers are many, their skills and power great. In *Public Opinion*, Lippmann rightly evaluated the modern news service as working effectively in reporting those matters where there is "a good machinery of public record," but deficient in reporting those events not "scored," data not publicly recorded or else hidden at the source, or those involving personal and conventional opinions. These kinds of events—the substantial tides of change that move unreported below the surface of frothy whitecaps that the media episodically cover as "news"—do not get reported, Lippmann observed, "until somebody makes an *issue of* them." For example, our growing environmental crisis did not become "news," until Rachel Carson wrote her series of jolting articles in the *New Yorker* headed, "Silent Spring," in 1962.

This, he said, is the "underlying reason for the existence of the press agent." This sagacious journalist-philosopher asserted:

> The enormous discretion as to what facts and what impressions shall be reported is steadily convincing every organized group . . . that whether it wishes to secure publicity or to avoid it, the exercise of discretion cannot be left to the reporter. It is safer to hire a press agent who stands between the group and the newspapers.

Journalists tend to cover that which moves. For example, it is much easier and more salable for the news media to report on President Ford putting English muffins in a toaster than it is to probe the internecine struggle between Nixon and Ford men in the Ford White House.[13] Most newsmen agree that the media focus far too much emphasis on the personal activities of the first family. Journalists helped build the "imperial presidency."

Given the growing power of public opinion and the constraints it imposes on all institutions, news sources have become more sophisticated about the power of news and more skilled in its management.[14] In January 1975, CBS News sent a reporter, Andy Rooney, to see how a new reporter finds his way around the maze of our overblown national government. In his concluding remarks, reporter Rooney told a nationwide audience: "Everyone has a public relations person who is more interested in obscuring the truth than in revealing it. Every time you ask a question, you get the impression they aren't thinking so much about what the honest answer is, but about what answer would make them look best."

News Sources More Sophisticated

Rooney's conclusion is a half-truth to be sure, but it does reflect the growing public relations sophistication of news sources. This has intensified the media-public relations struggle. Increasingly, executives have realized that the press's definition of "news" determines the agenda of public debate, and thus public decisions.[15] The power of the media to ignore "news" is equally influential in setting the public agenda. Rachel Carson's "Silent Spring" illustrated this. Both the newsman and the practitioner are deeply involved in determination of public opinion.

Although the rationalization for the public relations function in government is valid, it should be ever kept in mind that the government information machine has as its primary purpose advancement of government's policies and personnel. The information machine is the mechanism through which all sorts of information—some neutral in content, some political in purpose, and some not wholly accurate—is transmitted to the press and the people. The major objective is to gain support for the incumbent administration's policies and maintain its leaders in power. Government has the opportunity to make news and has elaborate publicity machinery to publicize that which it wants widely known. It also has the weapon of secrecy.

In the Miltonian concept of freedom all ideas must get a full and fair hearing in the "free marketplace" where the validity of an idea or cause is determined by its ability to gain acceptance. Too often today the fleeting public attention the busy citizen has to give to public affairs goes not necessarily to those most deserving of attention but to causes and ideas with practitioners skilled in gaining public attention. The democratic marketplace too often is tilted by the defaults and derelictions of the news media on one hand, and by the "news management" of government practitioners on the other. Ways in which the governmental machinery can be misused are laid out in David Wise's book, *The Politics of Lying*. The marketplace appears to be weighted in favor of government nowadays. Little wonder TV news executive William Small said that "The press is hard put to deal with government."[16] Many government practitioners, public employees, do not measure up to their responsibility to inform the public they are hired to serve.

Those who govern and those who aspire to govern depend primarily on the news media—print and electronic—to convey their ideas and criticisms. A continuing dialogue between governors and governed filtered through the nation's news machine is a distinguishing feature of democratic politics. This filtering process inevitably produces oversimplification and distortion. The men and machinery of the news media provide the common carriers for the two-way flow of information and ideas which is essential in democratic government. The press is the only institution in a large society equipped to disseminate political information quickly and universally.

The role of the news media has been enlarged and enormously extended by television, now the number one news medium. Television greatly heightens citizen awareness of the conduct of public institutions and emphasizes the impersonal, interdependent nature of his environment. It also creates a sense of frustration for the citizen, who is witness to much that he cannot control—be it a senseless war in Vietnam or senseless bloodshed in Northern Ireland or Lebanon, a crippling railway strike, or wretched life in the black ghettoes of our inner cities. This frustration in being witness to events beyond the viewer's control leads to anger, apathy, or, ultimately, alienation. Each component in our nation's public information system has some serious soul-searching to do.

It ought to start with television, especially at the network level, because that is where the greatest power is. The impact of television on our lives, on our values, on our politics, and on our economic system is awesome. Its reach and impact are plainly visible although efforts to ascertain cause and effect—such as violence on the screen translated into violence of children—are not wholly satisfactory. David Halberstam, in two perceptive articles in the *Atlantic*, sees network TV as the shaper and creature of politics, both a maker and a prisoner of public tastes. Television network news, which must cover the wide, wide world in a scant 4000 words and 22 minutes each night, has become, for ill or good, our most popular and credible source of news—despite the distortions imposed by its format. Its importance is made larger in the United States than in other Western democracies because we have no national daily newspapers in the sense that Britain does, for example.

Television news, because of its power and the money at stake, is largely confined to the hard-news, page-one format style of our two press services—the AP and UPI. [These wires are major sources of information for most Americans, whether they get their news on the car radio, from the nightly news show, or from their newspaper.] TV is not equipped for investigative reporting save for the rare documentary—and these are getting rarer. CBS's "60 Minutes" is a welcome exception and proves there is an audience for substantial news. Despite the lessons taught by the Vietnam War and by Watergate, TV news goes on its bland way as though these traumatic events never happened.[17]

The political power of network television was first clearly seen by John F. Kennedy and Richard Nixon. When Nixon skillfully used TV in his now famous "Checkers Speech" in 1952 to save his political life, he became convinced that he could win any battle by going directly to the people over the heads of the news reporters he intensely hated. This led him to accept the challenge of John F. Kennedy to TV debates in 1960. Kennedy's clear superiority in that first TV debate—it was more a "Meet the Press" show than a debate—which brought partisans of both candidates into the same hall was clearly a major factor in Kennedy's razor-thin victory over Nixon. He, too, had sensed TV's power. He went on to develop a pattern for political leaders: exploitation of this new and powerful instrument. Halberstam writes:

> Kennedy understood that television executives respect power and television producers love film and thus that the President and the executive branch could virtually go into the business of producing their own shows. The President's travels to other countries were events, special affairs that reporters and cameras would follow, not just dutifully but enthusiastically. . . . The farther the President was from Washington, the less he was seen as a domestic political figure and the more he was a kind of national symbol of all the people.[18]

As presidents move abroad with their large public relations staffs, it becomes easier for them to manage the news. Correspondents with them become less knowledgeable and weaker in access to other sources of information. The network reporter's time on the air increases as his ability to understand what is going on decreases. As Halberstam notes, "In countless ways John Kennedy wrote the book on television and the presidency." As he did, Richard Nixon was watching. Thus Nixon's trip to China in 1972 became the ultimate example of this capture of the networks' power. That trip to China was the most effective thing Nixon did in his campaign to win reelection.

We also saw a repeat in President's Ford's trip to China—a trip clearly undertaken more to win election than to achieve diplomatic gains as subsequent events in China made abundantly clear. When a president goes to China or to Europe, the powerful voices of TV—Cronkite, Chancellor, and Reasoner—go with him. They go, not because they expect major news to break, but because their competitors go. Little wonder the accompanying press corps gets frustrated. This frustration surfaced against Ron Nessen, Ford's press secretary, on the China TV spectacular. A committee of the National Press Club's appraisal of President Ford's press relations said,

> Press Secretary Ron Nessen, who has consistently had grave problems with foreign affairs, plunged to his nadir on the recent China trip by what many White House reporters believe was the most inept performance in modern times in handling press relations on a president's mission overseas.[19]

Thus we have the media event which news sources, particularly the national government and political candidates, can create at will and to which the media quickly respond in Pavlovian fashion with their standardized news values and news processes. Typical of such media events was that created by the Ford administration in the wake of the murder of CIA agent Richard Welch in Greece. Unlike the some 30 CIA agents who gave their lives in the nation's service before him and went to their graves without fanfare, the return of Welch's body to this country and his TV burial in Arlington National Cemetery were clearly orchestrated by Ford's public relations staff to dramatize the president's public support of the much-battered CIA. In this orchestration the administration repeatedly focused public attention on its assertion that Congress and the press, by exposing CIA's misdeeds and law violations, were endangering the lives of CIA agents and the work of the agency itself. We must constantly remind ourselves that public relations is a weapon of power.

Public Relations Official Essential

Nonetheless, without the government information officer, the news media could not function as effectively and as economically as they do in reporting government. Let there be no argument on these points:

1. The news values of the press unduly emphasize conflict over concord, political personality over political issue, and thus require balancing for a constructive democratic dialogue;
2. These news media do not have the reportorial and editorial manpower, either in terms of depth or in terms of specialized knowledge, to adequately and accurately cover today's broadened, complex government news spectrum. For example, the Associated Press Washington Bureau—by far the largest one in the nation's capital—has 57 reporters in the field as of a few years ago.[20]

Spread these reporters across two news cycles and big government and you can readily see the government's public relations officers have them outgunned by about 100 to 1! As a consequence, the role of the public information officer in the public information system is steadily expanding though the function may still be regarded as a stepchild of bureaucracy. Little scholarly or public attention has been paid to the fact that an ever-increasing share of the news content of newspapers, newsmagazines, radio and TV newscasts is coming, often unchanged, from the government officer's typewriter. More and more of the governmental news reporting task is abandoned to the practitioner who supplies the information in professional ready-to-use packages.[21]

Newsmen are reluctant to admit their growing dependence on the information officer. If the positive news of business, government, cooperatives, universities, or voluntary agencies is to be fully, constructively told, these agencies must provide their own reportorial manpower to do the job. The news media, particularly the thinly staffed press associations, cannot do the full reporting job without public relations assistance. The task has outrun their resources. Newsmen would be on stronger ground in condemning the threat posed by the public relations practitioner to the free flow of reliable information if they would admit and correct this deficiency. Given the scope and complexity of today's political issues and government functions, the assumption that the present corps of reporters covering government in London, Washington, or Atlanta, Georgia, can do the aggressive and meaningful reporting job that needs to be done if citizens are to understand and improve their governments is an assumption of doubtful validity.

Public relations practitioners understand, better than lay viewers or readers, that the press's quest is for profitable sources of prepackaged stories, not the search for the truth. Lippmann saw the root of the problem when he made the distinction between news and truth. "The function of the news is to signalize an event; the function of truth is to bring to light the hidden facts, to set them into relation with each other and to make a picture of reality on which men can act." Our news media have neither the time nor resources to do the latter.

The news media are quite contradictory in their attitudes toward this new element of the nation's public information system. They condemn public relations for impeding the flow of public information and for extravagant waste of tax dollars, yet eagerly scoop up public relations handouts with their reportorial arms. Some years ago, the Associated Press, in a slanted exposé of government public relations, made much of the U.S. government's army of information officers in the Pentagon, but remained silent on the fact that the AP's military reporter is quite dependent upon the Pentagon's several hundred information officers in reporting the news of that complex, gargantuan establishment. This dependence on the information official gives more and more control of the shape of the news to the source which has its axes to grind. Further, the news served up ready-made to reporters tends to make them sluggish. This happens to police reporters, to sports reporters, and to Pentagon reporters—a place where the stakes are higher.

Examples of Media Derelictions

In 1969 when President Nixon and Secretary Kissinger made the decision to bomb defenseless Cambodia, they also made the decision to keep the bombings secret—and got away with it over the next two years because our military reporters were more lap dogs than watchdogs. The first news we had that we were engaged in clandestine bombings of Cambodians came May 9, 1969, when the *New York Times* carried a story it had lifted from the *Times* of London. That morning Secretary of Defense Melvin Laird and his public relations aide, Daniel Henkin, hurriedly discussed how they would meet this break in their cover when they met reporters at the daily 11 A.M. briefing. They worked out a series of fall-back positions. They were never pressed to these. Some 20 Pentagon reporters assembled at 11 A.M. in the Pentagon briefing room. The first one asked, obviously in response to the *Times'* story:[22]

Q. Are we bombing Cambodia?

A. If you are referring to the *New York Times* story this morning, this is a speculative story and as such I have no comment on it. As you know, MACV has announced that we are hitting targets near the Cambodian border. Beyond that I have no additional information for you.

Q. Are we using B-52s?

A. Yes.

Then the reporters went on to other questions. No follow-up by the news media then or later—until the story became front-page news in July 1973, after the United States invasion of Cambodia which led to that country's devastation. Also typical of the passive way the press responds to the public relations official's handouts is the way the invasion of Cambodia was constantly referred to by the media as an "incursion." Also the way it picked up Nixon's public relations terms for lying us out of Vietnam, "Vietnamization." Little wonder he had contempt for the press.

Richard Nixon knew, as many news sources knew, the press's weakness for the simple lead, the quick scoop, the terse headline or air bulletin—characteristics that don't permit time for reportorial probing or space for qualifying facts. As David Halberstam wrote some years ago:

> Few news sources see reporters as they really are, for good or evil: prisoners of the mechanics of their craft, the pressure of deadlines, the limits of the definitions of news; often brighter than they write, often restless with the form.[23]

The media, all too often in the tradition of news objectivity, accept by and large what is said and pass it on to readers and viewers—swiftly, uncritically.

This kind of in-house reporting occurs at all levels of government. For another example look back to New York City's "perils of Pauline" financial crisis. Just months before the *New York Times* editorialized that the city was sliding into bankruptcy with a deficit as high as a billion dollars, its city hall reporters had accepted Mayor Beame's press releases to report in deadpan fashion that Mayor Beame was going to balance the city's budget. A study of the *Times'* failure to uncover New York's impending crisis shows an uncritical use of handouts from city hall.[24]

Another example of the press's lap dog tendencies can be seen in a study of the way Henry Kissinger kept the nation's diplomatic writers in his hip pocket for seven years by sharing with them his inside information and his booze. A former assistant of Kissinger summed up his capture of the press this way:

> Partly as a result of Kissinger's energetic accessibility, the media, while covering Kissinger and what he has concentrated upon, have a tendency to ignore what he ignores. Not only do we lack an accounting of the weaknesses or oversights of a singularly powerful secretary of state—more important, there is the danger that public and congressional attention will not fasten on issues—even urgent ones—that are not to Kissinger's taste. Foreign economic policy is probably the most significant case in point.[25]

The classic example, of course, of the capture of the media by a public relations apparatus was that of J. Edgar Hoover's FBI public relations machine. By means of skillful public relations, Hoover was able to perpetuate the myth of an intrepid, noble fighter for justice until he died—a myth that we now know to be a gross distortion. The media dutifully reported the "news" of the FBI in Hoover's years but never dug into the full truth of the FBI. The media—even the sophisticated Washington press corps—can be conned. There is a wide, wide difference between news and truth.[26]

Public Relations Has Gained Upper Hand in Capital

It is at the Washington level that the government public relations apparatus clearly has gained the upper hand. But nonetheless, at the state and local levels, too, the outnumbered news staffs must of necessity rely heavily on public relations handouts. This leads to frustration among newsmen.

A former wire service statehouse reporter wrote me some years ago:

> I watched the situation you so vividly describe develop through eight years of wire service reporting and three years as an editor. I watched my state government grow and grow, until there were twice as many agencies to cover, yet the same personnel to do the job. Finally, the only people you had time to see were the PR people who were developing stories and putting them in shape for the newsmen until you felt more like a garbage collector than a reporter.

On the other hand, the record must be balanced by the fact there are countless examples of aggressive public affairs reporting at the local and state levels of government which have exposed corruption, waste, and inefficiency in government.[27]

Several studies have been made which show the news media's dependence upon public relations sources. One, conducted by the American Institute for Political Communication, found:

> Daily newspaper dependence on government releases and related oral statements is considerably greater than the Washington press corps assessment would indicate. ... The analysis of 22 key papers, which publish in 11 major metropolitan areas representing every section of the country, reveals that one-fifth of the stories published in both the foreign affairs and health, education, and welfare fields are traceable in whole or in part to formal releases or statements issued by Executive agencies involved. The overall averages were 21.2 percent for foreign affairs articles, 21.3 percent for HEW pieces.
> If White House statements and press conferences also are considered, the figure jumps to 38.6 percent for foreign affairs articles. . . .[28]

This study concluded that "The daily press is heavily dependent upon the Federal Bureaucracy's generative capacities for the news it carries and this dependence is more the product of broad revolutionary forces operating on the American society than of reportorial habits, editorial biases, or the nature of the press itself."

The same situation exists at the state and local levels. Permit me to cite one illustration from local government and one from state government. The dependence of the press on public relations personnel and the latter's resulting influence on press content is clearly shown in a study of school districts in Ohio. Robert L. Rings selected from Ohio's city school districts a sample of 35 districts with public information officers and a matching sample of 35 districts without such an officer. These districts were well matched in every other respect. He found:

> The school districts with public relations personnel did receive *significantly more* (italics mine) news coverage than the districts without the public relations directors. This included the number of different stories as well as the amount of space. Likewise, the majority of coverage in the public relations directors' districts was of nonsports articles. In contrast, the majority of the coverage in the nondirector districts was devoted to athletic activities.[29]

The value of this public relations-supplied news coverage to the schools is seen in the fact that the public relations directors' districts received more financial support than those districts without public information officers. "Financial records indicated that the director systems' current average operating millage was two mills above the state mean, whereas the nondirector systems' average operating millage was four mills below the state mean. In local support per pupil, the director sample averaged $375 to the nondirector sample average of $275."

I think it fair to assume that public relations-produced news coverage contributed to these results. Rings found "The districts with the directors had a higher proportion of student and public affairs stories whereas the nondirector districts had the higher proportion of articles concerning the school's administration and sports." This illustrates anew that most newspapers will cover administrative changes and spectator sports, but will not do the more time-consuming reportage of curriculum developments, and so forth—unless it is supplied. And the price of this dependence upon the source is that news comes with the sponsor's slant.

Evidence of the press's dependence upon news sources for much of its content is found in the development of public relations machinery in the Wisconsin legislature, dating roughly from 1965. Today the four party caucuses of the legislature are served by full-time information specialists. In addition, a growing number of legislators employ administrative assistants who, in addition to other duties, assist with their legislator's publicity. Alan Rosenthal of Rutgers University made a study of the impact of professional staffs on the Wisconsin legislature and found greatly increased news coverage of the legislature to be an important result. Rosenthal found, as a result of these full-time publicists in the employ of the legislature, that "From 1961 to 1967 the total number of column lines reporting leadership statements or activities almost doubled."[30] He added:

> In the 1961 session 13 percent of the total coverage received by Republican leaders and 28 percent of that received by Democratic leaders derived from press releases. In the 1967 session the proportions had risen to 19 percent and 37 percent respectively. The growth is surely a product of the publicity endeavors of the Assembly analysts.

Rosenthal noted that

> Effects were not only direct, they were indirect as well. The staff helped familiarize leaders with techniques designed to capture the attention of reporters. One analyst taught leaders for whom he worked how to approach capitol correspondents and how to be aggressive rather than passive in communicating the news they want printed.

A subsequent study by a graduate student found that the public relations assistance provided both parties and individual legislators had greatly increased and that news coverage by the state's print and electronic media had grown correspondingly.

Does "Handout Reporting" Serve Democracy?

There is a genuine public question involved in whether the "handout reporting," increasingly characteristic of American journalism, meets the citizen's need for accurate, complete information. The National Council of Churches of Christ in the United States sponsored a study of the 1959–60 dispute in the steel industry. This report said, in part:

> Both sides in this dispute indulged in one of the most spectacular utilizations of mass communications media to be employed in an industrial conflict. . . . The methodology for influencing public opinion is full of ethical issues and it is to be noted that during the steel dispute no way was available whereby the public could obtain an objective evaluation of the claims which were being pushed so energetically by both sides.

If this is true, the news media failed in their assignment. We must frankly acknowledge that the public relations officer is a paid advocate who is employed primarily to influence people, not to educate them, contrary to any claims she may make. Other elements in the information system must serve as checks on the advocate to insure that we have advocacy with integrity. If there was a failure in the steel strike coverage to provide the whole story in meaning and in depth, it was more a media failure than a public relations failure.

Professionals Must Inform Selves as Well as Public

The lesson here is plain—both for the reportorial and public relations components of our public information system—to face up to their common responsibilities in what clearly may be a life-or-death matter for us all. Whether both information system components have the expertise and will to meet their obligations is a serious question. James D. Carroll has written that ". . . the public order of industrial society is not particularly well structured for identifying, publicizing, and resolving in public forums political questions implicit in technological processes."[31] The weakness of the media in such areas has been well termed "the conspiracy of complexity" by John DeButts, Chairman of the Board of AT&T.

Vermont Royster, former editor of the *Wall Street Journal*, which represents journalism at its best, thinks the problem is "compounded by an all-too-prevalent habit of mind among newsmen":

> That habit is not to recognize what they do not know and to be content with a smattering of ignorance. They grow so accustomed to leaping from story to story with perhaps a quick briefing from the files, that they are reluctant to take the time to really find out what they are writing about.[32]

The media's outmoded fetish for speed is also a part of this problem. Aristotle saw our problem centuries ago: "The environment is complex, man's political capacity is simple. Can a bridge be built between them?" Perhaps not, but both the news media and the public relations practitioners who have made themselves influential parts of the nation's public information system have the obligation to be more professional, more competent, and more honest than they have been in the past.

One of the long-standing criticisms of public relations is that its practitioners have cluttered our news media with the debris of trivia and corroded our channels of communication with cynicism. There is validity in both charges. However, the media gatekeepers must bear the ultimate responsibility for such effects because those in control of the media make the final decisions. The media must be more resolute in resisting the economy of the public relations handout—both the press release and the junket—and must be willing to invest more of the profits made by the media in reporting that enables the bewildered citizen to know the *truth* of nuclear power, not just the *news* of a new plant siting. Most importantly of all, the media need to break out of the rut of routines and news values ground for them decades ago by James Gordon Bennett and his successors.

James McCartney, Washington correspondent for the Knight Newspapers, has posed the challenge in these words: "The press must not turn itself over to those who would use it. Editors and writers must seek out the questions that require answering and set out to find the answers for themselves."[33]

Similarly, the craft of public relations, slowly inching its way to professionalism, must address itself to its responsibilities in making the nation's public information system work. Practitioners must recognize that as they corrode and debase the news media they are eroding the credibility of the channels of communication upon which they must rely to inform and to interpret the positive, complex news of their institution.

Let me renew my effort to balance the record because ethical, honest public relations has made substantial contributions to our society and to our public information system. There are many pluses in the public relations balance sheet. Contrary to what many editors say, the public relations person has opened more doors than he or she has closed. Despite the noise it has caused in our channels of communication, public relations has contributed substantially to the flow of useful, honest information in our news media.

Moreover, public relations is making voices for the public good articulate and understandable. Public relations is being used to create support for mental health research and treatment. Public relations was used to raise the funds that financed the research that ended polio as a crippler of our children. Public relations is used to make government more meaningful and more useful in the lives of our citizens. Public relations is used to muster direly needed support for schools, colleges, and universities. Public relations is used to pave the way for ever-accelerating technological change, to gain acceptance of progress against the ingrained resistance of mankind to change. The public relations practitioner can take pride in the many honest, ethical, and useful endeavors that have been carried forward by those professionally motivated. The practice and practitioner are essential to our way of life, to making our public information system work. But they need closer scrutiny of the news media and scholars if the public interest is to be protected.

These two of the several components of this nation's public information system—the journalist and the public relations practitioner—need to do some hard soul-searching on their responsibilities to each other and, more importantly, to the society they were created to serve. The need for this critical introspective look is made clear by the eroding credibility of both institutions—the press and public relations—and by their collective failure to provide citizens with the information required by today's complex, technological society. As Ashmore suggested, we can't dispense with these new forms and structures. We must make them function in the interest of the common good.

Notes

1. Lecture, "The Pentagon Papers: A Case History of Government by Public Relations," given at PRSA Public Relations Institute, University of Wisconsin-Madison, July 1971.

2. One useful study in this area is William O. Chittick's *State Department Press and Pressure Groups, A Role Analysis*, published in 1970. Professor Chittick, now of the University of Georgia, studied the interrelationships of State Department policy officers, State Department information officers, foreign affairs reporters, and leaders of non-governmental organizations (pressure groups) and the impact of these relationships on the formation of public opinion about the nation's foreign policy. Another useful study which focused on two elements in this relationship was Bernard C. Cohen's *The Press and Foreign Policy*, 1963.

3. Typical of this constant pot-shotting are: (1) A lop-sided story in the *Atlanta Constitution* December 15, 1975, informing readers that "the voices of government cost you $23,760 a day." It was not made clear to readers that *Constitution* reporters could not possibly cover government and public education without the services provided by these "voices." (2) A series of stories in the *Washington Star* under the dates of April 12, 13, 14, 15, 1976, under these typical headlines: "The Cost of No 'Publicity Experts' Comes to About $92.8 Million," and "Our 'Hollywood on Potomac' Subsidy."

4. In a tribute to Justice Louis D. Brandeis at a memorial service December 21, 1942, which may be found in *Proceedings of the Bar of the U.S. Supreme Court*, 317 U.S. XI–XIV. More readily available in *Spirit of Liberty*, edited by Irving Dilliard, Vintage, 1959, p. 132.

5. It should be noted that except for personnel of the Robert R. Mullen & Co., a public relations firm which served as a CIA "front" during the 1960s and early 1970s, no professional public relations practitioners were involved in Watergate crimes. Those crimes were largely the work of lawyers and advertising men. Although Richard Nixon hired the largest White House public relations staff in the nation's history, he had only five on his high-level staff who had had prior public relations or media relations experience: Bryce Harlow, Herbert Klein, William Safire, Paul Costello, and Victor Gold. None stayed into the second term. Looking at the end result of Nixon's White House relations one is reminded of Arthur W. Page's observation in 1906: "Truth can be as elusive as ever despite the multiplying of her salaried ministers." This is not to say that there were not many useful public relations programs carried out in the Nixon administration; in fact, there were information programs on foreign policy objectives, revenue sharing, wage-price freeze, and so on.

6. *Professional Public Relations and Political Power*, p. 3.

7. *Political Parties in Western Democracies*, pp. 240–241. The ability to "sell" a candidate can be easily exaggerated, as it was in McGinnis' *The Selling of the President 1968*.

8. National Press Club, "The White House and the Press Under Gerald R. Ford," December, 1975. A study by the Professional Relations Committee (mimeographed), p. 4.

9. "Rebozo Investigation Focuses on $100,000 Hughes Gift," *New York Times*, June 20, 1974, p. C–33.

10. See J. Anthony Lukas, *Nightmare: The Underside of the Nixon Years*, 1976, pp. 113, 115.

11. Quoted in *Harry S. Truman* by Margaret Truman, p. 356.

12. An exception: Elmer E. Cornwell, Jr.'s *Presidential Leadership of Public Opinion*, published by the Indiana University Press, 1965.

13. For details of press coverage of Ford administration's first months, see Richard Reeves, *A Ford, Not a Lincoln*, 1975.

14. A brilliant young editor, Fred Barbash of the *Washington Post*, in commenting on this lecture, wrote: "I found your point about the willingness of reporters to buy whatever is sold by government and political public relations people to be very well taken, but I believe it is a declining practice. ... The sophisticated public relations people, especially at the upper levels of politics and government, have learned how to feed handouts to reporters without making them seem like handouts. The idea is to make the

reporter feel like he has come up with the story independently. . . . Not only does this eliminate the now prevalent revulsion many reporters have towards writing from handouts, it also gives the reporter an exclusive story, one the PR man knows will get a better play in the paper and still be picked up by TV and the wire service."

15. The role of the press in the governmental process was discussed in a thoughtful way in Douglass Cater, *The Fourth Branch of Government*, 1959.

16. For elaboration, see his *Political Power and the Press* (1972).

17. The struggle of professional newsmen and newswomen to hold the line against the "showbiz" influence on network news obviously suffered a setback when in April ABC hired Barbara Walters, more a celebrity than a journalist, at $1 million a year to coanchor the ABC Evening News. As former CBS executive Fred Friendly observed: "It's sort of a throwback to the days of Walter Winchell when news was done by name people who got a lot of money—but there wasn't much journalism in it." Professional journalists don't need press agents, hair dressers, and limousines, "perks" Walters's contract calls for.

18. "CBS: The Power & The Profits, Part II," *The Atlantic*, February 1976, p. 63.

19. National Press Club Report, *op. cit.*

20. Figure given in AP's Washington News Committee's 1975 Report to APME, Williamsburg, Va.

21. The extent to which the federal government's public relations machine dwarfs the Washington news-gathering machine can be readily seen in the fact that, according to the *Washington Star*, 12 major executive agencies are currently spending at least $92,836,927 a year for 3990 persons who fall under the heading "publicity expert." The fact is that no accurate count of money spent and numbers employed by the U.S. government on public relations has ever been made, or is likely to be made as long as the function operates in the shadows of dubious legitimacy. See the aforementioned *Star* article by John J. Fialka, p. 1, April 12, 1976. More money is undoubtedly spent by the U.S. government in disseminating news than is spent by agencies covering government news—by a wide margin.

22. Minutes of Press Briefing Conducted by Assistant Secretary of Defense Daniel Henkin, May 9, 1969, 11 A.M., The Pentagon.

23. "Press and Prejudice," *Esquire*, April 1974, p. 113.

24. Martin Mayer, "Default at The New York Times," *Columbia Journalism Review*, January/February 1976, p. 17.

25. Roger Morris, "Henry Kissinger and the Media: A Separate Peace," *Columbia Journalism Review*, May/June 1974, p. 15.

26. For one glimpse at the way the FBI used the media, see Paul Clancy, "The Bureau and the Bureaus, Part 1: The Press Barely Laid a Hand on Hoover," *The Quill*, February 1976. Corroborating evidence of Hoover's misuse of the press can be found in the Final Report of The U.S. Senate's Select Committee Report, *Intelligence Activities and the Rights of Americans*, issued April 28, 1976. This report details the way Hoover's agents tried to leak derogatory information about Martin Luther King Jr., to newspapers in an effort to discredit him. The FBI also tried to block news articles favorable to King, the Senate report states.

27. For support of this assertion see "Did the Press Uncover Watergate?" Edward Jay Epstein, *Between Fact and Fiction*. A series of provocative essays on the press.

28. The American Institute for Political Communication, *The Federal Government-Daily Press Relationship*, 108.

29. Robert L. Rings, "Public School News Coverage With and Without PR Directors," *Journalism Quarterly* 48 (1971).

30. Alan Rosenthal, "Professional Staff and Legislative Strength: The Case of Wisconsin." Unpublished manuscript in Wisconsin Legislative Reference Library.

31. James D. Carroll, "Participatory Technology," *Science* 171 (1971):647–653.

32. "More Competence Is What News Media Need Most," *TV Guide*, April 17, 1976.

33. "Must the Media Be Used," *Columbia Journalism Review*, Winter (1969–1970):41.

CHAPTER 4

Problems with Government Advocacy: A Journalist's View

Edward Cowan

In August, 1979, the chairman of the Federal Trade Commission (FTC), Michael Pertschuk, sent a letter to 12 federal agencies raising questions about representations they were making to the public in advertising and promotions. Pertschuk, one of the most activist regulators Washington has known, was writing as the head of the agency with responsibility for truth in advertising. Traditionally, the FTC has concerned itself with the honesty of commercial advertising. Pertschuk's letter, so far as anyone could remember, marked the first time that the FTC concerned itself with advertising by the government.

Pertschuk's letter invited the addressees to have their officials responsible for advertising confer with the FTC's advertising practices specialists. There was no hint of a formal complaint against any of the federal agencies. As officials were to concede readily when asked, the FTC does not claim to have jurisdiction over sister agencies.

The man-bites-dog aspect of the Pertschuk letter—that the government itself may be guilty of the very deceptive advertising practices it accuses some businesses of engaging in—was fascinating. It called attention to the fact that the government engages in advertising and promotion for a broad range of activities and services in much the way that private enterprise does. The Treasury spends $500,000 a year to prepare advertising materials for savings bonds, according to Jesse L. Adams, the deputy national director of the Savings Bonds Division. The armed services advertise to prospective recruits the advantages of a military career. The Post Office promotes its overnight delivery service at premium rates. Other agencies seek to sell the use of or the merits of their programs and publications.

Such advocacy is a routine function of government. It is government promoting itself, commending itself to the public. If that seems objectionable to citizens who prefer as little and as unobtrusive government as possible, at least the advertiser is offering a specific product or service.

Advocacy of a much broader and vaguer kind is also an everyday function of government. The president and the members of Congress routinely advocate their own reelection, directly and in countless indirect but unmistakable ways. They advocate the merits of their policies and legislation. They advocate the defeat of their political adversaries. They attack the claims of their adversaries.

Such advocacy by the elected members of the government occurs daily, although it may be understated in quasispiritual Christmas and Thanksgiving messages to the public. There are some limits in law on the expenditure of public funds in a reelection effort. The president, for example, makes certain avowedly political trips at the expense of his party; however, every president has made assertedly "nonpolitical" trips at government expense even though such trips were meant to contribute to his popularity and that of his party. A senator running for reelection is supposed to pay his campaign expenses out of his campaign treasury, not his senatorial office funds. Apart from campaign financing, there are few limits on the right of the political officers of the government—the president, vice president, the president's political appointees, such as cabinet officers, and the members of Congress—to advocate their policies and themselves.

Along with this steady stream of advocacy, there is an outpouring of information by the government that is beyond measure. From the daily Treasury statement, showing how much the government gets and spends, to the decennial census results, the government spends tremendous sums—billions of dollars a year—amassing and publishing what is supposed to be factual information free of advocacy. Such information includes reports on the weather, nutrition, pest control, foreign trade, resources, health care, foreign countries, crime, and countless other topics of interest to the American people generally or to some subset of the population with a particular interest.

Many, perhaps most, of these reports are free of advocacy and may be regarded as essentially factual. Occasionally, however, the intermingling of advocacy with assertedly factual information has caused confusion and doubt. From time to time, just such confusion and skepticism has resulted from announcements by the president or a cabinet officer in a political context of economic data normally published by the government in a wholly nonpolitical way.

A good deal of government advocacy is appropriate, or at least not illegal. The problem, for both political appointees and career officials, is one of separation, of publishing factual information in a manner that does not invite skepticism about its reliability. Sometimes, as the Pertschuk letter indicated, the problem is overly zealous prosecution of an agency's deeply imbedded institutional interests. *Fortune* magazine cited such an example of misplaced zeal in its April 9, 1979 issue. It quoted a radio commercial by the Environmental Protection Agency as saying:

> Tampering with the pollution-control device of your automobile is not only against the law but, contrary to what some ill-advised mechanics say, tampering can cost you more in gas mileage and upkeep.

Fortune observed that federal law prohibits a dealer or auto mechanic from removing a catalytic converter, but not the car owner. An EPA spokesman conceded that *Fortune* was right (but added that some state laws prohibit such action by a car owner).

In apparent response to publicity about the Pertschuk letter, the FTC received complaints about the recruitment advertising of the armed forces and about the Treasury's advertisements for savings bonds. The complaint about recruitment came from the Washington Peace Center. It contended that such advertisements raised excessive expectations in the minds of unsophisticated young men and women, for example, that by joining the service they would travel to interesting places around the world, learn valuable skills, and work at interesting jobs. On its face, the complaint seems to have some plausibility. One of this author's strongest recollections of two years of army service is meeting young men who said they had enlisted for three years, rather than be drafted for two years, so that they would be allowed to choose a particular type of training. But once in the Army, they found they were unqualified, or that there were no training slots open, or that the Army had an overriding need to prepare recruits for some other type of duty. The television and poster advertisements certainly do not disclose all these caveats—the fine print, as it were. One might hope that recruiting sergeants conscientiously explain the facts of life, but one cannot be sanguine that this is usually the case.

Similarly, the Treasury's promotion of savings bonds was faulted for failing to disclose certain information. Public Advocates Inc., a San Francisco law firm, complained that savings bonds advertisements fail to disclose that with the bonds earning 6½ percent interest, and with inflation in 1979 running at 13 percent, the bonds fail to maintain the nominal value of the money invested. The Treasury replied, as it has to critics before, that in advertising savings bonds it is selling the savings habit, not the rate of interest. By encouraging employers to make payroll deductions available to their employees, the Treasury said, the program helps to create a mechanism for the automatic saving and investment of small sums. "For five bucks a week, you can't beat savings bonds," says Jesse Adams, who after 29 years with the program is a believer.

What is instructive in these two situations—military recruiting and savings bonds—is the picture that emerges of agencies that are more concerned with the success of their own programs than with seeing to it that the public gets all the facts. This is only to be expected. Put someone in charge of selling savings bonds and the success of his or her effort is measured by savings bonds sales, not by satisfying the full-disclosure notions of bureaucrats in another agency. Recruitment for the armed forces is not much different; the test of success is enlistments, not full disclosure. Yet, none of this is to say that maintaining an adequate enlistment rate and encouraging the sale of savings bonds are not in the public interest.

No one would object on principle to the government's advocating compliance with the law, for example, observing the 55 mph speed limit or filing an honest tax return. Certain other kinds of exhortation are also broadly accepted. Energy conservation now is what "meatless Tuesday" was during World War II, a patriotic act of self-denial for the common good.

Politics Is Advocacy

The elected members of the United States government—the president, the vice president, and the 535 members of Congress—traditionally have practiced advocacy in many forms. Usually no eyebrows are raised. Members of the federal judiciary are expected to advocate their views in their court opinions. Occasionally, a justice of the Supreme Court discusses law and the administration of justice in a public speech before an audience of lawyers. It is rare that federal judges express themselves on public questions of any other kind except from the bench. Indeed, vigorous democratic politics requires incumbents and challengers to advocate their beliefs and policies so that the public may make informed decisions. One expects advocacy from elected members of the government. Successful democratic politics means successful advocacy.

Advocacy also is considered an appropriate activity of the president's lieutenants—his cabinet officers, subcabinet officers, at-large presidential troubleshooters, and the White House staff. Virtually all serve at the pleasure of the president and are assumed to be loyal to the president. When they find that they cannot conscientiously advocate his policies, they are expected to do so anyway, or quit. (If they don't quit of their own initiative, they are usually pressured into doing so.)

The president's lieutenants engage in advocacy on behalf of the administration every day they are on the job. When they testify before Congress, they appear as advocates for the administration. At considerable expense to the taxpayers, the president's lieutenants travel around the country to make speeches explaining and advocating administration policy. They pursue the same purposes at press conferences and on television interview programs. In all, it is probably fair to say that most cabinet-rank officers spend 90 percent of their time either shaping policy or advocating it. (Most leave the running of their departments to a deputy.)

Body Counts, Budgets, Credibility

Indeed, advocacy is so much a part of the everyday activities of the president's lieutenants that some reporters are reluctant to believe that they ever dispense honest, untainted, factual information. Press skepticism about the government's official information about the Vietnam war—the information withheld, for example, about the bombing of Cambodia, as well as the information published—became increasingly common and outspoken as the war dragged on. This may have been the first time that credibility of the American government was repeatedly impeached in the public's mind.

Even before President Johnson sent to Congress the 1967 budget, which proved to contain understatements about the cost of the war, other presidents were accused of publishing spurious budgets. That is, their budgets showed extra revenues or spending economies that could be realized only if Congress took certain actions proposed by the president in the budget message. Often, those proposals were known to be controversial and uncertain of congressional approval. Sometimes, they were proposals Congress had defeated or ignored the previous year. In his budget for 1980, Carter included several proposals for reducing Social Security expenditures, such as abolishing the lump-sum death benefit. The fact that Congress had rejected such proposals from Presidents Carter and Ford did not inhibit Carter from renewing the proposals. The several hundred million dollars of savings they represented helped Carter to fulfill his announced determination to submit a budget with a deficit below $30 billion.

The inclusion of conditional revenues and economies in the budgets of every president has caused the press to regard the budget warily. A common view is that the budget is "phony" because it includes tax revenues or spending economies that Congress is unlikely to authorize. Journalists (and others) are entitled to that view. To the extent that it colors their over-all attitude toward the budget document, it may be unfortunate because the budget is a treasure trove of reliable information about what the government does.

As the president's budget illustrates, the comingling of information with advocacy carries the risk of casting doubt on the accuracy and honesty of the information. Such doubts may be unfounded, but they seem to arise inevitably through a kind of guilt by association. When the public senses that a political figure is using economic data to advance his or her policy, program, or candidacy, the reaction is to doubt not only the conclusions the politician draws from the data but the basic information itself.

Reading the Data

The problem for the citizen and for the news reporter is to recognize the demarcation between facts and inferences about their significance. (This is a common problem for specialists in all domains, from medicine to arms limitation to securities markets.) It does not help the reporter or interested citizen to decide what to think when he or she discovers that the experts themselves disagree about the meaning of the observed facts. Just such a problem appeared to arise early in 1971 with respect to the Labor Department's monthly report on employment and unemployment. With the economy showing signs of softness, the Nixon administration was eager to find encouraging news in the economic data, particularly the monthly report on jobs and unemployment. The unemployment rate was the economic indicator judged to be more politically important than any other.

To appreciate the brouhaha that developed in the winter of 1971, a little background is useful. For about 20 years, or since the Korean War and the pressures it put on the American economy, the Bureau of Labor Statistics (BLS) had held two briefings a month for news reporters, one with release of the job figures and one with publication of the Consumer Price Index. Just as the BLS is essentially a technical agency charged with collecting and analyzing data, so the briefings by senior BLS and Labor Department officials were essentially analytical and free of value judgments and policy recommendations. (I do not mean here to suggest that such briefings never had policy overtones. That would be beyond reason to expect or believe. There is general consensus in the United States that unemployment and inflation are bad, and that successful policy avoids them. These beliefs were implicit in many of the questions raised by reporters and no doubt were reflected in some of the answers.)

The officials discussed what the figures showed and how much one could dis-aggregate the data to get at trends for particular categories of workers, job-seekers, goods, and services. The officials discussed problems of seasonal adjust-ment and of revisions of earlier figures. They tried to make sense out of seemingly contradictory developments, such as simultaneous rises in unemployment and the number of persons employed. (That occurs because the government counts as unemployed anyone who is without a job and looking for one. If the number of job-seekers increases in any month by more than the expansion in employment, both series register increases.)

Incidentally, the labor force figures and the Consumer Price Index rarely were leaked in advance of official publication, although that has happened—usually in some incomplete way—occasionally. The specialists who cover economic news recognize that normally, little is to be gained by publishing a partial report 12 or 24 hours in advance of the official release, and there may be the danger of inaccuracy. Occasionally, when interest in the figures has been intense—for example, during a period of high unemployment—the pressures to "scoop the report" have been great and there have been such efforts, sometimes successful.

The conflict between information and advocacy in the winter of 1971 began early in January, with the disclosure that the national unemployment rate had climbed in December 1970 to 6 percent, its highest level in nine years. James Hodgson, the secretary of labor, opined that the December reading marked a cyclical peak. As if such a forecast were not risky enough, because the unemploy-ment rate is difficult to predict, Hodgson ventured that by the end of 1971 the rate would be down to 4½ percent. That forecast was more optimistic than others of the time, according to a story in the *New York Times* (January 9, 1971). Hodgson was out on a limb.

February brought a set of job figures for January of a kind that can confuse reporters and the public. With respect to unemployment, there were two de-velopments: first, the rate had slipped by two-tenths of a percentage point in January; second, the entire series had been revised upwards by two-tenths of a point. That is, the annual revision of the series for the preceding year (based on recalculation of seasonal adjustments that take into account the year itself, and other factors) had lifted the December unemployment rate to 6.2 percent, with January at 6.0. What was significant was the January decline, not the recalculation of the series.

Labor Secretary Hodgson said the decline of two-tenths of a point was of "great significance." But at the regular press briefing, Harold Goldstein, an assistant commissioner of labor statistics, called the dip "marginally significant." Hodgson professed to see good news in an increase in the number of job-holders, a figure that also is seasonally adjusted. But Goldstein said the rise was of doubtful significance because the number of persons employed in retail trade had gone up in December by an unusually small amount. Accordingly, the actual January decline was small and the seasonally adjusted total showed an increase that was more statistical than real. "It is not an upthrust in the economy," Goldstein said. Helping reporters to find their way through such technical thickets was one of the reasons for the monthly briefings.

In March, there was further disparity between the interpretations of Goldstein, the career civil service economist, and Hodgson, one of the president's lieutenants. The facts: the unemployment rate dipped further, to 5.8 percent, but the seasonally adjusted employment total also dropped, by a substantial 325,000. (A more revealing comparison showed employment down 225,000 from a year earlier, a sure sign of economic softness.) Hodgson called the reduction in the unemployment rate "indeed heartening" and "an additional indication from the labor market that the economy is moving in a favorable direction."

Later, at the regular briefing, Goldstein called the February results "sort of mixed." Pressed to reconcile that unenthusiastic appraisal with Hodgson's findings, Goldstein said, "It is not my job to support the secretary's statement or not support it. It's my job to help you understand the figures." That comment appeared in the *Washington Post*, which brought it to the attention of much of official Washington. Had it appeared in any other publication, it would have been less embarrassing for Hodgson. Hodgson's discomfort may have been compounded by a comment by the new secretary of the treasury, John B. Connally. Emerging from a meeting of the president's economic-policy officials, Connally said they were pleased with the second consecutive monthly decline of the unemployment rate; but he also voiced "a note of caution about it; that this is not such an enormous drop that any conclusions should be drawn as to what the future holds."

The employment report for February 1971 was issued on March 5. Before the month was out, Hodgson—presumably with White House clearance—had dealt with his problem in an unexpected way: he abolished the twice-monthly briefings. Reporters learned of that on March 19, when the Consumer Price Index was released without a briefing. A Labor Department statement gave the following explanation:

> The new procedure, we expect, will permit earlier release of the data by reducing time needed for the scheduling and preparation for news conferences, avoid the awkwardness of subjecting the professional staff of the bureau to questions with policy implications and achieve a consistency with the method of release of all other statistical data by the executive branch.

Of those three reasons, the first and third were nominally true but of no significance. The second, disingenuously worded, was controlling. The "awkwardness" was not, it seemed, a problem for the officials but for the secretary of labor. He didn't like being contradicted publicly by his own career officials. (It is worth remarking that Goldstein, who worked for the commissioner of labor statistics, not the secretary—even though BLS is an arm of the Labor Department—appeared to be in no danger of losing his job. For better or worse—in this case, for better—civil servants have enormous job security.)

Nine years later, the briefings were not yet restored. I do not argue that the public interest is gravely impaired by this lack. Some reporters who work with the reports for a few months become familiar with the nuances and pitfalls. Officials of the Bureau of Labor Statistics are available to discuss the reports on the very day they appear; indeed their names and telephone numbers are printed at the top of the report. Usually, however, they prefer to be referred to anonymously, as "officials" or "analysts." Such attribution, in my opinion, may lend less authority to what the officials say than would attribution by name.

Something has been lost by cancellation of the briefings. Reporters tend to be a cautious lot, on the whole, and may tend to muffle in their copy interpretive points they might make more clearly if expert officials are available to support the interpretation. Surely, the briefings were useful for reporters filling in on the economics beat for colleagues, or who were assigned to a single story—the job data or the Consumer Price Index—when economic trends were regarded by editors as big news.

In a sense, the twice-monthly press briefings have been replaced by hearings held by the Joint Economic Committee of Congress. Initially, it began hearing the commissioner of labor statistics on the morning the labor force report was issued. The commissioner read a prepared opening statement (with copies for the press), then took questions. In 1979, the committee began hearing the commissioner a second time each month, on the morning the Consumer Price Index was released. The commissioner is usually accompanied by a couple of expert associates. When the committee adjourns, all three are usually available to reporters for follow-up questions.

The committee members, of course, are free to make their own interpretations of the data and advocate their own policy prescriptions. Very often, the members use the monthly hearings to grind a favorite axe. Senator Lloyd Bentsen (D-Tex), chairman of the joint committee during the 96th Congress, invariably found something that confirmed his wisdom in introducing bills to reduce business taxes by permitting faster depreciation of equipment and factories. Reporters learn to ignore such mechanical, repetitive advocacy.

Although cancellation of the briefings did not cut deeply into the flow of information from the government to the public, it was an arrogant step in the direction of less information and less honesty. The analysis of the career experts conflicted with the interpretation Secretary Hodgson wished to advocate, and so he abolished the briefings. In the post-Watergate era, with the public and press more sensitive to abuse of official power, it is difficult to imagine a cabinet officer doing what Hodgson did. In retrospect, the only way to understand how he could exercise his authority in such a way is to see his decision in the context of other abuses by the Nixon administration, notably the White House-authorized break-in into the office of a Los Angeles psychiatrist (Daniel Ellsberg's psychiatrist) and the effort, involving Nixon himself, to cover up the Watergate burglary and related events.

Forecasts and Optimism

In the summer of 1979, there came to light another conflict between economic analysis and advocacy. This episode involved the Carter administration, which was being buffeted by an accelerating inflation and a weakening dollar. On July 12, the administration—still very much committed to holding down spending and avoiding any tax cut—published its usual mid-year budget review. The review included, in addition to budget estimates, revised economic forecasts for the economy in 1979 and 1980. It had been plain from retail sales and other figures that the economy had turned soft in the spring of 1979, particularly auto sales. Some weeks earlier, administration economists had stopped saying there would be no recession in 1979. On July 12, in releasing the revised and less favorable economic forecasts, Lyle E. Gramley, the member of the President's Council of Economic Advisers responsible for forecasting, conceded that the economy had entered a recession in the June quarter. The new forecast anticipated that business activity would contract or just barely hold its own through the rest of the year, with the national unemployment rate climbing to 6.6 percent by the fourth quarter from the 5¾ percent level around which it had been fluctuating for months. Very modest growth was predicted for 1980, along with a further rise in the unemployment rate to 6.9 percent by the fourth quarter of 1980 (when a presidential election would be held).

All of this seemed a bit optimistic, but not wildly so. Private forecasters expected a deeper slump, but there were a few who predicted no meaningful economic recession at all. Before July was out, however, there came to light through leaks an unpublished forecast dated July 27, a forecast prepared by the very economists supposedly responsible for the mid-year review. That forecast was decidedly more pessimistic, anticipating that the unemployment rate would be in the vicinity of 8 percent by the fourth quarter of 1980.

Most significantly, the few new economic data that had become available between July 12 and 27 were inadequate to explain the difference in the forecasts. It appeared that the later forecast, the one not intended for public consumption, was what the administration forecasting group really anticipated and that the published forecast was disingenuous precisely because it was intended for public consumption.

A sophisticated comment about all this might be: "So what! The White House is always the most optimistic economic forecaster around. Why should the Carter White House be different from the others?" There is a germ of truth in such sophistication, but much less than the whole truth. It is arguable that a president's forecasts tend to be self-fulfilling, especially if they anticipate trouble. There is an old wheeze to the effect that it is much easier for a president to talk the country into a recession than out of one. With just that in mind, one of the most sober, responsible fiscal officials in the government said to this writer one day, "Of course, the White House puts out more optimistic economic forecasts than others do. Anything else would be irresponsible."

The official explained that he was not asserting that the White House had a right to publish recklessly optimistic forecasts unrelated to private opinions. At any moment, he explained, an honest forecaster can pick not a single number but a range within which any value is about equally probable. The White House, the official argued, has an institutional responsibility—whoever is president—to choose numbers close to the optimistic end of that range.

That the two July 1979 forecasts were disparate and only 15 days apart was the most awkward aspect of the situation for the White House. No one could explain, for example, what had happened in 15 days that called for revision of the estimate of the 1979 decline of GNP from 0.5 percent (July 12) to 1.4 percent (July 27). Similarly, the July 12 forecast anticipated a 1980 rise of consumer prices of 8.3 percent, whereas the July 27 figure was up to 9 percent.

On their face, both forecasts could not represent good-faith assessments of the economic outlook. It is ironic that the Carter administration should have been embarrassed in this way, because it seemed to be making in July 1979 an earnest effort to avoid the kind of mulish optimism that had impaired the credibility of other administrations. For example, in presenting the July 12 forecast, Lyle Gramley said that an economic recession had begun in the second quarter of the year. Gramley could have equivocated on the grounds that it takes at least two consecutive quarterly declines of the GNP to make a recession (in the popular definition; the scholarly version is more elaborate) and that the third-quarter results weren't in. But having no doubt that the third quarter would show a decline, he called it a recession.

One advantage of such forthrightness was that it headed off endless press questions about the administration's candor, prescience, and hopes, not to mention inevitable press badgering from week to week thereafter as to whether it was clear yet that a recession had started. (Three months later, in October, the government reported that the GNP had scored a gain in the third quarter. Where was the recession? Officials could say only that they had been right the first time, that the third quarter was an aberration and that further declines in the GNP were in prospect. In fact, the second-quarter was the aberration and the recession didn't start until the first quarter of 1980.)

The heart of the forecasting problem is that sometimes the most honest numbers don't support the policy advocated by the administration. For example, the July 26, 1979 forecast of a weaker economy in 1980 could be read as casting doubt upon the wisdom of the administration's determination to hold fast to its budget and monetary policies of restraint. Because of this policy, the president already was in considerable trouble with the left wing of the Democratic party. He did not want more such trouble; he did not want to hear months later recriminations that his advisers had told him as early as July that his anti-inflation policies would drive unemployment to 8 percent. There were risks in pursuing restraint, but the administration judged them to be worth taking for the sake of battling inflation and supporting the external value of the dollar.

Energy Data Demonology

In 1976, Congress addressed directly the proposition that advocacy and information should be held rigidly separate. The context was energy, a problem that burst on the United States in the early 1970s with disturbing implications. The essential lesson was that the United States, which always has regarded itself as richly endowed with natural resources, was becoming increasingly dependent on foreign countries for the crude oil and petroleum products that were providing half of the country's total energy supplies. In October 1973, Arab states attacked Israel in a war that was to last weeks. The United States began shipping military equipment to Israel, whereupon the Arab states announced an embargo on shipments of crude oil to the United States (and the Netherlands and South Africa, also allies of Israel).

Early in December, Nixon created an emergency energy office to take charge of supplies. Meanwhile, the effects of the embargo were beginning to make themselves felt as the country's refiners found their incoming supplies of crude oil diminishing. By January, gasoline lines had begun to form in some states; the scarcity of gasoline became an all-consuming topic. For the first time, the American public found that the fabled American standard of living so casually taken for granted was in jeopardy. Meanwhile, enterprising journalists in the United States and Britain began to write stories that suggested that the shortage was spurious. Such doubts were encouraged by left-wing critics of the oil industry, who wanted to mold public opinion in support of their purposes, such as breaking up the big oil companies and establishing a government oil company that would operate as a "yardstick" against which to evaluate the performance of the big companies.

Two types of issues concerning information emerged from the embargo. One was a complex and subtle question about how to read the data—whether high stocks of fuel, for example, amounted to significant evidence that the shortage was spurious. (By themselves, stock data do not permit drawing a reliable conclusion.) The second was the reliability of the information available to the government about oil production, imports, and stocks. That data came weekly from the American Petroleum Institute (API), a trade association. Although its membership includes many small companies, API is a creature of the big companies, such as Mobil, Standard of Indiana, and others. Members of Congress and the press expressed dismay or outrage that the government was dependent for vital data on the very industry whose motives and practices were under suspicion.

The government's only comprehensive data on natural gas reserves was coming from the producers, via the American Gas Association (AGA). With the interstate pipelines beginning to experience tightening of supply in 1970 following a hectic decade of growth and bullish marketing, attention was drawn to the AGA figures. They showed that in the lower 48 states, reserves hit a peak in 1967 and then started to decline. (There was a one-time upward bump in 1970, when gas in, Prudhoe Bay, Alaska, was included in the data, but then the downward trend resumed.) The industry, meanwhile, was campaigning for an end to federal regulation of producer prices of gas sold in interstate commerce. The producers contended that regulation was keeping prices artificially low, discouraging exploration and encouraging profligate consumption of gas.

Didn't policy-makers need more reliable data, or at least data that came from independent sources, some members of Congress and the critics asked? Wasn't there a danger that the industry's statistics, if not outright dishonest, had some sort of self-serving bias? Congress and many commentators thought the answer to both questions was affirmative. That the government's other economic and resources data—coal and uranium reserves, retail sales, industrial production, inventories, and so on—were based on company reports did not matter. There were availability and price issues in oil and natural gas, and so reserves, production, imports, and stocks were deemed to be matters the government should measure for itself.

In the 1974 act creating the Federal Energy Administration (FEA), Congress directed the new agency to develop many kinds of statistics. It was only two years later, in the 1976 act extending the life of the FEA, that Congress expressed concern about separating information from advocacy. In Senate consideration of the bill, Senators Floyd Haskell (D-Colo) and Henry M. Jackson (D-Wash) offered an amendment to create within the Federal Energy Administration what Haskell called "a professional Office of Energy Information and Analysis." Haskell, in a Senate floor statement, gave this explanation:

> One of the most important reasons why so many of the debates over energy choices in past years have failed to converge has been the widespread confusion with respect to, and outright distrust of, both basic background energy data and statistics and the analytical methods used to organize this information. Control of and access to energy information has been held tightly by the energy industry for years. . . .
>
> Both the industry and the F.E.A. have been involved in the energy debate as advocates. This automatically raises substantial questions about the reliability and usefulness of the energy information and analysis which is provided from these sources.
>
> I believe there is an inherent conflict of interest between the role of a policy advocate and that of one who attempts to serve as an objective provider and organizer of information. I believe that this conflict of interest has substantially inhibited acceptance of the real messages contained in the energy statistics. . . . Both the F.E.A. and the industry have often told us the truth. However, because of their advocacy roles, both the basic information and analysis and their policy advice has been perceived as slanted.

Haskell went on to say that the new Office of Energy Information and Analysis should be "explicitly separated from the energy policy role of the F.E.A." and should "serve as an objective, professional resource for the Congress and the public. . . ." Haskell essentially made two points: that there is a conflict of interest, and that the public's perception of this alleged conflict denied credibility even to honest, accurate statistics. The amendment was adopted, after virtually no debate, by a voice vote. The Senate-House conference retained it.

In 1977, the Haskell amendment was elaborated in Section 205 of the bill creating a cabinet-rank Department of Energy. Both the House and Senate bills contained such provisions, and they were easily melded. Section 205 created within the department an Energy Information Administration and included several provisions designed to protect the independence of the administrator. It specified, for example, that the administrator did not need the approval of anyone else in the department for the collection or analysis of information; nor, it said, did he need prepublication approval of any statistics or forecast "of any other officer or employee of the United States." That language included the president.

As is often the case in government, the background to Haskell's doctrine of separation of policy-making from data-collection was more particular and less general than the senator's statement implied. By June 1976, when extension of the Federal Energy Administration was on the Senate floor, the Democratic Congress and the Republican president, Gerald Ford, had clashed along essentially ideological lines on a number of energy issues—chiefly decontrol of prices of petroleum products and natural gas; breaking up of the major oil companies; and putting the government into the business of producing crude oil. On each of these issues, especially price decontrol, the FEA policy staff produced figures that purported to show that decontrol and higher prices would inhibit consumption and lead to more domestic production. Democrats in favor of controls (and quite a few, chiefly from producing states, opposed them) attacked these figures in any way they could. Inasmuch as the FEA's deputy administrator in charge of policy also was in charge of data collection, the Democrats questioned the objectivity of the data.

Haskell's assertion about "inherent conflict of interest" was, like most such charges, easy to make and difficult to refute. Even someone who thought that there probably was little or no deliberate skewing of the data collected by the FEA could recognize that the issue would be eliminated by a prophylactic separation of data-collection from policy analysis. Moreover, there is some logic to such separation: collection essentially concerns what has happened; policy analysis requires speculation about what is likely to happen if the government takes various policy paths.

One could point to other agencies in which there is such separation. For example, the Internal Revenue Service publishes annual volumes of data about income tax returns filed in the preceding year. These are dispassionate summaries and cross-cut analyses of numbers compiled from tax returns. Tax policy is made by the Treasury's tax staff, which prepares predictive estimates of the revenue effects of the proposed changes. I have heard no suggestion that the Statistics of Income volumes published by IRS have been distorted for policy purposes.

A large fraction of the government's regular outpouring of economic data comes from two statistical agencies whose independence is rarely challenged. They are the Labor Department's Bureau of Labor Statistics and the Commerce Department's Bureau of the Census. Each department has a policy-making apparatus that is separate from the data-collection functions. The two bureaus are staffed by career employees who owe their jobs to no president. Only the top job in each bureau is filled by the president, and there is a tradition that both the commissioner of labor statistics (sometimes a career person) and the director of the census are people of distinguished professional backgrounds. This was just the image that Senator Haskell had in mind for the Administrator of Energy Information.

Conclusions

Law and tradition in the United States give the central government scope for a broad range of advocacy. Yet, there are limits. The government can advocate morality in a general way, but not specific religions. Yet, it would not be illegal or unconstitutional for a president or a member of Congress to recommend a particular religion, but even as general exhortation such advocacy would offend many people and cause serious repercussions for the advocate. Similarly, there are limits to certain other kinds of advocacy. The government can advocate wage and price restraint, but it runs into objections and alleged equity issues when it attempts to lay down specific guidelines for restraint.

The government can advocate good health, but not a specific doctor, medical group, or hospital. (In a limited way, the Department of Health and Human Services (formerly HEW) and the Congress have sought to arouse public interest in and support for medical-practice groups known as health maintenance organizations. Federal grants and loans are available to help them get started.) There are interest groups that fear economic injury and mobilize effective opposition. The many hospitals in the United States defeated mandatory hospital cost-containment legislation in the 95th and 96th Congresses.

The government can counsel against smoking, but only in limited ways. Although only a few states grow tobacco, the Congress continues to subsidize tobacco growers. The executive branch makes only token efforts to discourage smoking. The government can advocate sound nutrition. But there is strong resistance from business when an effort is made to go beyond general exhortation, as the Department of Agriculture found when it tried to exclude "junk food" from school lunch rooms.

Each of these instances shows that there are substantial barriers to making advocacy effective. One is the resistance of groups that fear economic injury (the tobacco farmers, candy companies, hospitals). A second, more subtle barrier is the general public view that government should not become intimately involved in regulating the everyday lives of the citizenry. This view combines a traditional wariness of the power of government (see the Bill of Rights) and the 1970s backlash against federal regulation as unnecessarily complicated, troublesome, and expensive (to consumers, taxpayers, and business).

Energy conservation has become a motherhood issue, advocated by all, opposed by no one. But the Congress has been unwilling to adopt several energy-conservation measures—rationing, additional gasoline taxes, decontrol of gasoline prices, mandatory quotas limiting oil imports, a "gas guzzler" tax on big cars. Each means discomfort or economic damage. Instead, the Congress has authorized tax credits for persons who install insulation and other energy-saving materials or who put in solar-energy devices. Tax credits do not mean discomfort or economic loss to taxpayers individually.

Each of these examples of advocacy that has been frustrated—wage-price restraints, smoking, nutrition, energy—points up the difficulty in the United States of marrying program to policy, of advancing advocacy beyond words into institutions and behavior. The gap between advocacy and program often is pronounced and persistent. This gap raises a question about whether our system of government is adequate to the problems of the times. The founding fathers were ambivalent, seeing the need for strong central government but also fearing it. Over two centuries, the trend has been for the central government to expand its powers. Yet, there seems to be now a considerable inability of the government to realize in program and action the policies it advocates. Perhaps this is only a temporary period of adaptation to radically different problems, a period in which a new public consensus is being forged. One must hope so, because the inability of the government to realize the goals it advocates—stopping inflation or diminishing the country's dependence on imported oil—is profoundly disturbing.

LEGAL FRAMEWORK

All communicators must be sensitive to the laws and regulations which help shape their environment; no communicators must be more sensitive to this legal framework than government communicators. The six articles that follow define the legal framework for government information practice and delineate the differences of opinion and interpretation in the field.

Anne S. Runyan, who completed her undergraduate and graduate studies at McGill University, the University of Windsor, and The American University, and currently a doctoral student in international relations at American, opens the inquiry with a review of the "Development of Public Information Laws." Ms. Runyan compiled the data for this chapter while serving as a research associate with the Institute for Government Public Information Research at American. Her account demonstrates the cyclical impact of political factors on the laws affecting government information and the effects of these laws on the psychological climate surrounding government information practice and its practitioners.

The access to records legislation known popularly as the Freedom of Information Act (FOIA) is the subject of two personal accounts, one by a government information officer charged with carrying out the act's provisions, the other by a former journalist who used the act to help make public serious shortcomings in private nursing homes. Russell M. Roberts, a public information officer with the Department of Health and Human Services, discusses the procedures by which his department—long regarded as a leader in FOI implementation—carries out both the spirit and letter of the law. Roberts is a graduate of the George Washington University and attended law school there. Before entering government service in 1963, he worked at the *Washington Star* and with Warner Brothers Pathé News.

Mal Schechter, currently a special aide to the National Institute on Aging of the National Institutes of Health, describes the lengthy process he initiated to extract data on nursing homes from the Social Security Administration in the early 1970s. Schechter, who holds a master's degree from the Columbia University School of Journalism, is the former publisher of *Aging Services News* and former Washington editor of both *Hospital Practice* and *Geriatrics and Modern Medicine*.

Related to FOIA and the access issues it raises is the Privacy Act of 1974 and the protections it affords to individual citizens. Robert Ellis Smith, the foremost journalistic proponent of a strict privacy law, opens this discussion with a vigorous defense of his concept of the Privacy Act's intent—to protect people, not government agencies, from unreasonable scrutiny. Smith received his undergraduate degree from Harvard and his law degree from Georgetown University. President of the *Crimson* while at Harvard, he has eight years experience as a reporter. Smith has edited and published *Privacy Journal* for the last several years.

Discussing how his agency walks the delicate line between protecting privacy and disclosing illegal acts by private citizens is A. James Golato, assistant to the commissioner and national director of the public affairs division of the Internal

Revenue Service, Department of Treasury. A graduate of Temple University, where he studied both journalism and accounting, Golato has held IRS investigative and technical positions in addition to his public affairs work for that agency.

Dealing with the complex and sensitive subject of the effects of national security considerations on public information practices is George Carver, a senior fellow at Georgetown University's Center for Strategic and International Studies. Carver, who retired in 1979 as deputy to the director of the Central Intelligence Agency, holds an undergraduate degree from Yale University and a doctorate in philosophy from Balliol College, Oxford. His book, *Aesthetics and the Problem of Meaning*, was published by the Yale University Press in 1952, and he has published numerous articles on national intelligence in foreign affairs periodicals.

CHAPTER 5

Development of Public Information Laws

Anne S. Runyan

There is no more difficult task facing the modern democratic state than that of containing pressures toward excessive publicity, without at the same time encouraging practices of secrecy which choke off the flow of information about public affairs upon which the vitality of government by discussion essentially depends. These are among the central problems that arise in reconciling the conflicting claims of publicity, secrecy, and democracy.[1]

American government has yet to meet adequately this challenge Francis Rourke articulated in his 1961 text, *Secrecy and Publicity*. The failure to strike a delicate balance between publicity and secrecy stems from some attitudinal and institutional factors heretofore inherent in the democratic state. In America, these factors have been translated into concrete legal restrictions.

The Origins of Government Secrecy

Until the passage of the Freedom of Information Act in 1966, there has been a long-standing legal tradition for government *not* to communicate. In 1775, during the Revolutionary War, laws pertaining to military secrets were first promulgated. In the early days of the Republic, the "first assertion of a claim to secrecy on the part of the Executive was made in 1792 by President Washington on the occasion of an investigation by the House of Representatives into an Indian massacre of a military expedition under the command of General Arthur St. Clair."[2] From that time, as will be described in more detail in subsequent sections, the right of our government to withhold information which might endanger national security has enjoyed strong and consistent legal sanction.

Since World War II, we have witnessed the development of an elaborate American security classification system, outlined in four executive orders issued by as many presidents and codified in a wide variety of other statutes, such as the Atomic Energy Act and the National Security Act. Also, as the Watergate hearings of 1973–1974 demonstrated, there is increased recognition of the doctrine of executive privilege. Although each of these laws and executive prerogatives are generally justifiable in themselves, the bureaucracy has tended to use them excessively, either by overclassifying documents, failing to declassify them when warranted, or inappropriately withholding information which would not adversely affect either the national security or the public interest. In effect, the American government has created a secrecy system which is frequently unjustifiable and always expensive, as a House subcommittee reviewing use of the national security exemption during the first five years of the Freedom of Information Act's operation learned when an expert witness testified that over $100 million is wasted each year as the result of overclassification.[3]

Numerous theoreticians have analyzed the tendency toward executive secrecy in all democratic states. One compelling assertion was advanced early in the 1900s by the sociologist Max Weber, in his discussion of the characteristics of the modern bureaucracy.[4] Weber hypothesized that secrecy is a necessary function of bureaucracy. It is first a source of power for the individual bureaucrat who must move up the government career ladder on the basis of his unique "knowledge" and talent. Also, secrecy sustains a self-perpetuating bureaucracy which prefers to realize its organizational goals without outside interference.

Robert K. Merton preferred to view secrecy as a manifestation of a "dysfunctional" bureaucracy in which the participants are "so subject to structural constraints toward overconformity or trained incapacity"[5] that they become obsessed with rules and regulations, often at the expense of meeting the needs of those they serve. Regardless of the source of this tendency, it has hampered the passage and intent of laws designed for greater disclosure of government information. This we can observe from the legislative history of the Freedom of Information Act.

Legislative History of FOIA

The Freedom of Information Act (FOIA) was signed into law by President Lyndon B. Johnson on July 4, 1966, as Public Law 89–487 (codified at 5 U.S.C 522) and went into effect on July 4, 1967. Enacted as an amendment of Section 3 of the Administrative Procedure Act of 1946 (5 U.S.C. 1002), it was the first comprehensive legislation in defense of the "people's right to know." FOIA signalled the adoption of the policy that "'any person' should have clear access to identifiable agency records without having to state a reason for wanting the information and that the burden of proving withholding to be necessary is placed on the Federal agency."[6] In theory, this represented a radical departure from prior legal sanctions pertaining to the release of government information, all of which tended to work more in favor of secrecy than disclosure.

The first pieces of legislation in this area were the "housekeeping" laws of 1789 (now codified at 5 U.S.C. 301), passed not long after the first Amendment to the Constitution guaranteeing freedom of the press. As codified in the Revised Statutes of 1873, the provision authorized "the head of each department . . . to prescribe regulations, not inconsistent with law, for the government of his department, the conduct of its officers and clerks, the distribution and performance of its business, and the custody, use, and preservation of its records, papers, and property appertaining to it."[7] This explicit control over departmental documents constituted a major statutory shield for the perpetuation of executive secrecy. This shield remained solidly in place even after it was amended in 1958 (72 Stat. 547) through the efforts of Congressman John Moss and his Special Subcommittee on Government Information to increase public access to information. After great debate and much compromise, the amendment was reduced to one new sentence emphasizing only that the law did not authorize withholding information from the public.

The Administrative Procedure Act of 1946, which was amended by FOIA, generally required that official government documents be made available to the public, but permitted the withholding of records where there was involved "(1) any function of the United States requiring secrecy in the public interest or (2) any matter relating solely to the internal management of an agency" or simply "for good cause found."

Needless to say, the vagueness of these statutes afforded great latitude in interpretation. Such latitude rarely, if ever, resulted in a precedent for increased disclosure. Rather, it allowed for a congeries of excuses for withholding information. This tradition of executive secrecy severely jeopardized the passage and reduced the efficiency of the highly touted Freedom of Information Act.

> The Executive Branch agencies did not support the proposal and had it forced upon them; the President reluctantly signed the bill, indicating to top administrators a lack of sympathy for the statute's requirements; the *Attorney General's Memorandum* interpreting the Act reflected a bias against the true spirit of the law; and the departments and agencies, in allocating resources for the administration of the Act, failed to regard its dictates seriously.[8]

Similar resistance was met when FOIA was amended in 1974 and when FOIA's sister pieces of legislation, the Federal Advisory Committee Act (FACA), Public Law 92–463, which became effective on January 6, 1973, and provided for increased government review and public scrutiny of federal advisory committees, and the Government in the Sunshine Act, Public Law 94–409 (now codified at 5 U.S.C. 522b), which took effect on March 12, 1976, and required open meetings for some 50 federal agencies headed by collegial bodies, were introduced. The Privacy Act, Public Law 93–579 (now codified at 5 U.S.C. 522a), which became effective on September 27, 1975, is also considered a companion piece of legislation to FOIA and is discussed in depth in a later chapter, as is current interpretation of FOIA itself.

The Historical Stigma of Government Publicity

As if it were not enough that secrecy is the dominant tendency of government and, therefore, its most common *modus operandi*, government publicity has had historically the added burden of being held in absolute contempt by powerful critics both outside and inside government, particularly legislators.

> The publicity function has been under steady fire from journalists, from some members of Congress, and from anti-administration politicians in campaigns. . . . In part, the opposition is merely a reflection of the stereotyped irrational resentment of "propaganda" and "press agents" which has arisen in the current tensions of transition from rural primary to urban secondary association in the nation. This cultural suspicion of publicity as a formalized way of persuading people to do something when they do not know they are being persuaded is too familiar to dwell upon. The point here is that the general atmosphere of distrust in which the federal publicity agent works is a factor in his status and forces him more than any other staff official to justify his role.
>   The broad criticism of "propaganda" implicit in contemporary culture has led to tangible legal restrictions.[9]

The legal restrictions James L. McCamy refers to in his 1939 treatise, *Government Publicity*, were enacted mainly in the early 1900s and are still in effect today. These restrictions serve both to obscure the generic title and function of the government public information practitioner and to prevent the proper reconciliation of the principles of secrecy and publicity necessary to a democratic society.

Antipublicity Legal Precedents

A number of incidents led up to the legislation designed to limit, if not eradicate, government public information activities.[10] Commonly known as the Gillette amendment to the Deficiency Appropriation Act of 1913 (38 Stat. 212, now codified at 5 U.S.C. 3107), this rider to the appropriations bill specifically forbade the spending of appropriated funds to hire "publicity experts" without express congressional approval. It was triggered by the reaction of Rep. Frederick H. Gillette (R-Me) to a Civil Service announcement recruiting a publicity expert for the Office of Public Roads, Department of Agriculture.

The Agriculture Department had already been taken to task in 1908, by the passage of the Mondell Amendment, and again in 1912, when Congressman John Nelson of Wisconsin charged the department with prejudicing his resolution to investigate meat inspection in the department's Bureau of Animal Industry by the issuance of a department circular defending its position on the matter. Similarly, Rep. John T. Robinson launched a 1910 inquiry into the hiring of an eight dollar per day "special agent" by Census Bureau director E. Dana Durand to publicize the 1910 census. This time, however, the Census Bureau was able to prove its case and won at least tacit congressional approval for the position.

In any case, the Gillette Amendment, more than any other piece of legislation, has denied the public information function a legitimate place in the governmental process.[11] Ironically, a law intended to bring to the light of day—if not snuff out—any nefarious attempts at "propaganda" by federal agencies, instead at times has promulgated subterfuge. Since the Gillette Amendment's enactment, publicists and public relations professionals have continued to enter government service in great numbers due to the increasing desire of Congress and the greater need for the executive branch to explain complex government programs to constituents. However, they have done so under the slightly evasive titles of public information, public affairs, education, or administrative specialists.

These effects of the 1913 law were compounded recently, too, by Richard Nixon's 1970 presidential order demanding that all federal agencies curtail "'self-serving and wasteful public relations activities.'"[12] It is little wonder that a January 1979 General Accounting Office (GAO) report found that "evaluating public affairs activities has been, and still is, difficult because Government agencies do not uniformly define 'public affairs' and are not consistent in reporting and evaluating their public affairs costs."[13] What is surprising is that neither the legislators requesting the investigation nor GAO addressed the causal relationship between the 1913 law and the current problems with government public information.

Six years after the Gillette Amendment, two more statutes were enacted which further inhibited public information practices. The first is the so-called "gag law" of July 11, 1919 (18 U.S.C. 1913), which prohibits the use of appropriated funds for any form of communication designed to influence the direction of legislation. It carries with it a fine not to exceed $500 or imprisonment for not more than one year or both. Although communication between members of Congress and government officials through "proper official channels" or by request is exempted, and the law itself has not been enforced to the letter, McCamy noted that "an extreme interpretation would forbid the distribution to congressmen of much of the literature published by administrative agencies."[14] This law has also found reaffirmation in more recent statutes involving appropriations, such as Pub. Law 92–351, Sec. 608(a) enacted July 13, 1972, Pub. Law 93–50, Sec. 305 enacted July 1, 1973, Pub. Law 93–143 and Pub. Law 93–192 (both enacted in 1974), which essentially reiterate that no part of any appropriations shall be used for "publicity or propaganda purposes" to influence the direction of any legislation pending before Congress with the exception of presentations made directly to Congress.

The second law, enacted on March 2, 1919, is now codified under title 44 of the United States Code which encompasses public printing and documents. Section 501 of title 44 requires that all printing and binding for all government entities be done by the Government Printing Office. Exceptions can only be made with the approval of the Joint Committee on Printing. Although the original intent of the law was to create an economical and efficient clearinghouse for all government printing, the system more often results in a complete lack of control over the content and design of government informational material by the initiating agency, printing "bottlenecks," and inflated prices for government publications.[15] In addition, there is the government franking privilege restriction (39 U.S.C.A. 321n), which limits the use of the free mail frank by prohibiting any executive department from mailing material without a request.

Finally of note is the Federal Register Act which has an indirect, but nevertheless disquieting, effect on responsible public information practices. The act, which resulted from a bill (H.R. 6323) introduced by Representative Emanuel Celler (D-NY) during the 74th Congress (1935) and was amended in 1937 (50 Stat. 304), created the Code of Federal Regulations which are now up-dated daily through the *Federal Register*.[16]

As the primary vehicle for making all regulations public, the *Federal Register* has great significance to the public information practitioner. Too often, the information officer is not told by agency colleagues when certain regulations will be published, leaving no time to prepare adequate responses to media inquiries sparked by *Federal Register* announcements. And now, through electronic data banks, increasing numbers of interested members of the public can obtain virtually instantaneous access to regulatory announcements, magnifying even further the plight of the public information officer who seeks to inform lay people of the implication of such events.

In sum, the legal precedents indicate a history of general legislative and administrative inertia concerning government-initiated public information programs and materials, disrupted from time to time by congressional outcry over government propaganda. Further, as Cutlip and Center have observed, such strong but intermittent congressional reaction is a true manifestation of our constitutional system of checks and balances:

> This opposition comes from both the legislator engaged in a struggle for power with the executive branch and from the legislator of the minority political power seeking majority control.[17]

Indeed, the typical scenario for such a power struggle occurs when a member of Congress either initiates or cites antipublic information legislation, effectively attacking an agency stand on an issue by suggesting that propagation of that agency position be curtailed. Thus, we find an inherent paradox. Congress fears the manipulative aspects of government public information or propaganda. But by legislating against it, at least in the piecemeal and erratic fashion observed to date, lawmakers themselves have become the manipulators, allowing the public information function to flourish only where it is politically expedient or in support of policies which they favor.

A Legislative Double Bind for the Practitioner

Although secrecy remains a hallmark of government bureaucracy, the trend toward greater disclosure is clear with the passage and growing acceptance of FOIA, FACA, Government in the Sunshine Act, and other agency-specific information laws and regulations designed to increase access to government information. Moreover, it is important to note that, increasingly, the responsibility for administering disclosure law provisions is falling upon the shoulders of government public information practitioners. Paradoxically, then, the same officials who court congressional disfavor for disseminating information about government (either at the behest of their superiors or as part of an agency's legal mandate), are now often expected to provide assistance to the public when requests are made for records or access to policy meetings.

This awkward state of affairs was accurately summarized by William L. Webb, then president of the Government Information Organization (now the National Association of Government Communicators), in a statement to the House Subcommittee on Foreign Operations and Government Information (now the House Subcommittee on Government Information and Individual Rights) during hearings which began in June, 1971, on the effectiveness of the Freedom of Information Act:

> The Freedom of Information Act, when laid side by side with section 3107 of title 5 of the United States Code, creates a state of schizophrenia in the minds of many government public information employees. . . . Many government public information officers feel they are caught in the crosscurrents of these two statutory directives, and the public is the real loser. The Freedom of Information law clearly orders the Government to recognize the public's right to know what its Government is doing. Obviously there must be an effective and free flow of information from the Government to the public if we are to comply with this mandate. But the machinery to accomplish this obligation takes personnel and money, and section 3107 can be construed as outlawing funds and people for such purposes.[18]

Webb's argument did not convince Congress to take steps to repeal the 1913 statute (an action recommended by the committee report which never even resulted in a hearing). But the dilemma facing the government public information practitioner who must work under such conflicting legislation remains real.

Passive Versus Active Instruments of Democracy

To date, Congress has attempted to strike a balance between secrecy and publicity by legislating for passive instruments of democracy, such as the Freedom of Information Act the provisions of which must be triggered by a public request, and against active instruments of democracy, such as government-initiated public information programs. Conversely, the executive branch rails against FOIA and similar passive instruments and does everything it can to circumvent antipublicity laws. One might view this as a manifestation of a healthy balance of power. But when it comes right down to effects, one finds that the public is not informed well enough to participate in the democratic process to use, for example, the powers inherent in FOIA.

In the next chapter, Russell Roberts notes that relatively few FOIA requests are received from members of the general public, the press, and public interest groups. Either lacking the time or inclination to wade through and interpret "raw" government documents, Americans have come to rely on receiving the government information they need to carry on their daily living from sources who can explain and interpret government policies in an expedient and understandable fashion.

This is not to say that the passive instruments should be abandoned. They are essential to making all of government adopt an open stance, and they should be expanded. But the active instruments, if administered evenly and professionally, should also be allowed to coexist with and bolster the passive ones. Perhaps, in this way, the conflicting claims of secrecy and publicity might finally be resolved.

Notes

1. Francis E. Rourke, *Secrecy and Publicity* (Baltimore: Johns Hopkins Press, 1961), p. 17.

2. U.S. Library of Congress, Congressional Research Service, *The Evolution of Government Information Security Classification Policy: A Brief Overview (1775–1973)* [by] Harold C. Relyea (Washington, D.C., 1975), p. 2.

3. Ibid., p. 25.

4. See *Max Weber: Essays in Sociology*, edited and translated by H. H. Gerth and C. Wright Mills (New York: Oxford University Press, 1946), pp. 196–204.

5. Scott G. McNall, *The Sociological Experience* (Boston: Little, Brown, 1971), p. 87.

6. U.S. Congress, House, Committee on Government Operations, and Senate, Committee on the Judiciary, *Freedom of Information Act and Amendments of 1974* (P.L. 93–502), Joint Committee Print, 94th Congress, 1st Session (Washington, D.C.: U.S. Government Printing Office, 1975), p. 3.

7. Rourke, p. 16.

8. Harold C. Relyea, "Opening Government—The Federal Experience: Freedom of Information and Information Control" (commentary prepared for The Commission on Freedom of Information and Individual Privacy, Toronto, Ontario, Canada, November 10, 1978), p. 8.

9. James L. McCamy, *Government Publicity* (Chicago: The University of Chicago Press, 1939), pp. 5–6.

10. As elsewhere in this book, the terms public information, public affairs, public relations, publicity, and propaganda are used somewhat interchangeably as they differ little in actual denotation, only in connotation. Public information and public affairs, however, are the terms most often applied to the function as it is practiced in government because, as will be demonstrated, the use of the latter three terms in that milieu has been deemed taboo by the legislature.

11. Dr. Harold Relyea of the Congressional Research Service has suggested that Rep. Gillette would have argued that government public information (or publicity) has no place in lawmaking or administration and, therefore, has no legitimate part to play in the governmental process. However, as we have seen, the function, which is increasingly receiving managerial status within a far more complex and sensitive governmental milieu than in 1913, can and does play a vital role in both these realms. See also *Freedom of Information Act and Amendments of 1974* (P.L. 93–502), p. 59.

12. Samuel J. Archibald, "Access to Government Information—The Right Before First Amendment," *The First Amendment and the News Media: Final Report*, Annual Chief Justice Earl Warren Conference sponsored by the Roscoe Pound–American Trial Lawyers Foundation (1973), p. 73.

13. U.S. General Accounting Office, *Difficulties in Evaluating Public Affairs Government-Wide and at the Department of Health, Education and Welfare*, Report by the Comptroller General of the United States, LCD 79–405, January 18, 1979, p. i.

14. McCamy, p. 8.

15. For a more detailed critical analysis of Title 44 from the perspective of the public information practitioner, see Henry Lowenstein, "Statement on Revision of Title 44 Submitted on July 24, 1979 to the Committee on House Administration and the Senate Committee on Rules." *Journal of Public Communication* 5 (1979):15–19.

16. U.S. Library of Congress, Congressional Research Service, *Title 44, United States Code—Public Printing and Documents: A Brief Historical Overview* [by] Harold C. Relyea (Washington, D.C., 1979), Multilith 79–36GOV, pp. 34–35.

17. Scott M. Cutlip and Allen H. Center, *Effective Public Relations* (Englewood Cliffs, N.J.: Prentice-Hall, 1971), p. 544.

18. *Freedom of Information Act and Amendments of 1974* (P.L. 93–502), p. 50.

CHAPTER 6

The Freedom of Information Act

Russell M. Roberts

It has a nice ring: the Freedom of Information Act! It's a name intended, of course, to stir the patriotic soul. It was signed into law, symbolically, on July 4, 1966, by President Lyndon Baines Johnson, to take effect on Independence Day one year later. As with much legislation, the title promises somewhat more than the statute delivers. It's not precisely a Freedom of Information Act, but rather an access to records act. It promises records, not information. The Freedom of Information Act does, however, provide the basic authority and procedure for the public to petition the executive branch for otherwise unreleased documents and records in its possession. It recognizes that government runs the only game in town and ensures that the public, who must play the game, can find out the rules of the game, the score, who made the hits, and who made the errors.

The Freedom of Information Act was intended to force federal agencies to reveal information they were sometimes less than eager to disclose, information about their failures as well as their successes. The act resulted from 11 years of investigative hearings on government secrecy by the House Government Operations Committee's former Special Government Information Subcommittee (1955–1962) and legislative deliberations by the successor Foreign Operations and Government Information Subcommittee. It was also based on studies and legislative proceedings conducted simultaneously during this period by Senate Judiciary Committee subcommittees.

The new FOI Act repealed the so-called Public Information Section of the Administrative Procedures Act, which had permitted executive branch agencies to withhold government records "for good cause found" and "in the public interest." If no good cause could be found for withholding information, the section allowed the bureaucracy to release information selectively to individuals "legitimately and properly concerned." The FOI law established the "right to know" and abolished the requirement that seekers of information about their government demonstrate a "need to know." When President Johnson signed the new law, he said: "I have always believed that freedom of information is so vital that only the national security, not the desire of public officials or private citizens, should determine when it must be restricted." In fact, the record shows that President Johnson opposed various crucial aspects of the statute and successfully beclouded its intent by pressuring for a House report which was not only inconsistent with its Senate counterpart, but contrary, at some points, to the explicit language of the proposal.

To explain the proper procedures for granting access to public records under the new FOI act, the Department of Justice prepared a 47-page memorandum providing government-wide guidelines for implementation within the executive

This chapter was written by Russell M. Roberts in his private capacity. No official support or endorsement by the Department of Health and Human Services is intended or should be inferred.

branch. The Attorney General's Memorandum, issued in June, 1967, stated that the key concerns of the law are:

- that disclosure be the general rule, not the exception;
- that all individuals have equal rights of access;
- that the burden be on the government to justify the withholding of a document, not on the person who requests it;
- that individuals improperly denied access to documents have the right to seek injunctive relief in the courts;
- that there be a change in government policy and attitude.

Those lofty ideals were somewhat diminished, however, because the Attorney General's Memorandum further confused the intent of Congress by its own misinterpretations of the act and by its reliance on the politicized House report.

Despite the new law's high-sounding name, the public relations "hype" of the presidential signing ceremony, and the strong support of the media which had loudly proclaimed its belief in its First Amendment responsibilities to inform the public, minimal use was made of the law during the first few years. Government agencies, none of which had endorsed the legislation, developed cumbersome regulations to comply with the FOI act and assigned responsibility for its administration to lawyers or records managers. Implementation of the act was viewed by most agencies as simply a paper exercise, or a legal exercise, or both. The self-protective bureaucratic desire to play it close to the vest, and the lack of leadership or sense of priority by the administration, led agencies to circumvent the new law. Thus, they developed secrecy by delay, taking many weeks to answer an initial request for access to a public record. They developed secrecy by dollars, charging far in excess of costs for copying public records.

They also used the investigatory files exemption as a major shield of secrecy. The original FOI act included nine categories of public records which might be exempt from public disclosure. One category was investigatory files compiled for law enforcement purposes. Federal agencies often claimed their public records were investigatory files even though the investigation had been completed long ago. When all else failed, federal agencies forced insistent applicants for public records to go to court. It was easy to get a case into court, for the law required federal district courts to give FOI cases expeditious handling. However, litigation was expensive, and agencies knew public record applicants would be likely to back away from their demands for documents rather than go to court.

In 1972, the administration and operation of the Freedom of Information Act came under detailed congressional scrutiny. During 14 days of sworn testimony, the House Foreign Operations and Government Information Subcommittee heard various government and private witnesses discuss their experiences and difficulties with the public access provisions of the statute. The House committee concluded: "The efficient operation of the Freedom of Information Act has been hindered by five years of foot-dragging by the federal bureaucracy."

Senate Administrative Practice and Procedure Subcommittee hearings on FOI act operations supported the House subcommittee's conclusions. Congressional interest in how the act was being administered culminated in 1974 with the adoption of legislation strengthening the provisions of the FOI act. The amended FOI law included stringent time limits for responding to requests (10 working days for initial requests, 20 working days for appeals from denials); administrative sanctions against employees who "arbitrarily or capriciously" withheld records; assessment of litigation costs and attorney's fees against agencies whose refusal to provide records is overturned in court; revision of the investigatory file exemption to limit its use to withholding only when disclosure would interfere with law enforcement proceedings or cause other specified harms; and annual reports to Congress on agency FOI activities.

As in the case of the initial 1966 Freedom of Information Act legislative history, no executive branch agency spokesman endorsed the 1974 amendments when they were being considered by Congress. Moreover, while President Johnson's support of the 1966 legislation was uncertain until he signed it into law, President Ford's opposition to the 1974 amendments was such that he vetoed the measure. Congress overrode the veto.

The atmosphere in which the 1974 FOI amendments were adopted was considerably different from that in which the original law had been passed. A president had been forced from office, at least in part because of an attempted cover-up. There were disclosures of wire-tapping of National Security Council staff, of White House "enemies lists," of misuse of individuals' Internal Revenue Service tax reports, of spying on private citizens, and illegal use of the FBI and CIA in domestic political activities. These and the news media's coverage of President Ford's veto of the FOI amendments, the Congress's override of that veto, and media reporting of increasing numbers of court cases through which government was forced to disgorge records sought under the FOI act, all served to enhance public awareness of the law and greatly increased its use. There was, in fact, an explosion of FOI requests.

For example, the former Department of Health, Education, and Welfare got fewer than 1600 requests in 1973; by 1979 it reported 46,673 requests. HEW's experience was not unique. The Department of Defense (57,845 requests); Department of Justice (21,940); and Department of Treasury (18,440) all reported similarly increased demands. The cost in 1979 of processing these requests by more than 90 reporting executive branch agencies was $37 million. FOI had become big business.

In addition, the provision in the 1974 amended FOI act allowing recovery of court costs and attorney's fees by requesters invited litigation. By 1979 more than 650 FOI cases had gone through the judicial process. The government lost many more cases than it won. A backlog of cases began building up, and the staff resources of the Justice Department's Litigation Division were severely strained. On May 5, 1977, Attorney General Griffin Bell warned executive branch departments and agencies that the Department of Justice would no longer defend an agency in litigation involving withholding of records unless the agency could establish that:

1. The records fell within one or more of the nine specific exemptions to the FOI Act's mandatory disclosure rule, and
2. That disclosure would result in demonstrable harm.

The attorney general told agencies that the mere fact that records could be withheld because they were technically exempt from disclosure was no longer—if it had ever been—a sufficient basis for denying access to those records. Because of this new standard requiring them to demonstrate that harm would result from disclosure, agencies were forced to consider other than legal factors in deciding whether to permit public access to records. While some executive departments and agencies, after passage of the 1974 amendments, had placed administration of the FOI act in the hands of public affairs officials or at least insured public affairs participation in the decision-making process involving FOI requests, the attorney general's new advisory prompted others to reconsider their procedures. HUD, VA, and other agencies began developing plans to move administration of the act out of the hands of their attorneys. The problem is where to place the responsibility—with program officials, records management or administrative service officials, public affairs officers, or others—and at what level. The experience of the Department of Health and Human Services (HHS), formerly Health, Education, and Welfare, would be a useful example to those and other agencies in making those decisions.

One Agency Experience

HHS's policy has evolved from the agency's attempt to carry out the spirit as well as the letter of the law. As a result, the agency's procedure has consistently been to interpret and implement the act's provisions for access to information in the broadest and most open fashion. No request for records is denied unless the records are legally exempt from disclosure and there is a compelling need to withhold them.

In 1965 President Johnson directed federal establishments to provide for better public access to government information sources. Johnson named John Macy, chairman of the Civil Service Commission, to head a task force to study the problem. On November 1, 1965, the president issued a directive to all federal agencies in which he recommended establishment of information centers which would be accessible to the people. John W. Gardner, then secretary of health, education, and welfare, placed responsibility for implementing this program of expanded services with HEW's public information officials.

When the Freedom of Information Act was signed into law by President Johnson eight months later, Secretary Gardner established a task force charged with developing recommendations for ensuring compliance. That task force— composed of attorneys, program administrators, management officials, and public information officers from HEW's operating agencies—presented three major recommendations which were adopted by the secretary. Each succeeding secretary has reaffirmed these recommendations:

1. That Department policy call for the fullest responsible disclosure consistent with those requirements of confidentiality and administrative necessities stated by the Freedom of Information Act itself;
2. That responsibility for administering the Freedom of Information Act be placed under the department's chief public affairs official; and
3. That access to requested records never be denied unless there were both a legal basis for the denial and a compelling need to withhold the requested information.

To ensure strict compliance with the last requirement, no denial is issued without a three-party consideration of the issues. The department's attorneys provide legal advice as to whether a requested record might be withheld; program administrators advise on the compelling need to withhold (for example, if disclosure would interfere with or impede effective program administration of government operations, interfere with property or privacy rights, etc.), and public information officials determine whether HHS will comply with FOI requests.

Authority to deny access to records requested under the FOI act was limited to only 16 of the chief public information officials at headquarters and in the field—one in each of the agency's ten regional offices and one in each of the six principal operating components in Washington. The secretary's decision that the Freedom of Information Act would be administered by public information officials recognized that those officials are the primary point of contact with the news media, the public, and the many special-interest audiences that the department serves.

In the 1972 hearings on the government's administration of the Freedom of Information Act during the first four years of its existence, Chairman William S.

Moorhead of the House Subcommittee on Government Information and Foreign Relations commented:

> HEW is the only agency in which the public information people appear to control public information. When the FOI Act was passed, HEW set up a special office to help administer it. This was part of HEW's continuing effort—going on ever since the Department was created—to gain some semblance of coordination over the diverse agencies which made up the Department.

Later, Moorhead and more than a dozen colleagues introduced a bill which would have required all federal agencies to establish a position of principal public affairs officer, having the title of assistant secretary for public affairs—or assistant administrator, commissioner, or other equally appropriate title—among whose chief responsibilities would be administering the FOI act. The proposed legislation was never acted on.

First as HEW, now as HHS, it has been the agency's experience that, placing administration of the FOI act with the public information officials, it avoided problems that might have arisen by placing it with either the department's attorneys or its program administrators. Program officials, it might be argued, have a vested interest in withholding records that might disclose inefficiency in administration or mistakes in judgment. Government attorneys, consistent with their role in other matters, limit their participation to advising whether records might be withheld because the records come within the legal definitions and court interpretations of one or more of the nine exemptions to mandatory disclosure. They do not make policy determinations as to whether such documents should be released or withheld.

HEW tried to ensure that each request—whether granted or denied—was handled promptly. Anticipating in the early 1970s that Congress would enact changes to strengthen the law, HEW's attorneys and public information officials began an extensive revision of the department's public information regulation, first published on June 30, 1967. In August, 1973, while the Congress was still considering proposed amendments to the FOI act, HEW published its new regulation. It reflected many of the changes in the law that would be incorporated in the amended FOI act passed over presidential veto on November 21, 1974. The most significant of these were self-imposed time limits of 10 days on the initial handling of FOI requests and 20 days on appeals from denials of FOI requests.

Each denial was made not only promptly but also with a full explanation of "why"—citation of the exemption (with cross-reference to HEW's implementing regulation) and the rationale for it. This was on the assumption that reasonable people respond to a reasoned reply. Nothing, in fact, can arouse more understandable hostility than an arbitrary reply—and surely government ought always to be at some pains to explain the decisions it reaches.

Another policy decision in the spirit of the law was that HEW administer the act without dependence on precedent. It quickly became clear that each case was best evaluated on its merits, with consideration not only of its legal but its public relations aspects. There is a normal administrative tendency in any organization to seek precedents. This is a natural outgrowth of government by law and it is, obviously, a way of life in the executive branch which must administer congressional enactments. Precedent can also be an easy and safe way out of unpalatable situations. Avoiding reference to precedent in the over-all administration of the Freedom of Information Act, however, has had the important advantage of continuously accentuating the positive approach throughout HEW.

Literal interpretation of the exemptions in the act could also seriously nullify the law's effectiveness. This is not to say that certain exemptions are not vital:

particularly those which cover the preservation of personal privacy, of legitimate trade secrets, and the need for government officials to exchange views *in camera*. In HEW, these exemptions had particular relevance for the Social Security Administration and some elements of the Public Health Service, particularly the Food and Drug Administration. A rigid and legalistic attitude toward them, however, could defeat the purpose and intent of the FOI act. This was distinctly not HEW's posture, as evidenced in the extensive 1973 revision of the agency's Public Information Regulation. HEW's self-imposed time limits for responding to FOI requests and denial appeals added impetus to the spirit of openness, and accomplished reduction of average response time from the 54 days reported to Rep. Moorhead's subcommittee to only 16 days.

Of the more than 46,000 requests received by HEW in 1979, only 1,082, less than 3 percent, were denied. For the most part, these were partial denials only. By comparison, other agencies reported refusal rates as follows: Defense, 15 percent; Justice, 15 percent; Treasury, 18 percent; Commerce, 15 percent; and State, 23 percent.

Who Uses FOIA?

Much is being made these days of what many consider the disproportional use of the Freedom of Information Act by business and industry, or by attorneys representing these businesses and industries, compared with the fewer number of requests from the media, public-interest organizations, and individual citizens. Some government officials have voiced concern that there is widespread use of the FOI act by commercial interests to obtain confidential data which, if disclosed, would provide them with an advantage over their competitors—competitors who have given that commercial and financial information to government agencies in confidence. One regulatory agency, for example, claims that 80 percent of all FOI requests it receives are efforts at "industrial espionage." Many of that agency's FOI requests, however, come from companies whose facilities or products the agency has inspected and which want to know the results—and the consequences—of those inspections. An attorney requesting information about a product or a company that produces it, rather than representing a competitor might, instead, represent a client believed to have been harmed by the product.

Concern is expressed, too, over industry's use of the FOI act to obtain government information which it then sells to its clients. Fee-for-services companies are making FOI requests for clients who either did not wish to be identified—there are even FOI requests asking who is making FOI requests—or who find it preferable to buy such services for whatever reasons. There is certainly nothing new about selling government information. Long before there was a Freedom of Information Act, companies were compiling and selling directories of government contacts, offering assistance in applying for social security benefits for a fee, or putting a new cover on the *United States Government Organization Manual* and selling copies of a "New Encyclopedia of Federal Agencies" at $20 to $50 a copy. As far as the use of the FOI act by business and industry to gain advantage over the competition is concerned, some undoubtedly try to do so. It is totally unfair, however, to attribute ulterior motives to all businesses and industries who use the FOI act.

Companies seeking to do business with the government or applying for research funds also make use of the FOI act to obtain copies of successful bids or grant applications so as to improve the quality of their own submissions. If the quality of contract proposals and grant applications is improved and legitimate competition enhanced as a result of such requests, the government—and ultimately the public—benefits. Or FOI requesters may be trying to assure themselves that a competitor beat them out of a contract because of the merits of the competitor's bid and not because of impropriety on the part of a government official. Surely, that kind of scrutiny is exactly what was intended to be provided by the FOI act.

As far as alleged industrial spies are concerned—whatever percentage of requesters they may be—exemption number 4 of the FOI act, aimed at protecting trade secrets and commercial and financial information provided in confidence, is intended to thwart their efforts. Moreover, it should be remembered that a single FOI request from the media, a public-interest organization, or an individual citizen is of far greater importance and has the potential for influencing public opinion, the decisions of government, or the health of our nation a hundred times more than a thousand requests by one business seeking a competitive advantage over another.

The Role of Public Affairs

While it may not be necessary to place administration of the Freedom of Information Act under the agency's public affairs officer as the Department of Health and Human Services has done, it is obvious that public information officers have a significant role to play in any agency's effective implementation of the act. There is a public relations impact to virtually every decision to disclose or to deny access to records. The public information officer can best assess that impact and its news value.

CBS's Mike Wallace once considered a segment on the high rate of default in the Guaranteed Student Loan Program for his program, "60 Minutes." He knew that the Office (now Department) of Education had collected, from thousands of lending institutions across the country, status reports on every student loan showing whether those loans were current, deficient, or in default. Wallace wanted a list of the 100 lending institutions having the highest rate of default. Office of Education officials pleaded for the protection of any of several FOI exemptions. First, though, they argued that the FOI act did not require them to compile or create such a list from their raw data. That was correct, the FOI officer ruled, but they might be required to provide the raw data and let Wallace compile his own list of 100 having the highest rate of default.

Next, Office of Education officials pleaded for invocation of the exemption pertaining to financial institutions, but the application of that exemption could not be stretched to fit the facts. Protect personal privacy, the officials demanded. Delete names, ruled the FOI officer. One by one, the applicability of the nine exemptions to mandatory disclosure of the FOI act were explored and discarded. It was only then that the real story came out.

The Office of Education had stored the information on 30 computer tape reels. Only 26 of these could be located. The fact was that the integrity of the information was compromised and the Office of Education had no way of determining an accurate answer to the Wallace inquiry. The FOI officer told the agency officials that they did not have a Freedom of Information problem, but they certainly had one hell of a public relations problem. Together, though, they discussed it with Wallace and admitted the blunder. The worst that could have happened was that Wallace might have taken 60 seconds or so of extremely valuable prime-time air time to point an accusing finger at another incident of bureaucratic blundering. But by this time, perhaps, stories of incompetence in government had so glutted the market that they were beginning to lose their news value. In any event, Wallace never mentioned the situation on the air.

In the dozen or so years that the Freedom of Information Act has been on the books, there has been a noticeable change in attitude throughout government. From a disposition to conceal, there has been a swing to the impulse to reveal. This is not, of course, all-embracing; and there have no doubt been acts of nullification which have never surfaced. Nonetheless, changes there have been.

The sometimes monumental, sometimes minuscule effect that disclosure wrought by the Freedom of Information Act may have had upon our society awaits history's perspective. Can we withstand the knowledge that J. Edgar Hoover had feet of clay and that Joseph A. Califano had a cook? Regardless of history's answer, it is clear that federal officials today appear to be less apprehensive about and less resistant to the Freedom of Information Act and the concept of open government. The doomsayers who predicted that letting a little sunshine into the bureaucratic workings of government would cause it to wither and die have not, at least to date, been right.

CHAPTER 7

How the FOI Act Has Been Used

Mal Schechter

On March 1, 1972, I entered a U.S. Postal Service substation in the U.S. Treasury Department building in Washington, D.C. This is the building depicted on the back of a ten-dollar bill. For much less than that, I initiated that day a Freedom of Information Act action that led to one of the first FOI lawsuits by a journalist for information that the federal government refused to divulge. I won that lawsuit in U.S. District Court. But that didn't stop the Government from declining, as its attorneys so elegantly phrased it, to "acquiesce" in the decision. I then filed a second lawsuit and eventually won it in a circuit court. As a result of this decision and decisions in several other jurisdictions in suits filed after mine, any individual can obtain the Medicare inspection record of any hospital, nursing home, home-health agency, or independent laboratory that participates in the program of health insurance for the elderly. As a result of my lawsuit and others based on the FOI act, Congress in 1972 changed the Social Security law governing Medicare and Medicaid to require that inspection records be routinely made public in the future.

Here's one way those records have been used. The National Council of Senior Citizens (NCSC), a labor-backed group representing millions of elderly persons around the nation, obtains the inspection records of Medicare and Medicaid nursing homes in the metropolitan Washington area. To this data, it adds fee structures and other information it gathers on its own. Anyone who wishes can look at these records and make comparisons among the facilities, just by visiting a model center which makes conveniently available information the government has gathered at taxpayer expense. Before 1972, the government obstructed such an effort—in defiance of the public's right to know the conduct of its own business, a precept articulated in 1966, when the FOI act was passed by Congress.

This is the story of the lawsuit I brought. When the Medicare amendments to the Social Security Act were passed and signed into law in 1965, they carried an implicit promise to open up windows on the nation's health-care establishment. It would not be long, I thought, before comparative information on the cost and quality of service in hospitals, nursing homes, and other providers of care would be known on a broad scale, regardless of the penchants of doctors, administrators, and technicians to keep such information confidential.

There was never any question that the Social Security Administration would make aggregate data available. Congress and the public had to know the total costs of the Medicare program so that tax rates could be set. The pattern of utilization of benefits by beneficiaries upon the instigation and advice of their guardian providers had to be known for policy as well as cost reasons. The intricate, limited benefit structure—it did nothing to cover outpatient drugs and long-term care in nursing homes, for example—was considered an installment on a more comprehensive system. Expansion of the program would occur as experience was gathered on costs, outcomes of care, and priorities of need for service.

In the early years, it became clear that costs were rising more quickly than expected. Questions were raised about the quality of care in facilities receiving Medicare payments, and nowhere were the questions so hot and heavy as in the nursing home sector. As a senior editor for the physicians' monthly, *Hospital Practice*, I undertook to follow and report on the administration of Medicare and Medicaid. An early article concerned the abuse of a provision under which payments for emergency hospital care could be made to an institution outside the Medicare system. Curiously, this provision was most often used in the South, where, also curiously, a number of hospitals were not in compliance with Medicare requirements.

One requirement had to do with the 1964 Civil Rights Act. No federal assistance could go to an institution unless it assured it was unsegregated. The Medicare law, however, allowed for payment for services covering a beneficiary if he or she needed them in an emergency and a fully qualified institution was not accessible. Segregated Southern hospitals had an unusual number of emergency Medicare patients, according to statistics given out by the Social Security Administration (SSA). I asked for them because an SSA official told me they would be the opening wedge for a key story on Medicare implementation.

Other officials assured me that the unusual cases were justifiable admissions to segregated hospitals. How did they know that? Well, they had the physicians' admitting diagnoses. Who checked on the validity of these? Why, nobody, really. No federal officer had authority to examine a patient. About all that could be done was to review the paperwork. If it was internally consistent with the concepts of "emergency" and the inaccessibility of a fully qualified Medicare hospital, then Medicare had to pay.

As the story turned out, thanks to inside sources, there were inconsistencies in the paperwork. For example, one patient's chart carried the physician's note that the patient could go home at night and return the next morning, if the patient wished. Another "emergency" patient was found to have been taken by ambulance past a Medicare hospital to a segregated hospital miles down the road.

With that information unofficially provided, I wrote a story about the abuse of Medicare and lax federal administration. Soon after its publication, the Social Security Administration produced tough regulations covering emergency admissions. As this source of payment dried up, a number of previously recalcitrant Southern hospitals suddenly joined the program.

Another investigation disclosed that, again contrary to the 1964 Civil Rights Act, Medicare hospitals in Louisiana were discriminating by race in making transfusions. Specifically, they were using blood labeled by race of donor and giving it only to recipients of the same race, contrary to scientific findings that in all but the most rare instances race makes no difference. A Louisiana law requiring transfusions to be given only with same-race blood was in effect. But the state health department informed hospitals to overlook it after my story appeared in *Hospital Practice* and was reported in the mass media. The American Red Cross chapter in Alabama, which shipped blood into Louisiana, stopped labeling by race; an honorary member of the Red Cross national board of governors happened to be the secretary of health, education, and welfare, the official responsible for the administration of Medicare.

I mention these stories for several reasons: (1) to show that journalism can lead to proper administration of the law, (2) to show that while officials sometimes profess to be unaware of administrative deficiencies, access to the data will demonstrate the deficiencies, and (3) to point out that there are often officials who will use the press to influence, even embarrass, their higher-ups into carrying out the law.

I might also mention that sometimes data are not gathered or are kept fragmented because of the potential political repercussions. For a Medicare official to carry out the mandate of the 1964 Civil Rights Act would mean the possibility of a clash with the chairman of the Senate Finance Committee and the House Ways and Means Committee. In the late 1960s, they were, respectively, Russell B. Long of Louisiana and Wilbur D. Mills of Arkansas, a state which had only lately abandoned its blood segregation law. In both states, and in other Southern states with powerful members of Congress, too, physician and hospital interests not only hated Medicare but were segregationist as well. Medicare officials, trying to get their program off and running, were tempted to look the other way.

It was highly important for Medicare in its organizing years of 1966 and 1967 to sign up as many hospitals and nursing homes as possible, so that the promised statutory benefits would be available to people. The political problem of low-quality hospitals was, in effect, resolved in the Medicare statute: any hospital accredited by the Joint Commission on Accreditation of Hospitals (JCAH) was deemed to meet the Medicare standard of care. JCAH happened to be the creature of the American Medical Association, American Hospital Association, American Surgical Association, and American College of Physicians. In essence, the statute let the public interest lawsuit in the District of Columbia and in San Francisco demonstrate that some JCAH hospitals were unworthy to be in Medicare. Congress subsequently allowed the secretary of health, education, and welfare authority to inspect JCAH hospitals to test whether they were indeed up to the Medicare standard.

In the case of nursing homes, there was no commission comparable to JCAH. One of Medicare's pioneering efforts at standard setting concerned nursing homes. The program issued its own standards and applied them through state health departments, working under contract. Rumors abounded in 1967 that HEW was admitting many nursing homes that did not meet its standards or the 1964 Civil Rights Act.

My early efforts to obtain inspection records to get a sense of what was going on were met by rebuff. No, I could not have these records. The authority for denial was Regulation No. 1 of the Social Security Administration, backed up by Section 1106 of the Social Security Act. Here is what that Section said:

> No disclosure . . . of any file, record, report or other paper, or any information obtained at any time by the Secretary of Health, Education, and Welfare . . . or by any officer or employee of the Department . . . in the course of discharging these respective duties under [the Social Security Act] . . . shall be made except as the Secretary . . . may by regulations prescribe.

This meant that, unless the secretary—actually, the commissioner of Social Security—established a regulation allowing the disclosure of a class of information, nothing could be disclosed. The agency had, by regulation, allowed for the disclosure of statistical information. It had not done so for Medicare inspection records. But it could; the choice not to do so was theirs. And so I argued off and on with SSA in letters in 1968, 1969, and 1970.

At the same time, I was corresponding with Arthur Flemming, a former HEW secretary (under President Eisenhower) who had become, while president of a midwestern college, head of the Social Security Advisory Council. Flemming, a former journalist, turned out to be sympathetic to disclosure. He continued to relay my correspondence to SSA and ask them for their view. SSA became more and more defensive.

Perhaps the most definitive statement of SSA's view is contained in a May 20, 1972, letter by Commissioner Robert M. Ball to me:

While we agree with this objective [of helping physicians and patients make sound judgments about institutions], we believe that widespread and indiscriminate dissemination of information about deficiencies in all participating institutions . . . may have some undesirable effects. Since certification is denied if institutions have deficiencies which constitute hazards or potential hazards to the health and safety of patients, public disclosure of the existence of other deficiencies in institutions which are certified might create unwarranted concern that particular facilities may be unable to provide adequate patient care. Such adverse public reaction could severely hamper an institution's efforts to maintain patient-loads while effectuating needed improvements.

In other words, SSA expected outsiders to take its word that it was carrying out the law, that no dangerously unsafe facility was in the program, and that to allow the public to make judgments about minor problems would hurt the income of the institutions.

In retrospect, it appears I was arguing with SSA on irrelevant grounds. There was the FOI act, passed in 1966, effective in 1967. I did not realize that it required SSA to turn over the inspection records I wanted. I had not really studied the act. I had a vague understanding of the kinds of information it exempted from disclosure. One of these stated that information specifically exempted from disclosure under prior statutes need not be disclosed.

My view until late 1971 was that the only way to get the records from a reluctant SSA was to change the Social Security Act. I began discussions with the staffs of the Finance and Ways and Means committees. They turned out to be sympathetic.

Jay Constantine, whom I had known since the early 1960s when he was on the staff of the Senate Special Committee on Aging, was particularly encouraging. As the health insurance expert on the Finance staff, he had produced a penetrating criticism of Medicare administration in 1969. Its disclosure of timid policy-making helped to strengthen the program. In 1970 and 1971, the Finance Committee was at work on a fresh round of Medicare legislation largely based on this report. Constantine saw the need for public disclosure guarantees, but, with an eye to getting a slate of reforms approved, did not want to push for disclosure of all past records. There was too much bureaucratic resistance. He thought SSA would go along with disclosure of records made in the future.

However, Constantine referred my proposal to amend Section 1106 to an aide to Sen. Abraham Ribicoff (D-Conn), a Finance member. My proposal would have limited secrecy to those SSA records identifying beneficiaries; all other records would be open. The senator introduced an amendment to this effect but, because of his wife's illness, was absent when Finance considered the subject of disclosure. Sen. Frank Moss (D-Utah), not a member of Finance, introduced an amendment applicable to Medicaid nursing home records, based on the staff work of Frank C. Frantz; this amendment and the approach approved by Constantine became part of the 1972 Social Security law.

While Congress was working slowly on Social Security legislation, the *Washington Post* in September, 1971, published my article, "Medicare's Secret Data." In it, I explained that Section 1106 was being misused. When the provision was enacted in 1939, the names of beneficiaries of federally aided welfare programs were being given out by state agencies. They gave the names to tradesmen and even allowed the names to be posted in an evident attempt to humiliate beneficiaries and deter potential recipients from applying for aid. Congress agreed with the then-Social Security Board that the privacy of these individuals and the objectives of the program needed statutory protection.

This was a valid purpose. The section actually restated Regulation No. 1, which the Board adopted as part of the wholly federal program of retirement benefits for the elderly. Twenty-five years later, in 1965, when Medicare was added to the

Social Security System, Section 1106 was automatically applied to Medicare information, including data from the program's corporate servants as well as its beneficiaries.

The *Post* article was read by Ralph Nader, the consumer leader. Nader was interested in the nursing home industry. And when we met by chance on an airplane after the *Post* publication, Nader said he was interested in the article. He suggested I bone up on the FOI act and said that if I thought I ever might need assistance, I should contact a legal assistance group he was just then establishing in Washington.

In January, 1972, I met the "group," consisting of Alan Morrison and a bicycle, in a small office on Fifteenth Street. Morrison thought I had overlooked the power of the FOI act. Soon after, I was introduced to Ronald Plesser, who quickly became a friend, adviser, and exponent. I told them that *Hospital Practice* was in no position to help me finance legal action. They said they would do the legal work without charge, but I would have to pay any court or transcription fees.

On March 1, 1972, I went to the Treasury Department building's Postal Service substation on Fifteenth Street, a block from the National Press Building. I registered a letter to SSA Commissioner Robert Ball requesting access to inspection records on 15 Medicare nursing homes in the Washington area. This was the text:

> Dear Commissioner Ball:
>
> On Jan. 9, 1970, a fire at a Medicare approved nursing home in Marietta, Ohio, took 32 lives. In preparing a story at the time, I became aware of the SSA policy, based on Section 1106 of the Social Security Act, to hold confidential the Extended Care Facility Survey Report. I was denied access to the report on the Marietta facility, Harmar House.
>
> I am now preparing a follow-up report bearing on Medicare inspections of extended-care facilities.
>
> Hoping that your confidentiality policy may have changed, I ask to be permitted to inspect and copy the latest Extended Care Facility Survey Report on Harmar House.
>
> In addition, I ask to inspect and copy the survey reports on ECFs named in the attachment.
>
> I would appreciate a reply within 30 days. . . .
>
> Sincerely,

The request was denied, I thought, in a March 28 letter from an HEW official. Morrison and Plesser immediately began to draft a complaint. On May 12, 1972, a letter from Commissioner Ball also denied my request, saying: "We favor in principle, and, so far as legally permissible, carry out in practice, the concept of making available to the public information regarding the operations of the Medicare program." Nevertheless, he concluded Section 1106 prohibits disclosure of the material I was requesting.

The reply was both laughable and infuriating. Ball or the secretary of HEW might at any time untie their own hands by issuing a regulation. They wouldn't say why they wouldn't do this.

On June 20, my lawsuit was filed under the FOI act. It argued that Section 1106 did not specifically apply to the kind of record I was requesting, and therefore it was invalid to argue that the FOI act exemption of statutory secrecy authority applied to my request. "To allow the continued non-disclosure," my complaint said, would be to negate the purposes of the Freedom of Information act, which has been proclaimed to provide the greatest possible access to information.

U.S. District Court Judge Joseph Waddy ruled in my favor on July 17. Ironically, for an information case, the ruling did not become known until September. A clerk had not notified us of the decision. I was not the only person involved in opening up Medicare program records. Suits similar to mine were filed in Florida (with a similar result) and in California (where the government won).

Within HEW, meanwhile, a battle was going on between those who wanted aggressive implementation of the FOI act and those who wanted to wait and see what would happen in terms of public and press use of the act and congressional pressure. Among the proponents of aggressive implementation was J. Stewart Hunter, associate director of information for public services, HEW. In testimony March 6, 1972, before the House Government Information subcommittee, Hunter declared that "Section 1106, as it now stands, squarely contradicts the Freedom of Information Act. As long as it exists, it will constitute a barrier to obtaining information on that agency's operations." And Robert O. Beatty, HEW assistant secretary for public affairs, also noted the conflict. "I'm sure the Subcommittee recognizes the difficulties inherent in administering legislative mandates which are in conflict."

My lawsuit and others could be understood as attempts to resolve that conflict. Congress could be accused of having legislated without a clear enough mandate for disclosure, and the courts were being asked to rectify the situation. As Nader appeared to understand so well, the FOI act would be given a cutting edge in the courts, and he intended that the public interest, as he saw it, should prevail.

So, SSA turned over to me the 15 nursing-home inspection records, at first attempting to charge me almost $100 for copying them. The records showed that several Washington area nursing homes had problems which the public, if not SSA, would consider serious. One, for example, did not have enough clean linen. Another advertised but actually had no rehabilitation facilities. Indeed, the records suggested that the nursing homes had entered Medicare more on promise than reality of compliance. There was more than enough evidence to convince me of the correctness of rumors that many nursing homes had been accepted into Medicare for political reasons.

On September 2, HEW announced proposals to change Section 1106. The announcement was in expectation of a legislative provision awaiting enactment in the 1972 Social Security Amendments. Inspection records made in the future would be disclosed after 60 days in which the facility could add comments or rejoinders. The records would then be available on request at the Social Security district office serving the area in which the facility was located.

The proposed regulation eventually became final, and the 1972 Social Security amendments became law. Unfortunately, both were silent as to pre-1972 records, and this silence was fashioned into another barrier to disclosure, not only to me but to others. The Camden (N.J.) *News-Courier* sought nursing home inspection records and was refused, even though it cited the decision in my case.

How was it possible for an agency of government to decline to follow a principle established in court? Apparently, the Department of Justice had decided that the government would not "acquiesce" in the ruling by the U.S. District Court for the District of Columbia. According to the Solicitor General, the government's chief lawyer, the Justice Department had withdrawn a notice of appeal to the decision in my case for two reasons: (1) SSA has published a disclosure regulation relative to future inspections, and (2) Congress had passed a disclosure provision in the Social Security amendments, at the time pending the president's signature. Or, as the Department put it in a memo, "for response to inquiries": "This measure if it becomes law, would be determinative of questions such as those involved in the Schechter case."

Moreover, The Solicitor General has advised [HEW] that his determination not to pursue the appeal . . . does not indicate the Government's acquiescence in the ruling of the District Court or any agreement that it correctly states the rule of law applicable to requests for disclosure such as that by Mr. Schechter. Rather, it was a determination that the Schechter case, in the light of the considerations just described [the SSA regulation and the amendments], was not an appropriate vehicle for raising the issues in the appellate court.

Thus, having decided that his chances for winning an appeal were not as good as he might wish, the solicitor general not only decided to ignore the court ruling but advised HEW to be guided by its current regulations prohibiting disclosure. "This means," the memo concluded, "that for the present, the Department of Justice will oppose any further efforts to obtain court orders for the disclosure of nursing home survey reports that have already been prepared."

This decision applied to inspection records for any Medicare facility, not just nursing homes. When I filed an FOI request for the inspection records of a clinical laboratory and a hospital on October 16, 1972, it was denied. "[HEW] has not acquiesced" in the court ruling, said a letter from the assistant commissioner for public affairs of SSA on November 15.

Actually, HEW was not "acquiescing" in rulings made first in my case and subsequently in a case in Florida, where it was appealing. HEW now based its denials on the regulation and new law. HEW contended that Congress could have legislated to open past Medicare records but did not. This silence was interpreted to mean that Congress agreed with past nondisclosure policy. So HEW asserted, adding that Congress never provided for disclosure of Medicare inspection records prior to 1972 although it had "every opportunity to do so."

I put the question of what Congress meant about past inspection records to the chairman of the Senate Finance Committee, Sen. Russell Long. In a letter to me, he explained that the disclosure provision in the new amendments "was not intended to estop any disclosure which otherwise might be required under other relevant Federal law—such as the Freedom of Information Act—with respect to present, past, or future surveys."

It wasn't until June, 1973, that my second disclosure suit was finally heard in U.S. District Court, this time by Judge George Hart. The judge found the HEW arguments acceptable and, while ruling against me, said he hoped my attorney would appeal the case. We did.

On October 3, 1974, the appeals court decided in my favor, 2–1. The decision, written by Senior Judge Charles Fahy, completely rejected HEW's argument concerning Section 1106. "Read as a whole, section [1106], vests complete, uncharted discretion with respect to disclosure to the Secretary rather than being a specific exemption by statute." The decision noted that the Florida case had by this time been decided against HEW in the appeals court and that a New Jersey case had been decided against HEW in a district court. Other cases had gone likewise.

What had been won? First, access to Medicare inspection records and other records maintained under the Social Security Act, except for personal records, was assured. Second, the FOI Act was visibly strengthened by the courts, which appeared to say, in effect, that the partisans of secrecy now had an uphill fight to retain it. The cases also demonstrated, I think, that there was an articulate, enthusiastic band of FOI supporters with sufficient resourcefulness to carry the day in court. Somebody really cared about FOI—the act and the principle—and would take on censorious officials.

The cases also showed the need for administrative and court procedures to toughen the FOI act. What Plesser, Morrison, and their associates in Nader's litigation group learned from cases like mine eventually was applied in FOI act modifications. Years later, when I asked for information, there was no hint of resistance or foot-dragging. If a journalist knew what to ask for and knew the act and the regulations, he or she would get the goods.

The episode was personally illuminating. In a direct and concrete way, I had seen public accountability at work: the government had been forced to produce records for me. The FOI act, as made effective in the courts and by amendment, continued to help me to research stories about the making and implementation of social policy. In the three years it took for my cases to run their course through the courts, I had sensed the contribution journalism can make to social policy, not only in the field of health care and insurance, but also in administration, through the power of disclosure.

A few days after I had mailed my registered letter to the Social Security Administration, the House subcommittee concerned with the FOI act, chaired by John Moss (D-Calif), was taking testimony on the act's implementation after seven years on the statute books. J. Stewart Hunter of HEW began his assessment this way— and it is as good a point as any for my conclusion:

> We can begin, I believe, with the premise that no government can exist which is totally open. It is equally true that representative government cannot possibly exist in a closed society. People's right to know is, in fact, less important than their *need* to know if they are to reach reasoned decisions for social action. This has been my consistent view as a government information officer, and it is what gives the government information function meaning and substance.

CHAPTER 8

Government's Role in Protecting Privacy

Robert Ellis Smith

The law of libel has always placed a limitation on what government public information officers, like anybody else dealing in information about people, may say. A government spokesperson is subject to a libel suit for disseminating false information that tends to damage the reputation of an individual. Less commonly realized, the developing law of privacy also places limits on what one person may say about another. A government spokesperson who discloses private facts that can be shown to invade an individual's privacy can face a lawsuit for invasion of that individual's privacy.

Both the libel and the invasion-of-privacy limitations evolved from court-developed law, the privacy limitation being codified in federal statutory law by the Privacy Act of 1974. The act limits the disclosure of personal information by a federal agency, both to outsiders and to other federal agencies. There are exceptions. An agency may release information with the consent of the individual. In the common law, the consent of the individual always obviates a claim of invasion of privacy. The Privacy Act also permits the release of personal information to another agency of government for civil or criminal law enforcement, to a committee or subcommittee of Congress, to anybody pursuant to a court order, and, most importantly, to anybody "for a routine use . . . for a purpose which is compatible with the purpose for which it was collected."

The Privacy Act was prompted first by organized public reaction to a 1965 proposal for a "Federal Data Center" that would have consolidated all of the government's records about individuals in one computerized system. Further pressure for privacy legislation resulted from disclosures of army surveillance and dossier-keeping on citizens who participated in political controversy during the Vietnam era and revelation of the Watergate abuses during the Nixon administration.

So, it was the fear of computer networks and a distrust of government in general, not abuses by the public information office, that led to passage of the act in 1974, less than six months after Richard Nixon had vacated the White House. Because the public information officer daily makes decisions about the release of government information, concerns about privacy invasions are now of paramount legal importance. There is a criminal fine of $5000 (plus civil sanctions) for wrongful disclosure of personal information under the act.

The law caused great consternation among public information officers in the federal agencies, and it inspired great hostility among bureaucrats generally. One of the government's foremost legal representatives called it "the worst drafted law ever." The very first response of federal civil servants after the law became effective was to deny information to congressional "case workers" who work with federal agencies to solve individual problems for constituents of a member of Congress—delayed Social Security checks, veteran's assistance, Small Business

Administration redtape mostly. That misreading of the Privacy Act was quickly straightened out, but antipathy to the law persists. Part of the confusion is due to an apparent conflict between the Privacy Act and the Freedom of Information Act.

Upon first glance, the Freedom of Information Act and the Privacy Act do seem contradictory. The thrust of the first is to open the government to scrutiny by citizens; the thrust of the latter is to protect government information, at least government information about people, from outside scrutiny. But upon reading the laws in concert, responsible officials who implement information policies should find no real conflict.

The Privacy Act, in fact, was passed as an amendment to the Freedom of Information Act. The FOI act *requires* the government to release documents upon request, with the exception of classified defense information, trade secrets of a business, internal memoranda, and certain other materials. These exceptions are discretionary. The government *must* release documents unless they fall into one of the exempted categories, in which case the government *may* still release the information, but *need not do so* if it wishes not to for policy reasons. An important exemption to the mandatory FOI act is "personnel and medical files and similar files the disclosure of which would constitute a clearly unwarranted invasion of personal privacy" [5 U.S.C. 552 (b) (6)]. Thus, information of this sort, under the act, *need not be* released.

The Privacy Act amended the FOI act to require government agencies not to release personal information about individuals. Naturally, there are exceptions, as we have mentioned. One of those exceptions is *when disclosure is required under the Freedom of Information Act*. This means that unless personal information falls within the so-called "(b) (6) exemption" of the FOI act, it must be released upon request to a third party, in spite of the Privacy Act.

This exemption "does not protect against disclosure every incidental invasion of privacy—only disclosures as constitute clearly unwarranted invasions of personal privacy," according to the U.S. Supreme Court in 1976, *Department of the Air Force v. Rose*, 425 U.S. 352 (1976). The *Rose* case involved a request from journalists for descriptions—with names deleted—of the violations of the honor code at the Air Force Academy. The Court ruled that the government was required to comply with this Freedom of Information request, even though it involved information about people, involved student records (covered by a separate confidentiality law passed in 1974), and involved extremely sensitive information. Still, its release was neither "clearly unwarranted," nor, in the view of the court, an "invasion of personal privacy."

This last is the hard part, because courts have given specific and problematic guidance. One court ruled that the names and addresses of employees voting in an NLRB representation election must be disclosed to two law professors researching voting patterns. But another court ruled that the names and addresses of all persons who have registered with the Bureau of Alcohol, Tobacco, and Firearms to make their own wine at home were *not* disclosable to a retailer who wished to market products directly to this audience.

These court decisions present a dilemma for the disclosure officer, because the legislative history of the FOI act indicates that "any person" should have access to identifiable records without having to demonstrate a need or even a reason. But the courts seem to be looking to the use of the information—and the function of the requester—to decide whether the intrusion upon privacy caused by the disclosure is clearly warranted or not.

Another court has said that the names and addresses of persons filling out customs declaration forms upon returning to the U.S. are entitled to privacy protection. The Supreme Court has more than once said that the constitutional right to privacy extends only to "matters relating to marriage, procreation, contraception, family relationships, and child rearing and education." Then, in a 1979 case that may be an aberration, our highest court said that the results of employment tests and probably other personnel records are entitled to privacy protection.

Still, it's not hard to find federal information officers whose reflexive action is not to release the name of a particular agency employee, or a criminal suspect, or accident victim, or prisoner. Why? "Because of the Privacy Act." This is a misreading of the act, and reporters ought not to stand for it. In reality, the protections of the Privacy Act would be fragile enough, even if government officials were enthusiastic about it. Unfortunately, the pattern seems to be that an agency will either use the act as an excuse for not releasing information that, for other reasons, it wishes not to release or the agency will ignore the act if it really wants to release the information. Two examples prove the point:

Prior to his ill-fated trip to Guyana in 1978, the late Congressman Leo J. Ryan wrote to the Department of State requesting information about Jonestown, the community established by the Rev. Jim Jones and his cult followers. Ryan wanted information about Jones's encampment and the whereabouts of some of Ryan's constituents. Relatives had complained to the congressman that cult members were being held against their will, that Social Security checks had been misappropriated, and that it was impossible to confirm just who was living in Jonestown.

The State Department rejected Ryan's request, citing the Privacy Act. To confirm whether certain persons were at Jonestown or to describe what was going on there would invade the privacy of those individuals, the department said. In fact, the department would have had to provide the information had Ryan gotten his subcommittee chairman to make the request, because requests from subcommittee chairman investigating something within their congressional jurisdiction are exempt from the Privacy Act restrictions on disclosure.

Next-of-kin themselves had repeatedly asked for confirmation of who was living in Jonestown. The Department of State turned down these requests, citing the Privacy Act, even though both these requests and Ryan's for "locator information" seem to fit within an exemption to the act that says the government may release the last-known address of an individual in "compelling circumstances affecting the health or safety of an individual." The affidavits submitted by defectors from Jones's cult were ample evidence to qualify for this exemption.

But the American embassy in Guyana had no legal counsel on hand and only a two-page advisory on this relatively new law. Its reticence regarding the requested information is understandable, but the refusals from the State Department's people in Washington are less excusable. My suspicion is that they simply didn't want to get involved, or didn't have the information, and used the Privacy Act as a convenient excuse.

On the other hand, the State Department was able legitimately to use the Privacy Act to justify its lack of full knowledge about Jonestown; one provision in the law prohibits the government from keeping information about how individuals exercise their First Amendment rights of free speech and free religious practice.

That was legitimate, but the same is not true of State's excuse that it could not compile accurate information about this curious collection of Americans in the middle of the Guyanan jungle because under the Freedom of Information Act and the Privacy Act, Jones himself could (and did) obtain copies of information in State Department files about him and his cult. This means that an agency has to make certain that the information in its files is accurate and fair. It does not mean that an agency should abdicate its responsibility to keep the information it needs to do its job, in the name of some false concept of privacy.

The second example shows the opposite tendency. If a government agency wants to release personal information, it will simply release it and wink at the Privacy Act. Secretary of Health, Education, and Welfare Joseph Califano discovered in 1977 what many citizens had feared all along: computer systems filled with personal information about people can make government more efficient if linked with other computer systems with other personal information. Congress clearly intended to discourage such linkage when it passed the Privacy Act, which prohibits exchanges of personal data among federal agencies, as well as release of that information by federal agencies to outsiders. One of the exceptions to this general rule is for a "routine use . . . compatible with the purpose for which [the information] was collected."

Califano launched "Project Match," whereby computer tapes of the federal civilian payroll would be run against tapes of District of Columbia welfare recipients. The HEW computer would easily pick out names of persons on both lists—"hits." These people were in trouble, although it was later found that individuals in certain low-paying jobs are legally entitled to welfare payments as well.

The Civil Service Commission, keeper of computer files on the federal government's workers, ruled that giving its tapes to HEW for Project Match would violate the Privacy Act, but it provided them under the Freedom of Information Act! This was strange because federal agencies had never been regarded as beneficiaries of the FOI act. The computer check turned up only 50 possible violators out of 2.8 million federal employees, but Califano was apparently elated by the results. He asked the Pentagon to supply the military payroll. The Department of Defense reluctantly agreed, saying this was a "routine use" of the data, even though it was clearly not compatible with the use for which the information was originally gathered.

Califano went on to ask private employers for their computer lists, apparently without realizing that he had that information already in his own Social Security Administration. Once the precedent had been established for the popular goal of catching "welfare cheats," HEW began encouraging states to conduct their own matches. The department then asked Congress to pass a law authorizing such match programs, and Congress promptly complied in 1977.

It was precisely these "wholesale" disclosures of personal information that the Privacy Act was intended to discourage. Yet such exchanges increase in number in spite of the act. It was precisely the "retail" disclosures of information like the Jonestown situation that the Privacy Act was not directly aimed at. Yet these disclosures are apparently curtailed by very strict, and often erroneous, readings of the act.

In spite of congressional policy against exchanges of personal information by federal agencies, there are plenty of large-scale exchanges going on. In fact, while it was passing the Privacy Act in 1974, Congress passed a separate law creating a Parent Locator Service in the Department of Health, Education, and Welfare, and authorizing it to query any of the government's computer systems to track down a parent who is not supporting his or her children. The system was intended to save welfare costs by finding fathers who had abandoned support of their children and left them on public assistance. Its services are available to nonwelfare spouses as well. The Parent Locator Service's prime sources of last known address, of course, are the Social Security Administration and the Internal Revenue Service. Each agency can also find easily your last known employer. Each agency normally handles inquiries of that sort from other persons and agencies by forwarding a letter to the person's last known address, but not revealing the whereabouts to the inquirer. Each agency is required by law, however, to provide that information directly to the Parent Locator Service.

The National Driver Register in the Department of Transportation is a computer data bank storing names, dates of birth, and physical descriptions of 6.2 million drivers who have had their operator's permits suspended or revoked. The information is submitted by state motor vehicle departments. When an individual applies for a license or renewal at any of those motor vehicle departments, the departments will run the name through the National Driver Register in Washington to see whether the computer reports the driver as one who has a revocation or suspension in another state. If the information is timely and accurate, the system should keep bad drivers off the roads. Trouble is, it doesn't work as well as it sounds. State motor vehicle departments issue a license before getting a report back from the National Driver Register. By the time the report of a suspended or revoked license is sent to the state, the license has been issued and it's too late to get it back without a lengthy search.

There are also enough exchanges of computer data between federal agencies and private agencies to blur further the fading distinction between government and nongovernment. At least two private organizations have access to the FBI's National Crime Information Center. The National Automobile Theft Bureau, which is run by the automobile insurance companies, has direct computer access to the stolen car portion of the NCIC. Interpol, or the International Criminal Police Organization, is a private association of police officials from 120 nations that has direct computer access to the NCIC through the U.S. Department of Justice. This means that police in member countries—including Argentina, Chile, Iran, and Uganda—have access to computerized criminal histories of United States citizens without any legal restrictions at all.

Private insurance companies that process Medicare claims for the government have computer terminals on the Social Security Administration Data Acquisition and Response System (SSADARS), a nationwide computer network. The private carriers are supposed to have access only to Medicare information in the Social Security computer system. The Medicare portion includes claimants' medical condition and Medicare claims, and often the family composition, marital status, insitutional commitment, income, assets, and expenditures. The over-all SSADARS network includes data on the monthly Social Security retirement or disability benefits of more than 34 million Americans and data on Supplemental Security Income (SSI) payments to up to 4.2 million eligible blind, aged, and disabled persons. State medical administrators and several federal agencies have computer terminals on this same system. Social Security Administration officials see nothing wrong in the fact that profit-making insurance companies that rely totally on personal information have direct computer access to sensitive government records about citizens.

Banks feed information into the Federal Reserve System's computerized network for transferring debits and credits around the country. The Production Credit Associations that provide loans to farmers have their 130,000 loan accounts linked to a central computer at the federally supervised Federal Intermediate Credit Bank in St. Paul, Minnesota.

How did all of these computer systems come about? This ever-confining web of government data systems that makes us feel as if every aspect of our lives is recorded somewhere in Washington did not come about because of intentional national policy. It came about because of the separate decisions of separate agencies in the government.

It would be wrong to assume that hundreds of government officials deliberately set out to build a network of personal data to the detriment of American citizens. There are, however, hundreds of government officials whose first response to a perceived problem is to build a computer system for gathering information. There are hundreds of government officials who think only of efficiency, and not about threats to individual privacy and autonomy. There are hundreds of government officials who zealously pursue the information needs of their own agencies with no regard for the cumulative effect. There are hundreds of government officials who are titillated by the possibilities of computer technology and who feel powerless without increasing stores of information under their control. There are hundreds of government officials who find it more exciting to come up with a new way of collecting information than to administer creatively the programs and laws we have. The best way to resolve the apparent conflict between freedom of information and privacy may be for government not to collect so much personal information in the first place.

CHAPTER 9

The Right to Know vs. Protection of Privacy: The IRS Case

A. James Golato

The mission of the Internal Revenue Service (IRS) is to encourage and achieve the highest possible degree of voluntary compliance with the tax laws and to maintain the highest possible degree of public confidence in the integrity and efficiency of the IRS. Voluntary compliance, which is the heart of our tax system, means that taxpayers are responsible for assessing and paying their own taxes. The government gets directly involved in relatively few cases. For example, the IRS audits only a little over 2 percent of the 90 million individual income tax returns filed.

Privacy as a Component of Voluntary Compliance

Voluntary compliance depends on four key elements: taxpayers must understand the law; they must have confidence that others are complying with it; they must provide necessary information to the IRS; and they must have confidence that the privacy of the information provided will be preserved. The first of these elements, understanding the law, requires extensive and effective public information and communication efforts. Ever since the current income tax law was first passed in 1913, following the Sixteenth Amendment to the Constitution, which permitted the Congress to levy and collect income taxes, the government has been obligated to educate the public on the requirements of the tax law.

The importance of meeting that obligation becomes all the more evident in light of the many changes that Congress makes in the law every year and the extraordinary complexity of the Internal Revenue Code. Therefore, a major part of our information efforts—whether they be through the press, publications, or audio-visual means—is to communicate the requirements of the law in understandable language to the average taxpayer. Voluntary compliance depends to a large extent on the public's perception and confidence that the tax law is being administered uniformly and fairly, that all taxpayers are treated alike by the IRS, that one's neighbor is not getting away with not paying his or her share of taxes, and that the IRS is sensitive and responsive to taxpayers' concerns and complaints.

Gaining public confidence in the tax system, no less than conveying an understanding of the law, requires affirmative public information activities. The IRS, therefore, provides taxpayers with information that enables them to know their rights and responsibilities under the law and to be confident that no one pays more than is legally owed. Convictions for criminal tax violations also are publicized to assure honest taxpayers that those who cheat are caught and punished. This helps to deter others who would try to evade their tax responsibilities.

Public information also is used to help enhance the efficiency of IRS operations. If taxpayers make errors, those errors must be corrected by IRS personnel. Correcting errors is expensive. Sometimes it can be done by computer or other mechanical methods. Often, the IRS must correspond with the taxpayer. Obviously information that helps taxpayers to file complete and accurate tax returns, and reduces the need to correct them, is cost effective for the IRS and taxpayers alike. And the efficiency and accuracy of IRS operations greatly heightens public confidence not only in the way the IRS is administering the tax system but in how it is spending the taxpayers' money.

The other two of the four elements on which voluntary compliance depends— willingness to provide information and confidence that the privacy of that information will be preserved—are tied to the integrity of the IRS and the public's perception of that integrity. In other words, taxpayers must believe that the IRS safeguards the confidentiality of their tax returns and related information.

Now comes the rub. Like a triangle, disclosure of information has three distinct aspects that appear to point in different directions. The Freedom of Information (FOI) Act of 1966, the Privacy Act of 1974, and the amendments to the tax law made by the Tax Reform Act of 1976 (Section 6103 of the Internal Revenue Code) covering the disclosure of information, although sometimes complementary, frequently appear to be contradictory. As difficult as these disclosure laws make the public information job, they are crucial to a free society. We have had to learn to walk a tightrope between the people's right to be informed about IRS operations, which is the public's business and is necessarily related to freedom of the press—a First Amendment guarantee—and the individual's right to privacy.

The right to privacy, in effect, is equally as basic to a free people in a democratic society as the right of a free people to a free press. Although privacy rights are not specifically set out in the Constitution, the implication is obviously there. For example, the Third Amendment sanctifies the home by prohibiting the quartering of soldiers in a person's home without consent of the owner. The Fourth Amendment protects persons against unreasonable search and seizure and affirms the right of people to be secure in their homes, papers, and effects. Supreme Court Justice Louis Brandeis wrote in 1890 that the individual's "right to be let alone" is the most valued right of civilized man. Even without the legal sanctions, the IRS would have a moral obligation of confidentiality when you consider that in the very process of filing a return, taxpayers entrust much personal and financial information to the IRS. Taxpayers are entitled to assurance that what they have entrusted to the IRS will be safeguarded and will not be disclosed without legal sanction or taxpayer permission.

The IRS probably has more information about more people than any other agency in this country. Questions often have been raised about actual and potential disclosure of this information. A recurring concern was whether disclosure of tax returns or information on them—even to other government agencies for nontax purposes—breached the privacy of American citizens. This concern, in turn, raised the question of whether the public's reaction to this possible abuse of privacy would seriously impair the effectiveness of our nation's very successful voluntary assessment tax system.

Although the Privacy Act of 1974, which covered privacy in general, has had an impact on the disclosure of tax information, Congress did not specifically focus on the unique aspects of tax returns in that act. Prior law describes income tax returns as "public records" open to inspection under regulations approved by the president or under presidential order. However, as a result of what is now referred to as the Watergate era, Congress felt that tax returns and return information generally should be treated as confidential and not disclosable except in very limited situations. So a special provision covering disclosure was included in the Tax Reform Act of 1976.

Generally speaking, the Tax Reform Act considerably strengthened the previous confidentiality sanctions of the Internal Revenue Code. The code clearly states that the confidentiality of returns and return information shall be maintained, that "no officer or employee of the United States . . . or any state . . . or other person who has or had access to returns or return information . . . shall disclose any return or return information obtained by him in any manner. . . ."

The law provides for disclosure to other government agencies for uses related to tax administration. For example, disclosure of tax information to state tax agencies for tax administration purposes is permitted under negotiated exchange agreements. However, the Tax Reform Act of 1976 amended this provision to prohibit the disclosure of information to governors. Furthermore, the IRS has strict procedures for insuring that tax data, once in the hands of state revenue personnel, is subject to adequate security. If the IRS concludes that a state's procedures are inadequate, tax information no longer will be furnished—a strong incentive for a state to keep such information confidential. IRS disclosure officers visit each state agency semiannually to check on the adequacy of their security systems.

The Tax Reform Act also restricted the disclosure of tax information to White House officials. The law permits disclosure to the president, but the request must be in writing and personally signed by the president. White House employees may receive information only if designated by name in the president's written request. In addition, the request must state: the name and address of the taxpayer; the kind of return or return information to be disclosed; the taxable period covered; and the specific reason why inspection or disclosure is requested. A report by the Privacy Protection Study Commission, established by the Privacy Act of 1974, expressed satisfaction with the IRS's statutory safeguards, review authority, and the periodic reporting on them to the Congress.

The Dilemma of Privacy

During the Watergate era, the less stringent controls on the use of tax returns and almost daily allegations in the press about enemies lists and use of returns for political purposes had caused tremendous public relations problems for the IRS. In many instances, the IRS was unable to refute the allegations under the existing confidentiality requirements without compromising the privacy of individual taxpayers.

Now some people could assert that Congress has gone too far—that although the law now protects innocent citizens from the abuse of disclosing private information about them, it also, unfortunately, protects criminals. For instance, Internal Revenue agents who uncover evidence of other crimes during tax investigations no longer can pass this evidence routinely to the FBI or organized crime task forces. Other law enforcement agencies now must go through elaborate procedures to obtain tax information, and since the person under investigation must be notified, he or she is tipped off in the middle of the investigation. On the other hand, while we do not have conclusive data on the impact of the Freedom of Information, Privacy, and Tax Reform Acts upon general law enforcement, we have no reason to believe that these acts have not bolstered public confidence in the integrity with which tax law enforcement is carried out.

Here is another example of the dilemma that sometimes confronts the IRS in its efforts to integrate privacy protection and freedom of information. A few vocal, self-styled tax protesters receive considerable publicity for their misleading claims—often made at profit-making "seminars" they sponsor for a fee. These protesters, who travel the nation extolling the benefits of tax evasion, and who encourage people to disregard income tax laws, often give the false impression that there will be no consequences. They claim they don't file complete tax returns or pay income taxes. These people often tell of many others who do the same and they maintain that the IRS legally can't do a thing about it. What many don't admit is that they themselves file perfectly correct tax returns although claiming they don't, knowing full well that the IRS is prevented by privacy laws from acknowledging that fact.

Some tax protesters have counseled taxpayers not to comply with tax return filing or payment requirements of the law, arguing that these requirements violate the self-incrimination provision of the Fifth Amendment or other constitutional rights, yet they have been convicted for following their own advice. Some even now are being investigated, but the IRS is prohibited by the privacy laws from disclosing the truth about their particular tax situation. So the press and its readers are exposed only to the tax protesters' side of the story. All the IRS can say in rebuttal is that taxpayers who follow these tax protesters' misleading advice may find themselves on the receiving end of strict civil and criminal enforcement of the law.

Some people may not like the fact that they can't verify the tax protesters' income tax return with the IRS to determine if what they say is true, and the IRS is frustrated by having to remain quiet when it can easily rebut their outrageous allegations. However, I'm sure most taxpayers like the fact that their own tax returns remain just as confidential.

No legal prohibition carries much impact unless the law also provides a penalty for its violation. So there are heavy penalties for unauthorized disclosure of tax information. The law now provides for a penalty of up to five years in jail or as much as a $5000 fine, or both, for the unlawful disclosure of tax returns or information from those returns. Previously the maximum penalties had been one year in jail or a $1000 fine, or both.

A provision also added by the Tax Reform Act of 1976 permits a taxpayer to bring a civil action for damage against anyone—including government employees or officials—who willfully or negligently discloses information from the taxpayer's return. It provides that "in no case shall a plaintiff entitled to recovery receive less than the sum of $1000 with respect to each instance of such unauthorized disclosure." In addition, the defendant must pay the costs of the legal action.

The intent of the strengthened provisions of the law was not to impede or prevent the legitimate and orderly administration of the tax law, but to make sure that tax returns and tax information are not used for any purposes other than tax administration. Congress obviously strove to balance the IRS's need for information with the citizen's right to privacy and the related impact of disclosure upon our country's voluntary tax assessment system.

Related Considerations: Balancing Information with Privacy

IRS policy recognizes that beyond the routine receipt of forms and instructions, direct contact by taxpayers with the IRS generally is limited to those taxpayers who avail themselves of taxpayer assistance, or those who otherwise come in contact with IRS processing or enforcement operations. This leaves a sizeable majority whose direct contact with the IRS is minimal and who derive their knowledge and attitudes from mass communications media.

IRS policy affirms the importance of the media in carrying out this responsibility with this official statement:

> Mass communication which adequately informs taxpayers of their obligations represents a potential for reducing more costly efforts of providing direct assistance, correction of errors and follow-up on delinquencies. The IRS, therefore, will conduct a continuous and vigorous information program through the mass media in order to help achieve its

objective of enhancing voluntary compliance with the tax laws and regulations. . . . In view of the important contributions made by press, radio, television, magazine and other mass media toward disseminating tax information to the public, and otherwise facilitating administration of the tax laws, the IRS will cooperate with such media in every reasonable way permitted by law.

The IRS relies heavily on the mass media to inform the public about its operations and to explain tax laws, regulations, rulings, and procedures. During 1978, the IRS issued over 4900 news releases to the media covering substantive technical and procedural matters, forms and publications, statistics, speeches by IRS officials on important tax topics and organizational changes. Releases were issued to assist taxpayers in meeting due dates, properly filling out forms, and in understanding their rights and responsibilities under the tax law. Tax information material also was sent to more than 16,000 radio and TV stations, daily and weekly newspapers, magazines, and special publications. And IRS personnel also participated in over 16,000 interviews and answered nearly 19,000 media inquiries.

Four half-hour IRS films were produced for use by TV stations and civic organizations covering the history of American taxation, taxpayer audit and appeal rights and responsibilities, the tax aspects of running a small business, and how to prepare a tax return. These films, two of which also were released in Spanish, were shown some 500 times on TV across the nation in 1978 and over 3000 times before professional, trade, civic, educational, and other groups.

The IRS encourages its officials and employees to deliver speeches, participate in tax forums, and write articles for publications, but only to the extent that such activities promote taxpayers' understanding of their rights and obligations under the tax laws, and represent effective and efficient means of conveying the particular information to the public. However, no employee is permitted to receive an honorarium or compensation. Also, any travel and other expenses related to a speaking or tax forum engagement must be paid for by the IRS or the employee, not the inviting organization. The point here is to remove any possibility of a conflict of interest, which is consistent with the very strict rules of conduct covering all IRS employees. Although the use of radio and television to convey taxpayer information is encouraged, IRS policy prohibits commercial sponsorship of IRS programs or materials. And, the showing of IRS films must not be done in such a way as to imply endorsement of any product or service.

In obtaining the aforementioned news coverage of its enforcement activities—to deter others from violating the Internal Revenue laws and to increase the confidence of conscientious taxpayers that the IRS does catch violators—the IRS acts with due regard for an individual's right to a fair trial as well as the public's right to know. Although general information concerning the work of a particular organizational unit involved in enforcement activities will be furnished to the media, IRS personnel may not participate in press conferences, serve as spokespersons, or issue news releases in connection with pretrial actions, including indictments or the filing of criminal informations. And, of course, IRS employees may not disclose that a tax investigation or examination is or is not in progress on a specific taxpayer.

Reporters or news photographers are not allowed to accompany IRS employees on investigative, enforcement, or other similar assignments such as raids. Even information obtained with a search warrant is not disclosed by the IRS at the time of the raid. Only after the search warrant is returned to a judge or magistrate, does it become public information and the report on the warrant may then be disclosed to the media on request. Of course, information which is a matter of public record, such as pleadings filed with the United States Tax Court, or convictions in a criminal trial, is available to reporters.

Sometimes news reporters try to obtain identification of taxpayers and cases, but we have to refuse them to maintain confidentiality of information protected by law, including the identity of taxpayers. For example, we receive queries about whether certain public figures who had previously received publicity from non-IRS sources about nonpayment of taxes or who were involved in legal tax actions have ever paid their taxes. We must, of course, decline comment in these matters because of the confidentiality and privacy provisions of the law. Reporters rarely become antagonistic and critical when our adherence to confidentiality under the law spoils a good story for them. Most understand the restrictions under which we must operate. A few, however, do show their annoyance and displeasure. We sometimes remind them that part of the impetus for stricter disclosure and privacy rules initially came from stories and editorials in their papers.

Another example is when a taxpayer, or a witness, in the course of an investigation, requests that a newspaper reporter be allowed to "sit in" during an interview with an IRS agent. If a witness—not the taxpayer under investigation—makes the request, we have taken the position that the reporter's participation in the interview, even as an observer, would constitute an illegal disclosure, since there is no authority under the law to make the disclosure to the media. We are not prohibited from allowing a newspaper reporter to sit in on an interview with a taxpayer at the taxpayer's own request; however, we could exclude the reporter on the basis that his presence would interfere with tax administration.

I should add at this point that the taxpayer is always free to disclose information from his or her tax returns, including making available a reproduction of the entire return. For example, copies of the tax returns of various political figures, including presidents of the United States, have appeared in the press along with discussions of various items on the return. This publication has come about because the taxpayer released the information, not the IRS.

Privacy and Freedom of Information

The paradox is that as privacy laws receive more attention and are aimed at tightening controls on information such as that which the IRS possesses, the IRS is striving for more openness and assistance to taxpayers to make them aware of their rights and obligations under the law and to maintain public confidence in the administration of the U.S. tax system. Another paradox is that at the same time that Congress is calling on the IRS to provide taxpayers with telephone tax assistance, IRS also is being directed to tighten up on granting tax information by telephone.

The recent discovery by a news reporter that the confidentiality of an income tax return could be breached by an imposter by simply providing a taxpayer's name, address, and social security number in a telephone call to the IRS has caused us to set up extensive procedures to make certain that the person asking for information about his tax situation by telephone is in fact the taxpayer and no one else. Since no telephone identification system is foolproof, most specific taxpayer information will have to be requested in writing so that the signature on the letter may be compared with that on the tax return. General tax information will be furnished by telephone.

The IRS will grant, under the Freedom of Information Act, a request for a record we are not prohibited from disclosing by law. The administrative cost and impact on operations involved in furnishing the requested record or records will not be a material factor in deciding to deny a request, unless the cost or impact would be so great as to seriously impair IRS operations.

Another aspect of disclosure involves so-called letter rulings. The IRS National Office issues thousands of private letter rulings, on request, to taxpayers advising them of the tax consequences of financial transactions they may be planning. These letter rulings apply only to the taxpayer to whom they are issued and can not be relied upon by other taxpayers. Some law or accounting firms, primarily in Washington, obtained copies of many of the letter rulings and were able to detect the thinking of the IRS in certain tax areas and advise their clients accordingly. This was an advantage small out-of-town firms and individual taxpayers did not have when attempting to gauge the possible tax consequences of a contemplated transaction not clearly covered in the tax code, regulations, published rulings, or IRS publications.

To avoid this apparent favoritism, the IRS now makes available in its Freedom of Information Reading Room "sanitized" copies of these letter rulings—copies that delete all taxpayer identifying information, references to trade secrets and other information, such as national security material, which by law cannot be divulged. We also made available to the public copies of more than 100,000 past letter rulings. Copies of these letter rulings now are also regularly published in a number of newsletters and tax-oriented periodicals.

When the Freedom of Information Act became effective in 1967, most requests for information were handled or coordinated by the Public Affairs Division, which conducts and oversees IRS public information and related activities. The assignment of the Freedom of Information activity to Public Affairs was, under the circumstances then existing, an appropriate one. Public Affairs had long been an advocate of more openness in the IRS. Those of us with a public affairs or public information background had long known from direct experience that secrecy, or even the appearance of secrecy, breeds suspicion.

As a result of the increase in requests under the Freedom of Information Act for records and information from the media, lawyers, accountants, researchers, and taxpayers, the FOI responsibility was placed in a separate Disclosure Operations Division with a nationwide field network. Public Affairs only gets involved when requests come from the news media.

Responding promptly to requests for documents under the Freedom of Information Act is an important part of IRS's service to the public. During 1978, the IRS processed 7600 requests for access to records under the Freedom of Information Act in field offices. Of the requests requiring extensive search and analysis, 4300 were granted in full and some 1000 were granted in part. The national office FOI Reading Room responded to 27,000 requests to copy or inspect records already placed on reading room shelves, a 45 percent increase over the year before. This increase was due primarily to the release of private letter rulings referred to earlier.

Under the Privacy Act, individuals made over 500 requests for access to records about themselves. The IRS permitted full or partial access in nearly all of these requests. The law permits disclosure of some information, under strict requirements, to federal, state, and local child support enforcement agencies to aid in collecting child support obligations and also disclosure to the federal commissioner of education to locate individuals who have defaulted on student loans.

In recognizing the people's right to know how tax laws are administered, IRS officials will make all reasonable efforts to provide requested information, disclosure of which is not specifically forbidden by law or policy. The prohibitions that exist are not to be used as devices to avoid disclosing information. It is recognized that many areas of information lack specific guidelines regarding disclosure. In these situations, the factor of judgment is needed—judgment which protects confidential tax returns and tax return information within the scope of the law. The mere fact that disclosure of certain information may be embarrassing to the IRS is not, and should not be, a sufficient basis for withholding it.

For example, the IRS decided that it was good judgment in 1975 to abolish an information system then existing called Technical Information Releases (TIR). This information system, aimed originally at technical publications, unintentionally had grown to a mailing list of 17,000, mostly lawyers and accountants who, over a period of years, had asked to be placed on the TIR mailing list. Thus a well-intentioned attempt to provide the public with legitimate tax information had evolved in another source of apparent favoritism, like the private letter rulings mentioned earlier. These technical information releases provided the more sophisticated tax practitioners with special mailings not accorded the press and taxpayers in general. The technical information that used to go out in targetted releases is now published in general news releases for all of the press and communications media. The nonmedia tax practitioner mailing list no longer exists.

The Public Affairs Division of the IRS reflects the attitude and the activities of the organization as a whole. Fortunately, the Internal Revenue Service has an enlightened attitude toward the people's right to know what their government is doing and is committed to providing all information possible. But it will do this without violating the confidentiality provisions of the law or jeopardizing the privacy of individuals. The IRS has a high level of sensitivity to the public impact of actions it takes in disclosing information and in otherwise administering the tax laws. It fully recognizes that the willingness and ability of the public to adhere to the voluntary compliance system depend largely on IRS effectiveness in its performance and in the public's satisfaction with the way the tax laws are administered. In other words, in carrying out a public affairs program, the IRS keeps in mind the public relations wisdom of Voltaire: "What you do speaks so loudly that I cannot hear what you say."

CHAPTER 10

National Security: The Limits of Public Information

George A. Carver, Jr.

Two basic concepts are essential to the effective functioning of our constitutional system of government. One is the concept of "checks"; the other, the eighteenth-century concept of "balance." Over the past few years, especially among journalists, there has been such focus and concentration on the former—checks—that the equal essentiality of balance has been obscured, if not forgotten. Many of America's current problems and adversities, both domestic and international, have been exacerbated (or, indeed, caused) by the fact than in many areas of our national life, critically important elements of "balance" have gotten badly out of kilter. In perhaps no area is a sense of balance, with its associated concepts of perspective and proportion, more necessary than in assessing the proper "limits of public information" in matters affecting national security.

World War II could never have been won or the Nazi nightmare ended—including the holocaust and the gas ovens implementing Hitler's "final solution to the Jewish problem"—had the Allies not been able to mount a successful, cross-channel invasion of Hitler's "Fortress Europe." D-Day was one of the great successes in military history, but things were very much touch and go in the initial hours (even days) of the June, 1944, Normandy landings. D-Day and World War II could easily have had different outcomes had the Germans, on Hitler's direct orders, not kept the Fifteenth German Army and the Panzer reserve away from Normandy's beaches and hedgerows until after the allied foothold on France was secured. Hitler gave those orders because, along with most of his general staff, he was convinced that the Normandy landings were a feint—intended to mask the "real" invasion, which was coming across the narrowest part of the English Channel in the Pas de Calais.

This stubborn belief, which Hitler did not abandon until it was too late to keep the Allied invasion from being successful, was molded (deliberately) by a complex, brilliant, and successful deception operation with the overall name of "Bodyguard."[1] The component of "Bodyguard" known as "Fortitude South" involved dummy encampments in central England, extensive use of falsified radio messages intended for German ears (sent either in the clear or in codes the Germans were known to have broken), the skillful use of doubled German agents, and numerous other techniques—all designed to convince Berlin that the "real" invasion would be spearheaded by an army under the command of General George Patton. Did the American people have a "right to know," at the time, that no such army existed, or that "Fortitude South" was nothing but a tissue of ingenious fabrication? There may be a few absolutist First Amendment purists who would argue "yes"; but most Americans (even in our current revisionist era) are doubtless profoundly thankful that Hitler was so successfully deceived, even at the price of simultaneously deceiving all the Allies' media, their consuming public, and, hence, "the American people."

We are not now in an openly declared war, but we would be well advised to reflect on whether it would be possible to execute a similar deception operation successfully, even in wartime, in a television-dominated era and in a climate of opinion such as that now prevailing—a climate which puts such a high premium on investigative reporting and advocacy journalism, and in which any thought of limits on "the people's right to know" is instinctively rejected.

Such questions also have peacetime applicability. When the Iran hostage rescue attempt had to be aborted in mid-course, President Carter felt he had to "go public" with most of the story immediately. From the standpoint of overall U.S. interests, it might have been better to say nothing about the failed attempt—even deny that any such attempt had taken place—in order to allay Iranian suspicions and preserve some chance of launching a better prepared and executed second attempt at some later time. In the current press and media climate, however, this was simply not a realistic option. That the government was able to get as far as it did without secrecy-destroying leaks and publicity borders on the miraculous, and there was no chance whatsoever of keeping the initial attempt's failure quiet— even though publicity about it gave the Iranian "government" a propaganda windfall, put the American hostages at greater risk, apparently caused their dispersion, and greatly diminished the chance of America's being able to effect a future rescue of its imprisoned citizens and diplomats.

Delicate covert action operations are fraught with risks under the best of circumstances. In the current political and journalistic climate and under currently operative laws, such as the Hughes-Ryan Amendment to the Foreign Assistance Act of 1974, these inherent risks are enormously increased—especially the risk of the kind of premature public disclosure which would eliminate any chance of the considered operation's being successful.[2]

In the current climate, it would be extremely difficult to conceive, plan and prepare any such operation without there being some leakage of critical information about it. At that point, two sets of virtually irresistible journalistic pressures would come into play: the competitive and the "prudential." No journalist, newspaper, magazine, or TV network could professionally tolerate being scooped on such a story. "Morality" would provide a ready, always available, rationalization for heeding competitive instincts and inclinations. The net result of these twin pressures would be that any executive branch official or member of Congress, or of a congressional staff, who was aware that any such operation was being contemplated and who was personally opposed to it (for any reason)—in tandem with any cooperative editor, publisher, TV network executive, or reporter—could scuttle the operation by leak-engendered publicity, with impunity and no legal risk.

For a variety of ideological and historical reasons (including "Watergate," and all that term has come to symbolize), the very notion of governmental secrecy is currently very much out of fashion. Such a premium is currently put on openness that, in many quarters, any governmental effort to preserve secrecy—in any field—is instinctively viewed as something intrinsically suspect, an irresistible (legitimate) challenge to any investigative reporter worth his or her professional salt.

There are, of course, some areas in which a need for secrecy is generally, if sometimes grudgingly, acknowledged and even afforded a measure of legal protection. As Americans, we cherish "fairness" (at least in abstract theory) almost as much as we value "openness." We do not consider it fair for advance, "inside" knowledge of public information to be exploited for private financial gain. Crop statistics—of which advance, pre-general-publication knowledge would enable one to make fortune in the futures market—are (accordingly) much more tightly protected by laws relatively easy to enforce than highly sensitive military or intelligence information. Effective legal protection also shields the privacy of grand jury deliberations, partly because there is a general consensus that the innocent—or at least those whom a grand jury does not feel it has sufficient evidence to indict—deserve to have their reputations and privacy protected.

Ironically, however, the areas in which governmental secrecy now tends to be most publicly suspect, hardest to preserve, and most difficult to protect by realistically enforceable statutes are those in which any government's right to and need for secrecy have the greatest degree of traditional, historical sanction and support—even in our own society: military matters, diplomacy, and intelligence.

Part of the difficulty involved here is rooted in fruits of modern technology that First Amendment absolutists often seem wont to ignore. Because of the pervasiveness and speed of modern communications, there is no way anything, or any information, can be told to or discussed by "the American people" without the fact (and that information) being almost instantaneously known to every concerned or interested government and general staff anywhere in the world. This is no argument for forgoing the advantages of our open, democratic society—or of open public discussion and debate of policy issues which concern us all. Even less is it an argument for "covering up" errors and misjudgments of our government, the representatives whom we elect, or other governmental officials whom our elected representatives appoint (directly or indirectly). Nonetheless, this is a fact which has to be taken into account when assessing "the limits of public information" in connection with matters and issues which affect our national security—and over the last two decades of this difficult century, could well affect our chances of national survival.

Military Matters and Issues

Harry Truman was a president whose devotion to democratic principles is beyond serious question. With typical salty directness, he put his finger on the nub of the problem when he said:

> Whether it be treason or not, it does the U.S. just as much harm for military secrets to be made known to potential enemies through open publication as it does for the military secrets to be given to an enemy through the clandestine operation of spies. I do not believe that the best solution can be reached by adopting an approach based on the theory that everyone has a right to know our military secrets and related information affecting the national security.[3]

The problem President Truman was addressing is real, and has grown more grave and complex in the almost three decades that have passed since his words were uttered. In this sphere, the "espionage statutes" (Sections 793 and 794 of Title 18 of the U.S. Code) are almost useless as practically effective protection for sensitive national security secrets. Obtaining a conviction under these statutes requires convincing a jury "beyond reasonable doubt" that the accused knowingly passed information to a foreign power with *intent* to harm the United States or benefit another nation. "Intent" is something extremely difficult to prove in court. The espionage statutes, furthermore, do not really touch anyone who passes sensitive military information (almost no matter what the information may reveal about U.S. military capabilities, weaknesses, plans, or intentions) to an American newspaper, magazine, radio station, or television network—even if that information is promptly published or broadcast and, hence, made available in full detail to every interested party throughout the world. Nor, in such a situation, would our government have any viable legal recourse against any American journalists or media organizations who had a hand in publishing or broadcasting the information in question.

The weak thinness of the legal arsenal available to our government for protecting sensitive military information is but one component of this particular problem. Another is human nature, and the full range of normal human emotions—including vanity, pride in accomplishment, desire for recognition, ambition, and institutional loyalty. Defense contractors naturally want to advertise their respective firms' wares, achievements, and abilities. Individual services, and groups or people within them, want to be well thought of by the American public, and by Congress—especially when the latter is marking up appropriations bills. Our free, feisty, vitally competitive open society gives scant acknowledgment, and fewer rewards, to individuals or institutions (in the governmental or the private sector) that hide their lights under bushel baskets.

Such factors, among others, make it possible for any foreign embassy or military attaché to obtain from Congressional publications or the unclassified version of the Secretary of Defense's annual Posture Statement or for the price of a newspaper, or subscription to any of several defense-oriented magazines—or by simply watching television—information about America's defense and military capabilities and plans which our government would have to spend literally millions (if not billions) of dollars to try to collect about rival foreign powers who are at least potential enemies.

Diplomatic Matters and Issues

A related (though slightly different) set of considerations makes it even more difficult for our government to protect diplomatic secrets than military ones. This is partly because many who might acknowledge that our government has *some* right or need to protect at least certain types of military information and data would not acknowledge any comparable governmental right or need in the diplomatic field.

The conduct of American foreign policy is of such interest and concern to so many groups in our society—including journalists who make their livings and professional reputations by covering it—and so directly affects the equities of so many, that there is an enormous, understandable reluctance to allow it to be conducted with any measure of secrecy, or even privacy and discretion. There is also an "internal" governmental factor in this equation. Several executive branch components (each with its own often competing groups, factions, or senior officials) and many congressional committees—not to mention individual members of Congress, and of congressional staffs—all have (or think they ought to have) a significant measure of direct participation in the foreign policy process. In such an environment, the temptation to advance one's own foreign policy proposals or preferred courses of action—or combat, preempt, and undercut those of rivals or opponents—by the tactic of leak and counter-leak is virtually irresistible.

Understandable as such considerations may be, they make it extremely difficult for our government to conduct delicate, difficult diplomacy or (especially) diplomatic negotiations. In the many contexts in which the conduct of modern diplomacy resembles various forms of "international poker," it is almost impossible for our government to execute a successful bluff, or win any particular hand or pot by subtle strategy. Our negotiators and diplomats (even the one who occupies the Oval Office) are usually in the position a bridge player at a tournament would be in if all his hands were put up on a screen before a crowd of kibbitzers, who dissected them and debated various plays' merits or chances of success in a way that immediately conveyed all of this information to all other players in the tournament.

Intelligence Matters and Issues

On 26 July 1777, General George Washington wrote a letter to Colonel Elias Dayton (the Continental Army's intelligence chief in New Jersey) in which our country's father said:

> The necessity of procuring good Intelligence is apparent & need not be further urged—All that remains for me to add is, that you keep the whole matter as secret as possible. For upon Secrecy, Success depends in most Enterprizes of the kind, and for want of it, they are generally defeated, however well planned & promising a favourable issue.

The need for intelligence which George Washington recognized is even more important in our strife-ridden era—an era in which thermonuclear warheads with more explosive power than all the bombs dropped during the Second World War can be impacted on American population centers minutes after being launched from lands or open oceans half a world away, and in which our economic well-being hinges on an assured supply of imported oil, at economically sustainable prices, produced in this planet's most politically fragile and volatile regions. The degree of secrecy which Washington astutely recognized as essential to the acquisition of needed intelligence is also even more essential today, partly because of the technological revolution in communications which has occurred since George Washington wrote that letter to Colonel Dayton.

No government, including ours, can have the sensitive intelligence it needs unless it can protect three things: the fact that it has such intelligence, and the sources and the methods by which it acquires that intelligence.

In any adversarial—let alone wartime—situation, what one adversary knows about the other's capabilities and intentions is invaluable information for the latter. This is a fact often lost sight of, or ignored, in our public debates and discussions about the capabilities and intentions of current or potential adversaries, or of the capabilities and effectiveness of America's intelligence services. Such considerations are not arguments against the kind of free and vigorous public debate on major national security policies or concerns which is essential to our open society's democratic form of government, and which our Constitution specifically protects. This, nonetheless, does not alter the fact that awareness of what any country (ours included) knows about another can often pinpoint the methods by which the information was probably acquired.

The judgment calls that have to be made in this sphere often hinge on the extent and level of detail involved. That America collects information on the troop movements and other military activities of many nations, including the Soviet Union, by satellite photography is no secret. The "fact of" such reconnaissance activity, indeed, has been publicly acknowledged by President Carter. If America is to be kept safe from surprise attack, however—or if America's intelligence services are to be able to monitor compliance with any SALT-type treaty with a degree of precision adequate to merit the confidence of the American people, or their elected representatives in the Congress—it is essential that others (including the Soviets) not know *precisely* how good our satellite cameras are, or other details of their *precise* capabilities. This is essential because if others had such knowledge, it would greatly facilitate the development of any deceptions or countermeasures toward which they might be inclined. Stories published in American newspapers or technical journals which go into details and specifics, consequently, can seriously jeopardize the continued effectiveness of collection capabilities America needs in this sphere for our nation's security—if not indeed, its survival. That is fairly obvious. What is less obvious but equally germane is the fact that by knowledgeable (foreign) intelligence professionals, capability assessments can be worked from a different point of departure. A leak-based published (or broadcast) news story, or an open congressional debate which goes into too much precise detail about *what* we know, can easily help current or potential adversaries figure out how we acquired that bit of detailed information, what our collection capabilities must be for us to have obtained it, and (hence) point them in precisely the right direction in their efforts to develop countermeasures capable of denying us such information in the future.

Intelligence sources—especially human sources—are even more vulnerable than intelligence methods to compromise, negation, and (sometimes literally) destruction through damaging public disclosure. This is important because despite the wonders of modern technology, sources—particularly human sources—are still essential to acquiring the full range of intelligence that our nation needs to protect the interests and security of all American citizens.

Over the past three decades, technological innovations (some bordering on the miraculous) have revolutionized many, but not all, aspects of intelligence collection. Oversimplifying slightly, technological collection is magnificent, often indispensable, for monitoring other nations' *capabilities*; but it frequently sheds little unambiguous or even useful light on their *intentions*. No potential adversary's compliance with a SALT-type treaty could be adequately monitored without technological collection; but orbiting satellites provide little useful enlightenment on intelligence problems such as assessing the challenges, dangers, and probable outcome of evolving political situations such as the one in Iran. For *this* kind of intelligence, and for reliable information on the *intentions* of foreign groups or nations, any intelligence service (ours included) must have *human* sources—of the right type, properly placed, and with whom secure, timely communication is feasible.

It is for this reason (among others) that intelligence officers are just as touchy about their sources as are journalists, and even more determined to protect them. Intelligence officers have to be. Without their human sources, intelligence officers—and services, and their countries—are effectively blind in critical, even vital areas. Furthermore, there are two additional considerations defining "necessary conditions" without which human sources can never be developed or maintained: prudence and honor, or good faith.

Any lawyer, accountant, doctor, or psychiatrist—or any partnership, firm, or organization for which any such professional works—that develops a reputation for indiscretion will soon have a steadily diminishing number of clients or patients. Any journalist with a reputation for indiscretion about his or her sources—or who works for a newspaper, magazine, or TV network whose senior executives acquire such a reputation—will soon have very few, or none. The same holds true, in spades, for intelligence officers. (Here, perceptions become as important as "facts." If foreign sources or cooperative foreign liaison services come to believe that American intelligence officers or services are no longer willing or able to protect foreign secrets, arguing facts—e.g., contending that a given Congressional Committee's track record on leaks is, to date, excellent—is of little avail.) That is the "prudential" consideration. The "moral" one, of honor, is even stronger. An intelligence source, particularly a good one, invariably puts his or her reputation, career, livelihood, freedom, even life (plus, often, that of any such source's family) in the hands of the intelligence service—and officers—with whom that source works and cooperates. As I know from having been a professional intelligence officer for more than 25 years, the element of trust involved can be chillingly awesome in its dimensions and potential ramifications.

The point here involved was well and succinctly put by yet another American president, James Polk:

> In time of war or impending danger the situation of the country may make it necessary to employ individuals for the purpose of obtaining information or rendering other important services who could never be prevailed upon to act if they entertained the least apprehension that their names or their agency would in any contingency be divulged.[4]

The vulnerability of human sources (especially strategically placed good ones) to compromise by inadvertent, unthinking public disclosure of seemingly innocuous information is hard for nonintelligence professionals to comprehend, let alone appreciate. One who has never handled human sources, for example, would not be inclined to regard a joke as anything possibly "classified." A good one—even if first heard at a sensitive intelligence briefing—would be more than likely to be passed along to friends or colleagues, put on the party circuit, and perhaps wind up in a gossip column. This could be disastrous, however, if the joke in question was one told by a foreign leader at a small, high-level meeting attended by an irreplaceable source.

Historical and Philosophical Impediments to "Balance"

Some of the reasons why it is currently so difficult even to perceive the need for, let alone strike, a proper balance in many areas of current public concern— especially in determining "the limits of public information" in national security matters—are deeply rooted in our history and cultural traditions. The founding fathers who initially drafted and adopted our Constitution were steeped in the heady philosophical wine of the eighteenth-century Enlightenment. These brilliant gentlemen were idealists; but by and large, they were also very broad-gauged, clear-eyed, and hard-headed pragmatists, who put a high premium on common sense and on using it judiciously in implementing even the most noble philosophical or political doctrines and theories. Many Americans subsequently prominent and influential in our nation's political, cultural, and intellectual life have, unfortunately, had a much narrower approach to central political issues, have been much less willing to be pragmatic, and far less willing to temper the concrete application of beloved theories with judgment or practicality.

One strand of Enlightenment thought has been a major thread in the whole fabric of our nation's cultural and intellectual history—the intellectual approach expounded by the French philosopher René Descartes. Whether or not they have ever heard his name, many Americans are intellectually Cartesians—instinctively wanting to focus on ideals, concepts, issues, and "problems" sequentially, pursuing each in tunnel-visioned isolation to its ultimate logical conclusion. Another such strand—indeed a taproot of our cultural and intellectual heritage—is a reverence for law. In the abstract, this is one of our noblest, most admirable national characteristics. In the concrete, it has often given lawyers what many nonlawyers (myself included) have considered a disproportionately strong voice in our political life, arrangements, and approaches to national issues—plus, at times, engendered a wistful, childlike (even childish) belief that legislation can somehow provide an answer to all of our nation's, or life's, serious challenges and problems.

The legal taproot of our national heritage has had special manifestations and consequences because it, in turn, is grounded in British and Anglo-Saxon notions of (and approaches to) law and jurisprudence. Perhaps the central notion of this legal tradition is a concept of law as an adversary process in which truth and/or justice will eventually win out if each combatant pursues his or her "case" with unflagging zeal and every possible resource, just as far as courts or legislatures permit that case to be pursued.

It was their broad-gauged, commonsensical pragmatism which led our founding fathers to erect a constitutional edifice on the twin conceptual foundations of checks and balances. Balance, however, is hard to preserve—indeed, it generally goes out the window—when people of Cartesian intellectual bent (whether they be legislators, journalists, or public-spirited citizens) pursue goals and ideals with a zeal fueled by an adversary approach to legislation, law, and legal issues. If you blend a Cartesian intellectual bent with an adversary approach to law, stir in populist notions incorporating a healthy, ingrained suspicion of any governmental secrecy,[5] and ferment this yeasty brew in a post-Vietnam, post-Watergate climate of opinion—you inevitably get some rather bizarre results, including some strange varieties of political "Kickapoo joy juice" as potent and potentially lethal as anything the late Al Capp's Hairless Joe and Lonesome Polecat brewed in their mountain hollow near Li'l Abner's Dogpatch.

One such result is the Freedom of Information Act, in its present form and with its present language. No other country—including any other democracy—has any such legislation on its statute books. The Freedom of Information Act confers its entitlements and benefits impartially on foreigners and American citizens alike. Under its provisions, the head of the KGB has just as much legal right, enforceable in our courts, as any American citizen to request (nay, demand, for any reason whatsoever) sensitive military, diplomatic, or intelligence information—which our government is legally obliged to provide unless it can demonstrate (to a court's satisfaction) that the information requested falls under one of that act's specific, limited exemptions.

The Constitutional Perspective

In impassioned debate over the limits of public information where national security issues are involved—or indeed, whether any such limits can or should be drawn in our open, democratic society and under our Constitution—two salient facts often tend to be forgotten or ignored: "freedom of the press" is a subject to which only seven of the First Amendment's 45 words are devoted,[6] and there is considerably more to the Constitution than the First Amendment.[7]

The overall purpose of our Constitution, and the governmental system it created, is quite explicitly stated in the Constitution's preamble:

> We the People of the United States, in Order to form a more perfect Union, establish Justice, insure domestic Tranquility, provide for the common defence, promote the general Welfare, and secure the Blessings of Liberty to ourselves and our Posterity, do ordain and establish this Constitution for the United States of America.

Our strife-ridden era is marked by steadily expanding thermonuclear, and steadily proliferating nuclear, weapons capabilities; by weapons delivery systems capable of spanning transcontinental ranges at supersonic speeds; by nearly instantaneous global mass communications; by a global interdependence such that virtually all foreign and domestic policy decisions interact and affect each other, in which traditional distinctions between "foreign" and "domestic" concerns become virtually meaningless; and by a national need for imported energy supplies to preserve our society's economic foundations. In such an era, our government simply cannot "provide for the common defence" or "secure the Blessings of

Liberty to ourselves and our Posterity"—or "promote the general Welfare," or even "insure domestic Tranquility"—unless some effective limits can be imposed on the public disclosure (which, because of mass communications technology, inevitably means global disclosure) of sensitive information relating to our military, diplomatic, or intelligence capabilities and actions. Discharging the basic responsibilities with which our government is charged, and for which it was established, by our Constitution is not "unconstitutional." There is no constitutional proscription against exercising judgment or common sense; and as Mr. Justice Jackson wisely observed, "the Constitution is not a suicide pact."

How to Go About Setting Needed Limits

In our open society, and under our constitutional system of government, setting limits on public information in any area—even to protect information whose public disclosure could be significantly prejudicial to our nation's security—is a delicate, difficult undertaking requiring nicely balanced judgments heavily salted with common sense. To cope with the problems and dangers created by the harsh realities of the world in which we have no choice but to live, however, we should consider at least four sets of actions.

The Supreme Court took a long stride in the right direction on February 19, 1980, when it issued a 6–3 decision in *Snepp* v. *U.S. No. 78-1871*. This decision upheld the government's contention that the secrecy agreement all Central Intelligence Agency employees sign in initially accepting CIA employment, as a condition of that employment, is an enforceable contract—whose enforcement does not (of itself) raise First Amendment issues.[8]

The provision of the CIA secrecy agreement at issue in this case was one requiring all CIA employees or former employees to submit the manuscripts of anything they desire to publish to the CIA for prepublication security review. (Mr. Snepp was a former CIA officer who had been stationed in Saigon, subsequently wrote a book about Vietnam entitled *Decent Interval*, and did not submit his manuscript for prepublication review as required by his secrecy agreement.) Understandably and inevitably, there has been a great deal of impassioned criticism of this Supreme Court decision, the CIA's secrecy agreement, and—particularly—this provision of that agreement. Much of that criticism, however, has been flawed by factual error or a misunderstanding of the questions at issue.

No one is obliged to work for the CIA. Anyone who does not like the terms or conditions of CIA employment is perfectly free to seek employment elsewhere. Accepting such employment, therefore, and signing the secrecy agreement upon which it is (in part) contingent, are voluntary acts. The Supreme Court's ruling was just, because no one can legitimately complain at being held to the terms of an agreement he or she freely and voluntarily accepted and signed.

The Supreme Court's decision was also sound, wise, and necessary—if the U.S. government is to have any effective ability to protect legitimate intelligence secrets. Mr. Snepp's basic defense (argued by the American Civil Liberties Union) was that his secrecy agreement did not apply in this case because nothing in *Decent Interval* was classified. The Supreme Court (rightly) upheld the government's argument that that defense contention—whether or not it was true—was irrelevant. That, too, was a sound ruling. No one, including any present or former CIA employee, has any private right to determine what intelligence information can safely be put into the public domain, or whether such information needs the continued protection of classification. The right to make such determinations is institutional, vested in the United States government. Legitimate intelligence secrets can hardly be protected if every current or former CIA employee is granted a private right to make declassification determinations individually and unilaterally.

One action that could help set meaningful, needed limits to damaging public disclosure of sensitive national security information would be expanding the circle of those required to sign secrecy agreements similar to that which all CIA employees must sign if they want to work for the CIA, even to the point of including all government employees given access to classified information in national security fields. Here, however, we would have to be very careful—to avoid solving one problem by means which create others equally serious.

I know from my own experience, on both sides of this fence, how CIA's prepublication security review of current or former employees' manuscripts actually works, and the strict canons which govern and sharply delimit it. (As a deputy to two directors of central intelligence, I was a senior official reviewer of such manuscripts for three years; as a now-retired private citizen, I have submitted several of my own manuscripts for such review.) That review is not "censorship." It focusses, and can legitimately focus, on one thing only: whether, in the Agency's institutional opinion, anything in a manuscript under review (if published as there phrased) would reveal information that needs to be kept classified to protect sensitive intelligence or intelligence sources and methods. Such review does *not* consider criticism, accuracy, personal opinions, or anything else—only this.[9] It would be unfair, and unconstitutional, to interpret or apply secrecy agreements in any other way—or ever allow them to become instruments of criticism-stifling censorship which would indeed infringe the constitutionally protected First Amendment rights of current or former government employees.

Another set of needed actions involves constitutionally acceptable ones which can have some real efficacy in inhibiting "leaks"—from all governmental components and echelons. (Our ship of state has been termed the only one afloat which leaks primarily from the top.) Here, it might be useful to expand the ambit of Section 798 of Title 18 of the United States Code—only in very carefully controlled, specifically delimited, and judiciously phrased ways. In its present form, Section 798 is narrowly focused on communications intelligence and communications security matters. Within that narrow field, it is a much more effective bar to "unauthorized disclosures" than Sections 793 and 794 of Title 18 (the "espionage statutes") because unlike the latter, Section 798 does not require the government to prove intent (to injure the United States or advantage a foreign nation) on the part of someone being prosecuted in order to make the case stick in court.

A third set of needed actions involves ones which curtail the flow of, and access to, highly sensitive military, intelligence, or diplomatic information. One example of the kind of action necessary in this sphere is current executive and legislative branch endeavors to modify the Hughes-Ryan Amendment to the Foreign Assistance Act of 1974—under which, eight congressional committees (which, with their staffs, total over 200 people) have to be informed of any "covert action" operations the executive branch undertakes, or may want to undertake. In theory, the Hughes-Ryan Amendment may have many defensible virtues; in concrete, real world practice, it leaves our government with almost no feasible foreign policy options between sending diplomatic notes and sending in the marines.

Then there is the most constitutionally delicate set of all such actions—ones which could make our media assume at least some measure of responsibility for national security damage done by what American media print, publish, or broadcast—including damage done by printing the identities of Americans serving their country abroad under various forms of "cover." Here, obviously, the First Amendment ice gets very thin indeed; but the basic concept involved is not revolutionary. We have laws of libel which make our media take some responsibility for damage unfairly or unwarrantedly done to private reputations and endeavors. The constitutionality of libel laws has been tested, and upheld, in our courts on many occasions. If it is constitutional to protect private citizens in this way, there must surely be some analogous, equally constitutional way to protect our government's ability to discharge the responsibilities for whose discharge it was constitutionally "ordained and established"—including its responsibilities to "provide for the common defence . . . and secure the Blessings of Liberty to ourselves and our Posterity."

Our forefathers fashioned a system of constitutional government which has stood all the tests of two difficult centuries, during which, the world known to those who drafted our Constitution has changed in ways and to an extent they could never have envisaged. As they knew, but we often seem to forget, the constitutional government they devised cannot function unless it and its workings are pervaded by a sense of balance, as well as a focus on and exercise of checks. In many critical areas—including that of where the limits of public information in national security matters should be drawn, or how they should be set and enforced—there is no "perfect" balance (for we live in an imperfect world), and no two American citizens may completely agree on precisely what balance should be struck. Our whole political process, however, was deliberately fashioned to decide—not resolve, decide—precisely such basic disputes, in a democratic way. Where information affecting our national security is concerned, the essential first step to deciding democratically where and how it is in our net national interest for such limits to be drawn is to accept the fact—no matter how unpalatable it may be—that we cannot be secure as a nation in the world in which we now live, and may not survive, if some such limits are not set on public information in these fields.

Notes

1. A code name derived from Churchill's famous Teheran Conference remark: "In war-time, truth is so precious that she should always be attended by a bodyguard of lies."
2. In the unsuccessful Iran rescue attempt, the Carter Administration largely finessed the technical requirements of the Hughes-Ryan Amendment, and got inevitable political flack and static for doing so. During the 1979–80 legislative session, there was considerable talk of revising if not erasing the Hughes-Ryan Amendment; but as of 1 September 1980, it was still on the statute books.
3. From a statement read by President Truman at a 4 October 1951 news conference.
4. From a message President Polk sent to the House of Representatives on April 20, 1846.
5. That is, any reluctance to divulge what our elected representatives, or other governmental officials appointed with these representatives' direct or indirect sanction, are doing with our money collected in taxes.
6. In its entirety, the First Amendment reads:
   Congress shall make no law respecting an establishment of religion, or prohibiting the free exercise thereof; or abridging the freedom of speech, or of the press; or the right of the people peaceably to assemble, and to petition the Government for a redress of grievances.
7. Seven Articles and 25 other Amendments (besides the First), to be precise.
8. I published a comment on this decision—outlining its background, rationale, and ramifications—in the March 17, 1980, issue of *Newsweek* (as that issue's "My Turn" column).

9. Other safeguards are also deliberately built into the CIA's review mechanism and system to ensure that the First Amendment rights of current or former employees are not infringed upon. Even within the Agency, several levels of appeal (up to the director himself) are available to putative authors who dispute the legitimacy or rationale of first (or lower) echelon determinations of which of their manuscript passages require the protection of continued classification. Furthermore, prepublication review decisions are seldom "yes or no" fiats. Every possible attempt is made to work cooperatively with an aspiring author to see if particular passages—sometimes sentences, clauses, or individual words—can be rephrased in a manner which simultaneously satisfies the author (with respect to intended sense and import) and the review board (with respect to, and only to, classification).

TECHNIQUES OF PUBLIC INFORMATION

In the following chapters, authors with extensive experience in their fields discuss techniques of government public information practice. In discussing staffing needs, Kenneth Rabin works his way through a thicket of job titles and grade levels, offering clues on how the job of government information is seen by its practitioners themselves and by others. Rabin, who is director of public affairs at E. R. Squibb & Sons, Inc., and former associate professor of public relations at American University, Washington, D.C., has worked for government agencies both as consultant and as employee. He has a doctorate in university administration, and has done extensive research in mass communications.

Margaret Rhoades looks ahead to the future of mass communications and sees intriguing developments in the 1980s and beyond. Cable television, satellite communications, and TV "superstations" are part of the changing scene she envisions. Mrs. Rhoades, who is associate commissioner for public affairs at the Social Security Administration, served for six years as an associate producer of TV documentaries for NBC. Before joining Social Security, she directed the public affairs program at the HEW Office of Education. She has a doctorate in comparative politics from Georgetown University.

Lewis Helm demonstrates in his chapter how the whole panoply of media tools can be melded into a single, purposive public information campaign. He stresses that no single medium, such as a newspaper placement or a TV spot, should be viewed as an end in itself, but rather as one of many means at a communicator's disposal to achieve his communications objectives. Mr. Helm served seven years in top government positions, including assistant secretary for public affairs of Health, Education, and Welfare and assistant to the secretary of Interior. He holds an M.S. degree in public relations from the American University and is president of a Washington, D.C., public affairs agency, Capital Counselors, Inc.

Government agencies are coming to view their own employees as a key audience for their messages, writes Michael Naver. They are organizing their public communications so as to offer both internal and external audiences high-quality products. Since 1968, Naver has directed, in succession, the publications program, the press office, and, more recently, the internal communications of the Social Security Administration. Before entering government service, he was a reporter and editor on the Baltimore Evening Sun for ten years.

Using special events as an adjunct to other communications is Bernard Posner's subject. Posner, who is executive director of the President's Committee for Employment of the Handicapped, has staged his share of special events for his organization since 1960, and offers practical advice on how to proceed. Earlier, Posner was assistant director of information at the Veterans Administration.

Advertising by government agencies comes under scrutiny in two chapters. First, Rabin discusses issues arising from the use of paid vs. unpaid advertising. Then, Robert Cuccia writes about planning and producing public service ads as a cost-effective way to reach large audiences. Cuccia, who is special assistant to the director of information at the Labor Department, has produced 40 television Public Service announcements (PSAs), more than 300 radio PSAs, and six films in a Labor Department career that began in 1969. He teaches communications courses part-time at the University of Maryland.

Rabin explains a new tool that can be used in communicating government programs—social marketing. He uses the National High Blood Pressure Education Program of the National Institutes of Health (NIH) as an example of how this new marketing approach has been used.

The technique of lobbying on Capitol Hill for an executive department is Michael Dolan's subject. Dolan, who is deputy assistant attorney general in the Justice Department's Office of Legislative Affairs, writes that sensitivity and common sense in dealing with congressmen and their staffs are as important to the lobbyist as knowledge of his subject. An attorney in private practice before he joined the Justice Department in 1971, Dolan assumed his present position in 1979.

Finally, Hiebert and Rabin address the oft-ignored area of planning and evaluating public information programs. They urge federal agencies to pay more heed to this important area, and see signs that they are. They offer practitioners some practical methods to measure the success of their programs.

CHAPTER 11

Factors Affecting Government Communications Staffing

Kenneth Rabin

It is a significant management task to plan and direct a public information program that can fulfill a federal agency's needs. One must write job descriptions for each of the specific personnel required to carry out that program. One must find new talent that will blend with existing staff and assess what types of training will keep each staff member up-to-date in a field that is currently subject to some technological change. In addition, one must help agency leaders define and carry out the organization's mission. This chapter explores how Civil Service standards overseen by the U.S. Office of Personnel Management (OPM) and related factors shape the roles of government information people, affect the image and self-perception of these men and women, and present those who manage the information function with a complex set of administrative tasks.

The Standards for Public Information Officers

The current Civil Service Position Classification Standards for public information workers were established in 1961 and were under intensive review in 1980 by the Office of Personnel Management, successor agency to the Civil Service Commission. According to the April, 1961, standards for the "public information series" (GS–1081–0), the holders of these jobs occupy "positions engaged in disseminating information about the activities of the Federal Government through the newspapers, radio, television, periodicals, and other information media, or through employee periodicals, and in furnishing advice to management concerning the information needs of the public. Positions in this series," the standards add, "require a knowledge of public information potential of written materials, illustrations, photographs, exhibits and radio, television and motion picture materials."

Government jobs which fall under the umbrella of the "1081 series" are:

1. Positions responsible for organizing, planning, and directing a public information program in a department or agency.
2. Positions whose incumbents maintain liaison with representatives of the various information media . . . to gain their cooperation in keeping the public informed of agency activities.
3. Positions whose incumbents maintain liaison with national or local public and private organizations.
4. Positions whose incumbents organize and conduct public information programs . . . directed toward the local communities in which Federal establishments are located, or toward . . . employees.

However, jobs which involve only "writing, rewriting, or editing" general materials used for public information purposes "do not require the public information knowledge and skills of the Public Information Series . . . and are classified to the Writing and Editing Series, GS–1082–0."

Writers and editors who must be experts in the specialized field they work in are further separated and designated "classifiable to the Technical Writing and Editing Series, GS–1083–0." Finally, foreign information specialists, audiovisual specialists, and "support or clerical information positions" were assigned in 1961 to a special GS–010–0 Information and Editorial Series.[1]

In addition to positions formally assigned to the various information series, some of the top managers of information offices are under the "GS–301–0" administrative series. With these, their work experience is more heavily in managerial positions with less activity in information areas.

The "1081 series" differentiates internally between public information officers (PIOs), who generally manage the function, and public information specialists, who carry out specific informational activities.

PIOs perform a broad range of tasks. The PIO must understand all of an agency's programs, suggest which publics and modes of communication should be employed to inform various groups and individuals about these programs, and "advise on what the general public reaction to the information is likely to be." To accomplish these ends, the PIO is expected to confer with other agency managers to discover "how the objectives of the laws and functions of the organization and the general public interest in the program may be furthered through the public information program."

Additionally, a PIO is expected to prepare information plans guided by management objectives, maintain good community relations, perform writing and editing tasks personally, and (depending on the size of the information staff) "exercise considerable administrative and supervisory skill in organization and directing."

Role of Specialists

In contrast to public information officers, public information specialists "direct their activities primarily toward the various information media" and "are responsible for assuring that the information material designed for a particular audience will meet the requirements of the information media that reach such an audience." As might be expected, "characteristically, public information specialists work under the direction and guidance of a full-time information officer or a management official who is responsible for planning and organizing a public information program as part of his total responsibility."

As part of this differentiation, the standards list the following job titles for people whose jobs are in the "1081 series":

> Public Information Officer
> Public Information Specialist
> Public Information Specialist (Press)
> Public Information Specialist (Radio)
> Public Information Specialist (Television)
> Public Information Specialist (Organizations)
> Public Information Specialist (Magazines)

Not all information officers or specialists have the same levels of experience, skill, and responsibilities. For this reason, the standards differentiate among these factors to determine which GS (or General Schedule) grade, and hence what pay and status, is appropriate to a specific job.

Most civil service jobs not filled by political (Schedule C) appointees are graded at a precise level on a scale of "GS-1" to "GS-18." Jobs at the levels of GS-1–4 are generally clerical. Professional-type positions at the GS-5 and GS-7 levels would be considered entry-level jobs (GS-6, GS-8, and GS-10 jobs are senior or supervisory clerical jobs by and large). GS-9, GS-11, and GS-12 jobs are reserved for junior and midlevel professional specialists. GS 13–15 jobs are middle management positions and GS-16–18 jobs are filled by "supergraders" who now make up the government's "Senior Executive Service."

The standards for public information officers include guides for writing PIO position descriptions at the GS-5, GS-7, GS-9, GS-11, GS-12, GS-13, and GS-14 levels. The lack of a specific guide for a GS-15 public information officer position description (although several such jobs and some at "supergrade" levels do exist) is taken by many as an indication that public information officers, although deemed professionals, are distinctly "second class" professionals in government service. Certainly it makes "downgrading" a PIO less hazardous than reducing the grade of, say, a lawyer.

Senior PIOs: Political Appointments and the Lack of a GS-15 Standard

Early in 1975 the Civil Service Commission took action to downgrade the ten regional public affairs directors at HEW from their GS-15 positions. Commission auditors explained that the top rating of GS-14 covered the responsibilities of the GS-15 and that, to retain the higher grade, greater responsibility need be proven than the expansive requirements under the GS-14 standard.

Then HEW Secretary Caspar Weinberger protested vigorously to the chairman of the Commission that the present salaries and rank of these positions were vital to the flow of public information. He called attention to the fact that some of the regional offices placed more than $12 billion in direct aid to individuals, groups, states, and cities and that the highest caliber of public affairs personnel was required to explain these programs in a way that they could be understood by both the recipients and the taxpayers. "It seems incongruous to me," he wrote to the chairman, "that while we are relying more heavily than ever on these public information activities to carry out the President's policy of open government, the standards now being applied by your regional offices are causing downgrades in this crucial function."

The HEW (now HHS) regional public affairs officers, in addition to handling press briefings and news releases, are also the Freedom of Information officers for regional activities; handle speaking and media assignments for the secretary and top White House personnel; handle relations with mayors, governors, and interest groups; and develop the region's public affairs plans and other high priority activities. The Commission assured Weinberger that the downgradings would be considered on a case-by-case basis, not as an over-all policy.

Weinberger left office in August, 1975. Shortly thereafter downgradings were put into effect. By 1978 all but one of the HEW positions had been reduced from GS-15 to GS-14. The New York regional public affairs person remained at the GS-15 level because that officer was required to be in contact with major publishing and television headquarters.

A later HEW secretary, Joseph A. Califano, Jr., obtained Civil Service Commission approval to change the jobs to "Schedule C" positions, out of the career structure, so that persons without government experience could be hired; this is a widely recognized method of making room for "political appointees." The incumbent career employees were transferred, downgraded and/or accepted political appointments. This system still remains in effect. Many of the supervisory public affairs positions in government are held not by career employees but by political appointees.

In 1980, there were five assistant secretaries for public affairs in government. These were nominated by the president and confirmed by the Senate to head public affairs at the departments of HHS, Education, Defense, State, and Treasury. Because of their rank as a member of the president's subcabinet, they carry considerably more influence within their own departments and outside than do other public affairs executives. They are the president's appointments, not the department head's, although they do receive their direction from the secretary of that department. Only the president can request or accept their resignations.

Below the assistant secretaries for public affairs are deputy assistant secretaries and other persons appointed to "noncareer positions" of a "confidential nature." That is another term for political appointees who can be brought into government to help implement administration programs and policy.

Under the Civil Service Reform Act, these positions now are intermingled with the top echelon of career positions, the Senior Executive Service. Limitations are imposed on each department as to what percentage of Senior Executive Service people can be appointed from outside the career structure. Persons holding these positions are considered by the Administration to be more responsive because they can be transferred more readily than lower-level career employees. However, they do have some basic rights of tenure.

In departments and agencies without assistant secretaries for public affairs, the top public affairs position may be an assistant to the secretary who also has the title of director of public affairs, or associate administrator or associate commissioner. This level of appointment is normally made by the department head with White House approval. Incumbents operate under civil service regulations related to the "do's" and "don'ts" of career service. The assistant secretaries though are expected to become involved in promoting the president's programs, decisions, and actions, speaking openly in a political vein. They, however, cannot spend appropriated funds for support of political activities, although they are not covered by the Hatch Act as are other "political" appointees.

The Current Cohort of Public Information Practitioners

As the foregoing section suggests, the public information person is affected both by partisan politics and the politics of organizational hierarchies. These practitioners, moreover, are little understood participants in the federal workforce. Two recent studies, one congressional and one academic, help shed light on the characteristics of public information practitioners in government, and their attitudes towards the job function they perform. As shall be seen, staffing regulations have an apparent effect on many practitioner attitudes.

In 1971, Rep. William Moorhead (D-Pa), a father of the Freedom of Information Act, asked federal agencies about the backgrounds of their information personnel. From a sample of 400 biographies of agency public information heads and their deputies, Moorhead and his committee staff learned that the person who runs a day-to-day government information program is likely to be a male with a college degree and some graduate work, with professional experience as a reporter in print or broadcast journalism and a political, as opposed to GS, appointment.

The Moorhead study did not, however, go into any detail about the attitudes or opinions of this group of information officers.

The first set of useful findings about the opinions of public information practitioners about their work came from a 1979 study of a large sample of members
of the National Association of Government Communicators (NAGC) conducted
by Dean DeBuck, a specialist in the U.S. Department of State, Office of Public
Opinion Analysis and Plans, working under the aegis of the American University's
Institute for Government Public Information Research.[2]

From the membership rolls of NAGC, 445 names of individuals whose "affiliation with a Federal agency was evident from the mailing list" were selected. Findings reported here are based on 229 responses, a rate of 51.2 percent, received by
April 18, 1979. It can be claimed that (1) these findings are representative of the
demographics and attitudes of NAGC members and (2) the findings will be generally applicable to all Federal government information practitioners, of whom
NAGC members are likely to be a more experienced and "aware" subgroup.

The mail questionnaire consisted of 32 attitude statements, 16 demographic
questions, and 13 multiple-choice and open-ended questions. The questionnaire
content evolved from issues raised in the literature on government information
practitioners and the written responses of 75 information people attending the
1978 NAGC annual conference to a single open-ended question about "their
views on the status of government public information and bureaucracy in general." The questionnaire was pretested on American University public relations
students and several Department of State information officers, primarily to clarify
and winnow out the number of attitude statements.

Based on the 229 responses, the findings showed DeBuck's

> typical respondent is male (60 per cent) and in the Civil Service (91 per cent). He is paid
> at the GS-13 to 15 level (45 per cent) and has worked less than 11 years as an informa-
> tion officer (51 per cent). He is a public information specialist under the Civil Service's
> 1081 series (45 per cent) with a master's degree or more (35 per cent) in English or
> journalism (44 per cent). He works for an agency responsible for natural resources,
> energy or science (31 per cent).

Practitioner Attitudes Toward the Job

As was anticipated in the selection of NAGC members as an expert sample, the
survey respondents were indeed of a far higher average grade than representative
of the universe of "1081 series" officers on the Office of Personnel Management
rolls.

DeBuck found that "the strongest correlation exists between attitudes that
managers do not consult information officers on policy decisions and attitudes
that managers outside of the information area make the decisions about the
direction and emphasis of information programs." Yet, when the information
office tried to advise top management, the majority (71 percent) of the respondents found management receptive. Moreover, most (85 percent) of the respondents believed it was their job to advise management and almost all (95 percent)
"agreed that they would not hesitate to advise management." Clearly, the responsibility for making the overtures to top management lies with the information
people.

Although research and evaluation remains on a fairly weak footing in government public information work, DeBuck found that 84 percent of the respondents
do believe they should be able to demonstrate achievement of objectives and 83
percent "think opinion research should be available for use by information
officers."

A hopeful sign, too, was the high correlation between respondents who valued
measuring effectiveness and those who were prepared to alert management to

potential problems. But, as DeBuck puts it, "there appears to be an urgent need to measure effectiveness in view of the attitude among 52 percent of the respondents that 'government misspends a lot of money on information programs.' " Finally, like most civil servants, information officers tend to feel that political appointees get the best jobs in their areas.

Although some public information officers tend to feel they are "second class citizens" relative to other managers, the DeBuck study asserts that "no strong relationship exists between feelings of being 'second class government profession- als' and job performance. . . . In fact, they may feel that their job performance will improve their status, if only they are given more opportunity and more authority to demonstrate their abilities."

Information officers tend, however, to be more confident of their knowledge of their public (86 percent) than they are of their agencies' substantive programs. In the latter area, "30 percent admit that their knowledge of these issues is not what it should be." This, of course, would place the PIO at a significant perceived disad- vantage vis-à-vis "policy" or "program types."

Sure as they are of what the public needs, moreover, the survey respondents "were also aware of the need to educate themselves . . . in new techniques." In the open-ended questions on this subject, desire for training in the audio-visual media was cited most frequently. This, coupled with managerial, research, and evalua- tion skill needs, defines the respondents' training preferences. The preferences are also quite understandable in light of the findings that "62 percent of the respondents agreed that they rely too much on the print media to communicate," and—as is common in private sector public relations also—most of them were trained in print-oriented communications programs "including journalism (27 percent), English (17 percent) and public relations (12 percent)."

Skill shortfalls within the population of government information officers— some of which are deliberate choices made by management to avoid equipment purchases and maintenance—are also reflected in the frequency and types of outside consultant use: "56 percent of the respondents indicated that their agen- cies use outside consultants for communications services. . . ." Graphics was most often contracted out, followed by audio-visual services, opinion research, photog- raphy, public service announcements, exhibits/special events, advertising.

Practitioner Attitudes Towards the Public

Although almost all (92 percent) of the respondents felt better communication programs could help restore public confidence in government, a very substantial majority (82 percent) felt they "could do more to transmit public concerns to management." This would indicate that the ideal of two-way communication is not yet achieved.

A substantial minority (39 percent) felt that the information they provide served the government's needs first. Nonetheless, almost all (92 percent) of the respondents said they would provide even "embarrassing" information to the public, and solid majorities of the respondents feel that government needs no independent ombudsman (59 percent), that "incentives should exist for those who report government mismanagement, waste and illegal activities" (63 percent), and that whistleblowers are *not* self-serving individuals.

The last question on the survey asked respondents whether or not the function they performed was defined adequately enough to allow them to "fulfill their responsibilities to the public and to their agencies." Those (58 percent) who felt the public information function needed change recommended these starting points: revise job standards; gain greater recognition of the public information function by management; gain more participation by information officers in management; require written objectives for information work; get Congress to "legalize" the jobs; and place less emphasis on what might be called "flackery" or "press agentry."

Conclusion: Coping with a Difficult Environment

An unnamed OPM administrator has said that no set of proposed Civil Service standards has engendered more outside comment—either from government workers or civilian practitioners—than the 1980 standards for the public information series, mentioned earlier. There should be no wonder at this. If the new standards remain in force for the same length of time as the current ones, they will shape the staffing of government public information offices into the first decade of the 21st century.

The present standards have not worn all that well. As indicated in this chapter, the government information officer today is as likely to be expected to edit an assistant secretary's speech as to do a program budget for a multi-million dollar operation employing a full range of specialists and equipped with sophisticated graphics and audio-visual hardware. While expected to influence top management on the effects of disclosing information on a vital current issue, that same officer, perhaps because he or she is too closely associated with the "arts and crafts" of public information, is often operating as a less than equal peer of the "policy" managers. As other research suggests, many information officers come from a news reporting background. The skills they bring to the job rarely involve the skills of program management, a shortcoming reflected all too often in how they, in turn, select and manage subordinate information staff. The partisan political nature of executive branch leadership, including most top information jobs, also grinds hard against the possibility of staffing for planned, objective opinion research and information dissemination.

In short, the public information function and, hence, the credibility of the information the public receives, is affected greatly by staffing considerations and the staff attitudes these considerations generate. Public information officers will, of course, never be fully dissociated from such environmental pressures. But it is evident that practitioners must be better armed to deal with them. Part of the answer lies with ongoing preparation for each member of the staff, developing a broad range of technical and managerial skills. As much lies in the care with which senior political and career managers in government learn to assess the role of the function and the staff which carries it out.

Notes

1. "Public Information Series" (U.S. Civil Service Commission Position Classification Standards, April, 1961). Later, better defined categories were created for visual information specialists (1084), foreign information specialists (1085), editorial assistants (1087), and audio-visual production specialists (1071).
2. Dean J. DeBuck, "Toward a Definition of Government Public Information: An Attitude Survey of Federal Information Officers" (unpublished directed study, American University, May, 1979).

CHAPTER 12

Potentials in Use of the News Media

Margaret Rhoades

The news media serve as the government's principal channel of information to the public. Although traditional news outlets are still the basic means of transmitting information, there are exciting new developments in the communications industry. New technologies will change the way we communicate in this country and therefore expand the opportunities for government agencies to communicate with their specific constituencies and with the country as a whole.

Traditional News Outlets

Government agencies target their information either to a specific group or to the broader public they serve. The messages themselves range from specific issues of interest only to a small group to those of importance to the general public. The latest information about the audiences reached by different news outlets indicates that 67 percent of adults rely on television for most of their news, followed by 49 percent for newspapers, 20 percent for radio, and 5 percent for magazines and word of mouth.[1] The more traditional media will be considered first, followed by the electronic media, which will lead into new developments in the electronic media in the second section.

Wire Services

Today, teletype machines speed the news from points around the country to virtually every print and electronic news outlet in the United States.[2] There are 108 AP and 110 UPI bureaus around the country. More than 2000 reporters work for these services in the United States.

Giving a press release, story, or interview to the wires is the best way for a government public information office to reach the largest number of people in the shortest time, since all the media have access to wire service stories. Therefore, the typical story given to a wire service reporter in Washington is a national story that should reach a large number of small town as well as big city newspapers and broadcast news programs. Typically, these stories are used by the more distant newspapers during the period of a week after a story is released in Washington. So a press spokesperson may react to the same news story from different states for a week.

This national news network provided by the wire services also operates in reverse, by bringing local news stories to the attention of government agencies, and by attracting national attention to a story of local importance that relates to national policy. Often, the government will take action on a matter of regional or even national scope because of a problem or issue that emerges in a local story.

Newspapers

Advertising by government agencies is prohibited except for the military services to recruit for the all-volunteer forces. Nevertheless, print is still the basic medium for government agencies to use in informing the public.[3] Of course many wire stories and government press releases end up in local and national papers. But beyond that, several of the leading newspapers have syndicated news services (for example, the *New York Times, Los Angeles Times* and *Washington Post*). These are used by smaller papers without the national staffs and bureaus of the new large papers.

Furthermore, several key national syndicated columnists (James Reston, Jack Anderson, Evans and Novak, for example) write in-depth articles, usually on the editorial or op-ed page of a paper, that present a more philosophical approach to an issue or set forth the results of a detailed research effort or investigation.

Obviously, giving a story to one of the major papers, which has its own news service, or to a syndicated columnist, widens its usage far beyond the readership of that newspaper alone. Besides giving specific stories to reporters, government agencies may take another approach which is increasingly important today— background meetings with the editorial staffs of papers. Government agencies are facing many complex issues, involving broad economic, political, social, and often highly technical matters. Some journalists already have the background to enable them to understand these issues and write about them easily. Many others ask for the background information necessary to write about the broad implications that a particular story may raise about a complex program.

One way to increase understanding of the complex issues we face today is to arrange meetings with newspaper editorial boards as key agency officials visit different cities. These meetings typically include reporters who cover the particular area of the official's expertise, as well as members of the editorial board. The purpose is not to generate an editorial or a story, but rather to provide the background information against which future news stories can be better understood.

Periodicals

This is probably the area that is the most underutilized of all the possible outlets for government information. Of course, news magazines carry stories similar to those that appear in newspapers. Also, they often do feature stories in which the writers explore one subject in great depth. Washington information offices provide material for these major stories in news magazines.

Two other kinds of magazines provide important outlets for disseminating information about government programs to a wide audience. One, which is used far too infrequently, is the series of columns and question-and-answer pages in monthly magazines. These publications do not have to relate to the specific field of the government agency. They are magazines with large national circulations and are an excellent way to reach a wide public.[4]

The other type of periodical which is very important to most government agencies is the trade publication. The trade publications number more than 4000, including both newsletters and magazines. Virtually every major subject area is covered by one or more publications, often based in Washington. In almost every field, from elementary education to space exploration, there are important trade publications which are read by everyone across the country who works in that field. These audiences are the particular constituencies which a government official often wants to reach. For example, he or she may want to be sure that the impact of proposed legislation is understood by the people who will be affected by it. The appropriate trade publication will receive a telephone call and send a reporter to do an interview. In this way, news about the budget, legislation, and important regulations gets to the people who need it.

Radio

Radio reaches a larger audience than any other medium. Radio broadcasts reach 98.9 percent of the American people. There are radios in 76.5 million households in this country, with at least five sets in the average American home. The number of listeners is high in each age group: 99.4 percent of teenagers, 96.2 percent of adult men, and 94.6 percent of adult women listen to radio stations each week. Radio has fully recovered from the arrival of television, and in fact seems to be entering a new period of growth.

The numbers tell a story of expansion and prosperity. Advertising revenue increased 12 percent in 1978, to almost $3 billion. The number of stations has been expanding, with 2700 new stations going on the air in the last decade, bringing the total number to 8653. Stations are increasingly turning to specific markets, targeting their material to certain groups. As a result, there are more stations on the air that are all news, all talk, all rock, or good music. In 1979, NBC announced a new radio network, "the Source," designed to appeal to the 18–34 age group. A few months later RKO announced a similar network geared to the interests of this same market.

Radio offers vast opportunities for sending information to specific or general audiences. Government agencies must now do the research work necessary to provide public service announcements designed for different kinds of stations and audiences. The wide variety of programming formats presents both an opportunity and challenge.

At the present time, stations offer free time for public service announcements from both public and private organizations. This is an invaluable opportunity for government agencies to reach large audiences. A government agency wishing to reach the young adult, for example, can package its announcements in a format tailored to the new networks and the all-rock stations. Research and understanding of the varied formats of the thousands of radio stations will result in broader use of public service spots that fit smoothly into the stations' programming.

The second important public affairs use of radio time is through interviews with government officials. This may be done as part of a news story, in a longer news interview show, or as part of a talk show. While an item receiving a great deal of attention from reporters will bring requests for interviews, it is also a good idea for government agencies to contact local stations and suggest a subject of interest to many listeners. For that reason, it is crucial to know in advance whether or not there is a special audience that radio station is reaching. This technique of generating coverage is probably more effective on a local level than trying to reach network news at a national bureau. Bear in mind that an interview will be particularly effective if local listeners can call in their own questions.

Television

Television, which today reaches 75.7 million households, is almost as pervasive as radio. One of the most important recent developments is that news programs are now rated among the most popular television programs. There were regular evening news programs almost from the time television appeared in the 1940s. But, in 1961, Newton Minnow, President Kennedy's appointee as chairman of the Federal Communications Commission, declared television a "vast wasteland." This widely publicized criticism caused the networks to begin a new form of television news journalism, the documentary series. Today, CBS's "Sixty Minutes" is rated among the top ten programs. Other news programs are also proving more popular than ever before. In 1979, a record number of people watched the evening news.

Television is probably the least familiar and most difficult medium for many government agencies to work with, and yet this is perhaps the most important medium for public information. Many agencies simply do not have stories that will be considered for the evening news or the Sunday interview programs. Even their press conferences may not attract more than local coverage.

Two other kinds of television programs should be considered. One is the morning news programs, which can be approached with material of interest to a significant number of people, and for which there is a "newspeg," a reason that people should pay attention to that story on a particular day. The second type of program is the talk show. Daily and weekly TV shows reach a wide variety of audiences, on local stations, public broadcasting—both local and national—and on the three major networks. Often these shows are geared for a particular audience, such as women, and would be interested in government officials discussing a public program of interest to this group. Some of the talk shows are news discussions and regularly welcome government and outside experts to mix with representatives of the media. Public affairs offices should keep the producers of these shows informed about breaking stories that will fit in with their formats and offer people who can discuss the issues. A wide audience is reached. And perhaps equally important, government officials learn what is troubling the press and the public, particularly if there is a studio audience. This kind of exchange helps them to be more responsive.

New Developments in Communication

This is a time of tremendous change and innovation in the communications field. Some of these new developments may well change the face of the communications industry by the end of the 1980s. A few of the new techniques, such as the QUBE system in Columbus, Ohio, are on a rather small scale, while others, such as cable television and satellite communications, are growing rapidly nationwide. At the same time, videodiscs may bring homeviewers the kind of program freedom that has begun with currently available technology for program duplication.

Cable TV

Cable TV should be of particular interest to government information officials because it has been growing rapidly, and it offers new sources of TV programming that can be adapted for public information purposes. Subscribers to Cable TV have risen dramatically, from 2.8 million in 1968 to approximately 15 million subscribers today. This means almost 20 percent of American homes with television now receive cable TV. Cable's 4100 systems serve 10,000 communities across the country. Projections indicate that as many as 25–30 million households will have cable TV by 1985, or 30–35 percent of all American homes with television. Obviously, this addition to the traditional television stations cannot be ignored.

Cable provides a new multichannel source of programming, not just to isolated communities where existing television does not reach, but to urban and suburban communities as well. Not only does it expand the number of viewers, it opens up new sources of programs compared to the handful of traditional stations.

Cable stations are giving their subscribers a range of new information not included in more traditional programming. For example, some stations offer weather reports with radar pictures, while others present a list of grocery prices at area supermarkets. Of greater interest to a public affairs office is the option some channels offer, to receive the UPI news headline service or audio news reports accompanied by still pictures. A channel in the Washington, D.C., area offers complete coverage of the proceedings in the U.S. House of Representatives. Another station features a bulletin board with public service announcements plus ads from the subcribers—a kind of video shopping center. This expansion of cable TV programming offers important outlets for government information.

Cable is already big business, with $2.5 billion in assets, and it promises to get even bigger. The number of additional channels available to the home viewer differs with the system. Most of the companies offer 6 to 12 channels, while some offer more than 20.

An important feature of cable television is the access channels. In 1972, the FCC ordered cable TV companies to provide several channels for the free use of citizens, schools, and government agencies. The FCC reasoned that cable could be used for "much-needed community expression." The full promise of access has not been met, with fewer than 400 communities having access channels. Some local officials have not agreed to access channels. In those communities where they exist, access channels air a wide variety of programs, from those captioned for the deaf to phone-in forums on local issues. Clearly, these outlets offer wide possibilities for public affairs offices.

Satellites

By freeing television from land lines and turning to satellites, communicators will usher in a new era of television. WTBS, an independent station owned by Ted Turner, is a UHF station distributed by cable systems. Turner has also developed a new system, the Cable News Network (CNN), started in 1980, to provide news 24 hours a day.

The land lines, or "local loops," are either telephone lines or microwave links. They are controlled by the networks. Satellites free television from the network-controlled loops and replace them with so-called "earth stations." The broadcasting station owns the receiving antenna. Several programs can come in at once by satellite, broadening the station's choices. At the same time, there is no guarantee that any of these possibilities will mean expanded public service potential.

The changes will come rapidly in this area in the 1980s. Already there are 1164 earth stations now receiving programming for cable TV; another 914 licenses have either been granted recently or are still pending before the FCC. Thus there are 2078 FCC licenses granted or pending for earth stations. CNN has already signed up Cox Cable, Storer Cable, and United Cable TV Corporation. Their plans call for lengthy news programs in the evening, and 50 percent new stories within each 24-hour period.

The extensive combination of cable systems and satellite transmission will bring less expensive and more varied programming. The individual broadcasting stations will have more of a choice in what they air, and the viewer will have a wider choice of channels. It is simply not possible at this time to analyze the new forms of broadcasting and say how much public affairs time will be available. There are trends, but they are mixed. There are news shows in the top ten rated shows today, and more viewers for the evening news. At the same time, there are more comedy shows. One of the new so-called "superstations," the Entertainment and Sports Programming Network, is planning to offer sports programming 24 hours a day. We do not yet know the real meaning of access channels. Still, there is a potential that more time will be made available for public service.

QUBE

In Columbus, Ohio, Warner Cable offers an experimental service called QUBE. This is an interactive service in which the viewers can "talk back" to their television sets. The television viewer presses different buttons to answer "yes" or "no" when questions are asked of the audience. Those answers are fed into a computer. For an extra charge, people can add this feature to their cable service. The subscribers receive a console with 30 buttons: 10 for conventional channels, 10 for specialized channels provided by the system (sports, community news, educational children's shows, etc.), and 10 channels for pay TV.

QUBE offers the viewer a chance to participate, to be heard, to have his or her vote tallied instantly. This kind of instantaneous survey took place in Columbus during the time American hostages were held in Iran. Following a debate, the viewers were asked to "vote" whether or not to return the Shah to Iran. They voted three to one against returning him.

If QUBE expands into other cities and attracts large numbers of viewers, obviously the possibility will exist for instant public opinion polls. At the same time, people appearing on a station with this "talk-back" feature will also find out quickly what people think of what they are saying. The public affairs possibilities are wide open. The privacy issue should also be carefully considered, so that the people who decide to have this service in their homes are aware of the possibility that information about them and their opinions could one day be available to others.

Conclusion

The public is demanding that government be more open and responsive to the people. Working through the news media in the forms discussed in this chapter offers government agencies the potential to fulfill these demands. What is called for today is a higher level of involvement on the part of the public affairs offices in understanding the changing processes of disseminating information. In this area, we can expect both new potential and added challenges.

Notes

1. These findings were the result of a Roper poll. The total of all the figures exceeds 100 percent because some people cited several outlets as prime sources of news.
2. For example, AP reaches over 1300 papers and more than 3600 radio and television broadcasters in this country alone, while AP International reaches more than 10,000 outlets of all types in 110 countries. UPI reaches more than 1150 newspapers and 3700 broadcasters in the U.S. and over 7100 news outlets worldwide.
3. The circulation figures for newspapers on an average weekday is now 61.9 million, with a drop to 53.9 million on Sunday. The total readership is larger, reaching 109.3 million, during the week, and 107.1 million on Sunday.
4. The circulation figures for some of these magazines show how large an audience they reach: 18.3 million for *Reader's Digest*, 8.3 million for *Family Circle*, 8 million for *Better Homes and Gardens*, and 8 million for *Woman's Day*.

CHAPTER 13

Strategic Use of the News Media

Lewis M. Helm

Media are means, not ends.[1] This is perhaps the most difficult lesson for practitioners of public affairs and public relations to understand. The ultimate objective is to *communicate* with people needing information about programs and services. And yet, it is widely accepted practice to point with pride at what has often
been considered to be the final product—piles of news clips containing the agency's name or that of the boss, appearances on television and radio shows, or
skillfully phrased explanations of agency activities in slick "house" publications.

This faith in tangible, physical proof of effort detracts from professionalism
more than any other false idol of public affairs. Further, it is a fallacy perpetuated
by the mass media because of its faith in its own efficacy. The placement of
information is only one phase of the public affairs process. Other phases include
the development of a public affairs plan, identification of target groups, selection
of the means to reach them, delivery of a realistic message, and assessment of
results.

George Beveridge, *Washington Star* ombudsman and media expert, wrote in a
column that "much of the output of the huge federal information apparatus has
little to do with stories which reporters and their editors are interested in chasing;
in some agencies only a small portion of the information force has anything to do
with 'press relations.' "[2]

The fact that piles of clips are generated does not show that an issue has
reached intended audiences or is understood. It merely shows that publications—perhaps the wrong ones for the message and intended audience—carried
the story. Likewise, an appearance with a Medicare message on a radio station
that appeals to youth is a waste. Then, too, the wrong medium might carry the
wrong message—as vividly illustrated in the famous Jimmy Carter interview in
Playboy.

The Print Media Tradition

Somewhere during the evolution of government public affairs, print media became the dominant outlet. Except for the 1930s, when film became a primary
medium to generate support for depression programs, print has remained the
most-used mass communications vehicle. It also has remained the primary emphasis of some public relations agencies, including Carl Byoir and Associates,
whose Chairman, George Hammond, still openly ponders, "How would Carl
handle this problem?"[3] Because of this faith in print media, other vital aspects of
public affairs have suffered, and the ability to communicate has been drastically
decreased.

David S. Broder, one of the most widely respected observers of the political
process, wrote that the press is "too often guilty of a kind of consumer fraud . . ."

through its claim to maintain an all-encompassing coverage of events. "The flag-ship of our business, *The New York Times*, flies that famous slogan, 'All the News That's Fit to Print.' It is a great slogan, but it is also a fraud," Broder wrote.

> Neither *The Times*, nor *The [Washington] Post* nor any other newspaper—let alone the nightly network news shows—has space or time to deal with all the actions taken and the words uttered in the city of Washington with significance for some of its readers or viewers—to say nothing of what is happening every day in the rest of the country and the world.[4]

Thus, even though it is impossible to convey government's messages sufficiently through newspapers, public affairs practitioners continue to try. And they are aided fully by the media's own narcissism. The comfort that comes from estab-lished rapport with reporters and the security of proving effectiveness by pointing to a pile of news clips has become the hub of the information cycle, dictating public affairs plans rather than the better approach of plans dictating the medium.

Components of the Orchestra

Newspapers resemble violins in a symphony orchestra. They can perform excep-tional solos, are vital to most major movements, and compensate when other instruments fail. However, all instruments of an orchestra must add their own unique qualities to produce the harmony, strength, and beauty that truly reach an audience. Therefore, what follows is a critical examination of the various media and methods at the disposal of the practitioner with an emphasis on the interplay of these tools. Also included are a number of suggested approaches to particular government public affairs tasks, which are based on my public affairs experiences.

Media Considerations

A wide variety of actions can be taken to convey information depending on the answers to these questions:

- How important is the announcement?
- What audience will be affected most?
- How complex is the issue?
- In what context will the announcement be made? This would include other related concerns, the history of the subject, and plans for future releases.
- What reaction is anticipated?
- How does the announcement fit into the over-all public affairs plan?

Media characteristics are important also.

Television is the only source of news for almost two-thirds of all people—but it is not suitable for the explanation of complex issues and cannot focus on a well-defined audi-ence.

Radio is a "hot" medium that can generate emotional support. However, it suffers a malady similar to television in that it cannot deal with complexity.

Newspapers can deal with story details in slightly more depth than broadcast. It is a medium where information can be seen in print and reproduced or clarified.

Magazines lack the timeliness of other media but they can treat material in depth. They also can be selected to reach well-defined readers and can be reproduced in quantity for secondary distribution to target groups.

Since media characteristics can affect an announcement's content, media selec-tion should be considered with the message as a package, not separately. What is the announcement intended to create in the way of action and by whom? Is congressional support wanted? If the program is a "no smoking" campaign, should the message be directed toward cancer patients, smokers, Congress, business leaders, and/or tobacco growers in North Carolina? And what modification of the program, if any, will be anticipated from public reaction?

The Instruments

The following are the instruments available to public affairs practitioners to orchestrate messages to selected audiences. Many of these tools are also used by private sector public relations professionals, but they are discussed here only as they apply to the government experience.

News Release

This is the most basic, but perhaps the most overused, tool of government public affairs and private sector public relations. In the case of the former, it can set forth the specific facts of an event, permitting an agency to go on the record with an issue the way it wants the issue to be presented. It can be distributed at a news conference. It can generate follow-up media interest and be used to answer subsequent inquiries. Since these are generally directed to the news media, they should be in a format which would appeal to a reporter or editor (i.e., typed, double-spaced, with wide margins, written in the journalistic pyramid style with a strong lead). Unfortunately, this principle can be lost in the preparation of government releases when an agency, in the name of conservation, imposes certain restrictions on the production of releases. Too often government releases are rendered unreadable by the necessity of having to describe complex issues on one page, forcing the use of single-spacing and both sides of the paper. This reduces the chance that even important government releases will be noticed or used by the media, which are deluged with releases from every conceivable source daily. Therefore, a telephone call to the paper is often necessary to generate interest in important events. Conversely, lack of a phone call can be taken to mean that the event is not important, thereby decreasing coverage. News releases are print-oriented in that they do not emphasize the photo or broadcast potential. Therefore, a personal conversation with editors also is frequently necessary.

Press Conference

This permits broad dissemination of announcements, a detailed explanation of complex issues, focus on events, personal identification of an official with the issue, and participation by all media. Negatively, it permits the presiding official to "misspeak" either intentionally or unintentionally, requires extensive preparation for participants, emphasizes shortcomings in the speaker's delivery, requires major public affairs support to manage, and permits little control over the message once it is released. Further, if used too frequently, its attraction for reporters diminishes unless there is a major running story to discuss.

Press Briefing

This is a less formal means of accomplishing what the press conference does. Normally, a limited number of reporters is invited. Ground rules can include everything "on the record" (fully usable), as "background" (without attribution by name), "deep background" (written as the reporter's own thoughts), and "off the record" (the discussion never took place). Only selected media are invited and ground rules permit the official to respond without public attribution. However, an increasing number of reporters no longer participate in any but "on the record" sessions, for this very reason. Another negative is that nothing said, even though it is termed "off the record," can be guaranteed as secret.

Press Availability

This means the official will be present and answer a broad range of questions and pose for photos or television. It normally is used in connection with an event, but adds informality to the occasion to the degree that it might become too low key to attract media—except in the case of a president or other very top personality.

Radio Actuality

This at one time was considered as the radio version of a news release. Agencies tape the voice of an agency official, then telephone it to radio stations. Other agencies connect the tape with a "call-in" telephone number so that stations can make their own tapes of an announcement as though they attended the news conference. This practice resulted in a 1974 congressional investigation because of radio tapes' use in the "Battle of the Budget." Most agencies discontinued the practice. However, during the Carter administration use of radio actualities widely returned in the promotion of administration programs. *Chicago Tribune* reporter Raymond Coffey wrote in 1978 about a HUD radio actuality: "That message illustrates the fine line that is not always drawn between political promotion and public enlightenment."[5]

Television Actuality

This device, equally controlled as its radio counterpart, is a TV news clip produced by the agency and mailed to interested television stations. (Regulation[6] prevents dissemination of such material to media unless the media has requested it. This barrier can be overcome by sending postcards to stations asking if they are interested in material. Most answer affirmatively.) Television clips generally provide feature material since they cannot be timely for breaking news. Smaller stations are prime users since they lack a capability to develop material independently. A negative is that a member of Congress might accuse the agency of "propaganda" if he or she disagrees with the issue being publicized. Another is high cost.

Op-Ed Pieces

These are major "thought" pieces written by opinion leaders about some aspect of policy or the manner in which a program is being carried out. Normally, they are about 500–700 words long and gain their name by appearing on the page opposite the editorial page. Use of this communications vehicle came from recommendations of some leading journalists concerned about communications, including James Reston, who wrote: "We need more open pages, preferably next to the editorial pages, where the best minds of the world could give their analyses of current developments."[7] This is a highly controlled form of communications and is capable of expressing in exact and detailed form the intent of the official. However, its audience is limited, the piece rarely can be developed on a timely basis, and the number of publications using this form of communications, while growing, is very limited.

Features

Feature material always is sought by publications and broadcast media. There-fore, agency research into a different "angle" could potentially interest media reaching a variety of audiences. The difficulty here is that considerable effort must be invested on speculation without commitment of interest from the media and, further, the material is liable to rewrite once released. There is also a poten-tial for charges that the agency is attempting to "promote" a policy or a service through propaganda.

Conferences and Seminars

These are used to develop in-depth understanding among the media and related groups. The Department of Health, Education, and Welfare developed these as major public affairs initiatives during 1973 through 1975. Various forms of media seminars were used by other agencies during the Ford administration in 1975–1976 and by President Carter in his town meetings. Negatives include the amount of effort required to plan and conduct the meetings and the inability to control what is said and how it is reported.

Magazine Articles

In many ways these are similar to op-ed pieces. However, they can more directly focus on interested groups. For example, articles by the secretary of the Interior can be placed in conservation-oriented magazines if they are directed toward a controversial issue affecting that group. Considerable work is needed to prepare magazine articles and work almost always must be done on speculation. Further, timeliness is rare unless the article is an integral part of a long-term public affairs plan.

Special Interviews

Scores of media representatives normally have requests pending for personal interviews with the head of an agency. Therefore, selection can be made by issue, by region, and by interest group. Depending on the familiarity of the interviewed official, preparation can range from minor to very major. Knowledge of the interviewing medium is most important. For example, *U.S. News & World Report*, showing a desire for the interview to reflect the official's position accurately, sends a final draft of the interview to the official for his or her review and editing. However, some media—most notably television specials with predetermined story lines—frequently will interview an official for upwards of an hour, then use only a small segment that reflects their story line. Often this is the worst part of the interview. Many governmental officials now refuse to participate in TV specials unless they retain some form of control over the segment that is finally used.

When this demand is made, that medium generally reports that the official refused to be interviewed, misrepresenting the circumstances but adding to the thrust of the story line. Other government officials have simply learned, or been taught at some expense, how to voice all their big thoughts in terse (30 seconds or less) noneditable terms.

Congressional Testimony

Seemingly, this should provide one of the best opportunities to communicate a point of view to the legislators and to interested publics. However, in practice it usually is the worst. First, the Office of Management and Budget (OMB), in representing the president, has the responsibility of reviewing and approving all testimony before it is given. Because of changing circumstances and the press of other agency business, draft testimony rarely is sent by the agency to OMB more than several days in advance. Similarly, OMB rarely approves the testimony until shortly before it is to be delivered.

Since testimony is normally drafted by attorneys and approved by budgeters, the final product can be totally incomprehensible to the general public. Further, protocol demands that Congress see the testimony before the media. If members disagree with it, they may "leak" selected parts in advance of the agency's appearance and refute those parts publicly before the hearing is held. The actual testimony can become a nonevent. Two dozen hearings might be under way at the same time, decreasing any possibility of news coverage. Also, only a portion of the full testimony normally is read by the witness, with the balance inserted into the record.

Reporters on deadline do not have the opportunity to hear testimony on complex issues before they must write their stories. Therefore, coverage of committee hearings often consists of reaction statements about stands which have never been reported initially. One way to overcome this system is to hold a background news briefing the afternoon before the hearing so interested reporters can write a story in advance, holding release until the hearing time. The whole system of testifying works against a sound communication between the executive and legislative branches.

Brochures

These are excellent vehicles for reproducing definitive articles about agency issues and conveying information to target groups without the use of mass media. Brochures range from inexpensive to high quality slick pieces. Printing control of these, as discussed later in this chapter, remains under the Government Printing Office. Brochures are also another product, like the pile of news clips, which can have the purpose of showing "action" by the public affairs office.

Periodicals

Some very useful information is contained in periodicals published by government agencies and directed toward those they serve. These are vehicles to maintain contact with groups that have a continuing interest in programs and policies. However, the periodical can be used to promote programs in an effort to generate increased funding for an agency. For this reason, OMB approval is needed to start a periodical. An annual periodical review is also required, although often ignored and rarely enforced. Proliferation of periodicals by one agency has a tendency to occur as target groups multiply and the ability to reach them becomes more difficult.

Displays

While in Europe emphasis is placed on the use of displays, only minor use is made of them in the United States. Displays can be one of the most effective means of communicating a "point of sale" message such as "Join the Army Here" or "Try Stamp Collecting." However, the cost per contact is far higher than communications through mass media. So, use of displays should be limited to very specific purposes.

Speeches

Speeches could serve as the basic activity around which other public affairs activities are built. For example, if a speech is to be given about the economics of smoking by the secretary of HHS before the Detroit Economic Club (one of the most sought-after forums for political and governmental leaders), it can be merchandised through other available outlets. During the trip to Detroit, an evening dinner session with top editors and reporters about the politics of the issue might precede the next day's speech. Early the following morning a live television show appearance might be possible. This could be followed by a visit to a newspaper editorial board.

Speech copies and accompanying news releases could be distributed in advance to the media and made available at the club itself. Copies then may be reproduced in brochure form and sent to interested target groups. Because of the speech's broad impact, copies also could be sent to other administration officials and editorial writers. At a minimum, reporters covering that agency should receive copies of all out-of-town speeches. In other words, while the antismoking speech would reach only a limited number of influential people at the Detroit Economic Club, proper handling of the secondary audiences should bring high returns.

Slide Presentations

These can be effective in support of explanations of complicated issues. However, there is a risk of losing the audience when the lights go out unless the presentation is very professionally handled and the slides add interest, rather than compete with the speaker for interest.

Films

Washington, D.C., has often been called "Hollywood on the Potomac" because of its massive outpouring of films. There are films to describe agencies, films to promote an issue or service, films to show how to care for teeth, babies and most other health-related activities. Films help to train military personnel on new weapons systems. Films are developed for placement on television, for use by speakers, and for general distribution to interested groups.

All told, the General Services Administration (charged with coordination of federal film purchasing from outside sources) estimates that about $500 million a year is spent on "audio-visual" activities, primarily film production. Further, there has been about $1 billion invested in plant facilities and equipment. In 1972 the federal government produced 593 films and 2339 television clips. There have been 13 different films on safe driving and 22 films on tooth-brushing produced since 1960. The Defense Department alone has 45 audio-visual production studios. The federal government has 75 in Washington, D.C., and 37 in Southern California, alone. Most film funding comes from program money, not from "line items" in congressional appropriations. Like brochures and newsclips, films can be proof that a public affairs office has been active without necessarily proving that an audience has been reached.

Congressional Record

Another instrument uniquely available in government to reach the audience, and one that brings great prestige with it, is a statement by a member of Congress in the *Congressional Record*. When a member is persuaded that an agency has done an outstanding job in an area of interest, the member will write a laudatory statement for inclusion in the *Record*. Sometimes the member will insert a statement written by the agency. Prior to 1979 it was not possible to tell whether the statement was a speech on the floor or merely an inserted statement. Now they are differentiated, although it is necessary to understand the code to tell the difference. The agency, then, can reproduce the statement and use it to answer inquiries about the program with the answer attributed to a member of Congress. This serves the purposes of the member and the agency. The 34,000 daily copies belie the true impact of the *Record*. It is closely followed by staffs of almost all Washington opinion leaders with relevant items called to the official's attention.

Federal Register

Whenever an agency goes through rule-making procedures, it is legally required that the public be informed about the pending action. *The Federal Register* serves this purpose with its 49,000 daily copies. A frequent oversight by many agencies is the fact that an item becomes public once it is filed at the *Register*, not when it is published. Thus many news stories have been broken prematurely because of a reporter's use of this knowledge.

The Government Printing Office (GPO)

The Government Printing Office (GPO), which began operations in 1861, serves as the focal point for the purchase, printing and binding of all publications developed by the federal government. Of the $591 million spent through the GPO during Fiscal Year 1978, about 60 percent was contracted outside to private printers.[8] In 1978 56 million publications were sold by the GPO for $43 million. The GPO, printing the equivalent of a 60-page newspaper daily, produces everything from telephone answering pads to slick four-color magazines and the *Congressional Record*. Federal agencies cannot by law contract outside for printing. Everything must be processed through the GPO under rigid costs and quality criteria. There is one exception to this publication processing. In 1950 Congress directed the Secretary of Commerce to establish a central clearinghouse for technical information. The legislation, entitled "The Technical Information and Services Act," established within Commerce a clearinghouse to collect and disseminate "scientific, technical and engineering information." In 1970 the *National Technical*

Information Services succeeded the clearinghouse. The NTIS produces fewer copies of each publication than the GPO but has a wide variety of limited-appeal titles available. Its funding for 1973 exceeded $10 million. A competitive situation has been growing between the two agencies because of the ill-defined sphere within which they work. As a result of this and other recent demands on the Government Printing Office, legislation was being considered in 1979 to make the Government Printing Office an independent agency with greater but more fully defined powers.

A Typology of Leaks

No discussion of media tools would be complete without a nod to that classic Washington device: the leak, or planted story. This section reviews several kinds, including those that work as part of the agency public information campaign, and others that work against it. The difference depends on who does the leaking and why.

A Candid Leak

During the 1979 Carter administration cabinet shuffle, one high-level public affairs official was quoted as saying that it was a toss-up as to who would be fired first, he or HEW Secretary Joseph A. Califano, Jr. The article spent two columns discussing how he had "survived" under five presidents being a candid conduit of information to reporters—while still remaining loyal to his immediate boss and the president. It quoted him as saying that during the final days of the Nixon administration Ron Ziegler, the president's press secretary, tried to bring him into the White House press office to help—and that he managed to avoid the assignment. The article failed to point out that the reason Ziegler attempted to bring him into the White House was to bring him under close scrutiny, to stop leaks. Thus, while claiming to convey "truth," this type of self-serving relationship with media tends to separate the public affairs official from the agency.

Leaks That Float

An often used but entirely different type of leak is the release of information with the intent to "float" an idea, to obtain a reaction which will be used to make program decisions. Early in the administration of former Interior Secretary Walter J. Hickel, it was necessary to emphasize that Hickel was proconservation, a viable representative of the interests that had opposed his confirmation during heated Senate hearings during January, 1969. He was being closely scrutinized by Congress and the media.

On January 28, 1969, a giant oil spill from a well operated in California's Santa Barbara Channel began to destroy some of the West Coast's most beautiful beaches. Assisted by two attorneys from the Solicitor's office, I attempted to create a new legal concept that oil companies would become "absolutely liable" for any spills that occurred. And yet, because of the radically new approach to pollution problems, Hickel did not want to announce the actions directly himself without first testing reaction.

Therefore, a staff member leaked the decision (to promulgate rules making oil companies liable) to a knowledgeable, interested reporter from the *Washington Post*, who verified each aspect of the planned action and developed a comprehensive story from the leak. Nothing, it was agreed, would be attributed to the Hickel staff. The exclusive *Post* article resulted in far wider media interest than if a news release had been distributed. Congress reacted favorably. An editorial appearing in the *Post* declared:

> The actions of the Interior Department this week in proposing tighter restrictions on offshore drilling and in placing full liability on the oil companies are certainly steps in the right direction. Secretary Hickel . . . seems to be responding well in this first test of his interest in protecting the Nation's natural resources.

Six months later, on August 21, the final regulations were published, enforcing decisions leaked in February. By that time, all considerations had been aired publicly and reactions of the media, Congress, industry, and California residents were well known. The regulations went into effect with minimal opposition.

Leaks from Torpedoes

Another type of Washington leak is one directed toward "torpedoing" a planned agency action. A classic example occurred during late 1970 when an Interior official, acting on instructions from the Office of Management and Budget, attempted to abolish the Bureau of Mines' mineral research centers in the western states. An Interior information officer took the exploratory order, attached an analysis of which members of the Senate and House of Representatives would have constituencies affected, then covertly gave the entire package to a friendly reporter from United Press International. A wire story appeared in every city with an office that would be eliminated. There was an initial wave of news clips from the West. This was followed by a second wave of negative editorials. This was followed by a third wave—letters from irate members of Congress. And finally came the decision to continue operation of the research centers.

Leaks and Swamps

In another form of "leakmanship," Secretary Hickel's staff recommended that he visit the Florida Everglades for the overt reason of checking alligator poaching. An expedition was planned with an overnight stay on an island in the middle of the swamp. Accompanied by National Park Service rangers, Hickel would go on a moon- and lantern-lit search for the beasts to see how they were easily trapped. The timing was perfect. During the spring of 1969, Hickel still was highly controversial, good news copy. Half a dozen leading Interior reporters gleefully accepted the invitation to go with him.

While on the island, chatting over a fire, Hickel established himself as a concerned conservationist. But more importantly, just as planned, he laid the groundwork for media support to block Department of Transportation attempts to build a jetport in the Everglades. The reporters had become interested participants in Hickel's personal focuses without knowing at the time that the jetport was his primary reason for the Everglades trip.

Full Orchestration

These, then, are the instruments available to deliver an understandable message to agency publics. How the instruments are used is dictated more often by the agency's degree of understanding than by budget, audience selectivity, and message content. It is quite possible to convey a one-shot message by relying on a well-placed leak or by distributing a news release or through a one-on-one interview. But to maintain a campaign to develop an understanding of a major issue among an array of publics, all of the instruments available should be polished for possible use.

If, for example, the Detroit speech appearance by the HEW secretary discussed earlier were a part of a major campaign to stop smoking, every instrument in the orchestra could be used. A *press conference* before leaving Washington, D.C., for the Detroit Economic Club speech could announce the anti-smoking campaign. This could be preceded by in-depth *press briefings* by an assistant secretary for health and the key program people related to the issue. A *press availability* at the National Cancer Institute could be set up so that photographers and television could shoot footage of the secretary examining the facility to accommodate the results of smoking. The *news release* would be distributed at the press conference in Washington with a second one in Detroit. A *radio actuality* could be added by taping the press conference and the speech. Likewise, *TV actualities* could be developed.

In advance of the press conference, an op-ed piece could be written and selectively placed in target parts of the country to support the press conference announcement. *Feature articles* about the history of anti-smoking campaigns could be prepared in advance for placement in consumer-oriented magazines. Likewise, *trade press* articles could be placed in publications of the health-related industry. *Seminars* on the issue could be held for health writers at the White House or in HHS so that they could obtain enough information to cover the campaign accurately.

In addition to Detroit, *special interviews* could be granted for target media and areas. *Congressional testimony* would naturally follow as Congress exercises its oversight prerogative. *Brochures* containing positive editorial comment and additional information about the issue could be widely distributed to editorial writers and interest groups. Both internal and *external periodicals* written by HHS and printed by the GPO could feature the issue fully. *Public service announcements*, including both radio and television, could be distributed widely to promote the benefits of not smoking. *Exhibits* could be used at every available health show during the period of controversy. *Films* and *slide presentations* could be developed to accompany speakers. Every top departmental official could be assigned to give a *speech* before target groups in different parts of the country and then to make media appearances similar to the one made by the secretary in Detroit. Supporting comments could be placed in the *Congressional Record* by friendly members of Congress.

Every instrument could help to orchestrate the flow of information to the various publics—and there would be no violation of law since the activities would not be directed at pending legislation. Making this information available to the public would be part of HHS's congressional mandate to inform the public about the dangers of smoking. The flow of information would be propaganda because of its intensity and because it advocates a position. But the public affairs official would be carrying out his or her mission fully and effectively as directed. The media would be the means. The end would be persuasion of the public to act.

Notes

1. In his book, *Understanding Media* (McGraw-Hill, 1964), Marshall McLuhan develops the insightful theory that "the medium is the message." I don't agree fully with his thesis. A medium can be the message, but it is also a means to an end.

2. The *Washington Star* published a series of four articles beginning on April 12, 1976, about "The Selling of the Government" through advertising and public relations. A wave of protest from public information and other government officials about the articles' "imbalances" resulted in a column on April 20, 1976, by George Beveridge, "Federal Information Needs Defining."

3. Carl Byoir, founder of Carl Byoir and Associates, died in 1957.

4. David Broder, "The Press Is Guilty of Consumer Fraud," *The Washington Post*, June 3, 1979.

5. Raymond Coffey, "Taxpayers Footing Bill for Army of Admen," *Chicago Tribune*, April 23, 1978.

6. Title 39, United States Code Annotated, paragraph 321n, Government Franking Privilege, limiting use of free mail frank by executive agencies without requests.

7. James Reston, *The Artillery of the Press: Its Influence on American Foreign Policy* (New York: Harper and Row, 1966).

CHAPTER 14

Government Media for Internal and External Audiences

Michael R. Naver

The use of public information by management for problem-solving among its various publics is not new to government or private industry. More recent is the notion that the employees of a government agency ought to be regarded as one of the important publics the agency serves. Just as government information executives have found that the post-Watergate, post-Vietnam climate spawned a public that is more restive, more critical, and even more hostile towards government than ever before, those same managers have discovered that the employee public, once taken for granted as sharing management's goals and attitudes, can no longer be so viewed. This change is not really surprising; people who work for the government grow out of the same environments as their friends and neighbors in private industry.

One major implication is that government communicators are not likely (if they ever were) to achieve their goals with employees through the mimeographed house organ and its Polaroid photos of a smile and a handshake. The same professional, well-planned, well-designed problem-solving communications used with outside publics are equally useful with internal audiences. Another implication is that employees are viewed not only as an audience in themselves, but as a medium to reach other publics. At Social Security, for example, we're always impressed by the knowledge that if each of our 85,000 employees communicates with only three friends and neighbors in a week's time, that's an opportunity for Social Security messages to reach a quarter of a million Americans—a sizeable public in itself. That the design and content of those messages is a matter of some importance is not lost on our top managers.

Employees and Their Needs

What do we know about today's work force, and what challenges does it pose to the government communicator?

First, it's the best educated work force in history, and therefore best equipped to question management's policies and judgments.
Second, it's been nurtured by the implicit "right to know" of the television generation.
Third, it's sophisticated about using the law and the full range of employee rights mechanisms against management.
Fourth, it demands a "free speech" environment where open discussion of views is always possible.

At the same time, recent research suggests that today's employee so equipped brings a set of attitudes toward the organization that is probably more negative than ever before. The Opinion Research Corporation (ORC), which has been gathering information about employee attitudes for 25 years, has some distressing news for management communicators. (The research has been conducted in private corporations, and opinions might differ about whether the findings would apply to government.) Here's a summary of the conclusions:

- Most employees believe their company is not as good a place to work as it once was. The percentage of managers perceiving improvement in their companies has steadily decreased over the past 17 years.
- A downward trend is evident in employees' ratings of how equitably their company treats them. Expectations of job advancement are the lowest they've ever been.
- The gap between the job satisfaction expressed by managers and that of hourly employees is as wide as it has ever been. That's not because managers are finding increased job satisfaction. Rather, it's because satisfaction is *decreasing* among hourly employees while managers' attitudes have remained about the same.

"The findings," according to the ORC authors, "lead to the conclusion that employee values are changing and that dissatisfaction is increasing. This is not a myth; it is an emerging reality. As such, it provides a major challenge for management in the 1980s."[1]

In addressing these realities, government communicators find it helpful to understand what employees look for in their agency publications. In general, they find that employees are asking for more hard news about their organizations; more information about plans and trends in their particular specialties; more about salaries, benefits, and promotional opportunities; and finally, more upward communications—a climate in which "their suggestions and complaints can be heard, understood, and acted upon if possible."

Some research has gone further and has found that the nature of employee information needs varies not only with the kind of work an employee does, but the kind of organization where he or she does it. Highly innovative and creative organizations generate curiosity and interest among their employees about the organization's products and services; in organizations where the work is viewed as repetitive, however, employees find news about Susie Jones's marriage more interesting. Within a given organization, a similar pattern develops; employees in blue collar jobs tend to prefer news about employees or about administrative change to news about the agency's research projects, while management and professional employees react the other way.

Management Needs

Fortunately, signs are growing that management is becoming more sensitive to government employee needs and is willing to meet them, at least in part, through effective internal communications programs. In a 1979 poll of more than 2700 members, the International Association of Business Communicators, consisting of both industry and government practitioners, found that 49 percent of responders placed "worker needs and interest" at the top of the list of management challenges in the next two years. Also, 63 percent found "worker satisfaction" as the most important issue before communicators in the same two-year period. A like number (62 percent) forecast a wider role for communications programs in the next two years.

These results are not startling, considering the group surveyed. What is perhaps surprising is the extent to which management's communications goals for internal audiences are beginning to approach those used for the external publics.

Management's goals in government public communications programs have generally been predictable, particularly in large benefit-paying or tax-collecting organizations like the Veterans Administration and the Internal Revenue Service, where the agency's actions impact upon individuals either as beneficiaries or taxpayers. At the Social Security Administration, for example, our public communications goals are likely to be articulated in such terms as:

- Inform the public about their rights and responsibilities under social security.
- Support effective administration by building understanding of administrative processes.
- Facilitate change, as when changes in law require new administrative procedures.
- Promote the public's "security" in their ability to know ahead of time that a benefit check will be paid at retirement, as well as in their having the economic "security" of the check itself.

These are not very different from a set of goals that might be enunciated for an employee information program.

Also, evidence exists that the *limits* of the public information role, both for employees and for external publics, are similar. To the extent that top management would like to use the public information function to change attitudes, both of employees and other publics, recent research indicates that this may not always be a realistic goal. These findings point to a conclusion that communications programs can be useful in placing "agenda items" before a public for its consideration, but not in shaping attitudes toward those items. In other words, communicators can influence employees and other publics in what to think *about*, but not in what to think.

A good approach to setting realistic communications goals was developed by the Bell Telephone System. The company decided to measure the success of its 1978 employee publication against the following standards:

- Does it *reach* all employees?
- Does it create *awareness* of management messages?
- Does it have a reputation for *reliability*?
- Is it written so that the material can be *understood* by the intended audiences?

Missing from this checklist are such time-honored employee communication maxims as "promoting employee morale," "improving employee attitudes towards management," and the like.[2]

Locating the Internal Communications Function Within the Agency

Another sign that top management is viewing its internal and external communications in the same light is in the way those functions are organized within the agency. Most major departments and agencies house their public communications functions within an "office of public affairs," which is generally staffed by professional communicators. The internal communications function, on the other hand, has in the past been relegated to the administrative side of the house and operated by people whose specialties are in fields other than communications. This picture is changing in the 1980s.

Two examples make the point. The Navy's SITE (Shipboard Information, Training, Entertainment) system is located in a division that reports to the chief of information. So does its program of publications and other communications for sailors at shore installations. At the Social Security Administration, the internal communications function was shifted at the end of 1979 from the Office of Management, Budget, and Personnel to the Office of Public Affairs. In his memo to the executive staff announcing the change, Stanford Ross, then commissioner of Social Security, gave as his reason the "complementary nature of external and internal information programs; i.e., public understanding of social security is achieved to a large extent through informed employees." Margaret Rhoades, associate commissioner for public affairs, puts it another way; "We've brought all the communicators together."

Implicit in the change is the expectation that both the Navy and Social Security will bring to the task of internal communications the same high-quality skills and products it uses with outside publics. Many large private organizations have long operated successfully under this strategy.

Using Media

Virtually every communications manager in a large government program has a variety of controlled media at his disposal, in contrast to the mass media of press, radio, and TV, on which he also depends. How well he uses government media with internal and external publics depends largely on how well he matches the three major elements in his communications programs: audience, message, and medium. This chapter is not the place for a full description of the catalog of media available to a communicator—films, slides, brochures, periodicals, posters, car cards, television spot announcements, and so on. Instead, it will highlight some selected uses of government media that offer promise to communicators in the 1980s.

Videotapes

As the newest communications medium, television is being used increasingly by government communicators in a variety of ways for external publics and, more recently, for internal audiences. The recorded public service announcement, blessed by the Advertising Council for use in commercial programming, is the most ready example. But communicators are finding that videotape is widening their horizons beyond PSAs.

Videotape has a number of advantages. It can be produced (and changed) virtually instantaneously; production costs are low; the tape can be reused; it allows a variety of formats. Some examples:

- The "talking head," in which a speaker on camera talks directly and simply to the audience.
- "Employee press conference," in which employees can quiz the boss on matters of concern for instantaneous or later showing to coworkers.
- Panel discussions, in which complex issues of program or administrative change can be communicated by experts in a relatively informal setting.
- "Magazine of the air," in which the agency develops a full-scale feature production in an entertainment format that yields small doses of useful management information.

In its SITE shipboard program mentioned earlier, the Navy placed TV sets aboard half of its 500 ships, and expects that TV will be on board all ships by the mid-1980s. These television sets do double duty as communicators of management information by day and purveyors of popular TV programming at night, thanks to the Armed Forces Network. Navy public information managers find it effective to communicate Navy news and policy to sailors through the same medium by which they are used to getting their entertainment. Videotape does that job.

At Social Security, television sets are installed in all 1400 field offices across the nation. Potential audiences include employees in a training setting as well as members of the public who visit the offices. In some offices, monitors are set up in the employee recreation room for viewing during coffee breaks. In other offices, TV sets can be set up in the waiting area for viewing of social security messages by people while they wait to be interviewed about their claim. At Social Security, the video tape production crew is part of the Office of Management, Budget and Personnel, but responsibility for planning public affairs tapes and some internal information tapes (those that are not explicitly for "training") rests with the Office of Public Affairs.

Recorded Telephone Messages

These are proving effective in several ways; the recordings can be used by employees, by the public, or news media. Proven uses have been found for all these audiences. The American Telephone and Telegraph Company, aptly enough, set up a recorded "hot line" for employees as a rumor control device during a strike several years ago. It proved so effective that the company continued using it after the strike. Government agencies, such as the Office of Education, provide recorded material for radio news programs. Congress uses recordings to give its employees and the public information about the progress of legislation on an hour-by-hour basis.

Telephone recordings have several advantages: messages can be mounted and changed quickly; distribution is as fast as the receiver wants it to be, since she decides when to pick up a telephone to listen; the messages are accessible to people across the nation; and are adaptable to a variety of publics. The prospects are that communicators will make increasing use of it in the 1980s. A cautionary note: The use of some government recordings on radio has been criticized in the past for giving listeners the impression that the radio station participated in a news conference, when in fact it did not.

Weekly News Bulletins

Many government and private organizations publish attractive monthly newspapers and magazines, but are discovering that the monthly schedule is not frequent enough to keep audiences informed. As a result, they have gone to weekly, and in some cases, daily news bulletins. These have proved popular. They can be produced quickly and cheaply, using typewriter type and no graphics. The formats permit quick reading and throw-away afterwards. Their brevity prevents management from editorializing, which so often creeps into longer publications, so employees or other publics can have confidence that they are getting "just the facts."

Where the work force is highly concentrated in a few locations, rapid distribution is possible and the newsy quality maintained. Where the agency has far-flung field installations, one news bulletin to serve all of them is often not possible. In these cases, management can use the bulletin for headquarters employees and develop standards for field installations to use in producing their own news bulletins. These projects require careful planning and proper internal approvals to assure there's no duplication of activity. The bottom line: Less versatile than video tape or telephone recordings, but cheap and easy to use as an adjunct to other communications in the right organizational settings.

Magazines

The old employee communication workhorse—the "house organ"—is finally catching up, both in government and industry, with the lush, colorful "externals" for key outside publics. It's getting harder to tell them apart. The employee magazines range from small-circulation, black and white, in-house foldouts to four-color periodicals on glossy stock. At last look, the Government Printing Office counted more than 350 external periodicals, and no one could estimate the number of internals government wide. These latter range from the small-circulation, one-color foldouts printed in-house to the glossy full-color armed service magazines. Within HHS alone, that department's publications office estimates 500 internal periodicals. Government-wide, the total undoubtedly runs into the thousands. (These figures demonstrate the importance of continuing evaluation of publications to assure that they meet real needs.) The number of large-circulation, national employee magazines, like Social Security's *Oasis* and the air force's *Airman*, probably stands at less than 100.

To limit the profusion of externals, the Office of Management and Budget requires, in general, that they be distributed on the basis of paid circulation. Approval of a free distribution magazine can be made in some cases. There is no comparable regulation governing internals, other than those imposed by individual government department.

Is the magazine still an effective communicator in an electronic age? Recent research indicates that it is. A study by the *Opinion Research Corporation* (for the Magazine Publishers Association) reported that people are more likely to look to magazines as a source of knowledge and usable information than to other media, even though they may spend more time with those media, especially television. And they are more likely to take action on a magazine than on a television commercial.

A survey by the Social Security Administration of its *Oasis* magazine found that 74 percent of employee respondents said the magazine made them feel more like a part of the agency. Lower-grade employees were slightly more likely than higher-grade employees to find it useful as a source of information about new work procedures, employee activity, and consumer news. The bottom line: Well-produced magazines that can target messages to key publics, both internally and externally, are here to stay in government.

Making Messages Effective

Communicators usually agree on the elements that make messages effective in the media we've described. The problem is often one of convincing top management in any given case that these elements should apply. This is not because top managers don't want messages to be effective, but because they are prone to insist on insertion of elements that weaken effectiveness. Communicators are on solid ground when they argue with top managers for these elements in communications to internal and external publics:

- Messages must be *clear*—that is, presented simply and in good style, and with nonessential, potentially confusing elements kept out.
- Messages must be *credible*—that is, presented so as to be factual, balanced, fair.
- Messages must be *timed* to reach audiences when audiences are likely to be listening. This means being careful not to communicate too early, before the receiver can reasonably take action, and certainly not too late for him or her to act.

- Messages must be *repeated* to be effective. Don't expect to achieve full awareness with your first message.

Employee Feedback

Of all the communications skills public affairs managers learn, the weakest is usually the art of listening to others. Their training emphasizes how to say it well, not how to listen well. Fortunately, that's changing. More and more organizations, public and private, are placing emphasis on feedback from their audiences.

The signs of change abound. Sperry Corporation runs full-page ads in business magazines to tout the art of effective listening. Major organizations set up an ingenious variety of devices, called "hot lines," "open circuits," "speak out," "employee mailbag" (with replies mailed confidentially to the employees' homes), and the like. All these efforts are intended to give employees a voice in their organization's decision-making process. Some attempts succeed better than others.

Feedback helps in several ways. Management has found that the benefits reach out not only to evaluating how well the employee magazine is read, for example, but also to shaping strategies on what should go into the magazine. Feedback can also tell communicators about the level of audience *awareness*, and thus help them fine tune *messages*. It can tell management where employee problems exist and don't exist. Some communicators belabor a point when the audience is already on their side; others downplay the seriousness of a problem. Feedback helps.

Feedback helps communicators select the right *medium*. On some issues, you'll need such one-way communications as recorded cassettes or leaflets. On others, two-way vehicles, such as workshops, open meetings, and employee "press conferences," fit the bill. Feedback helps management decide where to place its training resources and how incentive programs are working. Employee input to these activities may improve morale and productivity.

Feedback is a mixed blessing. Once management has opened its doors and its ears to employee views, it's hard to close them later. Knowing how to use feedback is an important management skill, and misuses should be avoided. Some common misuses of feedback include:

- Using the wrong feedback mechanism. For example, don't hold an employee gripe session unless you are prepared to act on what you hear.
- Design surveys carefully. Look for a representative sample of your audience, rather than simply listening to the raised voice. Make sure you hear from the "silent majority" who never volunteer opinions, but will respond if asked.
- Don't ask the wrong questions—the ones you unconsciously hope will provide answers reinforcing your preconceptions. To avoid this trap, consider using a professional survey item to design your questionnaire on important surveys.

The traditional view of employee surveys is to use them as a management information device. A new approach treats them as a legitimate form of upward communication. Management can, under this approach, give employees a chance to take part in shaping the questionnaire. Find out what questions they'd like answered and design them into the survey. Feedback the survey results to employees. Continue the two-way process by asking employees to generate proposed solutions to the problems identified in the survey. Evaluate the proposed solutions and report back management's response. This approach won't automatically solve all problems, but one result could be a measurable change in the way employees view management's attitude toward them.[3]

Conclusion

Through technology, and through more sophisticated understanding of the needs of audiences, communicators are equipped to do the best job ever in the 1980s. At the same time, the challenge posed by a range of publics as critical as any in history will demand from public affairs managers their best efforts. If the net result is a freer flow of communications, both downward and upward, there can only be winners—top management, communicators, employees, clientele publics, and most important, taxpayers.

Notes

1. Michael R. Cooper, Brian S. Morgan, Patricia M. Foley, and Leon B. Kaplan, "Changing Employee Values: Deepening Discontent?" *Harvard Business Review*, Vol. 57, No. 1, Jan.-Feb. 1979, p. 118.
2. James F. Tirone, "Measuring the Bell System's Public Relations," *Public Relations Review*, winter, 1977, Vol. 3, No. 4, p. 31.
3. Cooper, Morgan, Foley, Kaplan, p. 125.

CHAPTER 15

Special Events for Government Communication

Bernard Posner

Early each March the Department of Labor invites its employees into the cavernous departmental auditorium in Washington, D.C., for the presentation of awards. The program never changes: welcoming speech by the secretary of labor; plod, plod, plod of employees marching across the stage; flash, flash, flash of an overworked camera recording each sweaty handshake and toothy grin. Year after year this event plays to a packed house.

Its objective is to create at least a mild sense of family among employees. Has it worked? The Labor Department cafeteria and coffee bar still buzz with gripes about pay, bosses, promotions. Yet attitude studies do show that most employees do feel there's more to their jobs than the cardboard paychecks they're not supposed to bend, spindle, or mutilate; and the feeling is strongest in March.

In Washington in the late 1970s a White House Conference on Handicapped Individuals took place, preceded by statewide conferences in every capital city. The former Department of Health, Education, and Welfare handled the conference; a dozen other agencies helped. The president spoke amid whoops and crutches being tossed in the air. So did congressmen and cabinet heads. Three-thousand resolutions were passed. Then it was over. The handicapped people went home and waited for things to happen.

Nothing happened. Nothing? True, there was not a spate of new laws and programs as the handicapped people expected, but there was something else. The White House Conference convinced the people that they had a voice and they had power. A vigorous handicapped activist movement sprang up, impelled by the conference. What if 3000 recommendations didn't get implemented? Instead, handicapped people found their strength. The planned objective didn't emerge, but the conference succeeded all the same.

The Veterans Administration decided to close a small veterans' clinic in an eastern city because patients could get better and cheaper care at a well-equipped VA hospital on the other side of town. But you don't close a clinic capriciously; veterans groups, Congress, and the medical profession would protest loudly. So VA handled the entire closing as though it were a special event. It planned an entire series of advance meetings to share the planned move with all who might be interested—congressional delegation, union, veterans' organizations, employees, medical association. Before the closing, it found other jobs for all whose jobs would end. It called a press conference, answering all questions openly and fully. There were no surprises. There were no protests. There was virtually no press coverage. A special event that did not create a ripple; that was its objective.

"Nothing Happened." "Nothing . . .?" "Happened . . .?"

A yearly awards ceremony, a White House conference (several occur each year), the closing of a clinic—hardly the raw material of news. They certainly don't rank with world treaties, defense budgets, or medical breakthroughs. But they don't compete as news. These are events that do not spontaneously happen. They are created and engineered. They exist not for their own sakes but for definite preconceived purposes behind them. Machiavellian? Not necessarily. The Boston Tea Party was a special event. So was the massive march on Washington in the sixties protesting Vietnam. So is Pasadena's Parade of Roses and the Salvation Army bands at Christmas and the annual potted plant sale of the local garden club.

Government makes skilled use of special events. Remember the Bicentennial? And Armed Forces Day, and National Hospital Week observed by every government hospital, and the 200th Anniversary of the Customs Bureau, and the 10th Anniversary of the Department of Housing and Urban Development? There is a constant kaleidoscope of special events in America. They may not be news, but they add zest and fun to our lives.

Plusses and Minuses

There are some strong plusses and minuses to special events. One plus is the fact that it is not always easy for a government agency to break into the news with the good it does. Americans basically distrust their institutions, government agencies included; they would much rather read about the bad sides of agencies than the good. One Labor Department employee indicted for taking bribes is worth a hundred honored for exemplary service.

So one way to gain public attention for the good is through the special event. Another plus is the fact that a special event enables us to bring together all the constituencies and supporters and friends of the agency, creating a bond indicating that government does not operate in isolation but rather is a living part of society.

A big minus has been expressed by Daniel Boorstin, Librarian of Congress, in *The Image*. He contends that special events cloud truth and distort realities. Too many are like living in a vast Disneyworld rather than a real world. Nonetheless, a rich variety of special events stand ready to serve your agency. Here is a small sampling:

Anniversaries

Anniversaries of the creation of your agency can be observed as special events, and they need not only be in multiples of ten years. A perfume manufacturer once staged an imaginative observance of its 32nd birthday. Why the 32nd? "Because we felt like it."

Also, anniversaries of the creation of major government programs can be commemorated—U.S. Savings Bonds, the GI Bill, Rural Electrification, FHA home loans. There is a temptation to use anniversaries as occasions for backpatting. Don't. The emphasis should always be service to the American people, and the huge army of forces other than the agency itself which cooperated to bring it about.

Days, Weeks, Months, Even Years

In establishing special days, weeks, or months, many agencies seek either presidential proclamations or joint resolutions of Congress. These do not assure success; only you do. The promotion of a special day or week or month can require months of planning and coordination.

Rather than create your own day, week or month, it is always possible to ride the coat-tails of events already established. The President's Committee on Employment of the Handicapped has created National Employ the Handicapped Week the first full week of each October. Other agencies use this week for their own ends. VA uses it to promote jobs for disabled veterans; the President's Committee on Mental Retardation uses it to promote jobs for retarded people; Rehabilitation Services Administration uses it to promote jobs for those who have gone through the rehabilitation process. A good starting point for establishing your own or using someone else's: *Chase's Directory of Annual Events*, Apple Tree Press, P.O. Box 1012, Flint, MI 48501.

Annual Meetings

Many agencies hold them. They need not be dull recitals of current personnel practices or managing by objectives. Rather, they can be imaginative meetings bringing together constituencies and supporters; and recharging commitments and enthusiasms. Treat them as events, not as bores.

Awards

There can be awards to people inside the agency as well as to people outside. They are gracious ways of expressing appreciation and recognizing achievement. Don't forget local neighborhood newspaper coverage.

Contests

The limit here is the extent of your imagination. Some agencies give awards for the best letters written each month; some sponsor essay contests in high schools; still others hold contests for specific purposes. (Once the president's committee sponsored a contest for the invention of a stair-climbing wheelchair.)

Open House

Hold them whenever possible, but be sure visitors have something worth seeing. No point staring at green file cabinets. Open houses can build the bonds between agency and community.

Landmark Events

Some major events fall into your lap for special event treatment: the appointment of a new head of the agency; enactment of an important new law; closing of an old program; an agency moving to another city. Make the most of these; they don't occur often.

Confrontations

Confrontations can be a form of special event if handled properly. These days, government agencies are the butts of citizen protests of all kinds—energy, the environment, mental health, physical health, nuclear reactors, seat belts, affirmative action, education, welfare.

If protests happen to your agency, don't hide behind locked doors and terse "no comments." If at all possible, top management should extend its hands to try to build bridges. This can be done by inviting protestors in or by meeting them outside. You may not build acceptance, and you may not bring about a meeting of the minds. You will at least shore up the process of communication. The agency may not win the argument; it may win respect and approbation.

A few warnings about special events and your agency:

First, they do not merely happen because a president or the Congress issued a proclamation. They take months of planning by people in and out of the agency.

Second, there should be no such thing as just one single event, period. They should occur at intervals, perhaps yearly. They have a way of pyramiding one on top of the other.

Third, special events do not exist solely for the purpose of media coverage. Certainly, it is desirable, but there are deeper purposes.

Fourth, special events need agency-wide commitments, top down. Top management has to *believe* in the event as being more than a publicity-seeking plaything. This requires a purpose that clearly is essential.

Fifth, no single agency alone can create a special event. Events are the products of many forces working together. The agency has to keep them all happy; has to give plenty of recognition; has to keep everybody marching in step.

These 12 rules for special events will not guarantee success but they might improve the odds:

1. *Objectives*

Every special event should have a clear-cut objective that gives it direction and coherence. The objective must also be attainable. Consider the 25th anniversary of an agency. What is the objective? "To stage a successful anniversary celebration?" Useless and formless. "To make the entire nation aware of the agency's contributions?" Self-serving and unrealistic. Or rather: "To recognize all the non-government forces which have worked hand-in-hand with the agency over the years, enabling it to serve the people." At last; an objective with direction and meaning. A guidepost.

2. *Publics*

Special events should not be aimed at every man, woman, and child in America. Instead they should be aimed at specific publics, groups of people that, for good reasons of our own, we have decided we particularly want to reach. Through the selection of specific publics, our special event gains precision. We are communicating with human beings, not with shadowy creatures belonging to something called "the general public."

3. *Opinion-Molders*

Even carefully selected specific publics may not respond to our blandishments. They may listen to us with half an ear, read our output with half an eye; but they look back over their shoulders for a reassuring nod from someone they trust. That someone is an opinion-molder. A voice of respect and authority. A person or persons whose judgment is leaned on. Opinion-molders are not always easy to identify. Who do teachers listen to, principals, unions, parents? What about businessmen? Labor leaders? Health food purchasers?

4. *Media*

Special events are more than events within themselves. They are a means to an end, a vehicle for getting across concepts and ideas to some specific publics. These publics are reached through media—not indiscriminately selected, but fine-honed to head straight for their targets. This means it isn't necessary to think of *Time* or *Newsweek* or AP or UPI or the "Today" show. *Barber's Journal* may be more appropriate; or the suburban press surrounding a big city; or a mimeographed house organ; or a tiny college radio station. Publics come first; media are selected to reach publics.

5. *Personal Involvement*

One basic fact of effective communications is that there is no substitute for person-to-person getting-together. The mass media can create awareness; personal confrontation makes the impact on human minds. Some sort of personal involvement can be arranged for any special event. Even a speaker who stumbles over words at a meeting is superior to a slick address on TV. At the Labor Department's award ceremonies the secretary of labor speaks in person. At the White House Conference on Handicapped Individuals, the president spoke in person. At the closing of the VA clinic, the administrator of veterans affairs made the announcement in person.

6. *Cooperation*

No single agency can run any kind of special event without enlisting an entire corps of friends and supporters and constituents. A first step should be a list of cosponsors and cooperators, and the wider the representation the better. This becomes more than a list; it becomes the basis of an across-the-board planning committee for the event. Be sure all get due public credit for their help.

7. *Budgets*

Even simple special events do cost money. Can your agency's budget cover some of the expenses (exhibits, travel, printing, and so on)? Can funds be raised from nongovernmental sources to cover expenses? Here, it must be absolutely clear that there would not be the slightest trace of conflict of interest. Money does raise its head. Better solve the money problems early.

8. *Name That Event*

An eye-catching name would help, if possible. It could grip people's minds and reverberate a long time.

9. *Timing*

When should the special event take place? Every event is unique. Consider an open house, in establishing the matter of timing: On a Saturday so school children can attend; weather not too hot or not too cold; no other major community events the same time; stay away from Super Bowl Sunday and World Series Week. Plan far enough ahead, and timing can be worked out satisfactorily.

10. *Pacing*

A special event is more than a two-dimensional event where you pull out all the stops and make a steady din for as long as you can. The event has peaks and valleys of activity. You must be aware of them.

Back to the open house: there would be an initial peak of activity with the formation of the planning committee; then quiet for a while as plans develop; then another peak as special events for the open house are announced in advance; then a crescendo of publicity building up public interest in the open house; then the event itself, hopefully with a peak of public attention; then it's over, and another flurry of follow-up activity, which leads to . . .

11. *Thank You*

The event is over. Prompt "thank you's" should go to everyone who took part— the planners, the implementers, the participants, everyone. Some agencies give warm personal letters; some give plaques to those whose efforts stood out.

12. *Measurement*

Many people spent scores of hours putting together a special event. It is over. Was it a success? Measurement is not easy. If objectives have been defined with enough precision it may be possible to evaluate whether they were reached. You can count press clippings and radio and TV coverage. You can count people at an open house. You can count a surprisingly large number of things.

But it is possible that these measurements do not dig deeply enough. What minds were reached? What opinions were changed? We may have to develop our own kind of a bottom line: The fact that a special event took place and was carefully planned and implemented is *perhaps* some indication that it did what it was supposed to do.

Special events—manipulative contrivances, or fragments of history? Fancy or fact? They are what we make of them. They are legitimate tools of the communications process, awaiting the use we put them to. They have earned their place; they are used universally. They have acquired dignity and respect. Use them. Use them well.

CHAPTER 16

The Rising Role of Advertising

Kenneth Rabin

The federal government in 1978 ranked as America's twenty-fifth largest advertiser. Buying media time and space to attract military recruits, Amtrak passengers, foreign tourists, and express mail customers, and producing messages for free media time and space for countless other purposes, the government in 1978 exceeded the *combined* expenditures of such highly visible commercial advertisers as Exxon, American Airlines, and Schlitz beer.

The government became a major paid advertiser rather suddenly, acquiring the role in 1973 as a byproduct of the shift from the draft to an all-volunteer military force. Advertising expenditures have since risen to an annual range of $115–130 million. Moreover, although congressional action to restore the military draft could reduce these costs with haste, the government's swift incursion into paid time and space has had an indelible effect on the way federal agencies approach *both* paid and public service advertising. In these areas, the government is becoming both a more knowledgeable client, and a more sophisticated persuader.

Free vs. Paid Media Time and Space

The earlier and more common form of government advertising is public service advertising, in which the time or space for the advertising message is donated to the sponsoring agency by the media. The print media—newspapers, magazines, display, and transit—donate space entirely as a goodwill gesture. The electronic media—commercial radio and television stations licensed by the Federal Communications Commission (FCC)—are required by the Communications Act of 1934 to program in the "public interest, convenience, and necessity," and are expected to give free time to public service announcements (PSAs) from government and nonprofit agencies. The FCC dictates no set amount of time, time of day, or specific types of public service messages to its licensees. However, the FCC does require a station up for license renewal, a triennial process, both to substantiate public service announcement activity over the last three previous years and to answer questions about its plans for the upcoming license period.

Government public service advertisements gain free broadcast time either directly through the stations or indirectly through network feeds accepted by affiliated stations. PSAs may be prepared and distributed to the media by a government agency itself, by an advertising agency or producer under government contract, or by an advertising agency working with the government through the Advertising Council, a consortium which has dominated the national PSA picture since World War II.

Paid time and space obviously increase the government's control over when, where, and how often its advertising messages appear. But buying media is quite expensive, and too dramatic a shift to the paid approach might all but close the door to free time and space for government causes.[1] For this reason, the government has been quite judicious about its incursions into paid media, restricting its activities to either military recruiting or the quasi-business endeavors of tourism, postal services, and rail transport.

Debate over paid versus free time remains intense, and some new paradigms could emerge. The U.S. Postal Service has successfully split its advertising between paid ads for the sale of stamps to collectors or the promotion of express mail and mailgrams to business customers and public service ads encouraging everyone to mail early for Christmas. Nutritionists in the Department of Agriculture in 1979 awarded a contract for a test campaign to change children's eating habits. According to *Advertising Age*, "materials would be tested in three markets under various media patterns. One market would probably use paid ads, for example, while another would rely on donated public service time and space."[2]

But at the same time Agriculture got permission to experiment with paid media for government ads, a paid media campaign by the Commerce Department's U.S. Travel Service to encourage potentially profitable foreign tourism faced extinction due to White House budget cuts. Moreover, another Commerce Department agency, the Bureau of the Census, decided in 1978 to shelve earlier proposals for using paid media to convince minority audiences to fill out 1980 census forms.

Human Factors Influencing Government Advertising Messages

Government advertising presents some unique problems with respect to the acquisition of media time and space. Less unique, but equally problematic, is the process by which a government agency decides what types of message and appeals it will use to "sell" a particular program or behavioral alternative to its audiences.

At bottom, *all* advertisers want their viewers, listeners, or readers to take a specific action in response to a received message. To get results, a message must be both clear and persuasive. The most memorable government advertising campaigns, like their commercial counterparts, certainly fulfill the clarity criterion:

> Don't Forget. Hire a Vet.
> Only *You* Can Prevent Forest Fires.
> The Marines Need a Few Good Men.
> 55. It's a Law We Can Live With.
> Join the People Who Joined the Army.
> The Navy. It's Not Just a Job. It's an Adventure.
> Take Stock in America.

Satisfying Decisionmakers

In-House Decisionmakers

As in the private sector, a government advertisement (usually at a preliminary stage of development such as layout, treatment, script, or storyboard) must satisfy certain decisionmakers. First, the government agency personnel who correspond to profit-sector product managers, brand managers, sales managers, vice presidents of marketing, and general counsel must all be convinced that (1) the PSA campaign proposal is defensible under the agency's legislative mandate and against charges of boondoggling from both Congress and the press; (2) the best message and media have been selected; (3) the sponsoring agency has not made any promises it cannot keep; and (4) the expense of producing the advertisement will be exceeded by the public and agency benefits produced.

In the last category, of course, we can observe the greatest difference between government and the profit-sector advertising message decisions. If an ad exists to sell a product, sales figures can be tracked. But, what if an ad exists to change public attitudes towards using seat belts or filing one's income tax on time? Some ads have measurable outcomes, as was observed in the 80 percent census test response in Richmond, but such possibilities are much less clear cut than dollars and cents. One of the time-honored government alternatives is to have the ad promote a tangible product—a brochure, for example—so that requests for the product can be traced. But does requesting a brochure mean that its content will be acted upon by the recipient?

Some government advertising is judged as successful if it receives frequent free time and space in competition with other PSAs. But measurements of this type also are not always accurately made. In short, government agency decisionmakers can interpret the cost/benefit implication of an ad in more ways than their private-sector counterparts. Government advertisement producers must decide what "the bottom line" really is before they propose the use and content of ads.

Media Decisionmakers or Gatekeepers

Both government and private-sector advertisements must also win the approval of decisionmakers who allocate time and space at the magazines, newspapers, television and radio stations, and networks. Such decisions are somewhat more clear-cut for the advertiser in or out of government who is paying for time and space. Only two questions need be addressed:

1. Is the advertisement in good taste and good technical form? No responsible media gatekeeper will accept an ad, even a paid ad, which will lower the quality of his or her over-all content or programming.
2. Will the advertisement expose the medium to legal pressures from individual consumers or organized protest groups? Many corporations have switched from product ads to "corporate" or "issue" ads. Broadcasters often reject these paid ads on the grounds that antibusiness groups may request free air time for response under the "fairness doctrine" established under the Communications Act of 1934.

For an ad message to get free time and space, then, these same two questions must be addressed by the public service media gatekeepers. Additionally, government agency advertising producers who seek free media time and space must also ask themselves:

3. Does the media gatekeeper know about my agency and the particular program we are promoting?
4. If the media person is local, does he or she know our impact on the local market—a major consideration in terms of current FCC licensing renewal policies?
5. Are some times of the year better than others to get free time and space?

This last group of considerations means that the producer of government public service advertising must know the mindsets of media gatekeepers and must be prepared both to produce ads that satisfy the media and to plan small campaigns to "sell" PSAs to media people.

Other Decisionmakers and Other Human Factors

Aside from internal agency decisionmakers and media gatekeepers, government

PSA producers must also tread carefully around Congress. What did Congress intend when it indicated that a law it wrote mandated some public information activity by a specific agency? Or, at the individual member level, will a PSA concept offend a member's sensitivity? A costly error in this latter respect was made in the mid-1970s by the Department of Treasury, which thought it had scored a public service coup by convincing actor Telly Savalas to do a "Kojak Caper" spot for Savings Bonds right on the set of the then-popular CBS show.[3] The spot was just about to go into national distribution when word of its content reached a congressman actively involved in Italian-American civil rights causes. He was offended by what he felt was Mafia connotations to Kojak's caper, and the spot was killed.

Racial and ethnic considerations also enter into decisions about which private-sector advertising agencies will be chosen to contract to produce advertising messages. Minority contract awards—referred to as "8-A" contracts—are, of course, a major component of federal equal opportunity policy.

Persuasive Techniques in Government Advertising

In their study of television public service announcements, David Paletz and his associates identified several persuasive approaches and techniques that PSA producers frequently employ:

1. PSAs often attempt to persuade through an appeal to the viewers' emotions. One method in past years, but now looked upon with disfavor, is the so-called scare tactic.
2. Another often used technique, humor or irony, is now considered a superior method of dealing with anxiety-arousing subjects such as smoking or drunk-driving.
3. Many PSAs attempt to persuade viewers through appeals to their self-interest.
4. Guilt is another emotion that producers of PSAs invoke to achieve the desired response on the part of the viewer.
5. Many PSAs invoke authority figures in an effort to lend credibility to their messages. In general, these authority figures fall into two classes: those with expertise in the subject being discussed, and celebrities from other fields.
6. Slogans are another way . . . producers of PSAs seek to make their spots more memorable.
7. Finally, some PSAs attempt to increase impact by providing viewers with an address or telephone number through which they can obtain further information. . . ."[4]

Paletz' assertions, however, do require some further modification. For example, the fear appeal in public service, or any other, advertising is by no means in total disfavor. The operating rule is never to employ fear to the extent that it will paralyze the audience into inaction. Thus, fear *is* employed if the problem raised is also shown to be soluble at an individual level. Humor is, indeed, an increasingly frequent device in PSAs, but the danger occurs when the humor blots out the message. And testimonials, or spots done by "authority figures," are also tricky. One must consider such things as (1) a senior official may be an authority figure in the agency, but he or she is generally not such to the audience the producer wants to reach, (2) a celebrity testimonial is generally ineffective if there is no clear link between the star and the cause endorsed, and (3) on-location celebrity testimonials will be used only by network stations or affiliates which carry the star's show.

In conclusion, the government PSA producer in the contemporary environment should remember this advice on persuasive devices from a 1949 rhetoric textbook: There are only two kinds of propaganda, uphill and downhill. Downhill propaganda is consonant with prevailing societal norms, opinions, attitudes, and beliefs. Uphill propaganda is contrary to the prevailing factors. The only uphill propaganda that succeeds, however, is that which resembles downhill propaganda.[5]

Role of the Advertising Council

The Advertising Council, certainly the major, if not the dominating, force in both government and nonprofit PSA campaigns, can either produce campaigns completely or endorse the media campaigns produced by others:

> If a group is lucky enough to become one of the approximately 25 major campaigns the Council undertakes each year . . . it will have a complete public service effort developed for it by one of the country's leading advertising agencies and be responsible only for expenses incurred in the production of advertising material. . . . The Council also provides assistance to some groups which do not obtain major campaign status by listing them in the *Public Service Advertising Bulletin*. This is published bimonthly by the Council and reaches roughly 13,000 media outlets.[6]

In essence, once a government agency's specific PSA campaign (Savings Bonds and Smokey the Bear being the traditional examples here) is selected as a major Ad Council effort, all the government agency need do is have a good liaison with the Council and the cooperating advertising agency. Creation, production, and distribution all follow. On the other hand, if the government agency's campaign—whether publicized in the Ad Council's *Bulletin* or not—is produced and distributed by other means, the government agency can more freely elect to have as great or as little a role as it wishes in the technical processes involved.

The only real limitation on a government agency working independently on PSAs is what Paletz refers to as an OMB inclination to oppose agency investment in sophisticated production equipment. Even so, a great deal of leeway is left in terms of concepts, storyboards, and even distribution. And if a production contract is let to a recording studio or filmmaker, for example, agency public information people may work as directors and editors in concert with the contractor's staff. Such an arrangement typifies PSA activity at the Department of Agriculture's Animal and Plant Health Inspection Service, a fiercely independent PSA-producing agency which exists under the same large roof as the United States Forest Service, home of Smokey, the Ad Council's bellwether.

More typically, a government agency producing a PSA campaign independent of the Ad Council will contract out as much work to its independently chosen advertising agency or production house as it would have to an Ad Council agency. In either case, the public information people may then begin to resemble contract administrators more than "creative" types.

Origins of the Advertising Council

During the 1930s all elements of American business were under siege; the advertising community was no exception. Fearful of increased regulation of both pricing and trade practices, representatives of the Association of National Advertisers (ANA), the American Association of Advertising Agencies (AAAA), and other groups convened in Hot Springs, Virginia, on November 14, 1941, to decide how to respond to what ANA President Paul West called "the continued charges that advertising is a waste, that it fosters a monopoly, that it is simply an added cost to the consumer."[7]

The assembled advertising executives were on the defensive until James Webb Young, a J. Walter Thompson executive with both academic and government experience, exhorted them to look on the bright side:

We have within our hands the greatest means of mass education and persuasion the world has ever seen. . . . Why do we not use it? Use it for consumer education . . . Use it to create an atmosphere in which business can hope and plan and dream again. Use it to confound the critics of advertising with the greatest demonstration of its power they have ever seen.[8]

Had not the attack on Pearl Harbor occurred just three weeks later, however, it is doubtful that so concerted an effort as the one which resulted first in the War Advertising Council, and then in the present Advertising Council, could have been mounted.

During the war, the council worked closely with the federal Office of War Information, which screened all PSA campaign requests first. Some of the war-time campaigns, conducted as they were in a period of virtually total national consensus, remain classic studies in mass persuasion: War Bonds, Victory Gardens, scrap drives, military and war worker recruitment, blood donations, even the birth of Smokey the Bear. At the war's end, the Office of War Information was abolished, and the War Advertising Council made its transition to peacetime. By 1948, the current organizational structure of the Advertising Council was in place.

At present, the Advertising Council serves best those government agencies which have a national campaign objective, need to reach the broadest possible audience, have a fair amount of money to spend, and are addressing a topic which falls into the category of "downhill propaganda." The government agency which fulfills these criteria can expect outstanding creative performance and excellent chances for free time and space. Indeed, one Advertising Council executive has estimated that the worth of free time and space given to council campaign materials was over $600 million annually.[9] This figure, however, is not obtained by the same means that commercial advertisers use to evaluate their purchases of time and space, and is conjectural enough to warrant some further investigation, as will be shown in the next section.

Does It Pay to Advertise?

As was mentioned earlier, some government agencies now pay for time and space. It was also noted that such decisions are under constant OMB and congressional scrutiny, and that agencies which buy time and space may damage their subsequent chances for free exposure. It is evident that the government (and the taxpayer) cannot afford to become an across-the-board paid advertiser. At the same time, the government agency should be willing to examine the risks and benefits of paid advertising in specific instances. The problem at present is the lack of a regular mechanism to make such public policy decisions. There is no internal government process for setting PSA priorities; the task is left to the Ad Council, which has merely fostered competition among government agencies for both Ad Council endorsements and—with or without such endorsements— limited free time and space. In effect, some government PSA campaigns are more important than others. Yet, currently, all PSA messages are prioritized informally, in a system largely extraneous to government.

In early 1980, eleven government advertising accounts used paid media. With their individual 1978 billings and advertising agency affiliations, these were:

1. The United States Army
   $36,300,000
   N. W. Ayer
   Lockhart & Pottus (minority recruiting)
   Uniworld Group (minority recruiting)

CSI Advertising (minority recruiting)
J. P. Martin Association (minority recruiting)

2. The United States Navy
   $18,000,000
   Ted Bates
   Burrell Advertising (minority recruiting)

3. The United States Marines
   $12,151,209
   J. Walter Thompson Company

4. The U.S. Army Reserve
   $9,600,000
   N. W. Ayer

5. AMTRAK
   $8,500,000
   Neeham, Harper and Steers

6. The United States Air Force
   $8,300,000
   D'Arcy-MacManus & Masius

7. The U.S. Postal Service
   $8,201,000
   Young & Rubicam

8. The Army/Air National Guard
   $6,505,000
   W. B. Doner & Company

9. The U.S. Army ROTC
   $4,900,000
   N. W. Ayer

10. The U.S. Travel Service
    $2,140,000

11. The United States Coast Guard
    $900,000
    Henry J. Kauffmann and Associates[10]

Congressional and OMB reservations about spending money on advertising time and space has been noted. This attitude is felt most strongly by the government's biggest ad spenders, the military services. However, since the end of the draft in 1973, policy-makers have found the fact that no military service is recruiting or retaining enlisted personnel sufficiently well more important, and, therefore, have allowed the services to begin using paid media regularly. Congressional budget trackers also urged the Department of Defense to consider combining recruiting budgets and, consequently, message and media decisions. This was tried for the first time on a large scale in 1979:

> The armed forces' first nationwide ad campaign to jointly promote all four major services is set for a January 1st launch with $9,700,000 budgeted to go into network tv, magazines and direct mail. . . .
> The campaign . . . is the product of the Joint Advertising Directorate of Recruiting (JADOR), a Pentagon committee of the ad directors for the Army, Navy, Air Force and Marines.
> Each of the four services transferred funds from its regular ad budget to finance the joint drive and the campaign is being put together by the four ad agencies that handle the armed services accounts.[11]

It is doubtful from a persuasive standpoint whether such a campaign will attract more potential recruits. The first print ads featured only a symbolic device—the American eagle—that all four services could agree on; the first television ad, seen during the 1979 Super Bowl, merely combined on split screen the four current campaigns and slogans. On the other hand, if the enlistment rates are unaffected negatively and the draft is not restored, JADOR could become a busy Pentagon operation.

New Approaches

One of the best prospects for paid media use by government agencies may lie in merging messages with advertisements from the private sector. One new proposal' in this area came from the Department of Energy in 1978:

> An unusual paid U.S. Energy Department advertising campaign opening in five markets next week will trigger promotions of energy-saving items by dozens of retailers, including local Sears, J. C. Penney Co. and Montgomery Ward stores. . . .
> The Energy Department will spend $400,000 on media for a five-week campaign in Atlanta, Syracuse, Minneapolis-St. Paul, Portland, Ore., and Denver using television, including prime time and news programs, magazines and outdoor. . . .
> The campaign's three 30-second TV spots, created by Evans & Batholomew, Denver, are humorous and close with the theme, "If it saves energy, it'll pay for itself." They promote the use of a variety of energy-saving devices. Magazine ads offer a coupon for more information.
> While the ads are directed to the consumer, it is trade reaction that the Energy Department is most interested in. . . .
> More than 500 retailers in the test cities have been recruited to participate and will display p.o.p. displays from the Energy Department explaining how energy-saving equipment saves money.
> The follow-up ad campaign next spring will be in the same five markets plus Houston, and will feature a sweepstakes promotion, local laws permitting, calculated to draw consumers into stores to pick up entry forms.[12]

The main problem facing government advertising specialists who wish to pursue this option is the problem of "good taste," as the U.S. Forest Service discovered when it loaned out Smokey the Bear to the makers of Bic lighters for a tie-in campaign with the message, "Please: Flick your Bic carefully in my woods." We tend to stand with *Advertising Age*'s editors on this one. "It builds a new momentum to Smokey's campaign," they maintain. "Listen to Smokey. He knows a catchy ad campaign when he sees it."[13]

Notes

1. There are different schools of thought on this issue. The Gallup organization, surveying radio and television station program officials nationwide for the N. W. Ayer advertising agency and the U.S. Army in 1971, found the preponderant majority of its respondents would be unwilling to give PSA time to the Army once the Army had established itself as a media-buying account. Donald Smith and I found in 1976 a 50–50 split among radio program and public service directors in response to the statement: "An organization that buys any media advertising should not expect PSA time." Yet, some experienced local government and nonprofit public relations people claim they have put together "package deals" with local broadcasters, obtaining quaranteed PSA time in return for a regular time buy for the same spots, thereby doubling or tripling the value of their purchase. This latter phenomenon is hard to document from the broadcasters' side, since it is decidedly against the spirit—if not the precise letter—of FCC regulations.

2. Richard L. Gordon, "NH & S Researcher Team for Nutrition Ads," *Advertising Age*, 50 (February 26, 1979):2.

3. In general, if a star does a PSA in costume and on the set of his or her show, that spot will only run on affiliated or owned and operated stations of that star's network. This limitation is a small price for the cost savings on set decoration and costume. Also a local station is more likely to air a PSA which serves as a promotion for one of its own shows.

4. David L. Paletz, Roberta E. Pearson, Donald L. Willis, *Politics in Public Service Advertising on Television* (New York: Praeger, 1977), pp. 56–58.

5. This advice is paraphrased from William Castle Hummel and Keith Huntress, *The Analysis of Propaganda* (New York: Sloane, 1949).

6. Paletz et al., p. 6.

7. Quoted in Harold B. Thomas, "The Background and Beginning of the Advertising Council," in *The Promise of Advertising*, ed. Charles Harold Sandage (Homewood, Ill.: Richard D. Irwin, 1961), p. 18.

8. Quoted in Maurice I. Mandell, "A History of the Advertising Council" (unpublished Ph.D. dissertation, Indiana University, 1953), p. 53.

9. Kenneth H. Rabin, "Network Public Service Announcement Feeds: How Many Do the Affiliates Really Use?" (unpublished speech, PSA Conference, Washington, D.C., April 18, 1979).

10. *Advertising Age* 50 (September 6, 1979):156–157.

11. "Armed Forces Join to Mount First United Ad Drive," *Advertising Age* 49 (November 20, 1978):6.

12. "Retailers Join U.S. Save-Energy Drive," *Advertising Age*, 49 (September 18, 1978):3.

13. "Smokey Flacks for Bic," editorial, *Advertising Age* 49 (April 24, 1978):18. In August 1979, a shift in Energy secretaries brought in Charles Duncan, a former Coca-Cola executive with a high commitment to paid advertising. His presence gave added strength to proponents of both cooperation and Department of Energy originated paid ads.

CHAPTER 17

Public Service Announcements as Free Advertising

Robert A. Cuccia

Radio, television, and print public service announcements (PSAs) are effective, economical communications tools used by many government agencies. Despite the emergence of the paid government ad during the 1970s, public service announcements remain a primary form of "advertising" used by the government. The tradition of televising, broadcasting, and printing PSAs in the public interest is still followed by all the networks and many newspapers, magazines, local radio and television stations around the country. At relicensing time the federal communications commission reviews a television or radio station's record of airing public service announcements produced for government or private-sector programs.

Radio and television network public service and broadcast standards executives say that those government agencies that buy time are less likely to receive public service time. But, the executives are quick to point out, and rightly so, that full consideration is given to all PSAs submitted for airing.

Public service advertising space in the print media is limited. There is no relicensing procedure for the print media, and they are not required to print in the public interest, although many profess that they are.

For the purpose of a more simplified discussion, this chapter will focus on radio and television public service announcements, which serve the largest markets.

Reasons for Using Public Service Ads

Many senior government public affairs/public information people and their bosses consider public service announcement campaigns to be a legitimate use of taxpayers' money. They realize that radio and television audiences are large and generally attentive. Government communications people realize that along with the PSAs run at odd hours "you get your share of drive time and prime time" if your product has universal appeal and is produced in a highly professional way. In this case "highly professional" means by network standards.

On balance, there are government communicators who doubt the value of the public service announcement as an effective tool because of its unpredictable use patterns or because of the communicator's lack of expertise in PSA use. Our experience is that a carefully conceived, carefully marketed, and carefully measured radio or television public services announcement series is a cost-effective means of communicating necessary information to the various publics the government serves.

The Anatomy of a Public Service Announcement

The most successful public service announcement is one that is interesting and informative. The most successful series is one which generates the planned action from the audience. Competition for available public service time on the major networks and in the 100 major market areas of the country is usually so keen that only one of 10 messages received by the stations is aired.

Interesting advertisements attract attention. Entertaining ads help retention and hold interest. Informative ads fortify an attitude and hopefully encourage the action you intended (a call, a visit, or a letter). Your PSA must have all three ingredients, perfected to suit the standards of excellence of the network broadcast standards executive, the program director, or the public service director.

The network executive, program director, and public service director are the first persons to preview your ads. They are professionals who choose which ads best fit their format and time restrictions. They are professionals with personal tastes along with many years of experience. The lesson here is relatively obvious. Meet with the network people and as many of the local station people as you can find to discuss their needs. Once you understand their problems and standards, your foundation for producing a successful spot is sound.

It is helpful to have a supporting framework, or formula, to add to your foundation. The formula which has worked successfully for me for more than a decade has at least eight major ingredients. They include:

- Enough planning time (including research, audience analysis, talking to station people)
- An interesting, useful subject
- A compatible, creative production staff and a creative composer
- Committed talent (celebrities, actors)
- A first-rate film or recording crew
- An attractive marketing package
- An effective distribution system
- A good feedback device

Operating without just one of the eight almost always results in an inferior product or result.

It is difficult to substantiate which of the eight ingredients is most important, but certainly without thoughtful, careful planning the entire project is likely to falter. To begin with, allow at least four months, after contract award, for the preparation of a series of radio or television PSAs. Identify *the* key element of the message you intend to communicate. The single element is stressed because simplicity generally results in your message being understood, retained, and, most importantly, used. For example, if the minimum wage has increased to a new level, concentrate on that dollar figure. Shy away from complicated descriptions of the various covered groups.

After you have a clear understanding of your message, the planning phase turns to the identification of audiences and their needs. If you are planning a TV spot series, defining your audience is somewhat easier than if you are planning for a radio series. There are fewer than 800 commercial television stations in the United States and most attract a varied audience. Radio stations, on the other hand, number nearly 6000 nationwide and generally attract more specialized audiences. This factor, of course, makes planning more challenging for the government communicator. But it also provides a chance to tailor a message to a specific audience. The resurgence of radio as a major communications tool in the 1970s is likely to continue into the 1980s. Experience dictates that most audiences can be reached through radio because of the many available specialized formats. A PSA on prime time TV, however, obviously reaches more people, but the audience is likely to be more heterogeneous.

Once the audiences have been defined and the primary methods of reaching them have been selected, it is time to consider the basic framework for each PSA.

For television PSAs, live action without a celebrity is usually preferred by the networks and the local stations. Most of the celebrities appearing in television spots usually owe their allegiance to one of the networks, thus limiting exposure on many otherwise willing stations. Competitors do not favor the promotion of another network's stars. Occasionally, a celebrity is so strongly identified with a cause or subject, and has no network affiliation, that his or her appearance would lend credibility to the PSA. Two recent examples come to mind: Bill Cosby on child labor and Tennessee Ernie Ford ("16 Tons") for black lung (coal miners disease) benefits.

Using a celebrity on a radio PSA is a different matter. Program directors, public service directors, and disc jockeys prefer a familiar name and an appropriate sound. More than 95 percent of the stations returning use reply cards in 1978 and 1979 indicated that they prefer celebrity spots specifically tailored to their format. Accordingly, our PSA discs and tapes have a variety of formats and sounds with a common set of messages. Rock, country, middle of the road, easy listening, swing, and Spanish language spots generally appear on each disc or tape distributed nationwide.

Selecting a Spokesperson

Selection of appropriate spokespersons is a critical step. Experience and taste mandate selecting someone with either musical talent or a readily recognizable name or voice. The best person often has a combination of musical talent, a familiar voice, and an interest in the message the PSA is to convey. A caution is appropriate here. Take care not to select a person who has limited appeal. "Rising TV stars" come and go, so to speak. Do not use their talents unless you will be satisfied with mediocre results at best. The plethora of famous people willing to lend their names and talents to an important public service campaign has always been reassuring. Bill Cosby, Ricardo Montalban, Lola Falana, Roy Clark, Johnny Cash, Mary Tyler Moore, Carroll O'Connor, and many others have willingly done radio public service announcements when asked.

Of equal importance in the early stages of preproduction is the establishment of a compatible relationship with the contractor. Nearly all of our radio PSAs are written in house. Some of the TV PSAs are created by staff, but most are created jointly by staff and contractors. This is the preferred way of doing business from our standpoint. In any case, the need for a creative contractor is critical. For radio, insure that you have a proven composer who can translate a verbal theme into a suitable, appealing theme with simple, meaningful lyrics. The musical theme should be translatable into a number of familiar musical formats. The formats can often be recorded in the same session with talented, flexible musicians. One rule that must be strictly followed—never use canned or prerecorded music. On the other hand, use only original music recorded by professionals and reproduced by professionals.

TV PSA contractors are selected from the combined list of certified television and film producers. Competitive bids are solicited once a suitable script or format has been approved. Once a contractor is selected, insure that a quality camera and sound crew are assigned and that experienced editors and a reputable laboratory are used to process the film or video tape. Request samples of past work and check references. Whether it is radio or TV, close, on-site supervision is vitally important to a quality product. It will save your agency time and money if an experienced information officer supervises each project from creation to measurement of use.

Once the PSAs are filmed, video taped, or recorded it is time to consider the final designs and packaging of the spots. For television spots you should consider releasing video tape or film copies to the networks. If you choose film instead of video tape, plan to shoot the spot in 35mm. The initial cost is greater, but the increased quality of 35mm over 16mm is definitely worth the expense. The networks will require 16mm prints for screening. Following approval the networks will ask for 16mm and 35mm prints for telecast. In addition to choosing a reputable lab to reproduce your television spots (if reproduction is not part of the original contract), insure that you order prints specifically for television. They're bluer than regular projection prints. The TV spots should be individually boxed, titled, and labeled with your return address. Scripts should be included with all TV spots.

Radio spots can be packaged in two ways. The standard 7 inch, 33⅓ disc is a favorite method. It can be an attractive package if you choose your photographs, graphics, and colors well. Station people, the program manager, public service director, or DJ are often attracted to carefully prepared packages, famous names, and high-quality production. Cassette tape is another suitable way to package radio spots, but experience indicates that more stations prefer discs to cassettes. The packaging advantages of the disc, along with its general acceptance by the stations, are strong arguments in its favor. It is much easier to insert a letter, verbatim script, and a reply card into a disc envelope than to package the same ingredients with a cassette tape. Stations usually transfer PSAs to a master cartridge or tape from discs and cassettes.

Distributing the PSA

PSA distribution is often left to contractors with preprinting mailing lists. While that approach might work well for some communicators with small staffs in the central office and around the country, the personal approach of delivering materials directly to stations has produced markedly better results. If you have the good fortune of a built-in distribution system of regional and area offices around the country, you have a powerful and useful tool available to you. As often as practicable we provide our field staff with enough prints of a specific TV PSA to cover all stations in their area. Since most TV stations are located in and around large cities, the system works well.

Hand delivering radio PSAs poses a different problem. The large number of radio stations (6000) and their locations in many small cities and towns prevents us from providing hand delivery. An up-to-date, nationwide mailing list is used to mass-mail to all stations. We do, however, follow up with personal visits to radio stations in larger cities to insure that the disc was received and will be used.

An important outgrowth of our personal delivery system has little to do with public service announcements but serves as a primary motivator for using such a system. Many of our people are asked to appear on radio and television talk shows to answer questions about the many government programs which affect the listeners and viewers. These talk and panel show discussions lead to requests for speakers before high school, college, community group, business group, consumer group, and labor audiences which might not have otherwise heard about our services.

Following distribution by hand or by mail, and the necessary follow-up, the next step is to evaluate the use reply cards and other comments received from the stations. Our approach to evaluating the use reply cards is rather simple. They are a barometer check on the general acceptability of our materials and they serve as an immediate feedback on planned use by stations.

It has been our good fortune over the last 10 years to enjoy the confidence of each of the major television and radio networks, and many local stations. Our PSAs have been telecast and aired during many prime and drive time shows. Their quality and acceptability have been verified. But quality and acceptability are fragile factors. Network and station executives change. Contractors and subcontractors change. Government agency information staffs change. These changes tend to negate any complacency. Rather, they mandate that every project be approached with renewed enthusiasm and candor *and* with the clear understanding that the evaluation of a creative product is a subjective matter.

Radio and television public service announcements are a proven means of communicating effectively with general and specific audiences. The studies we have done reveal that most of the audiences we are trying to reach get their information from radio or television PSAs rather than through pamphlets or brochures. And, equally important, the studies indicate that most of the people who ask for information nationwide are led to our offices or phone numbers by radio and television PSAs. That fact alone encourages our continued efforts in the public service announcements arena.

CHAPTER 18

Social Marketing: A New Tool

Kenneth Rabin

The term "social marketing" has gained considerable acceptance in less than a decade, and provides government information people with an advanced planning methodology of real promise. In this chapter, social marketing is both described and illustrated in terms of the best-known example of its application in the federal government: the National High Blood Pressure Education Program of the National Heart, Blood, and Lung Institute, Department of Health and Human Services.

The Genesis of Social Marketing

The application of profit-sector marketing techniques to the task of gaining acceptance for social ideas, though discussed in principle for many years, was not codified as "social marketing" until Philip Kotler and Gerald Zaltman published an article by that title in 1971.[1] This and related marketing applications are detailed in Kotler's recent and popular text, *Marketing for Non-Profit Organizations*.[2]

Basic Marketing Terminology

Kotler defines marketing itself as "the analysis, planning, implementation, and control of carefully formulated programs designed to bring about the voluntary exchanges of values with target markets for the purpose of achieving organizational objectives. It relies heavily," he adds, "on designing the organization's offering in terms of the target markets' needs and desires, and on using effective pricing, communication, and distribution to inform, motivate, and service the markets." Marketing managers employ the vehicle of *exchange*, as opposed to love or threat; they convince people to trade value for value. The variables that marketing managers manipulate are summarized as the "4 Ps":

1. *Product*, which can "include physical objects, services, persons, places, organizations, and ideas" and must be clearly defined in the marketer's mind before it can be portrayed to the public.
2. *Promotion*, which embraces what we consider the specific tools of public information people—advertising, publicity, personal contact or selling, and sales promotion.
3. *Place*, or distribution, the most cost-effective way of getting the product to its consuming publics. In the context of the subsequent example, place could be one's living room, car, doctor's office, clinic, medical library, medical classroom, medical conference, or mobile health fair. Place has many possibilities.
4. *Price*, which is affected by what the consumers are willing (psychologically and financially) to pay for a product, particularly in light of competition.

These basics can be adapted to settings recognizable to government public information practitioners.

Marketing Applied to Ideas

The exchange of values that takes place in the literal marketplace is, of course, much more straightforward than the exchange that takes place in the marketplace of ideas. The hard constructs of marketing are employed for less precisely measurable ends in social marketing, which Kotler calls "the design, implementation, and control of programs seeking to increase the acceptability of a social idea or practice in a target group(s)."

Social marketing differs from "business marketing" in three fundamental ways:

1. Business marketers typically try to meet the identified needs and wants of target markets; social marketers typically try to change the attitudes or behavior of target markets.
2. Business marketers typically feel that their major aim is to make a profit through serving the interests of the target market or society; social marketers typically aim to serve the interests of the target market or society without personal profit.
3. Business marketers typically market products and services through the medium of ideas; social marketers more typically market the ideas themselves rather than the products or services. In government, however, actual services can be marketed.

All three of these points underscore the relative "softness" of social marketing. There are also degrees of softness. Some social marketing initiatives will be more likely to succeed than others. Cognitive change—the increase of knowledge or awareness of ideas—is a relatively easy objective. Too, Kotler contends that "social marketing may also be effective in producing action change, that is a particular act." Indeed, it is the act of taking one's medicine on which the High Blood Pressure Education Program's public service advertising campaign—which is only a small, if highly visible, part of the project—focuses. However, when a single act cannot be chipped apart from the iceberg of habit—cigarette smoking, driving fast, overeating, failing to exercise—the social marketer's task becomes more complicated. And people's social values are even less susceptible to easy change than are their habits.

Social Marketing Differentiated from Public Information

It is noted elsewhere in this book that the extent of a government public information person's role in agency management is generally somewhat circumscribed, but that managerial status will tend to accrue to those information people who are both effective in crises and competent planners. Social marketing, as a planning system, can serve to confer greater managerial prerogatives on those who practice it.

Kotler, moreover, asserts that social marketing is a more strategic aspect of management than public information, which he dubs "social propaganda:"

> The social marketer differs from the straight social propagandist in a number of ways. The propagandist usually comes into social planning after the objectives, policies, and "products" have been determined. His job . . . is to promote the organization's objectives and products, using communications media. The social marketer, on the other hand, participates actively in the organization's planning. He advises what products will be acceptable to the target publics; what incentives will work best; what distribution structures will be optimal; and what communication program will be effective. He thinks in exchange terms rather than in one-way influence terms. . . . Whereas the propagandist

takes the product, price, and channels as given, the social marketer treats these as variables."

It is at least apparent that what might be called the "marketing mindset" can open up the planning options information people sometimes perceive as too limited, primarily by forcing a government program *and* its promotion to be considered as inseparable. Certainly, the High Blood Pressure Education Program exhibits how marketing strategy can be applied with encouraging effects to that subfield of social propaganda or public information once called health education.

The National High Blood Pressure Education Program

Scope, Mandate, Management

The General Accounting Office deems the National High Blood Pressure Education Program (NHBPEP) among the most successful current federal government information campaigns, and describes it as "a comprehensive effort aimed at reducing diseases and illnesses associated with . . . hypertension," a health problem which may affect as many as one in six Americans.[3]

As noted earlier, NHBPEP is housed within the National Heart, Blood, and Lung Institute (NIH). The Institute and NHBPEP do not act in isolation, however. One of the great strengths of this campaign is that it is the outcome of Institute cooperation "with 15 major Federal agencies, State health departments, and more than 150 national organizations, including professional societies, voluntary health organizations, the insurance industry, the drug industry, and labor and industrial organizations."[4]

NHBPEP gets its legal mandate from Public Law 92–423 (The National Heart, Blood Vessel, Lung, and Blood Act of 1972). Estimated program cost for 1973–1980 is $17.5 million, almost 60 percent of which is in the form of outside contracts. Some of the contract money is spent to obtain services from the types of private firms and agencies a corporate marketing or public relations department would be likely to retain: The Gallup Organization, the New York advertising agency (via the Advertising Council) of Norman, Craig and Kummel, and the Washington-based social marketing firm of Porter, Novelli and Associates. The largest single contractor NHBPEP has, however, is Kappa Systems, Inc., of Rockville, Maryland, a firm which specializes in health education and information project management.

NHBPEP operates within the Heart, Blood, and Lung Institute as an independent, multidisciplinary unit, not as a typical public information office. There are eight professionals in all: two sociologists, a public information specialist, two health educators, a biochemist, and a nurse. These NIH-based staff members decide on NHBPEP policy, do contact work with cooperating public and private sector groups, and manage or oversee the tasks performed by the contractors.

The primary contractor, Kappa Systems, initially employed one over-all manager and a supervisor for each of the following NHBPEP components: the High Blood Pressure Information Center, a Community Development Service, Educational Materials Assessment, Professional Education, Public Education (Mass Media), Special Projects, Special Studies, and Program Evaluation.[5]

In 1977, the NHBPEP components operated by the primary contractor were reorganized to include programs in communications, community program development, professional and patient education, consumer education through the mass media, special projects, and evaluation.[6]

While most of the remainder of this chapter focuses on the mass media as promotional implements in the social marketing process, one should keep in mind that the mass media represent only about 20 percent of project effort. Nor should we underestimate the impact of evaluation. While the GAO declined to infer causality from the reports NHBPEP forwarded, and felt that the work required to draw such an inference would be "time consuming, if not impossible," the government's fiscal watchdog was convinced that:

> Data provided by the Institute indicates that the cumulative effort to date appears to have contributed to a decline in the death rates from hypertensive disease and from strokes and coronary heart diseases related to high blood pressure. The stroke death rate, for example, decreased 9 percent during 1965–70 and 18 percent during 1970–75. In the past 5 years, deaths from hypertension-related disease have continued to decline at a much sharper rate than those from cardiovascular disease not related to hypertension.[7]

While no social scientist would argue a case for causality, the statistical trends just cited should at least encourage us to look more closely at how social marketing is employed in this project, using the "4 Ps" as a general framework.

Product: What NHBPEP Is Selling Public and Patient Audiences[8]

The social marketer cannot sell a service or an idea until everyone involved in the exchange process shares a similar notion of what *is* being offered for exchange. NHBPEP's program is based on a careful description of what hypertension is and is not, and suggests—in the form of a goal—the precise "product" NHBPEP is going to sell. The program is aimed not at one monolithic market, but a primary and secondary target audience. Many media—including health providers and planners as second level disseminators—are orchestrated. The plan shows marketer awareness of the advantages *and* disadvantages of the product, which is perhaps the greatest departure of all from traditional health education, which too often consists of the words, "Take this, it's good for you." In short, we begin with a heightened awareness of what the program has to offer consumers, and what "sales pitches" are most logical in this context.

The Marketing Problem

According to NHBPEP coordinator Graham Ward, approximately 35 million Americans have high blood pressure, or hypertension. By properly treating their high blood pressure and thereby reducing it to recommended levels, they can reduce their chances of stroke, heart disease and kidney disease.

However, although many Americans know they have high blood pressure and studies indicate that public awareness about it has increased, many who are aware of their problem fail to maintain the daily treatment necessary for control. This difficulty that "aware hypertensives" have in "taking their medicine" regularly is the marketing problem NHBPEP faces.

The Program's marketing research indicates several factors which compound the basic problem, usually by causing only occasional adherence to what should be a daily drug regimen. For example, while many people believe that high blood pressure has symptoms they can observe, this is not always the case. Too, even people who know that high blood pressure may occur without symptoms still think they can tell when their blood pressure is up—they confuse hypertension with tension. Others apparently confuse *control* of high blood pressure with its *cure*; some feel they can control high blood pressure without medication if they just make certain "life style changes" like salt-free diet, weight control, exercise, and smoking reduction.

Social Marketing Goal and Subgoals

NHBPEP describes the specific objective of the Program as "to reduce the morbidity and mortality attributable to high blood pressure by educating aware hypertensives to lower their blood pressure to recommended levels through proper treatment. Specifically the objective is to reinforce the behavior of people who are controlling their blood pressure and to help persuade those who are not to begin or resume proper therapy." To do this, NHBPEP seeks to decrease the number of aware hypertensives who have misconceptions about high blood pressure, improve how they see the benefits of proper treatment, and increase the support family and friends can give to aware hypertensives. All three of these subgoals, it should be emphasized, are *measurable* by the social marketer.

Target Audiences

NHBPEP's target audience for educational initiatives is people who know they have high blood pressure. These include those who are not treating their high blood pressure at all, those who are treating their high blood pressure inadequately, those who are newly aware that they are hypertensive, and those who are properly treating their high blood pressure (as positive reinforcement).

The Program's secondary target audience is the families and friends of those who know they have high blood pressure.

Promotion: How NHBPEP Persuades Audiences to Buy the Hypertension Therapy "Product"

Having carefully defined both their product and an appropriate strategy to gain heightened product acceptance by the four subgroups in the primary target audience, Ward and his colleagues set about the promotional task, using the multifaceted contractor approach described earlier.

A range of promotional activities alone, however, will not suffice. Such activities need to be linked thematically, to be consistent, to be clear, and to produce desired actions. For this reason, NHBPEP has several promotional "ground rules" or what Ward refers to as "considerations for communication." One example is that the word "hypertension," as alluded to earlier, may contribute to popular myth that high blood pressure is caused by simple tension and need only be treated when "symptoms" such as headache or "nerves" arise. Thus the term "high blood pressure" is used in communications with nonprofessional audiences.

Applying Promotional Considerations in the Public Service Advertising Context

William Novelli, a social marketing specialist who both consults with NHBPEP and teaches a graduate seminar in the subject, offers the following public service advertising case as an example of the thought which goes into all of NHBPEP's promotional messages.

All proposed television public service spots, prepared for NHBPEP by Norman, Craig and Kummel, a volunteer advertising agency assigned to the project by the Advertising Council, are pretested by the Health Message Testing Service (HMTS) for comparative effectiveness along the same variables any advertisement would be tested—viewer attention and idea recall being the two most important. The memo and illustrations from the case study show how an earlier theme or slogan, "Do It for Them," evolved into "Take It for Them" (the slogan used in the "Country Mother" test ad), thereby building on prior recognition. Problems with the ad's jingle are discussed and mention is made both of different versions of the "Do It for Them" spots with black and white actors and the possibility of using older talent in future campaigns:[9]

With Norman, Craig and Kummel now at work developing copy for the next campaign, it seems appropriate to outline findings from "Country Mother" in comparison to the white family message from the "Do It for Them" campaign that was tested and reported last September.

The two primary criteria for judging message communication in HMTS are *attention* and *main idea recall*. On the attention measurement, both "Country Mother" and "Do It for Them" scored comparably and were close to the HMTS norm (i.e., the average score of all public service advertisements tested).

	"Country Mother"		"Do It for Them"	
HMTS Norm	*Aware Hypertensives*	*Non/Unaware Hypertensives*	*Aware Hypertensives*	*Non/Unaware Hypertensives*
30%	32%	31%	29%	33%

On main idea recall, "Country Mother" fared better than its predecessor.

	"Country Mother"		"Do It for Them"	
HMTS Norm	*Aware Hypertensives*	*Non/Unaware Hypertensives*	*Aware Hypertensives*	*Non/Unaware Hypertensives*
35%	33%	46%	22%	34%

It may be expected that "Country Mother" would score somewhat better than the earlier message on main idea recall, since respondents likely have seen the campaign on the air; therefore, they would be familiar with the message line.

Nevertheless, it seems clear that this campaign, begun as "Do It for Them" and extended as "Take It for Them," has stopping power and is communicating its main copy point of taking medication for your family's sake.

Also, HMTS diagnostic data suggest that both messages are well received. They are well-liked (especially "Country Mother"), register very few dislikes, and score well on the characteristics of well done, interesting and pleasant.

Based on these findings, the idea of extending the campaign still further and building on the existing base of acceptance and information is appealing.

At the same time, there are several areas in which the campaign may be strengthened. First, there remains the question whether the most important point in the message—the need for daily medication—is understood to be medication *for hypertension* or simply the need for medication *per se* if prescribed for *any* illness. This question is raised by the verbatim responses for main idea recall and in the responses to what is worth remembering.

Second, and perhaps related to the first problem, is that respondents continue to have trouble understanding the lyrics, even after two exposures.

Third, while the campaign continues to hit singularly at the desired behavior (taking daily medication), it may lack the reason(s) why.... Clearly, it is impossible for a television message to dispel all the misconceptions and also stress the positive benefits of therapy maintenance. By asking the messages to carry too much information, we may communicate nothing.

Nevertheless, it seems necessary to begin now to go beyond the current stage and at least experiment with ways to address the barriers that may inhibit therapy behavior.

On a separate issue, we continue to see high levels of response to the question of whether anyone in the respondent's family has ever been told that they have high blood pressure.

"Country Mother"		"Do It for Them"	
Aware Hypertensives	Non/Unaware Hypertensives	Aware Hypertensives	Non/Unaware Hypertensives
87%	51%	66%	49%

With this suggestion of the size of such an audience, and with the added indications that:

1. The prevalence of hypertension is greater in older populations.
2. Family understanding and support is important in therapy maintenance . . .

it, therefore, seems appropriate to develop messages on the current strategy and campaign executional approach, but which feature older individuals and are aimed at an older audience. This would improve the overall mix of messages and hopefully appeal to older segments of the mass audience.

Place and Price: The Problem Areas of Social Marketing

The National High Blood Pressure Education Program is most successful in adapting the marketing considerations of "product" and "promotion" to the social context within which it operates. The program has had more problems, as might be expected, in translating concepts of "place" (or distribution) and "price."

The $17.5 million which was NHBPEP's 1973–1980 budget is, by anyone's reckoning, a great deal of money. Yet, it pales in comparison with, say, the United States Army's *one* year recruitment advertising budget alone. For NHBPEP to succeed, its product must be promoted freely by a loosely disciplined network of local, regional, and national government and private health agencies, physicians, pharmacists, and pharmaceutical manufacturers. All of these groups share NHBPEP's desire to curb hypertension, but many of them also compete in other spheres. Occasionally, their primary goals will take precedence over full support to NHBPEP, and occasionally, they will disagree with NHBPEP's promotional tactics, even though they do accept its strategy.

The following excerpts edited from a memorandum in Novelli's case study suggest clearly the range of sensitivities and needs the social marketer must consider in order to gain the most efficient product distribution possible. The issue of most appropriate public service advertising distribution channels to mass media has been discussed in an earlier chapter.

I. Background

On the opening day of the National Conference on High Blood Pressure Control, a meeting was held on *high blood pressure public information and education*.

Participants included representatives of The American Heart Association (AHA), The National Kidney Foundation (NKF), state departments of health, and community-based programs.

II. Summary of the Meeting

The representatives described public education activities in which they are engaged. . . .

In reviewing how NHBPEP might better assist state and community-based programs:

1. There was general agreement on the need and utility of a compendium or program digest. . . .

There were numerous suggestions of areas to be covered in this document including:
   a. Statistics on hypertension incidence . . .
   b. Information and examples on what the national organizations are planning and doing in public education on high blood pressure . . .
   c. Information and examples on what the state and community programs are planning and doing in public education . . .
   d. Data . . . that can be used to motivate corporations to set up control programs in the worksetting.
   e. Information on patient as well as public education. The differences between these two audiences are often blurred. . . .
   f. Resources that can be tapped for . . . further information.

2. The meeting participants appeared responsive to the concept of the NHBPEP developing prototype materials. . . . which local programs can shape to meet specific community conditions. Several representatives used the Program's Ad Council TV and radio public service advertisements (PSA's) as an example of poor coordination. Their contention was:
   a. Competition for PSA time is more intense than ever before. Local programs with strategies keyed to local efforts must compete with the AD Council spots.
   b. The Ad Council spots are mailed directly to broadcast outlets, not distributed via local program staff. This, the local representatives claimed, causes:
      1. Confusion among the media.
      2. Difficulties in localizing the Ad Council spots (if this is desired).
      3. Embarrassment to local programs, supposedly the community's focal point for hypertension activities . . .

3. Pilot testing and measuring public education efforts as part of an overall community hypertension control program was discussed. . . .

4. Ways to improve media coverage of high blood pressure were discussed. . . .

III. Conclusions

The participants at this meeting cannot be considered representative of all state and community control programs. However, they did represent a cross-section of such programs, and conclusions may be drawn from several areas covered at the meeting:

1. The diversity of public and patient-directed strategies and tactics in state and local programs is considerable. The NHBPEP can increase its support of these programs in three ways:
   a. Improve our contact with and monitoring of these efforts. The first step in supporting these programs is to be aware of them. Current outreach work is the key to this. But additional contacts are necessary regarding public and patient education. Two possibilities:
      1. Phone call and written follow-ups from other staff to increase communications and exchange ideas, materials, and information.
      2. Regional mini-conferences on public/patient education for the same purpose.
   b. Influence the state and community programs by providing sound direction and services that they otherwise do not have access to. One example is the Health Message Testing Service. . . .
   c. Serve as an exchange service so that state and community methods and materials reach other programs at the same level.

2. The proposed digest of public and patient information/education is worth undertaking. It appears that this document will be useful to state and local programs and will enable NHBPEP to increase its support in the ways outlined above (monitoring, influencing direction, and exchanging methods and ideas). . . .

3. We must address the problem of competition and lack of coordination regarding

Ad Council and state/local broadcast PSA's. While there is no indication of how widespread this problem is, it is likely to exist most frequently among the stronger, more advanced community programs.

4. The pilot testing and measuring of public education as part of an overall community hypertension control program should be pursued. . . .

5. Regarding improved media coverage, it may be concluded that:

   a. We can provide suggestions for news pegs on high blood pressure. . . .

   b. The state and local programs are as ambivalent about the value of High Blood Pressure Month as we are. Let the debate continue.

   c. Regional media coordination is best left up to regional managers. National media coordination will always be at its current state because the Heart Association views media access as a right and a necessity independent of NHBPEP.

Distribution, as the above indicates, often relies on good interpersonal and interinstitutional relationships in the non-profit or social marketplace. On the other hand, the profit sector construct of price, which is seemingly non-existent in this context, has very real correlates. In controlling high blood pressure, for example, there are dollar costs to the patients. Both treatment and medication must be paid by someone. And these costs fluctuate greatly, as does the frequency and—perhaps—effectiveness of treatment of less well-to-do patients. Certainly the public health setting is less likely to promote the sensitive counseling high blood pressure education requires.

None of these factors can be controlled by NHBPEP. Nor, as our private/public health care system functions, are they ever likely to fall under federal control. This, in fact, is why NHBPEP and its contractor spend considerable time reaching influential audiences with the health care system, to turn these people into understanding advocates of what would otherwise be a centralized and far more traditional information strategy, a distinction not to be overlooked despite the relative emphasis.

It is clear that by using the social marketing approach, NHBPEP has overcome a great many of the weaknesses evident in other federal public information efforts. Above all, they have been able to at least demonstrate a significant correlation between the growth of their efforts and the decrease in incidence of the health problem they seek to motivate Americans to understand and treat. Whether the same approach can work in less agreed-upon problem areas—GAO cites smoking and drug abuse as two unsuccessful health campaign subjects—is moot at this point. It is up to government information practitioners and top agency management to expand experimentation with this approach.

Notes

1. Philip Kotler and Gerald Zaltman, "Social Marketing: An Approach to Planned Social Change," *Journal of Marketing*, 35 (July 1971):3–12.

2. Philip Kotler, *Marketing for Non-Profit Organizations* (Englewood Cliffs: Prentice-Hall, 1975).

3. GAO, "Difficulties in Evaluating Public Affairs Government-Wide and at the Department of Health, Education and Welfare," LCD 79–405, January 18, 1979, p. 21.

4. GAO, "Difficulties in Evaluating . . . ," p. 23. The Posner article cited in section III, chapter 1 also emphasizes the importance of cooperation in government promotional campaigns.

5. Much of the detail on staffing was supplied in an unpublished paper written by an NIH staff member, Betsy Singer, April 1979.

6. A letter to Kenneth H. Rabin from Charles S. Lerner, Project Manager, Kappa Systems, Rockville, Maryland, 4 September 1979.

7. GAO, "Difficulties in Evaluating . . .," pp. 23–24.

8. "The National High Blood Pressure Education Program's Information and Education Strategies for Public and Patient Audiences," January 1979, and discussion with NHBPEP Coordinator Graham Ward are the basis for the contents of the sections which follow.

9. William Novelli, "Case: National High Blood Pressure Education Program" (University of Maryland, Course BMGT 750, Marketing Administration, Fall 1978). The Advertising Council's structure and the use of the "volunteer campaign coordinators" and "volunteer agencies" is reviewed earlier.

CHAPTER 19

Communicating with Congress: The Lobbying Function

Michael W. Dolan

The public misperception about the work of lobbyists is largely the fault of the lobbyists themselves, who, like most professionals, accentuate the arcana of their craft. That the average lobbyist is not a glib, cash-stuffing back-slapper, whispering his instructions into the ears of legislative chieftains, should come as no surprise. It should also be no surprise that the primary lever of the private sector lobbyist is information, not favors, campaign contributions, or friendship. Information—the supply of facts, statistics, forecasts, and argument—is the principal means by which the private sector lobbyist promotes and defends his or her organization's interests on Capitol Hill. What is not as well known, however, is that it is the only means by which the government lobbyist can operate in the struggle with his private-sector counterpart for the collective will of our national legislature. Why this is the case, and how the government agency directs information to the Congress, will be examined in this chapter.

Many agency legislative officers object to being described as lobbyists, pointing out quite correctly that they are government officials who represent the public and that they oversee the much-needed task, envisioned by our Constitution, of communication between the executive and legislative branches of the government. While these and other distinctions between the private and the agency representative to the Congress will become more apparent below, the nonpejorative term "lobbyist" will be used to describe the activities of both.

Although my focus will be on the transfer of information from the agency lobbyist to the Congress, it should be remembered that all lobbyists spend a great deal of their time getting information from, rather than giving information to, Congress. One has to know what members and committees are doing before one can affect what they are doing. And knowledge of what Congress is doing and not doing is not only important to the lobbyist-tactician, it is important to agency officials who, for better or worse, are often more aware of public thinking and attitudes through Congress than directly from the public.

Public vs. Private Lobbyists

Political scientists and other Congress-watchers will forever argue about how private-sector lobbyists operate. How important is the communication of information to the private lobbyist? To what extent are legislators influenced by campaign contributions? How much of the public's business is conducted in private conversations between lobbyist and legislator at social gatherings? How much constituent pressure is really lobbyist-generated? While these and other questions are difficult to answer when asked of private-sector lobbyists, the answers are relatively easy when the operations of the government lobbyists are examined. The agency lobbyist operates under constraints such that information is his or her only tool.

Before examining the ways of the government lobbyist, we should consider the differences between private-interest lobbyists and their lesser-known government counterparts.

First, one of the more significant differences between the operations of government and private lobbyists is contained in Title 18 of the United States Code, Section 1913 of which makes lobbying by government officials a crime. Fortunately, the so-called antilobbying act has been construed to be inapplicable to agency legislative officers who communicate with Congress at the specific request of members and their staffs.

But this statute has raised and will continue to raise questions about agency attempts to influence congressmen through their constituencies. The chief congressional affairs officer of every major agency can probably cite an example of an all-too-familiar situation: an agency lobbying campaign is finally paying off, and the lobbyist can now begin working the votes which will represent the margin of his victory. Suddenly, a congressional foe counterattacks with a charge that agency lobbyists are violating the antilobbying statute, immediately forcing the agency on the defensive, causing it to justify its actions when it should be pressing for a legislative triumph.

Unlike his private counterpart, the government lobbyist cannot make campaign contributions, and here one should remember that contributions may not only complete an information link between private lobbyist and legislator, but they also create social opportunities by the donor's attendance at fund-raising events. Such social occasions enable the lobbyist to use the member's name when seeking appointments with staffers, or permit the lobbyist to follow up her social encounter with a memorandum or letter to the member.

Government lobbyists carry another burden not borne by the private lobbyist: the public and congressional expectation that a major function of government agencies is to supply information to both the public and the Congress. A great deal, certainly more than half, of the time and effort of the typical agency legislative operation is spent responding to committee and member requests for information. While one may wonder why the opportunity to supply information should be a handicap, congressional requests have several drawbacks.

> First, they divert the lobbyist's resources from his priorities to congressional priorities. Second, the information often is not helpful to or may even detract from the agency's mission. The agency lobbyist, who usually finds himself on the defensive far more than on the offensive, knows that skillful committee staffs will respond to a one-sided agency lobbying campaign by forcing the agency to divulge facts and statistics which support the other side of the question.
> Third, although the lobbyist is responsible for supplying the information to the Congress, the material is usually in the hands of others—quite often agency employees in the field. Not all government employees are as sensitive to the need to be responsive to the Congress as are the agency's legislative affairs people, who are continually beseeching agency employees to handle congressional inquiries timely and accurately.

A further difference between government and private lobbyists is more difficult to measure. Although the executive from time to time makes much of congressional intrusions into executive functions, the constitutional principle of separation of powers can also be raised by the legislative branch. For example, when a private interest attempts to influence a member's assignment to committees—so important to a lobbyist's legislative fortunes—such an attempt may be viewed tolerantly by Congress as merely heavy-handed. But if the executive attempts to stack committee membership, the action will often evoke congressional howls of separation-of-powers violations. For the same reason, the executive is usually nervous about attempts to tamper with committee jurisdiction, while generally private interest lobbyists will not shrink from attempting to influence the all-important issue of which committee has jurisdiction over which matter.

The Constitution, of course, provides the agency lobbyist with his or her only major advantage over the private interest lobbyist—the president's veto. While the use of the veto is a White House decision, members and staffers are acutely aware of the fact that the agency will have an opportunity to review the enrolled bill and to advise the president whether it should be approved. Although the wise agency lobbyist never uses the veto possibility as a threat, he is aware of its looming presence in any serious dispute between the president and the Congress.

Too much has been made of the capability of agencies to manipulate members by selectively leaking information. Although there is surely a bit of truth in the popular reports that certain agencies, Mr. Hoover's FBI for example, were able to "keep" certain members by passing them information not in the possession of other members, these incidents are probably much more limited than the public wants to believe. More likely is the situation in which a disgruntled employee leaks derogatory information about his agency to a member or committee—"whistle-blowing" is the current euphemism. Agency lobbyists are not even in agreement on the ethics of such rather harmless practices as giving a member advance notice of a grant or other benefit going to the member's state or district. By announcing a grant or the opening of a government office, the argument goes, the member is able to imply that he had something to do with the agency's decision.

Communicating with Congress

Having compared the private lobbyist with the agency lobbyist, we can examine the means by which the agency lobbyist informs the Congress. First, let's look at the information itself, the nature of which is more often determined by the Congress than by the lobbyist. What type of information does Congress require? Committee chairmen and members, through their staffs, request facts and statistics for a number of purposes. Congressional staffs, contrary to a typical agency attitude, are not always motivated to embarrass the agency by using information to build a case against it. Quite often the congressional request is a function of its oversight responsibility. Of course, what Congress describes as its oversight responsibility is often viewed by unsympathetic agency officials as a fishing expedition. Congressionally extracted information, whatever its motivation, often proves to be quite helpful to the agency—much to its surprise.

Another type of congressional request is for information, usually sought by members rather than committees, which is responsive to inquiries made by the member's constituents—casework if you will. Where is the constituent's government check, loan or grant application, employment request, or what have you? What is the agency going to do about a specific instance of mistreatment of a federal prisoner, or misconduct of an agency employee? What happened to a month-old unanswered constituent letter?

Staff members who are close to their committee chairman will acknowledge that a prompt agency response to a constituent inquiry can be more important to a committee chairman than an agency reply to a committee request for technical data or agency policy on a piece of committee legislation. Unless a member is running for national office, he or she will prefer to be seen as an effective constituent problem-solver than as an effective legislator. It is often impossible for the agency lobbyist to describe the importance of congressional constituent inquiries to the agency employee ultimately charged with handling them—an employee who usually ranks so low on the government totem pole that he is unable to buck the "congressional" to anyone below him. Some agencies will probably give congressional mail a low priority, and agency line operations will continue to assign congressional constituent mail to their newer or less capable employees along with other projects viewed as of lesser importance.

The "Talking Paper"

How does the agency lobbyist get her information to the Congress? While technical data submitted in response to a congressional request can be in traditional letter or memorandum form, advocacy communications cannot. The lobbyist quickly learns that advocacy-type communications are best restricted to one or two pages at the most. The so-called "talking paper" (lobbyists are not known for their diction) is almost an art form. The paper is usually given to a member or staffer for his or her use in committee or on the floor or to brief someone else. Not only must it be concise, it must make the lobbyist's case in forceful, unrebuttable terms. Nevertheless, lobbyists are continually amazed at how quickly an inaccurate or over-reaching position paper will fall into the hands of their opponents.

Of course one should never assume that the lobbyist spends all his time selling a product. The salesman metaphor, while common, is inexact. Even accounting for the current antigovernment mood in Congress, most agency lobbyists spend the major portion of their time defending the agency from Congress rather than promoting their agency's legislative program. Here, of course, information is most useful. The master legislator Lyndon Johnson once remarked that "if the full implications of any bill were known before its enactment, it would never get passed." Alerting the Congress to those implications is the major weapon of the defensive lobbyist. Accordingly, a large amount of the information communicated to Congress is in the form of facts, statistics, and, most important, hypothetical case studies.

Although the Congress is much more influenced by the merits, as opposed to the politics, of a legislative position than popular folklore gives it credit for, the politics of any legislative situation cannot be forgotten. The word "politics" is used here to encompass all of the outside pressures that deflect congressional attention away from the merits of a legislative position. Legislative people at the Department of Justice, for example, are under continuous pressure from other department attorneys, themselves professional advocates, to make lengthy arguments to the Congress as if it were an appellate court able to rule on the merits of an issue in complete isolation from outside influences.

It is difficult to explain to the agency employee why it would be useless to file a 20-page brief with the committee about a minor issue in a major bill when the committee chairman has already resolved the issue against the agency. A proposed statute that would authorize an agency to conduct its own litigation in federal court may not make much sense to a Department of Justice attorney, but it may make a lot of sense to a committee staff attorney who is interested in the agency's legal affairs and who hopes to bolster the prestige of the committee by bolstering the independence of the agency that is the legislative responsibility of the committee. A federal prosecutor may be convinced that the government should have unrestricted access to filed tax returns, but the Congress, which may be guided by principles other than that of efficient law enforcement, may not be so persuaded. The work of our founding fathers, themselves supreme generalists, indicates a healthy suspicion of specialists.

Whenever agency information is communicated orally, the prudent agency lobbyist must always be wary of using an agency line person or specialist to give a technical briefing. The specialist may know the answers, but he'll usually either put his listeners to sleep or outrage them with arguments that demonstrate his insensitivity to the pressures felt by members and their staffs. A Department of Justice bankruptcy specialist, opposing legislation which would give child support debts a higher priority in bankruptcy than tax debts, once attempted to argue to a committee that "surely a man's obligation to his tax collector exceeds that owed to his family."

Credibility with Congress

A continuous problem for the government lobbyist is that of credibility—the lobbyist's stock in trade. Agency officers never realize that if their lobbyist is to maintain her credibility, the material relayed to the Congress must include the bad news with the good. Agency lobbyists have one advantage over their private counterparts—because agencies presumably represent the public, rather than a parochial interest, agency information should be entitled to a greater degree of credibility than that accorded to the information provided by the private sector. However, the agency's credibility is often beyond the agency or the lobbyist's ability to control.

In the halcyon days before Watergate, the Department of Justice rarely had to use personal contacts in its lobbying efforts, instead relying on official letters to effectively transmit agency views on pending legislation. During and after 1973 and 1974, the department's lobbying efforts were forced to become much more aggressive, and even personal visits could not keep up with the department's deteriorating lobbying effectiveness. Of course the more aggressively an agency lobbies, the more its motives are suspected. It may be decades before the department can regain its former possession of a credibility such that legislative views can be effectively supplied by official letter—the envy of every lobbyist.

Agency lobbyists continually fight rear-guard battles with their client agencies, which often press the lobbyist to subordinate credibility considerations to important agency objectives. This brings up the danger of the so-called single-shot lobbyist. Every agency contains special assistants, project managers, and line people who will attempt to lobby pet projects on their own. Unfettered by credibility concerns, the single-shot lobbyist, pulling out all stops, can be remarkably successful when compared with the professional lobbyist, who not only is limited by credibility considerations but may have dozens of bills competing for the same committee's time and attention. The penalty paid is a diminution of the agency's credibility.

For the lobbyist, credibility involves more than just the perception of honesty. An honest and well-intentioned lobbyist may lack credibility because his information is inaccurate or stale, or because the organization he represents is fickle or given to taking unrealistic positions. The lobbyist's information may be untrustworthy simply because he is thick-witted.

The Art of Compromise

Edmund Burke said that all government—indeed, every human benefit and enjoyment, every virtue and every prudent act—is founded on compromise and barter. Yet the rule of compromise and conciliation, so central to the art of politics and government, is often overlooked by agency policy-makers. Agency officials who are for the most part not only practitioners but masters at the art of compromise in their daily affairs are quick to march up to the Hill (or delegate the task to their legislative affairs people) to present "final positions" or "last offers" on pending bills. Such edicts and attitudes are not only reckless, they immediately label the player as unwilling to play by the rules of the game.

An illustration of the importance of compromise and of the role played by committee staffs occurred when the Department of Justice objected to legislation which would have restricted the use of so-called third-party summons in the prosecution of criminal tax cases. After weeks of arguing the department's position to members and staffs, the legislative people arranged a final meeting between a high department official and the key counsel of the committee that was to present the bill to the Senate floor that afternoon. The committee staffer, who had complete control of what was a relatively minor issue in a massive and complex tax bill, presented a compromise position which he had worked out with the staffs of opposing members the night before. After a moment of serious thought, the department official announced to the startled assemblage that he would not only refuse to compromise the issue, but that he thought he could win an up-or-down floor vote. The stunned committee counsel left without a word, and that afternoon the department official, sitting in the gallery, was treated not only to the spectacle of the Senate voting against his position, but was forced to watch the committee counsel moving about the Senate chamber, successfully lobbying against the official's position.

Another congressional phenomenon useful to lobbyists is the antipathy not only between houses but between committees. Bureaucratic infighting and petty jealousies are just as prevalent in the legislative as in the executive branch. Committees are suspicious of jurisdictional raids by other committees, and each house generally distrusts amendments made by the other. Lobbyists learn to take advantage of this phenomenon by waiting to attack an amendment made by one body until the legislation reaches the other body, or by tying up an unfavorable piece of legislation in a jurisdictional dispute between committees. Trucking deregulation legislation, for example, was stalled in the 96th Congress while the Senate Commerce and Judiciary committees battled over whether such a bill was really a trucking bill or an amendment to the antitrust laws.

Structuring the Lobbying Function

A few words should be said about the structural organization of the typical agency legislative affairs operation and how it relates to other agencies, the Office of Management and Budget, and the White House. Most legislative shops split their operations into two groups. One group, typically a group of legislation specialists in the agency general counsel's office, produce the technical agency views on legislation in response to requests from congressional committees and OMB. The Department of Justice receives over 2500 of these requests during a biennial Congress. The actual congressional liaison work and the coordination of the agency's response to congressional inquiries is frequently a separate operation, usually located close to the agency's policy-making components. Of course, to be effective, the agency's chief congressional liasion officers must be situated both organizationally and physically as close as possible to the agency's chief policy-makers. As with any information specialist, the lobbyist is only effective if her information is the most accurate obtainable.

All agency views on pending legislation must first be screened by OMB before transmission to Congress. This requirement, imposed by OMB, is often viewed by the agency as an unnecessary stage of bureaucratic review and by the Congress as a White House attempt to meddle in agency affairs. Actually, OMB's review of agency legislative positions presents the Congress with a coordinated administration position and serves to reduce the time agencies spend fighting among themselves. It also eliminates the need for committees to sort through differing agency positions.

Most legislation is technical and complicated; the Congress and the public benefit from the unique capability of OMB to sharpen the focus of legislative issues by defining the legislative positions taken by the executive branch. Most agencies soon realize that behind many of their legislative problems lie other government agencies.

Many Washington pressure groups can persuade at least one agency to represent their views, and the prudent agency lobbyist will try to neutralize that agency by arguing to OMB that his agency represents the real views of the administration. Department of Justice antitrust legislative proposals are often opposed by the Department of Commerce or by affected regulatory agencies. At times, Department of the Army Corps of Engineers proposals have been studied closely by the Council on Environmental Quality and the Environmental Protection Agency. A favorable administration position, hammered out by OMB, should keep opposing agencies from formally approaching the Hill.

Although large agencies separate their congressional liaison and their public information staffs, there are surprisingly few examples of informational mishaps caused by a lack of coordination between these functions. The congressional liaison staff quickly learns that public legislative positions must be immediately transmitted to the public information people, and the public information staff knows that information of interest to the public and the press will immediately be sought by the Congress. Slip-ups usually stem from an error in one office rather than from a lack of coordination between the two operations.

In 1978, the press office for the Department of Justice learned of a forthcoming Senate subcommittee press release claiming that it was department policy to retain attorneys for government employees accused of criminal conduct. The department's legislative people denied that such a policy statement had ever been given to the subcommittee, when the truth of the matter was that an ambiguous statement on attorney retention was contained in a mass of material transmitted to the subcommittee months earlier. The press officer, relying on the unfortunate denial by the legislative people, put out a similar denial—much to everyone's subsequent embarrassment.

The Importance of Coordination

The degree to which agency lobbyists formally coordinate their activities with White House lobbyists varies, of course, with the administration. The formal White House congressional liaison staff is a relatively recent phenomenon, having first appeared with the Eisenhower administration. The subsequent Kennedy years saw an increase in the numbers and activities of White House liaison officers under the direction of Lawrence F. O'Brien. President Johnson believed that the office was so important that he personally supervised its operations on an almost daily basis. The Nixon and Ford administrations, although faced with a Democratic Congress, fielded a liaison office that by most accounts was considered quite effective, an adjective the appropriateness of which is still being debated for the Carter administration.

As the importance of the White House liaison office increases, the need for coordination with the agency lobbyist increases. Most members would obviously prefer dealing with the agent of the president than with the agent of a cabinet secretary. The usual response to a White House entreaty, however, is a call back from the agency, because in most cases only the agency can solve the member's problem. As a general rule, agencies deal with the House and Senate leadership only through the White House.

A comparison of private and agency lobbyists, a look at how agency lobbyists operate and some of their problems, and a brief glance at the structure of the government's lobbying apparatus, amply demonstrate that there is nothing arcane about the agency lobbyist's profession. As with most information specialties, it requires nothing more than common sense and sensitivity—two qualities which agency officials who deal with Congress should always heed.

CHAPTER 20

Completing the Process: Research and Evaluation

Ray Eldon Hiebert and Kenneth Rabin

In the past, public information officers and their administrators have too often considered communication to be simply a matter of sending out messages, be it through press releases, publications, public service announcements, or special events. They were not concerned with the response from those messages—the feedback—or with attempting to understand the audience before they sent out the message in the first place.

Now we know more about the communication process, and we understand that communication cannot be effective without systematically understanding the audience and analyzing its feedback. That part of the process requires research and evaluation. Communication is not complete without these elements.

Research and evaluation are important to many parts of the public information process. They can help define goals, diagnose problems, identify publics, probe opinions, test programs, and evaluate results. They provide ways of going about the tasks of public information systematically. A good public information program should foster research and evaluation in all of its aspects. And research starts by developing a research attitude and a research habit in all employees. Snap judgments and quick hunches should be questioned. Proposals and position papers should be as fully documented as possible, with data to support all conclusions and recommendations.

And yet they are still too often forgotten, or sometimes neglected because of intimidation caused by press criticism, congressional influence, or the constraints of regulation. J. L. McCamy surveyed government agencies in 1937 and found that of the 36 responding offices, just "one had ever made a survey of its market in the manner of advertising surveys."[1]

Despite considerable government reliance on such social science research techniques as opinion polling of domestic audiences and content analyses of Allied and enemy media during World War II, McCamy's prewar findings were reiterated in John A. R. Pimlott's 1951 study of *Public Relations and American Democracy*. Conducting his research in 1947–1948, this British writer concluded that "interpretation of the public . . . has a subordinate place in the typical federal information office."[2]

Thomas Kell, surveying 15 "small, independent Federal agencies" in 1977 found that little had changed since McCamy and Pimlott's research. The types of research and evaluation government information offices *do* employ tend to be among the less sophisticated alternatives. In research prior to program planning, for example, PIOs are more likely informally to survey personal contacts and field personnel, qualitatively analyze incoming mail and clipping or broadcast monitoring service reports, confer with representatives of groups directly concerned with a problem, or assess trends in public usage of agency services. They seldom analyze national opinion polls, survey representative samples of particular publics, employ either depth interviews or focus group panels, or perform a systematic content analysis of their clippings or mail.

Justifying Research

Government agencies—at least in a democracy—have no more rights and privileges than nongovernment agencies. They must have the consent of the public to succeed. They must be publically accountable for their policies and their actions. In a democratic society, with a free press and public access to information, the public will sooner or later insist on a full accounting. Continuous evaluation must be done to provide the facts for such an accounting.

The public information office should perhaps be called the "office of public responsiveness." Ideally, it should have two branches, one to get response from the publics, and the other to respond to the publics. One branch should perform the evaluation function, the other the communication function. But they must work in concert, for they aid one another.

In a cost-conscious age, the public information function itself must be able to justify its expense. Here again, research on the effectiveness of the public information program will be increasingly important in a cost-effective analysis. Evaluation of the public information program has many important benefits in addition to justification.

One of the most important reasons for public information research is to provide mechanisms to insure feedback from the publics. Communication must be a two-way proposition, but mass communication in a mass society often precludes direct feedback from the audience. Continual research is the only means of assuring regular and meaningful response from those who receive our messages.

Lack of thorough research and evaluation in government public information can seriously affect public perception of the government as an effective instrument of the people's will. This useful generalization alone should argue the case for investment of money, personnel, and time in these processes.

Public information people can and should justify investment in these areas to top administrators in several ways: Without research, plans made in a Washington agency could be so out of line with public opinion that the agency could suffer serious harm by carrying out an untested program. Effectiveness of programs mandated by law cannot be evaluated without measuring public awareness of them. Severely limited public information resources may not be wisely invested unless the alternatives are carefully researched. And it is difficult to produce useful or competitive publications or audio-visual materials without the equivalent of public-sector marketing research.

Constraints and Alternatives

Congressional and press mistrust of executive branch "propaganda" has sometimes blocked full use of research and evaluation techniques. One manifestation of this mistrust is the requirement of the Office of Management and Budget that any agency wanting to conduct an internally initiated survey of more than ten members of the public must receive OMB approval, granted infrequently. Thus, sophisticated quantitative analysis of the American public is somewhat circumscribed.

There are, however, readily available alternatives. Public attitudes and opinions can be extrapolated through unobtrusive research, such as content analyses of public participation feedback. Opinion research of internal audiences can be undertaken. Opinion research is possible on external audiences that either (a) request such analysis or are (b) the targets of a campaign like military recruiting, which represents a major investment of public funds. And secondary analysis can be made of commercially marketed opinion research studies (e.g., Gallup, Harris, Roper, Caddell, Sindlinger, or Yankelovich).

Types of Research

We can identify at least three types of research that are essential for public information evaluation.

External Audience Evaluation

Research can help government in the analysis of publics: who they are, what they need and want, what their attitudes are, what their images are of government, what flexibilities and rigidities exist in their opinions. Survey research has become one of the most important types of evaluation research. Although the Office of Management and Budget review has a dampening effect here, we have already noted three ways by which survey research of external audiences may be accomplished: in response to external request, as a result of the size of government investment in a program, and indirectly, through secondary analysis of data purchased from commercial pollsters.

Survey research has shown the government what the public approves, and it can do so over a period of time. Michael E. Schiltz, for example, examined large numbers of opinion surveys over a 30-year period, 1935–1965, to determine public attitudes toward social security, for the Social Security Administration. He found that "most Americans most of the time have supported . . . social insurance programs . . . at least as a means of responding to the needs of the poor."[3] Without such support, government would be foolish to continue such programs.

Survey research has helped government learn what the public disapproves. In a famous public survey for the U.S. Senate in 1973, the Louis Harris organization examined public confidence in American government in a detailed 342-page report. The analysis ended with the conclusion that "the American people display much less confidence in their government than do their state and local leaders. But both the people and the leaders see a potential for effective, well-run government."[4] The study suggested many areas for new government policies to win public confidence.

Survey research has given government an idea of what kind of images exist in the minds of its publics. In 1973, the Response Analysis Corporation undertook a national survey of attitudes toward food, farmers, and agriculture. The results showed that nonfarm households had an image of farmers and their problems quite similar to farm households, especially on matters of costs, prices, conditions, and government control. But the nonfarmer image of agricultural use of pesticides was quite divergent from the farmer's. The study pointed up an area where the cause of a bad image had to be changed, or where a more effective communication plan had to be developed to explain a problem.[5]

Such research has enabled government to know where the public is misinformed and misguided. For example, in 1971, Louis Harris and Associates undertook a survey of public opinion on "American attitudes toward alcohol and alcoholics" for the National Institute on Alcohol Abuse and Alcoholism. They concluded that the public was aware of some basic facts, and that there was much fear and apprehension of the danger of drink. "But there is also misapprehension and some confusion as to the causes and possible solutions to drinking problems, all of which indicates the need for an intensified campaign of public education." The authors suggested a coordinated approach involving the courts, the police, and social agencies rather than depending solely on the judicial system to clear the backlog and confusion in dealing with alcohol-related cases.[6]

Survey research has helped government produce more effective communication. Donald Smith of the Veterans' Administration in 1976 developed a three-part questionnaire mailed to 250 public service managers whose stations were ranked among the top five AM or FM outlets in the nation's 50 largest markets. Findings from this study resulted in the Veterans' Administration devising a new PSA distribution format which personalized the packaging by emphasizing the *local* importance of the VA programs promoted. Eighty percent of the survey's 102 respondents agreed that local relevance of the cause being promoted was a primary factor in a spot's being aired.[7]

Another survey of external opinion leaders was initiated directly by the president of American Business Press, who visited the National Bureau of Standards to complain that "the volume of material produced by NBS was overwhelming and unmanageable, from an editor's point of view . . . There was simply too much information to process and, for the most part, the information that was available was too technical in nature to be easily converted into a form suitable for the readers of trade magazines."[8] From this request came a gatekeeper study of the preferences of 102 editors whose publications were produced by member companies of the American Business Press. From these findings, the NBS public information staff devised *NBS Update*, "an editor's guide to recent activities at the National Bureau of Standards."

Internal Audience Evaluation

Much government survey research is aimed at the internal public—the employees of any agency. This is critical since employees project the dominant "image" of an organization which has no tangible product on the marketplace.

The military services lead the way in this area. Typical was a 1977 communications study of a stratified random sample of individuals in the U.S. Air Force Systems Command. The survey showed that there were content and distribution problems with the command's internal newsletter for junior enlisted audience. It also showed the potential usefulness of base newspapers within the command as a means of carrying command-wide as opposed to local stories. It indicated strong sentiment for more meaningful inclusion of civilian employees in "Commander's Call" meetings. And it showed senior officer reliance on their peers as important information sources.

Another Air Force survey studied the effectiveness of selected internal information materials provided primarily to other information personnel for their study or adaptation to local internal or external media and messages. Three hundred respondents to the survey, stratified by the nature of their assignments, helped determine the relative utility of different products to information personnel in different types of commands, enabling some cost-efficient alterations in content and distribution.

One of the most useful studies of government employee communications was conducted on the employee population of the highly decentralized and research-oriented National Bureau of Standards. A random sample of employees was used to measure their perceived relationship to 14 different situations that might affect a range of employees, representing most content areas covered in employee publications, their readership habits in terms of 21 employee media, their own content preferences, and their specific recall of nine story items about NBS. A key conclusion was that—for all the different personalities and roles involved—the *Standard*, the bureau's biweekly employee newsletter, presented the most accurate picture of bureau events and people. However, the results also suggested that NBS employee media contain information about situations which employees do not perceive to involve them. The study also isolated four types of employee publics with different communication behaviors and different information needs, for which different communication strategies are necessary.

Message Evaluation

Research can also be focused on the messages governments send out. Without some systematic audit of what is said, government may not achieve its original objectives. Government can, for example, pretest the message with a small sample of publics, to make sure it conveys the images or the ideas desired. Government agencies have assembled small panels of consumers to look at storyboards or evaluate poster layouts before the agency makes a final commitment. This usually does not require high-level approval and it can help prevent the type of oversights that occur when a product is approved for mass production without disinterested evaluation. The materials used by the National Heart Blood and Lung Institute involving supermarket chains, for example, were reviewed at several stages by members of a consumer panel.

Quantitative message-testing of television public service advertisements has been used by the National Cancer Institute and the National Heart Blood and Lung Institute. They are codevelopers of the Health Message Testing Service. Working through a commercial market research firm, the testing service helps government PSA message producers discover if the message they have designed will attract audience attention; cause high recall of key ideas; or be considered relevant, believable, interesting, and informative. Moreover, the message testing service can discover which *parts* of the message are stronger or weaker. The effectiveness of proposed messages can be compared to established norms on several scales of attention, attraction, recall, and relevance.

Proposed PSA messages are shown to test audiences in representative markets. The messages are presented in the context of a "real" program, including other commercials. Respondents are interviewed before, between, and after test message exposures. Government can also posttest the message to find out what was said. Content analysis can be used to determine the real transmission and the gaps in transmission, which over a period of time can be lost in the day-to-day business of handling crises.

Message evaluation can also be undertaken through readership studies to determine what publics actually received. Sometimes the message isn't received at all, and at other times the message that is received is misunderstood. The Public Health Service undertook a readership survey of its employee magazine, a slick, expensive monthly called the *PHS World*. The organization discovered that only 44 percent of the PHS employees regularly saw the magazine on which it was spending a quarter million dollars a year.

Another sort of message evaluation can be obtained from systematic audit of the mass media. Content analysis of the mass media can reveal what messages got into the public media, and how the messages might have been changed by the media's gatekeepers as the words went through the media processes. Survey research of the media gatekeepers themselves can reveal reporter and editor attitudes, and detail their reactions to the kinds of messages sent to them. A news media survey completed for the U.S. Department of Agriculture showed the attitudes of editors toward a particular release. A detailed questionnaire was sent to food editors concerning "Food and Home Notes," a weekly release sent to 3500 food editors. The survey helped to determine how, why, when, and where these editors were using the release, and changes were subsequently made to increase the release's effectiveness.

Impact Evaluation

No doubt the most difficult but certainly the most important type of public information evaluation is the systematic study of how well government did its job. What impact did it have? To what extent did it inform, persuade, influence, or change public attitudes in the desired direction? This kind of evaluation is usually more expensive and time-consuming, often involving experts, or in-depth interviewing, or before-and-after studies where evaluation takes place over a period of time so trends and changes can be observed.

Experts or leaders can sometimes be brought together to provide meaningful evaluation of programs. In-depth interviews can provide a useful method of probing attitude changes, because it can allow the interviewer to go beyond the surface opinion to when and why and how the opinion developed. After the U.S. Post Office became a semiprivate corporation, its internal communications program was revised in order to try to cure growing personnel problems. Several years after the changes, the department sought to evaluate these efforts through in-depth personal interviews of a random sample of its middle managers around the country. The survey revealed that the department's internal communications media were accomplishing certain goals, such as building identification with management on the part of middle managers. But the probing uncovered areas of failure which were leading to discontent. For example, the in-depth interviews revealed a reservoir of resentment that communication channels were all one-way, from Washington to the local office. Channels were recommended to get feedback from the local level back to headquarters.

The most effective type of impact evaluation is probably the use of survey research, repeated over a long period of time, so policy changes can be clearly related to opinion changes and accurately audited. The Library of Congress Readings for the Blind program undertook such an analysis before and after a major public service announcement campaign designed to educate the public about the program. The impact study provided the library with a sophisticated method of measuring the successfulness of the campaign.

All public information evaluation—not just impact evaluation—should ideally be done on a continuing basis. The number of variables in audience and message are so great that the results of any one systematic investigation may have very limited application to any other situation. Research should not be an occasional or last resort, but an on-going and integral part of the process.

The Evaluation Process

Although the usual public administrators and public information officers are not going to be experts on research, they should know the basic considerations for conducting meaningful evaluation of any public information problem. They should have the basic outline of steps in the process firmly in mind, so they can direct the experts and not be directed by them. They should know the pitfalls and the problem areas, what is acceptable, and what is shoddy.

The list that follows is designed to include the essential considerations for completing an evaluation project. The important thing to remember is that each of these steps should be carefully thought out before the project is undertaken.

Stating the Problem. Evaluation is not a bandage that can be applied to a sore to cure the whole body. It can only be directed at one specific problem at a time, and that problem has to be clearly defined, with carefully stated limits. It would be foolish to carry out an evaluation effort for the stated purpose of "determining the most effective public information program." But by limiting the project, one might make it quite possible "to evaluate the effectiveness of health information for the elderly citizens of Pumpkin Center."

Designing the Evaluation. Knowing the problem and stating it concretely, we are ready to plan the project to achieve proper evaluation. Research design is a series of guideposts to keep us going in the right direction.

The design for a good evaluation project should include a working guide, budget, and timetable for the project. The design has to be practical. We should not plan to take on more than we can handle, in time, money, or personnel. The design should describe the needs for the project, and the steps necessary to bring it to conclusion.

Determining the Sample. Evaluation research is possible in public information largely because of the laws of statistics. If we have a proper sample, even though it might constitute a very small percentage of the total population we are studying, we can project the results of our study on the total population with reasonable accuracy. We do not have to interview the head of every household in the city, which would be an expensive and time-consuming task, if we can devise a representative sample of heads of households. The Gallup poll of national public opinion, for example, is based on about 1500 interviews to represent more than 200,000,000 people.

At least three main types of sampling can be used, although others can be identified. *Random* sampling requires the least subjective judgments. It's like shuffling cards and then picking them from the deck. Every card has an equal chance of being selected. A related and more convenient method is *systematic* sampling, which requires selecting every n^{th} item in the universe.

The other two main types of sampling are *stratified* and *judgmental*. In a stratified sample, an effort is made to get equivalent proportions in the sample to some known proportion in the universe. For example, if we know that our elderly population is 42 percent white female, 16 percent black female, 30 percent white male, and 12 percent black male, we would try to get a stratified sample with exactly those percentages in each category.

A *judgmental* or *purposive* sample can be used when practical considerations (perhaps small size of the universe) preclude the use of a probability sample. The investigator uses his or her best judgment to determine what would be representative. Such sampling should be used only when the possible errors from bias would not be serious, and when other sampling is impractical.

Gathering the Data. Although it might seem like the major part of research, gathering the data should actually be the simplest, or at least the most routine, aspect of the project. The real work comes in stating the problem, designing the research, and selecting the sample. In public information offices, the data can be gathered by nonresearch but trained lay persons. If the evaluation has been properly designed, the data that are gathered will not be affected by the person doing the gathering. The facts should be replicable no matter what individuals are involved.

The methods for gathering the data must be clearly laid out, whether in a questionnaire for survey research or in a schedule of items and categories for content analysis. The interviewers or itemizers should be thoroughly briefed on the project, understand the goals and objectives, and know the sponsoring agency.

Analyzing the Results. To make the results meaningful, the raw data must be analyzed, and this usually requires the help of machines—calculators, sorters, and especially computers. It is crucial that the project be designed with categories so the raw data can be coded or classified according to some systematic method. The set of categories should be derived from a single classificatory principle; they should be mutually exhaustive, and the categories within the set should be mutually exclusive.

Obviously, the more specific the raw data, the easier it will be to use a machine for tabulation and analysis. If questions are posed so the answers can be readily categorized—yes or no answers, or multiple choice answers, for example—the data can be easily coded for sorting or computing. If the questions are open-ended, with long notes from in-depth interviews, the results will have to be digested and categorized separately before they can be analyzed by machine.

There is a break-even point for machine tabulation. Generally speaking, if the number of items to be tabulated is under 500, it can be more efficient for a trained clerk to hand-tabulate the items.

Interpreting the Results. It is usually not enough simply to tabulate and analyze the results, showing averages, ranges, ratios, and relationships. That analysis must be interpreted. What does it all mean? How does it relate to other studies? How can the results be used? What are the limitations?

A problem in interpretation is the tendency to over-generalize. It is important not to draw conclusions that stretch the facts beyond their limits. And it is important to keep the interpretation objective, without the biases of the investigators, public information officers, or public administrators.

Reporting the Results. The results need to be reported in a meaningful way, or a lot of time, energy, and effort will have been wasted. Unless the results of the research are reported to the decision-makers so they can integrate the conclusions into policy, there is little need for such evaluation. Therefore, the report should be succinct, forceful, direct, with as many graphs and charts and other visual representations as possible to dramatize key points and emphasize salient features.

Good evaluation research can have the added benefit of providing promotional material for the program, because the results can be reported to the publics concerned as well as to the decision-makers. Such reporting can demonstrate the concern of the decision-makers for the attitudes, opinions, and reactions of the publics studied.

Methods of Research

One of the key decisions in the evaluation research design is what specific method should be used. Most often used in public information is survey research, although content analysis can also be useful, so we will discuss both here briefly.

Survey Research is a method of systematically probing public opinion and soliciting feedback and is growing rapidly in use and importance. Most survey research uses a questionnaire, with carefully worded and pretested questions, administered to a carefully selected sample of the population to be studied. The steps in the survey process are similar to the steps in the research process described above. We can identify at least three different modes of survey; each has its advantages and disadvantages, and these need to be examined in designing the research.

Personal face-to-face interview is probably the best mode, although it is also the most expensive. A trained interviewer must administer the questionnaire to each individual in the sample. The rate of response is usually the highest of the three modes, because the interviewer is paid by the interview and can persist until a satisfactory response is obtained. The chances of misunderstanding are reduced because the interviewer can explain the questions and use visual aids to inform and instruct.

Telephone interview is increasing as a useful mode of survey research, partly because it is less expensive than the personal face-to-face interview. In the past, telephone interviews could not have yielded a valid sample of the total population, however, because telephone ownership was not typical, certainly not among those in the lower economic strata. Today, however, the telephone is much more widespread, making its use in survey research practical. But it is still not without problems; a growing group has unlisted numbers, and there is still disproportionate lack of telephones in the inner city compared to the affluent suburbs. Finally it is important to make certain that the telephone interviewers are as carefully trained as those who work face-to-face.

Mailed questionnaire is probably the easiest and least expensive mode. It also has the advantage of providing more candid results because it can be completed in privacy and anonymity, without the stressful situation of a face-to-face interview. The chief disadvantage is the low rate of return and bias. Some social scientists feel that certain types of people are apt to return questionnaires and other types do not. If this is true, the results can be biased for certain characteristics. Efforts can be made to reduce possible bias from nonrespondents by follow-up mailings, telegrams, phone calls, and even house visits. Mailed questionnaires require a literate universe, and one that is highly motivated to respond.

Special Problems. A number of survey research problems should be noted. First of all, pretesting of questions and training of interviewers are essential. We can make sure our questions are not vague, misunderstood, and confusing only if we try them out on a small group in advance of the full-scale research. This trial run can save time and money and greatly increase the validity of the final results. Training sessions with the interviewers can also increase the effectiveness of the survey.

One should not overlook the dangers and pitfalls in survey research. Beware of questions on complex issues about which the respondents lack information. Beware of question wording—what is said or not said can be misleading. Beware of sensitive issues and questions that tend to elicit silence or misleading answers. Beware of nonrepresentative results if inadequate procedures are used. Beware of the problems of invasion of privacy which concern some respondents.

Content analysis is also a useful method of evaluation in public information. First of all, it can help audit the message. Such an audit can help determine whether we are meeting our objectives, and it can also help us see whether our messages are readable, listenable, and digestible for our audiences. Second, it can help us examine outside messages, about us or those we are interested in, especially in the mass media.

The United States Forest Service in the Department of Agriculture has, for several years, applied systematic content analysis to oral and written opinions solicited on issues related to its responsibilities. Agriculture's expertise was tapped by a government task force consisting of representatives from agencies such as HUD, HEW, and EPA, all of whom have public participation stipulations in their funding allocations to local entities. Emerging from the discussions was the draft of a detailed "Handbook for Public Response Content Analysis."

The task force sets five objectives for a content analysis of public responses:

1. To develop a document which displays public comment in an organized, systematic manner.
2. To extract verbatim opinions and reasons from response, keying those opinions and the associated reasoning to decision items or issues and organizing them in a way that clearly and accurately reflects the full range of public concerns as they relate to specific subject areas.
3. To be able to extract comments, yet retrace each to its source.
4. To identify sources of responses geographically and by affiliation categories, distinguishing one group from another within an opinion range.
5. To produce an accurate report that can stand on its own or be the basis for a highly valid summary report.

Questions to be considered and answered by the decision-maker and person responsible for the response analysis are: What information is needed? Who will your publics be? How will response information be processed? What time will be allowed for response? for analysis of response? for interpretation? evaluation?

The task force suggests that the process, best undertaken by a small team of employees either at lower or middle civil service grades, "but not a mixture," breaks down into seven key steps: "assigning response codes, making a respondent log, duplicating responses, analysis, organizing comments, formulating reports and typing."

Readability Tests can also be done by content analysis. The standard readability tests outlined below are discussed in a publication of the National Cancer Institute, "Readability Testing in Cancer Communications." In addition, there are computer programs based on the formulas for these readability tests which allow for instant feedback on the grade level of reading skill a particular piece demands from its audience.

Rudolf Flesch's "Reading Ease Formula" was the first readability test to gain widespread popularity. Assuming a minimum of 50 percent reader comprehension, the Flesch formula calculates readability in terms of the reader's school grade level. The key variables are the average number of words per sentence and the number of syllables per 100 words. The formula is: $-2.2029 + .0778 \times$ sentence length $+ .0455 \times$ word length.

Edgar Dale and Jeanne Chall published their formula in 1948, the same year the Flesch formula was first introduced. The Dale-Chall formula also is based on 50 percent reader comprehension, and also employs average number of words per sentence as one key variable. Instead of using the number of syllables per 100 words as a second criterion of difficulty, however, Dale-Chall counts the number of words in a passage which are not on a list of 3000 words familiar to most fourth-grade students. The formula is: $3.2672 + .0596 \times$ sentence length $+ .1155 \times$ unfamiliar word percentage.

Robert Gunning's approach, published in 1952, parallels the two earlier techniques in terms of level of comprehension and use of sentence length as a variable. His simplification is based on the replacement of Flesch's number of syllables per 100 words and Dale-Chall's percentage of unfamiliar words with his absolute number of polysyllabic words (that is, having three or more syllables) per 100 word passage. The revised Fog Index Formula is: 3.0680 + .0877 × sentence length + .0984 + percentage of polysyllables.

The National Cancer Institute itself, however, applies G. Harry McLaughlin's 1969 SMOG computation to its "pamphlets, flyers, posters, and magazine articles . . . designed to appeal to a wide spectrum of the American public." While the three formulas noted above will yield a grade-level score indicating only 50 percent comprehension of the material, the SMOG index will indicate "the material being tested will be *fully* comprehended by 68 percent of its readers who have reached a reading level within 1.5 grades of the SMOG score."

The SMOG calculation takes four steps:

1. Three ten-sentence samples are drawn from the piece to be tested—one sample from the beginning, middle, and end of the piece.
2. The number of polysyllabic words in all 30 sentences is counted, polysyllables again being defined as having three or more syllables.
3. The estimated square root of the number of polysyllabic words is computed.
4. A constant of three is added to the estimated square root, yielding the SMOG index grade level.

Special Suggestions

Public information evaluation itself needs to be evaluated from time to time. It can be useful to have outside experts come in to examine the work, to make sure the sampling procedures are adequate, to check that biases are not hurting the objectivity and validity of the results, and to examine the over-all design to make sure the right questions are asked about the real problems. Such an audit can also help to answer criticisms from the public or administration of the findings.

If the public information office can establish a research attitude toward its work, there are many ways in which the professionals can evaluate communication efforts without engaging in major research. The day-to-day flow of communication can provide material for objective evaluation without great expense. Outgoing communication—press releases, promotional materials, annual reports, and even public correspondence—can be categorized and filed by subject and theme, so that a running check can be kept on our messages as we go along.

Incoming communication can also be categorized, tabulated, and filed on a daily or weekly basis. Clipping services and broadcast monitoring services are useful expenditures, but if they are used only to send items to the administrator to show how we got into the media, the expense may not be worth it. Clippings and broadcast reports can be categorized and evaluated on a regular basis and charted for trends. Correspondence, complaints, and telephone calls can also be recorded and categorized. Contacts with media representatives can also be noted. It is useful to have a form on which employees can note such contacts with the public and press.

But several warnings are in order. First, one should not make the mistake of thinking that this miniresearch can take the place of regular, full-scale research projects. Also it is wise to remember that most public-initiated responses are negative. People write or call in with complaints much more often than with compliments. Such response is apt to be negatively biased. Finally, efforts to record contacts with the press have sometimes backfired, with journalists claiming that this is an effort to intimidate public officials or newsmen and violates the spirit of a free press. This can be easily avoided with adequate explanation in advance of starting the procedure.

Conclusion

If public information is to serve its real purpose in public administration, evaluation must be a vital part of the process. It should begin with the development of a research attitude on the part of all public information personnel. But it can and should go beyond that to the use of research experts for major evaluation on crucial issues at regular intervals. Only with evaluation can public message-sending achieve the feedback necessary for effective communication. Only with continual research can government remain in contact with and responsive to their publics. And only with research can the public information activity be evaluated for an accounting of the effectiveness of the taxpayer's dollar.

Notes

1. J. L. McCamy, *Government Publicity* (Chicago: University of Chicago Press), 1939, p. 35.
2. J. A. R. Pimlott, *Public Relations and American Democracy* (Princeton: Princeton University Press), 1951.
3. Michael E. Schiltz, *Public Attitudes Toward Social Security, 1935–1965* Washington, D.C., U.S. Department of Health, Education and Welfare, 1970, p. 181.
4. U.S. Congress, Senate, Committee on Government Operations, *Confidence and Concern—Citizens View American Government: A Survey of Public Attitudes* Washington, D.C.: Government Printing Office, 1973, p. 27.
5. Response Analysis Corporation, *What the Public Says About Food, Farmers and Agriculture*, Princeton: Response Analysis Corporation, 1973.
6. Louis Harris and Associates Inc., *American Attitudes Toward Alcohol and Alcoholics: A Survey of Public Opinion*, Washington, D.C.: U.S. National Institute of Mental Health, National Institute on Alcohol Abuse and Alcoholism, 1971, p. 202.
7. Donald R. Smith and Kenneth H. Rabin, "What Broadcasters Want in Public Service Spots," *Public Relations Review*, Vol. 4, No. 1, Spring 1978, pp. 29–36.
8. Richard S. Franzen, "Playing the Game by the Editor's Rules," *Journal of Communication*, 4 (Winter 1978).

MANAGING COMMUNICATION: THEORY AND CASES

In the past much of government's communication has been reactive rather than proactive. The government waited until something happened and then tried to organize some means to deal with the problem. The clear trend is away from acting after the fact, with no preconceived plan. In the first chapter in this section, Kenneth Rabin and Richard Franzen show how government planning in the communication process is growing. They use the communication strategies of the National Bureau of Standards as an example of the principle. Franzen, a former newspaper reporter, is chief of the editorial section, Office of Information Activities, NBS; he and Rabin have completed several research projects on government communication at the American University.

Planning for emergencies has become one of the most crucial aspects of public relations. Lewis Helm has been involved in a number of crisis situations as a public affairs official, and he uses his experience to outline 16 elements as a guideline for disasters. In three cases that follow, we have explicit examples of what to do and what not to do in disaster situations. In the case of the Agnes flood, Helm shows how an emergency could be used to communicate the interests of the White House and the effectiveness of the federal government. In the case of the Sunshine mine disaster, Helm shows how the government can work together successfully with the news media in a tension-packed situation. And in the case of the siege of the BIA building, Robert A. Kelly, former communications director of the Interior Department, concludes this section by dramatically illustrating the problems created for government communication when there is little central planning or coordination.

CHAPTER 21

Increasing the Role of Planning

Kenneth Rabin and Richard Franzen

There is a clear trend towards increased planning, as far in advance as possible, of federal agency public information efforts. However, this shift in orientation towards a planned effort in public communications is relatively recent. As a result, government communication planning technique lags behind both public relations planning technique in the private sector and planning in other functional areas (for example, electronic data processing systems, delivery of social services, weapons systems) of the federal government.

The Voice of Government, a 1968 collection of writings by government information specialists,[1] for example, underscores how new the concept of communications management planning is to the federal government. Four of the contributors to that collection address the subject of "practices of public information," the heading under which government agency communications planning might logically be addressed. The first chapter in the *Voice of Government* discussed "organizing an information office." The writer, former Department of Housing and Urban Development public affairs director Wayne Phillips, concentrated mainly on how to achieve the direct, centralized control the secretary wanted and needed for policy purposes, and at the same time maintain a close working relationship with the operating areas of the department.[2] In essence, Phillips believed correctly that the public affairs office needed to be organized to provide service to internal agency constituencies. But he stopped short of describing or even envisaging a public affairs office that might initiate its own design to assist the functional program areas in achieving agency policy objectives. In short, the 1968 public affairs office reacted to internal requests; it did not anticipate or shape them. Phillips acknowledged, too, that "one of the tragedies of government public information activities is that very few (if any) government public information men ever get initiated into the mysteries of budgeting and management."[3] Indeed, knowledge of these mysteries is a prerequisite to effective planning.

The second and third *Voice of Government* articles on public information practices dealt with limited, though vital, functions of an agency public information office, "Operating a News Room" and "Using Special Events" to create news in support of new agency programs mandated by law. Neither suggested any over-all planning scheme into which these activities might be integrated. Only the final chapter in the sequence, as its title—"Preparing Promotional Campaigns"—implies, deals with aspects of public affairs planning.[4] In this piece, Bernard Posner, executive director of the President's Committee on Employment of the Handicapped, focused on the promotional campaign ("government's megaphone") as a purposive effort with defined objectives and measurable outcomes.

Enduringly apt as it is, however, Posner's article dealt only with the structure of a single campaign and omitted the key internal staffing and budgeting factors that Phillips raised earlier. Only in the decade since *The Voice of Government,* then, has the trend to systematic planning of government public information become significant. Such planning in public information has emerged primarily as a by-product of dramatic growth in over-all use of computer-based planning and control systems as the basis for agency accountability in what might be termed "hard" program areas. The use of the term "byproduct" is deliberate here, since public information is usually viewed as one of the softest, most "political" program areas in government, since public information exists on such a tenuous and fragmented legal mandate, and since government public information persons are not likely to be trained as managers. In fact, many may even resent the intrusion of management systems on their domains.

Sound communications management plans exist today only in those agencies which are relatively free of such inhibiting factors. Specifically, where the agency involved is not a center of constant political shifts and pressures, or where the public information program involved has a relatively clear legal rationale, or where the public affairs manager has appropriate management training and style, we can expect to find prototypes of the systematic communications planning that may eventually prevail throughout the federal government.

An Agency Plan

The agency plan that follows is the outcome of such a confluence of positive factors. First, the agency involved—the National Bureau of Standards of the United States Department of Commerce—deals with issues that are vital, yet fundamentally apolitical. Too, the enabling legislation for NBS mandates information dissemination. Lastly, the techniques employed by the NBS public information staff to disseminate information are indicative of a management goal-oriented operation.

Readers not familiar with public relations management plans should note certain features which all such plans have in common. The first of these common aspects is the concept of organization-wide communication themes. These are message contexts proposed by the public information staff as appropriate general ideas about the organization as a whole. When top management agrees to these themes, the public information people have won powerful leverage over which aspects of organizational programs they will publicize *and* how the messages about those programs will be framed. This is a considerable advance over merely responding to often uneven internal demands for public information services. Such an advance, it should be added, can only be made if the public information staff is perceived as both competent and expert by other elements of the organization.

Other important aspects of the NBS strategy reflect points Posner raised in his article on promotional campaign planning, particularly the selection of clearly defined audiences, the delineation of precise media capabilities, and cooperation from all the other elements within the agency which need support from the communications staff. Finally, this document moves from strategic to tactical planning by demonstrating how themes, audiences, and media selected by the public information people work in concert with the goals of operating program staff to yield a list of specific public information objectives and projects or tasks relevant to an operating program. This, again, represents significant management control for the information people, who otherwise might diffuse their resources responding to spur-of-the-moment requests for a story here and a photo there. More than bureaucratic power for the communicators, though, a planned communications strategy is more likely to create consistent public awareness of, and response to, the major social and economic benefits an agency is trying to provide—despite an increasingly intense flow of competing messages in the society-at-large.

The National Bureau of Standards Communications Strategy[5]

NBS and Its Communications Output

With its headquarters located in a contemporary campuslike complex of offices, laboratories, and conference facilities in the Washington suburb of Gaithersburg, Maryland, the National Bureau of Standards has served as the nation's reference point for measurements in the physical sciences and engineering since 1901. To describe the nature and significance of its work to various audiences, NBS scientists communicate with their peers through such means as extensive publishing and conference programs. In addition, NBS performs a full range of more general public information activities. In just one recent year, the bureau's contribution to the over-all science and technology information explosion was a total of 2200 separate titles and 60,000 pages of scientific and technical information. This output did not include hundreds more pages of news releases, magazine reports, and other program descriptions prepared and distributed to nonscientific or general audiences.

This river of information carried words and images about hundreds of projects ranging from abrasion tests for masonry and stone to solar and stellar satellite astrophysics. Audiences ranged from scientists throughout the world engaged in basic research to suburban homeowners worried about fire protection. Clearly, some control needs to be exerted over so large an outpouring of facts. How can confusion be prevented? Which facts are the most useful to which people? Are external market forces—new fads and lifestyles—causing changing information needs? Which media can best describe which projects? What recurring themes or concepts tie the disparate research programs together?

Introduction

This communications strategy builds upon and strengthens the role traditionally played by the bureau in communicating the results of its scientific and technical research to a wide range of technical, semitechnical, and general publics. The strategy provides a focus for this activity by identifying three major communications themes and then describes how these themes can be consistently and continually reinforced by the application of a variety of communications activities to selected tasks being performed at NBS and directed at specified external target audiences.

The elements contained in this strategy reflect extensive thought and consultation with each individual member of the NBS executive board and other members of the bureau's technical staff and the Public Information Division. The strategy describes a conceptual framework for the coherent and effective use of limited public information resources in helping NBS fulfill its mission and achieve its programmatic objectives.

Themes

Traditionally, one of the difficulties in explaining what the bureau does and why it does it is that NBS has increasingly grown to be so many things to so many different kinds of people. Our scientific and technical advantage—diversity and multidisciplinary expertise—can also present problems when trying to communicate with the many individuals and organizations who should be aware of, or need to know, what we are doing.

Without interfering with the scientific and technical communications channels already firmly in place at the bureau, we have identified three major themes as representative of the broad interest and scope of the bureau's work. The selection of these themes does not limit the large number of messages emanating continuously from the bureau's hundreds of tasks and subtasks. What it *does* provide is an opportunity to create an understanding on the part of our principal audiences, through repetition and reinforcement, of the bureau's distinctive and unique characteristics and contributions. The key, then, to an effective communications strategy, is the consistent, long-term reinforcement of a limited number of themes. The three themes selected for the NBS communications strategy are described below.

Theme I: Assuring Technical Excellence. The bureau's past success in attracting and fostering excellence in a multiplicity of scientific and engineering disciplines has made it possible to respond rapidly to new legislative assignments, to carry out projects of national importance, and to work on the frontiers of science and engineering. Establishing, maintaining, and building areas of excellence devoted to long term experimental and/or theoretical studies in science and technology will provide the underpinning upon which both NBS and its user communities can rely for expertise now and in the future. Technical excellence makes it possible for the bureau to work in the *public benefit* and to *improve governmental and industrial* productivity.

Theme II: Improving Productivity. The bureau undertakes a large proportion of its projects to improve productivity in government (for example, Institute for Computer Science and Technology projects aimed at more efficient computer operations in government) and in industry (for example, the National Engineering Laboratory's work in manufacturing-related measurement assistance). Improving industrial productivity is essential to controlling inflation and maintaining U.S. economic health and standard of living. In the governmental area, improvements in productivity act in part to keep down costs of government and to help minimize escalation of costs. Improved productivity enables U.S. industry to compete more successfully in international markets in those areas where it is not now doing so, and helps maintain the edge in those areas where U.S. industry is successfully competing. Improved governmental and industrial productivity are tied closely to the Commerce Department's goal of successful economic development, industrial growth, and a better quality of life.

Theme III: Working in the Public Benefit. To quote a 1915 Annual Report from the Department of Commerce:

> The Bureau is an intensely practical service, bearing directly and daily upon the life of our people. At one end of its work is research into things as yet unknown. At the other end is the putting of things discovered and determined at the service of our people.

This quotation is equally true today. Many of the bureau's projects are aimed at serving the public—especially in the areas of health, safety, and consumer product performance. The bureau undertakes work at the request of other agencies and with congressionally appropriated funds to meet present and future needs of society.

Working in the public benefit arises from the dual mission of the bureau. There is the bureau's classic mission as a central reference laboratory for all kinds of measurements in engineering, physics, and chemistry. The bureau's other mission has been to apply this basic competence to solve problems. The two roles are complementary. The competences required to operate a successful laboratory can be drawn on to solve more specific problems. On the other hand, by working on such problems, NBS maintains the contact with many important areas that stimulate the work of the reference laboratory.

Audiences

On the basis of information supplied by various bureau staff sources, a total of 11 major audiences have been identified whose interests coincide with the NBS mission and objectives. The audiences are as follows:

Industry
Trade Associations   Professional Societies
State/Local Governments   Universities
Other Federal Agencies   Other Laboratories
Congress   Standards-Writing Organizations
General Public/Consumers   International Organizations

Information Activities and Staffing

There are numerous activities performed by staff members of the Public Information Division that are useful in conveying messages about the bureau to a variety of audiences, ranging from readers of trade and technical journals (nonarchival) to television viewers. The Public Information Division has a staff of 29 persons, grouped under five organizational units that perform 31 major activities. One of these units, for example, the Division Office, provides over-all management and guidance for the operation and is responsible for preparing the division's minimum, current, and proposed level of impact statements associated with zero-based budgeting as well as undergoing yearly program justification reviews and quarterly budget reviews.

The National Bureau of Standards was built as a collection of modern and well-equipped laboratories as well as a conference facility with two auditoriums and numerous meeting and lecture rooms. Public information staff are responsible for providing the logistical support for the 80 major technical conferences that take place at NBS each year. This support includes making arrangements for printing and distribution of programs, scheduling sessions, assisting with publicity, and planning for meals, travel, and accommodations.

The community outreach activities referred to as special activities involve an educational exchange program in which approximately three dozen NBS scientists make presentations of their work to elementary and secondary school students in the surrounding area. The staff also conducts career days for high school students. *NBS Update* refers to a biweekly newsletter sent to editors of business publications that presents digests of all significant work taking place at NBS and includes announcements of new publications, upcoming conferences, and significant organizational changes.

Dimensions/NBS is the bureau's magazine. It is published ten times a year and contains feature articles aimed at semitechnical and general audiences as well as more technical reports. *The NBS Standard* is the employee newsletter and is published every two weeks.

The public information staff also serves as a producer for the technical staff in the audio-visual area and contracts out the free distribution of the 35 films, slide shows, and videotapes that are listed in the NBS audio-visual catalogue. In addition, activities of the scientific and technical staff form essential communications links with the technical communities. These activities include:

> Technical publications
> Standard reference materials program
> Technical talks and presentations
> Standards and technical committee work
> Research associate, guest worker, and post-doctoral programs

Also, congressional testimony and speeches by bureau managers are an effective and frequently used means of communication with key interest groups.

Selected Tasks

In order to describe the communications strategy concept, one program has been selected as an illustrative example from each of the bureau's two laboratories, the National Measurements Laboratory and the National Engineering Laboratory, and from the Bureau's Institute for Computer Science and Technology. The examples represent the way in which bureau tasks can be used to implement a communications strategy through reinforcement of themes with target audiences.

Example 1: Metallic Corrosion

Improving Materials Durability

In response to a congressional directive, a study of the cost of metallic corrosion to the United States was undertaken by the National Bureau of Standards (NBS). The study showed that in 1975 corrosion cost the United States an estimated $70 billion—or 4.2 percent of the estimated Gross National Product for that year. Of this total, about 15 percent or $10 billion was avoidable. The corrosion process has a significant effect on many sectors of the American economy, since corrosion results in the use of materials, energy, labor, and technical expertise that would otherwise be available for alternative uses.

As a result of corrosion, users of metal products incur a wide range of costs, including painting and other methods of corrosion control; more expensive, corrosion-resistant materials; premature replacement of capital goods; larger spare parts inventories, and increased maintenance. Although some of these expenses could be reduced through the economical best practice application of available corrosion control technology, lessening the remaining costs requires advances in technology.

NBS Program

At NBS, metallic corrosion research is part of the larger program of materials science, which in part is directed at minimizing the adverse effects of the deterioration and catastrophic failure of materials to the economy and to public safety. Corrosion research is also necessary so that new and developing technologies in the areas of energy, transportation, defense, communications, environment, materials conservation, and food production can be used successfully and in the most cost- and materials-effective ways.

The corrosion research done at NBS by interdisciplinary groups of researchers supports three of the four sectors in the materials cycle: processing; design, manufacturing, and assembly; and user. (The Department of Interior has the governmental responsibility for the other sector—raw material extraction.) For the materials processing sector, NBS researchers are attempting to determine which features of composition and structure of materials that are built-in during processing should be eliminated or changed to improve durability. They are also working to provide measurement techniques needed to determine these features and assess their effect on durability.

In addition to determining the composition and structure required for optimum durability, the NBS program provides the design, manufacturing, and assembly sector with measurement methods, standards, data, and information that allow effective design and manufacture for predictable and optimum durability. For the materials user sector, the NBS programs are aimed at assisting product users in specifying and controlling durability by quantitatively relating lifetime in service to aspects of service conditions that limit service life and by providing effective maintenance procedures. In order to give the scientific basis for this, NBS researchers must determine the processes that reduce durability of materials as well as establish the measurement methods needed to monitor performance in service.

Themes

The metallic corrosion programs exemplify all three of our themes: technical excellence at frontier areas in the field, working in the public benefit, and improving both industrial and governmental productivity.

A number of researchers in the corrosion area are recognized internationally as experts. The competences required include chemistry, physics, electrochemistry, metallurgy, surface science, and materials science. Technical thrusts include development of theory and experimental methodology. The public benefit is served by making it possible for industry and government to increase the safety of products, such as bridges and pipelines. Much of the information acquired by researchers in this work is also useful directly to consumers in selecting products that will better resist corrosion, in preventing corrosion in household items, and in removing corrosion from objects. Lastly, the proper application of NBS research results in this area should lead to better utilization of materials, more efficient quality control in production, and standards development which in turn lead to improvements in both industrial and governmental productivity.

Audiences

The information gained in these programs is of value to a multitude of audiences including: manufacturers and industry, professional societies, other federal agencies, industry and trade associations, universities, Congress, standards-writing organizations, consumers and consumer organizations, state and local governments, other laboratories (private and public), and international organizations.

Example 2: Semiconductor Technology

Improving the Performance and Reliability of Integrated Circuits

Semiconductor technology is one of the most pervasive technologies in the United

States today. To quote *Business Week*, "It is not only shaping the future of many other industries, but is also creating whole new industries." The applications range from pocket calculators to cardiac pacemakers to sophisticated systems for industry and defense.

Within this industry, more so than perhaps any other, accurate measurements play a vital role. Impurities in the raw materials used to make semiconductor devices must be controlled to within parts per billion, dimensional control must often be measured in micrometers, and tolerances on the order of a wavelength of light are sometimes required. The NBS effort in this area has been to develop or improve the sophisticated measurement techniques needed by the semiconductor industry to maintain quality control and to improve manufacturing techniques so that semiconductor devices will be more reliable.

NBS Program

Significant NBS developments in this area have included:

1. Studies of semiconductor resistivity which produced the basis for five industrial voluntary standards and a Standard Reference Material. These developments have saved the industry an estimated $30 billion in commercial transactions alone over the past ten years;
2. Landmark developments in making and testing semiconductor wire bonds—known to be the major cause of field failures in semiconductor devices—that led to the use of new products and manufacturing equipment by the industry and a dramatic decrease (33% to 5–10%) in wire bond failures in the field;
3. The equally significant development of new test and measurement procedures for I-C line widths that has led to a new Standard Reference Material, great industry demand, and a new understanding in the theory of optics that has affected microscope manufacturers.
4. Work on solid state test patterns to increase production control in an industry plagued with production-line control problems.

Themes

This work exemplifies all three of our themes. The technical excellence of this work has been attested to by technical experts both in the government and industry. A wide range of competences are required including physics, chemistry, metallurgy, electronics, topology to name a few. The improvement in productivity and reliability wrought by NBS researchers is well-documented. The work is also in the public's benefit, since semiconductor devices are increasingly becoming general consumer items, such as fuel injection systems, electronic brakes, heart pacemakers, and "smart" appliances.

Audiences

Important audiences to be reached include:

1. The microcircuit manufacturing industry, including both those who make semiconductor devices and those who make the machines that make semiconductor devices;
2. Semiconductor consumers who are interested in the quality control of the products they buy (this would include both companies and general consumers, though they would probably be reached by different media);
3. The academic communities that are interested in electrical engineering technology and, to a lesser extent, the theoretical spin-offs (as in optics) of NBS research; and

4. The general public, which is presumably interested in what return it is getting on the tax dollars invested in NBS.

Example 3: COBOL Standards Program

Improving Management of Computers

COBOL (Common Business Oriented Language) is the computer language most widely used in business and industry as well as government. Its effective development has its greatest impact in the area of productivity. By providing new features in the language, such as allowing COBOL to be used in data management systems, the utilization and management of computers is significantly advanced.

NBS Program

The National Bureau of Standards has a special responsibility within the federal government for computer science and technology activities. The programs of the NBS Institute for Computer Science and Technology are designed to provide electronic data-processing standards, guidelines, and technical advisory services to improve the effectiveness of computer utilization in the federal sector and to perform appropriate research and development efforts as foundation for such activities and programs.

Establishment of COBOL as a Federal Standard in 1972 was a milestone, followed in 1974 by a revised American National Standard COBOL and a revised Federal Standard COBOL. Now, a new federal COBOL standard with further improvements is targeted for issuance in 1981. COBOL development and standardization is a cooperative effort, marked by interaction among CODASYL—the Conference on Data System Languages—federal task groups, and industry. As 1981 approaches, NBS will sponsor important technical conferences on the new standard with federal and nonfederal groups.

Themes

As noted, the development of COBOL standards has its greatest impact in the area of productivity.

Audiences

The audiences to be reached include federal agencies, industry and trade associations, computer professional societies, standards-writing organizations, state and local governments, manufacturing and business, research organizations, business management organizations, operations research groups, and Congress.

A Complete Strategy for a Single Specific Program Area

One project has been chosen in the area of metallic corrosion to demonstrate how the communications strategy concept actually works, although many similar examples could be chosen from throughout the bureau. The program is described, the three major themes are referenced, and specific audiences and communications activities and outlets are presented in the following section.

Example 4: Metallic Corrosion

Program

In a project for the Department of Energy, NBS is attempting to develop methods for the detection of dangerous corrosion conditions in buried concentric neutral cables used in the transmission of electric power. Tests are being conducted on laboratory samples and on actual cables buried at a special NBS site. Significant progress toward development of test methods for in situ detection of corrosion of underground power cables is expected by September, 1979, as is the evaluation of electrochemical noise measurements as a diagnostic tool for in situ detection of processes leading to cable corrosion.

Theme References

This program demonstrates all three themes in the communications strategy. The program requires the sort of excellence shared by the NBS scientists working on the problem who have received national and international recognition for their contributions in fields such as chemistry, metallurgy, and surface science. The results of the research have direct implications for improving productivity through extending the life of manufactured products. The public stands to benefit through increased reliability of underground cables and avoidance of costly and dangerous power failures.

Audiences, Information Activities, Outlets

All 11 NBS audiences are concerned with this program and are the informational targets of the proposed communications strategy. An appropriate illustration not reproduced here indicates representative examples of the kinds of informational activities that are appropriate to reach those audiences as well as the specific outlets through which the information could be most usefully and effectively conveyed.

Conclusion

Two items merit reemphasis here. First, the acceptance of this strategy by the agency's top management put control over communications goals, objectives, and tasks in the hands of the communicators. Second, the National Bureau of Standards strategy is by no means the only one of its kind. The increasing acceptance of the planning concept in government public information is a healthy indicator of growing professionalism and managerial expertise in the field.

Notes

1. Ray Eldon Hiebert and Carlton E. Spitzer, eds., *The Voice of Government* (New York: Wiley, 1968).
2. Wayne Phillips, "Organizing an Information Office," in Hiebert and Spitzer, eds., p. 250.
3. Ibid., p. 254.

4. Bernard Posner, "Preparing Promotional Campaigns," in Hiebert and Spitzer, eds., pp. 287–299.

5. Richard S. Franzen, *A Communications Strategy for the National Bureau of Standards* (Washington, D.C.: Approved by the NBS executive board, November, 1978). The introductory section summarizing NBS activities is adapted from Franzen's article, "Playing the Game by the Editor's Rules," *Journal of Public Communication* 4 (1978):19.

CHAPTER 22

Meeting the Problems of Crises

Lewis M. Helm

A basic function of government is to help people during times of crisis. Throughout its two-century history, the United States government has played major roles in bringing relief to victims of scores of major disasters and thousands of smaller catastrophes. With the advent of public affairs, however, government has obtained a new and important means for improving assistance. Since the time of the San Francisco earthquake, communication tools have so improved that victims are more quickly informed about available assistance and where to obtain it. Lives have been saved because of this increased ability to focus information.

Improved communications played a definite role in efforts to rescue 93 men buried up to one-mile deep in Idaho's Sunshine mine, which is the crisis case analyzed in Chapter 23, and in relief efforts after the $2-billion blow to northeastern states by Hurricane Agnes, the second case, described in Chapter 24. Unfortunately, there are also examples of how government has failed to use its communications capability, such as during the siege of the Bureau of Indian Affairs building in 1972, the final case, described in Chapter 25.

In recent years, it has become fashionable to focus on "proactive" government public affairs and the use of well-researched, planned, and evaluated long-range communications efforts. However, the true test of public affairs occurs during a crisis, a "reactive" situation, when all of the pressures of government and the media are packed into a tight timeframe, when public statements and actions result in lead television time and headlines around the world. In a "proactive" posture, it is easy to theorize whether one approach or another will bring better results. It is quite another matter during a tense, around-the-clock marathon, ringed by television lights, choked by outstretched microphones, and interrupted by spates of questions ranging from "Why are you hiding the facts?" to "Explain why there's not enough money to do the job that's needed."

And yet such moments also provide the opportunity to influence events in a way that can help people most directly and most visibly. Whether the public affairs practitioner can take advantage of the opportunity depends on that person's skill, determination, and, to a large degree, stamina. Even more, it depends on whether the top program official can be made to recognize that public affairs can help solve the crisis through clear communications with the public.

All crises differ but have enough in common so that basic contingency plans should be developed by government agencies before crises occur. For example, during the 1960s when federal troops were moved into riot-torn cities, they operated from contingency plans, including ones for the handling of information. Likewise, agencies charged with bringing relief to disaster areas follow plans that can be adapted to that specific situation.

The public affairs office of each federal agency should have its own annex to that agency's contingency plan. The annex should spell out how the flow of information will be channeled, who would be sent to the scene for various types of emergencies, and what the relationship will be with the top program official on the scene. The annex must have the full endorsement of the agency head.

Even with such plans at the federal level, however, there can be major overlaps and intense disagreements in implementation, such as occurred between the governor of Pennsylvania and the Nixon administration during Hurricane Agnes. When federal and state governments, plus private industry, are involved in a common disaster, such as the nuclear reactor emergency in 1979 at Three Mile Island near Harrisburg, Pennsylvania, massive confusion and misinformation can occur. However, it is possible for government and industry to work together as in the case of the Sunshine mine disaster.

Also during emergencies, even ones with well-designed contingency plans, the experience of the top program official and the public affairs head is the most decisive factor in determining the success or failure of attempts to communicate with the public. This was true in each of the three "reactive" case studies that follow. However, it is possible to establish specific guidelines which can be applied to the public affairs activities during emergencies. They may help to turn a potential public affairs disaster into a public affairs success.

Public Affairs Guidelines for Disasters

1. Personally verify all information before releasing it. Your word must be the ultimate authority.
2. When verification is not possible, quote an authority by name rather than releasing the statement under your own name. When the authority is capable of handling a media briefing without creating more problems than solved, make the authority available for questions—but maintain control over the session yourself. In this way detailed information will be released but you remain free to correct misinformation, if needed.
3. Respond quickly and authoritatively to media inquiries but do not rush into a response without full knowledge of your answer.
4. Speak candidly always. However, when information could cause panic or harm to innocent persons, select very carefully what is revealed and what goes unreleased.
5. Present facts; do not editorialize. Let the media draw their own conclusions about the government's actions. Editorialization is propaganda that frequently returns to haunt the speaker.
6. When facts are not available, help the media generate feature material. Reporters during a major running crisis *must* file stories. The lack of information often results in "creative" pieces based on misinformation, supposition, and rumors.
7. Centralization of the information function is essential. Otherwise, there will be confusion about the accuracy of comments and who is responsible for which actions. Decentralization increases intentional and unintentional misstatements. However, when queried, authorities should be free to answer media questions, knowing that ultimately they will be held accountable to their superiors if they pass along misinformation or comments which are detrimental to the effort, and then inform the public affairs officer about responses.
8. Establish a central location for the media to use for working and obtaining information. Attempt to "log in" media, listing their affiliations and *local* addresses so contacts can be made by your office about major changes in the situation.
9. Remember that your mandate is different from that of the media. Theirs is to report views; yours is to inform the public about actions, programs, and services. Generally, but not always, these two mandates run parallel on separate tracks.
10. The public affairs head must report directly to the top program official, participate in decisions, and have unimpeded access to all information, confidential and otherwise. Not only does this result in more responsive program decisions, it also builds credibility with the public and media.
11. Irrespective of the consequences, inject yourself firmly into *program* decisions if there is an overriding public interest to be served. Ultimately, your actions must answer the

dictates of your own conscience, and missed opportunities to serve higher ideals rarely return.

12. Use all available means to inform the people of the affected community. Expense is secondary during an emergency even if funds are not budgeted.

13. Insist that an ombudsman or similar independent channel of two-way communications be established so that the community can appeal bad decisions and circumvent needless bureaucratic entanglements. However, care must be taken that the appeals system does not overwhelm and supersede the normal handling of program activities.

14. When the emergency is over, leave as quickly as possible, allowing the flow of information to return to normal. Intrusion by the government for long periods into established communications channels can be extremely harmful. By its size and ability to dominate events, the government is capable of crippling the small news media of any community.

15. Keep a sense of humor—but don't show it. Humor can be misunderstood during a crisis and, after all, communities have their own comedians.

16. Enjoy the satisfaction of conveying information needed to save lives and property. After the emergency is over, everyone will recall the benefits and ills of program activities—but a successful public affairs program is never even observed.

CHAPTER 23

Agnes: The Politics of a Flood

Lewis M. Helm

Our Army helicopter settled onto a mud-splattered parking lot near the Mackin School in Wilkes-Barre, Pennsylvania. It was July 7, 1972, just after Hurricane Agnes had unleashed her $2 billion blow on the eastern seaboard of the United States. My party of four relief workers had flown in from Harrisburg, the state capital. Our flight party traced the wreckage-strewn course of the Susquehanna River to the center of devastation, Wilkes-Barre and the Wyoming Valley.

I recently had become top career public information officer of the Department of the Interior, an assignment which followed several years in government political positions and six months as a 1968 Nixon campaigner. On June 28, I had been assigned to Harrisburg by the White House to coordinate all federal public information in connection with Agnes—and quietly to develop recommendations to remove the faltering federal relief effort as a potentially negative presidential campaign issue.

As we climbed out of the helicopter, we saw MPs directing relief columns amidst emergency stock piles and field kitchens; the activity was much like that of a World War II army of occupation. We made our way to the Mackin School, a focal point of federal relief efforts. My party included Susquehanna River Basin Commissioner Thomas Webster, Army Lieutenant Colonel Robert Ragains, and Jan Corp, a representative of the minority leader's office of the state legislature.

Inside the school, flood victims sat dazed along dark hallways, calling out to us as we walked by. Relief workers from HUD, SBA, OEP, HEW, and other federal agencies, whose alphabet names meant little to the refugees, scurried about with sheaths of official-looking papers. Church groups, Red Cross and Salvation Army workers added to the sea of motion and noise. Odors of urine, vomit, and vegetable soup pervaded the air.

In a crowded basement room we found an army colonel surrounded by victims clamoring for his attention.

"What do you want? Who let you in?" he snarled. He had been at his post four nights and four days without relief. This colonel, whose regular assignment had been as an army reserve advisor in Pennsylvania, gave us our first detailed briefing on the Wyoming Valley situation.

The flood, he said, was a "200-year flood." The odds were against it happening more than once every two centuries. Yet 12 inches of rain had suddenly inundated the entire watershed of north-central Pennsylvania and lower New York. The water had rushed south, joining the weight of heavy spring rains near Wilkes-Barre, swelling tributaries and gullies, then plunging into the narrow banks of the Susquehanna and surging toward the Chesapeake Bay.

By early morning on June 23, the Susquehanna had swept over sand bags atop 35-year-old levees at an elbow bend in the river at Wilkes-Barre. A crest of 40.6 feet above normal turned the valley into an inland sea, its dozens of communities into islands.

Impact of Agnes

Elsewhere, Agnes's waters made murky messes of Pittsburgh, Philadelphia, Harrisburg, and most other river towns in Pennsylvania, New York, Maryland, Delaware, Virginia, and West Virginia. In Wilkes-Barre, only ham radios, army communications networks, and some broadcast stations on high ground provided contact with the outside world. Highways, railroads, telephone lines had been swept away. Local governments ceased to function, their leadership scattered among the 72,000 homeless in temporary shelters. The receding river had left 25,000 houses standing as small islands in the midst of silt, sludge, and black water.

The Federal Office of Emergency Preparedness had moved into place at the Mackin School to coordinate federal relief efforts. OEP was a small organization in the Office of the President. Each of its 10 regional offices normally was staffed by about seven persons. During a disaster, it assumed limited authority over personnel from other federal agencies. But OEP had too few people in Pennsylvania, or the entire United States, to cope with such a massive crisis management assignment.

The wide devastation made accurate information unobtainable. And since the facts just weren't there, no organized relief effort was immediately possible. Federal, state, and local governments lacked resources to find out exactly what Agnes had done and what types of relief were most needed. No one knew the numbers of dead and homeless or the degree of disruption to essential services. In fact, it took about a month to determine just how much Agnes had drained from Pennsylvania and poured into the Chesapeake. This delayed effective mobilization of relief at all levels of government.

Reports came from our pilot that more rain squalls were headed toward the Wyoming Valley, so we hurried back to the helicopter to return to Harrisburg. At heights of 200 to 400 feet our pilot circled the area. Smoke from smoldering culm bank fires put a deep haze over the valley. On most buildings a stain near the second floor windows showed where waters had reached at flood crest. Throughout the city American flags could be seen fluttering from windows, porches, poles in remembrance of July 4. A billboard on high ground proclaimed, "A Valley with a Heart . . . Coming Back Better Than Ever." I learned later that OEP had bought and distributed the flags. The billboard was leased to keep morale high in the face of depressing times.

Our helicopter rose, turned, and headed southwest. Sheets of rain sprayed against it as we climbed over the mountains. We were forced to land twice during the 75-mile flight back to the Federal Building in Harrisburg, the site from which the most massive domestic relief operation in history was soon to be launched. During the next six months, 12,000 federal employees and persons under federal contract poured into the flood area from almost every state. Two dozen or more federal agencies, in cooperation with state and local governments, took part in the recovery effort. In fact, just about every available office in the Wyoming Valley was leased for the use of the federal government, but that still was not enough office space.

The Department of Housing and Urban Development brought mobile homes from as far as the West Coast to establish mobile home parks for displaced residents. Other mobile homes were placed on lots next to ravaged homes for families to live in while they repaired their houses. In all, 8000 mobile homes were dispatched to the Wyoming Valley.

The U.S. Army Corps of Engineering repaired the levees, cleaned streets, connected utilities, and sealed homes for the coming winter. The Small Business Administration granted $500 million in easy-term loans to 60,000 homeowners and 3500 businesses to help them rebuild. Hospitals, schools, the elderly, disabled, and poor all were assisted by the U.S. Department of Health, Education, and Welfare.

The Agriculture Department worked with the farmers, Transportation with highway systems, Interior with recreation areas and mines, while the army provided safety and supply assistance. Free buses shuttled around the valley. Meals on wheels, schools, and mental health care were provided.

Money had become no problem once President Nixon proposed emergency assistance legislation following a thorough assessment of the damage. Additional funds were given to state and local governments to enable them to hire experts who knew the procedures on how to obtain even more funds. Sufficient labor was available although there were squabbles about union and nonunion workers. In fact, the recovery effort brought such an influx of workers that it was impossible to find a spare bed in 50 miles. Yet, as I flew back to Harrisburg from Wilkes-Barre that day, it was difficult to envisage that the federal relief effort would come together successfully.

Harrisburg

My assignment began on June 28 when Robert Hitt, Executive Assistant to Interior Secretary Rogers C. B. Morton, telephoned me to say that on White House instructions I would go to Harrisburg to coordinate the public affairs part of the flood relief efforts. Des Barker, special assistant to the president, would give further instructions the next morning before I left for Pennsylvania.

Des was succinct. The federal flood flood relief effort was not falling into place quickly enough. Philadelphia Mayor Rizzo, who probably would support the president's reelection campaign that fall, was on the phone every hour trying to stir up faster action. Governor Milton J. Shapp, a strong Democratic opponent, apparently had seized the flood relief effort as a campaign issue and was attempting to blame the administration for ineptitude and apathy.

My job was to help the White House "neutralize" the situation, to make it a nonissue. I was to see what was happening, report back shortcomings in personnel and programs, and focus public attention on the positive steps being taken by the administration. The president wanted his 1972 reelection campaign built around administration accomplishments, not flood relief—or any other shortcomings.

After meeting with Barker and John Whitaker, Assistant Director of the Domestic Council (the person who would handle program-oriented decisions), I drove three hours to the Federal Building in Harrisburg. OEP already had assembled its key people and others were coming in to support the centralized public information operation. William Tidball from OEP Dallas became my deputy. Carl Shaw was on detail from the Rural Electrification Administration as our backup. Other public information specialists—such as Willard Foist from SBA, Jerome Fitzpatrick from the Army, and Wynn Moseley from HUD—were assigned on their way to Harrisburg to help.

Each information specialist was charged with telling the public all of the things his or her agency was doing to help bring relief. Naturally, an organizational problem developed when I attempted to coordinate the flow of information from them through a central office in Harrisburg. I lacked the authority that only Washington-based agency information chiefs had to make assignments and exercise quality control. So, the White House occasionally was called on to intercede with the agencies to see their employees complied with the needs at the disaster site. Some uncooperative persons were reassigned away from the flood area.

Quelling interagency squabbling was necessary because it was essential to let the media know that one information office was responsible for all coordination of the flood information on which they based their news coverage. I began publishing a daily "Round-up" of federal assistance, releasing it to all media covering the flood. I held daily briefings at the state capitol building. A list of information officers, identifying their specialties and office locations, was also released.

We avoided any feature or "color" types of releases, opting for straight news announcements. This eliminated any potential criticism of us for trying to get cheap publicity from the suffering of flood victims. In the meantime Governor Shapp continued to press his attack on federal relief efforts. Time and again key media in the state quoted him as saying that the federal effort was as big a disaster as the flood . . . that Nixon was sending help "too little and too late."

We launched a public information counteroffensive. On Saturday, July 1, I developed a four-page mailer to be sent to every postal delivery address in the state. It explained where to apply for help, what emergency stations had been set up, and what aid could be expected. Its purpose was to tell what the president and his administration were doing to help. It read:

> President Nixon has ordered every federal agency to assist flood disaster victims as rapidly as humanly possible. To carry out his instructions, the following sites have been established to provide federal aid. Additional offices and changes in locations will be made as required to provide maximum service. Here is a detailed informational guide listing locations of federal agencies which you may contact for emergency assistance. . . .

I called the Harrisburg Post Office, only to find it had closed at noon Saturday. So, I tracked down the regional duty officer. I explained that it was vital to reach thousands of flood victims who had no real idea of where to obtain help. I explained that we had to make it known where food and shelter could be found and that a critical way to do so was through a swift and massive mailing to every business and residence in the state. The post office's help was desperately needed.

"We're closed for the weekend," he replied.

"I know. That's why I'm calling you at home now. We can't wait until Monday."

"You'll have to call back then. I can't help you."

"Let me restate the question," I exploded. "In 30 minutes I will be briefing two dozen reporters and facing a row of television cameras, telling about what we plan to do to help flood victims. You have a choice. I can tell them that the post office is cooperating fully on a massive mailing to everyone in the state . . . or I can tell them that you said the post office is closed for the weekend and won't help. Which way do you want it?"

The mailing, which turned out to be the biggest single one ever made, went out as planned. A two-year fight did ensue as to who would pay for it . . . OEP or the Post Office.

The White House staff also followed up on an early suggestion that they schedule cabinet members for a fact-finding mission to Pennsylvania, in a further effort to show presidential concern. An Air Force jet took off from Andrews Air Force Base on Monday, July 3, bound for Harrisburg carrying secretary of Labor James D. Hodgson, secretary of Commerce Peter G. Peterson, OEP Director George Lincoln, SBA Deputy Director Anthony Chase, and several others. A series of private and public meetings had been arranged for them, including a press conference at the Penn Harris Hotel.

A young special assistant to an assistant secretary of Commerce was assigned to advance the VIP trip while I arranged the meetings and worked with the media.

He didn't have time to heed advice that he should stick with the entourage. However, he did appear to have everything under control.

A motorcade with state troopers was dispatched to the Capital City Airport for the cabinet entourage's arrival at 8:10 A.M. The advance man waited with the rest of us at the hotel. It wasn't until 8:45 A.M. that the phone rang. It was the VIP party. The police had been sent to the wrong airport!

"Ahhhhh! I've been screwed! I'm dead!" the special assistant shrieked, as he appeared to crumple onto the floor of the press conference room. But despite the initial confusion, the VIPs took cabs and arrived a short time later. The special assistant survived and the state appreciated their visit.

Confronting the Governor

Governor Shapp stepped up his attack, charging the cabinet-level visit was not enough . . . the state didn't need a visit by superbureaucrats . . . if Nixon cared about people, he would have come himself. In our next telephone conversation, Barker and Whitaker both felt that it was essential to confront the governor more directly. Otherwise, our relief efforts would continue to be both unsupported and unappreciated.

We decided that I would give an "emotional" and spontaneous statement to the media about how the governor's continued sniping was counterproductive. The resulting news coverage would serve notice that, if he continued in his present vein, his own comments would be subjected to continued active rebuttal.

The operational head of OEP, I was instructed, should not be told about my statement until after the fact. He was to continue to concentrate on substantive program problems while I handled the public statement. I also was told the head of the Regional Council was not to make any public comment about what I released.

On July 5, at a 3 P.M. press briefing in the Capitol Building, I said:

> We are losing our patience with Governor Shapp playing politics while we're here to help the destitute people of Pennsylvania. He consistently ignores the facts. I have avoided replying until now but feel I must do so because these attacks by the governor cannot help but have a detrimental effect on the morale of the 12,000 federal workers here in this state, working tirelessly day and night to assist flood victims.

This was followed with radio interviews.

When I returned to my office, an SBA news release was on my desk. It had been sent out the day before, and it praised the high degree of cooperation between state and federal officials. This was in direct conflict with my recent statement. The author, who had failed to clear the piece, was quickly reassigned away from TDY in Harrisburg.

The OEP head called me to his office, too. He was shocked that I had made such a statement. He further said he planned to make his own statement to undo the damage I had done. I advised him that the White House's instructions were for him to say only that from his position as program chief, all sides were doing the "best we can to work together." He called OPE Washington, then reluctantly agreed with me. His agency superior, Retired Army General George Lincoln, had already been briefed.

The next day the governor's special assistant telephoned. "What message are you trying to give the governor? We want to kiss and make up."

"The only message not in the release," I replied, "is to quit pissing on us. Then we'll make up."

"It's a deal," he responded.

My White House contacts, Barker and Whitaker, both were relieved. "Lay off and see what he does. We'll play it straight in the meantime."

The next day Governor Shapp's press secretary confirmed what his colleague had said. "There aren't any problems. Why did we wait so long?" The flood relief effort continued. There were no more public exchanges. So I told Barker that it was time for me to return home. He agreed . . . but said I should wait several more days. That's when we took the helicopter flight to Wilkes-Barre, so I could give the White House a current and complete picture of the hardest hit area.

The night before I left Harrisburg our little group of information officers gathered on the Starlight Roof of the Holiday Motor Hotel. We celebrated and sang "Ole Man River" while viewing the still high Susquehanna. But as I drove back to Washington on July 9, I felt uneasy. I wondered what effect the skirmishes between federal and state officials had on the flood victims. It really could have turned them off the system. I also realized that my career position at Interior was gone, even though I did not violate the Hatch Act.[1] There would be no survival, whether a Democratic administration was elected in November, or not.

But most of all, it was great to be going home.

Return to Pennsylvania

Three days after my return, the president asked Congress for a vast amount of additional flood relief, the largest dollar sum of humanitarian assistance ever rendered by government. Before doing so, however, he met with key state and federal officials to discuss the proposals. A quiet Governor Shapp attended. I was assigned by the White House to greet him as he entered . . . and to attend the session with the president. The gubernatorial submissiveness didn't last, however. A new round of political warfare erupted two weeks later, and the White House ordered me back to Pennsylvania, this time to Wilkes-Barre, where the heaviest destruction still was leaving an indelible imprint.

The decision to press again for a stronger federal public affairs effort was based on news headlines such as: "Woman Questions HUD Inspections" . . . "HUD Snafu Continues" . . . "Camper Has Extra Hitch, Promised Hookup Fails To Arrive" . . . "Unable to Get Trailer, 9 Move into HUD Offices" . . . "Key Problems Hamper Work in Flood Areas."

I spent the night of July 29 in Harrisburg on the way to Wilkes-Barre. This time, I felt as though I might never be free from the flood.

Public information activity in Wilkes-Barre had been uncoordinated, to say the least. No plan had been developed for generating maximum coverage for the federal efforts. Programs available to victims were going unnoticed or misunderstood. Few new programs to solve specific problems had been generated. I called a 7 A.M. breakfast meeting at my Scranton hotel, some 20 miles from OEP headquarters, and outlined to the information staff how our activities would be handled.

No release would be sent without my clearance. A phone service for radio stations would be established through which they could call in and tape "actualities" daily for their news shows. We would have daily press briefings. No feature releases would be sent. Moreover, we would actively seek and recommend program changes, meaning we could function as ombudsmen.

I asked the White House to replace several information officers in Wilkes-Barre with one of my Harrisburg colleagues and with an Interior Department broadcast expert. They would be my deputies.

I urged Barker at the White House to send HUD Secretary Romney to Wilkes-

Barre, as much for his down-to-earth appeal as because HUD had the most problems. Romney arrived August 8. I met him at the airport to brief him about our plans for the next day. But he refused to see me. Not until the next afternoon did I realize that Romney was fuming because he had been ordered to Pennsylvania by a person he deemed subordinate—Domestic Council Chief John Ehrlichmann—and that the president had refused to talk to him about it.

Against my counsel, Romney met simultaneously with Governor Shapp, the media, and flood victims. The media event went something like this:

Shapp: "The federal government should pay off all the old mortgages of flood victims!"

Romney: "That's unrealistic demagoguery that's being used to fuzz up the flood recovery effort with political issues!"

Min Matheson, 63-year-old union organizer: "I don't believe you give a damn whether we live or die!"

Romney, a head taller, held his arm around Shapp's shoulder and grasped the latter's neck. Each time Romney wanted to emphasize a point he would squeeze the governor's neck and pull him back away from the cameras. Min stood in front of both and shouted throughout the hour.

Despite its length, the news conference included only three questions from reporters. I was squatted in front of Romney writing notes. He kept waving his finger alternatively at Shapp and me.

Finally, the conference broke up. When reporters followed the red-faced Romney, he turned and, flushed with anger, snapped, "The president told me to report to him, not to you!" The stiff-necked Shapp remained silent.

News coverage rated the two politicians an even draw. The flood victims got the sympathy.

In my subsequent call to Barker and Whitaker, we agreed that the recovery effort urgently needed someone in Wilkes-Barre who could personally represent the president and make immediate major decisions. That person had to be able to cause residents to identify with him *personally*, to see that he could help them mold bureaucracy to their urgent needs. To accomplish this, he also had to be both extremely knowledgeable about the ways of government and competent to make the relief effort work. Without such a person, the chief effort would be dissipated by endless squabbling such as between Secretary Romney and Governor Shapp.

Frank Carlucci, a native of Wilkes-Barre, and the hard-working, bright and young Deputy Director of the Office of Management and Budget, was stagecast for the job. He was a career government employee with a record of success in humanitarian concerns, particularly with the Office of Economic Opportunity.

Carlucci Arrives

Carlucci arrived on Saturday, August 12, by presidential helicopter from Camp David. He held a press conference that afternoon to introduce himself as President Nixon's personal representative. To help give the victims a recognizable government leader with whom they could identify, he took immediate steps to become a central figure in the effort. He would have a daily "open house" to hear the people's problems directly and to attempt to cut red tape.

At 11 A.M. each day there would be a "Report to the People," in which he would outline federal relief plans and answer media questions. He began walking through the valley for a minimum of one hour a day, to meet people, hear problems, and show the federal presence. All relief staff members were to follow suit in their public dealings.

Carlucci began to bring top federal officials into the valley regularly, to show interest, respond to questions, and solve problems. Each official would join him in front of the TV cameras at the "Report to the People." The media and public responded warmly and with relief to their native son. News stories, television, and radio coverage began to sound like this Wilkes-Barre *Record/Leader* article:

> Frank Carlucci, the President's personal representative, here to coordinate the federal flood recovery operation, had the blessings of at least 25 displaced persons late Monday afternoon after lending an attentive ear to their complaints.
>
> Carlucci sat with two aides and listened to each complaint in an office trailer at Scanlon Field, Kingston, where open house for flood victims will continue to be held from 4–5 P.M. daily.

From these personal meetings developed "Carlucci Specials," actions to help victims in emergency calls, which often required the federal agencies involved to alter their priorities and produce quick, visible results.[2]

Every day at an early staff meeting Carlucci met with key flood workers from each agency. Based on their reports of needs, plans were developed to create new programs. Carlucci, still acting with the authority of OMB, would contact the heads of agencies which could address the problems. Where a solution lay beyond agency authority, direct White House action would follow to put the program in place.

Every step of the operation was explained openly at Carlucci's daily "Report to the People." Following the staff meetings, a barrage of news releases was prepared for Carlucci's use at the daily press conference. During one typical day, August 29, the following were released:

> "Frank Carlucci, the President's personal representative to the Wyoming Valley, announced today the arrival Wednesday of the Honorable John Volpe, the Secretary of the Department of Transportation." The release outlined Volpe's itinerary including an appearance at Wednesday's "Report to the People."

> "The U.S. Department of Housing and Urban Development has lifted its ceiling of $200 on payments to flood victims who had their own utilities connected to mobile homes on individual sites, it was announced today by Frank C. Carlucci, the President's personal representative." The release then explained why the action was taken and how it would benefit victims.

> '"I have been assured that no major subsidence will occur in areas of the Wyoming Valley that were flooded during Hurricane Agnes," President Nixon's personal representative, Frank Carlucci, declared today during his "Report to the People." ' He then explained that the entire area had been surveyed by the U.S. Bureau of Mines and that it was safe from sinking into coal shafts.

> "Frank Carlucci, President Nixon's personal representative in the Wyoming Valley, said today that his office is still receiving many questions concerning the Internal Revenue Service ruling on casualty loss deductions, in those cases where an SBA loan is involved." It then explained the complex IRS ruling.

> "In summing up the municipal conference held Monday at King's College, Frank Carlucci, the President's personal representative, had the following words. . . ." He then explained how the federal government would help cities plan their economic development and where they could obtain funds for police, garbage collection, and so forth.

> "U.S. Department of Health, Education and Welfare has granted a total of more than $100,000,000 through federal, state and local agencies for the Wyoming Valley flood recovery program, according to Frank Carlucci, personal representative of President

Nixon to the Wyoming Valley." He then showed where the federal funds were used to help restore educational operations.

TV Coverage

Television crews would shoot the entire press briefing. One regular exclaimed, as his crew was tearing down, "Well, that's tonight's news show!" Radio newscasters rarely attended the sessions. Sophisticated tapings were made of each announcement. These were edited by a local former broadcaster. The spots were called directly to local stations and the tape was also connected to a local phone so that any reporter could obtain the edited messages by dialing a given number. Print media used almost all the releases verbatim. In one front-page article taken directly from our release, the *Recorder/Leader* even printed our instructions, to "See Attached," which referred to some appended statistical data.

The first major national media coverage of our progress under Carlucci was Mary Russell's piece in the *Washington Post*. In a front-page piece headed, "Carlucci Cuts Red Tape on Flood Aid," she wrote:

> Frank Carlucci has an assignment right out of "Mission Impossible."
> The Deputy Director of the Office of Management and Budget has been assigned by the President to return to his home town here and pick up the pieces of a federal flood relief program that has received almost as much bad publicity as the flood itself.
> So far, he has been successful to a large degree.

She then reported charges of ineffectiveness along with the facts about how and why the situation was handled as it was. She quoted Carlucci's response to Governor Shapp's charges of excessive publicity:

> "Good public relations is one of the area's most critical needs, along with a sense the government wasn't an impersonal, uncaring monster," he said.
> "I instituted a daily 'Report to the People,' where we began telling them everything government was doing. I think one of the main problems was the flood victims were not getting information about what was going on," Carlucci said.
> "Then I immediately made myself available at a particular period every day. I was under orders from the President to do that. He also ordered me to go out and walk and I have done that."
> "It is necessary to let people know that, as the President's representative, I'm interested in their problems."

Governor Shapp had renewed his intensive effort to discredit the relief effort, claiming that it was all public relations without substance. His Lieutenant Governor, Ernest Kline, spoke at a Wilkes-Barre press conference, September 8:

> Washington has publicly promised much and privately delivered little. The federal representatives have clearly orchestrated their public relations and have evolved a "minor league game plan" into a major league disaster.
> The Feds have concentrated on bringing in many PR men to lay down a barrage of slick Madison Avenue PR, to give the public the impression of a great deal of forward progress on the part of the Feds, but in reality have covered up their indecisiveness and inaction and unwillingness to bring to the resolution of the problem the vast resources which only the federal government has available.

Kline's attack was muted by what had become a trend of media support for our efforts. At the press conference, the Associated Press reporter asked him how his remarks tracked with the fact that federal relief was nine-to-one more than state relief.

Editorials told Shapp to quit quibbling. All this occurred just one month to the day after Romney's ill-fated visit. The turnaround took place because the Wyoming Valley people had faith in Frank Carlucci and, therefore, in the government that served them. The progressive programs the government had instituted were proof of what Carlucci said.

Carlucci, told that he would be summoned to Camp David for a meeting with the president on September 12, prepared a report detailing federal actions past and future to be released at Camp David. His memorandum to the president read:

> I've walked across the square in Wilkes-Barre back to my office from a meeting three blocks away. It took 45 minutes. Friends of my family would stop me. Others would shake my hand and say, "Tell the President he's doing great." Some would say thanks. Then, there were many who would ask for help.

Positive as it was, Carlucci's description of the recovery never became a news item. It was buried by a bigger story, the ultimate federal event.

A Presidential Visit

September 12 was a quiet Saturday morning. Des Barker's warning that I had better get some rest Friday night seemed meaningless. We had finished our information officers' staff meeting in which we mapped plans for Carlucci's return. The phone rang. It was Carlucci.

"Lew. Don't say anything. There isn't time. Just listen. We're leaving Camp David in five minutes. The president's coming. John Ehrlichman will be with him. Don't tell anyone. He wants it to be a surprise. He especially doesn't want Shapp to find out and meet him there.

"Arrange for six cars. Tell them to meet us at the Dan Flood School at noon. Work up where the president should go. Include a visit to the Scanlon mobile homes. Get that $4 million check for Wilkes College. We'll give it to Dr. Michelini. We'll leave from Forty Fort Airport.

"Don't tell the state police. Shapp will hear . . . and don't tell anyone else. Give the media a place to meet us for an important announcement. I've got to go now."

A presidential advance in a one hour time frame! He hung up and I started talking to the information officers still in my office.

"I can't tell you anything more than this," I began, "But we have to handle Frank's return as tightly and effectively as though the president were with him."

Jack Murphy took charge of the motor caravan meeting the president. Pat Patterson of GSA pulled together the cars, drivers, and police escort. Lieutenant Colonel Richard Hewitt from the Corps of Engineers took charge of communications and the headquarters.

Dick Whitaker was assigned to tape everything the president and Carlucci said. He, Agnes Mravcak, and John Bush called the media, saying we would have an extremely important story, that they should show up at Wilkes College at 12:30 P.M., and wait. We emphasized that it would be of national interest.

Jim Stueve of the Administration on Aging went with Bill Foist and Mary Murphy to the Carlucci office trailer in Scanlon Park. They alerted the people in that area that Carlucci wanted to have an important meeting at 1:30 P.M.

William Swarm and Bert Lane from OEP quickly got the $4 million check for Wilkes College and alerted the college president, Dr. Francis Michelini, to be ready to receive the check in front of the media at 12:30 P.M. He was asked to set up his conference room.

Everyone disappeared from my office; in the next hour a thousand mistakes could occur. I told Col. Hewitt that I'd go to Wilkes College, where the first and most important event would take place. If something went wrong, that's where it would be.

I arrived at Wilkes College. Most of the media had not even speculated that the president would visit. At 12:55 P.M. the phone call from the Flood School came.

"May I have your attention, please," I announced. "Earlier today Frank Carlucci was called to Camp David by the president. Mr. Nixon agreed to return to the Wyoming Valley with him. They have just landed at the Flood School and will be here momentarily. For security reasons, please remain where you are until he has arrived and then left Wilkes College."

The media roared approval. And they remained in place.

President Nixon, followed by Carlucci, arrived with a warm smile, a greeting for everyone. He called Dr. Michelini forward and presented the check "from all of the people of the United States with our best wishes for a speedy recovery."

Invitation to a Picnic

As he stopped speaking, Jill Garrett, a young, attractive, black relief worker, urged me to invite the president to the flood victims' picnic next weekend.

"You do it," I said and pushed her into the center of the floor in front of the president and the media. She did beautifully. Nixon responded graciously that he could not do so but promised to send the White House mess staff to cater the picnic. That delighted the crowd . . . and generated a wire photo used in papers around the country showing Jill and the president. (The catered picnic was a rare success too.)

He held no press conference. Instead, he shook hands with every worker and reporter. As I followed him out to join the motorcade to Scanlon Park, Helen Thomas of UPI spotted me and remembered my political campaign work from the past. She was one of two pool reporters chosen to accompany the president on that trip.

"I knew they were lying. You advanced this trip, didn't you? It really was not a spur-of-the-moment decision!"

"Sorry, Helen. It really was. I've been working up here for about three months handling the flood recovery public information. This was a surprise to me, too."

A crowd had gathered at the Scanlon mobile homes, eagerly cheering the president's every word. Again he took each outreached hand, voicing praise for their spirit and hard work. On the way back to Forty Fort where two helicopters awaited, Nixon spotted a wedding party. Daniel Conte and Catherine Pickering were just coming down the steps of the Forty Fort Presbyterian Church.

Nixon stopped the motorcade and approached the amazed couple. "Where's your marriage certificate," he asked, signing it on the witness line. He gave Rev. Harold Mante, the pastor, a $20 contribution for the church.

"Wow! When I have a wedding, I have a wedding!" the groom shouted.

This photo made the Sunday newspapers that Jill's did not.

After several more stops, the president made his way to the Forty Fort field. A local announcer, overwhelmed by the day's events, reported live to his listeners by way of a nearby phone:

> I can see the helicopters on the field now. They will take the President of the United States back to Camp David after this historic day. I can see the name on the first 'copter. It's name is "United States of America." I can see the second 'copter's name. It also is "United States of America." Both planes are named "United States of America"!

The President's visit was a total success. The Wilkes-Barre *Times/Leader* editorialized:

> Thank You, Mr. Nixon! Never before in Wyoming Valley's lengthy history was there a more spine-tingling spectacle than the unprecedented surprise visit here yesterday of the nation's Chief Executive. . . . Mr. Nixon, we thank you from the bottom of our hearts!

A spate of negative editorials about Lieutenant Governor Kline and Governor Shapp followed.

Reaction from the White House came to me in the form of a September 15 memo from Barker: "Inasmuch as I have not received a written report on your activities since the first of August, I will accept the attached story." It was a UPI wire story by Sara Fritz, datelined from Harrisburg, Pennsylvania:

> President Nixon has widened his edge over George S. McGovern in Pennsylvania with a polished campaign to tell voters what the Administration has done for the flood victims.
>
> Although the polls give Nixon a 17 percent lead, the President was losing face among thousands of flood victims last month as Democratic Governor Milton J. Shapp relentlessly criticized federal disaster aid.
>
> Both Democrats and Republicans now agree the trend was reversed by public relations and a surprise presidential visit September 9 [*sic*] to Wilkes-Barre—the state's hardest hit area during Tropical Storm Agnes. . . .

Winding Down the Effort

My main problem after that was keeping the Nixon Reelection Committee and the Republican National Committee out of the state to prevent them from boasting about flood relief successes. I felt that the victims and the campaign would be ill-served by heavy-handed "puffs" while so many still suffered. The White House agreed. All campaign efforts in Pennsylvania were stopped.

By October 1, it had become obvious that little more needed to be done. Our last problem was to extricate a large part of the federal team without having the flood victims feel they had been abandoned too soon. We carefully developed our strategy. Carlucci cut down the number of open-door sessions to every other day, then once a week. News conferences would be decreased similarly. Public reaction was minimal.

The only criticism thereafter came from investigative reporter Jack Anderson. HUD information officers had reported in October that Anderson was coming to the valley. They had heard he would focus on HUD's shortcomings. Carlucci and I both instructed HUD officials to give Anderson every possible courtesy, to answer questions fully and accurately, and, otherwise, to leave him alone.

Apparently, they followed other mandates from HUD Washington. On December 20, long after Carlucci and his key people had left Wilkes-Barre, Anderson wrote: "I was taken on a quick tour of the devastated area. Trailing my car, I later learned, were two of Carlucci's agents. They were Michael Guzzi and Larry Martin, who had been assigned to go where I went, see what I said and whether I left any reporters behind."[3]

Anderson then charged that Carlucci had caused havoc, failing to generate anything but publicity. Another Anderson story followed on January 1, using gossip from Carlucci detractors but lacking substance. The Wilkes-Barre *Sunday Independent* responded: "Anderson Badly Misinformed . . . The People Have Judged Carlucci, They Have Not Found Him Wanting."

Carlucci began to divide his time between Washington, D.C., and Wilkes-Barre.

By the time I returned home on November 2, Carlucci was visiting the valley only once a week. The initial recovery effort was over and the job of long-term rebuilding had started.

Notes

1. The Hatch Act, signed into law in 1939 by a somewhat reluctant President Franklin D. Roosevelt, specifically forbids civil servants from certain forms of partisan political activity.
2. Indeed, representatives of the National Institute for Mental Health found at this point that a marked increase in depression and threatened suicides noted in the wake of the disaster had begun to decline toward more normal levels. Those working on this project believed that the positive effects our highly visible program had on the flood victims helped expedite this trend.
3. Jack Anderson, "Bureaucratic Havoc in Agnes' Wake," *Washington Post* (20 December 1972), p. D. 19.

CHAPTER 24

Sunshine Mine: Handling the Media in a Disaster

Lewis M. Helm

Late in the morning of Tuesday, May 2, 1972, smoke and deadly fumes began to fill the Sunshine silver mine near Kellogg, Idaho. The 173 men on the morning crew tried to escape from depths of 3100 feet to one mile, but the evacuation was hampered as the carbon monoxide gas rapidly spread, killing hoist operators before most of the miners could reach the surface. Only 80 successfully fled, leaving another 93 trapped.

Although rescue efforts continued for nine days, only two trapped miners returned to the surface alive. They had been buried for one week in a tunnel 4800 feet below the surface, surviving by eating from the lunch pails of their dead companions and drinking water from an air conditioner hose.

Investigations into the disaster never determined its exact cause, but the fire apparently resulted from spontaneous combustion in piles of old timber stacked in unused portions of the mine. In any case, the disaster pointed out a myriad of deficiences in the Metal and Nonmetallic Mine Safety Act, not the least of which was that it failed to address the possible incidence of fires, previously thought only to occur in coal mines.

The act placed responsibility for enforcement in the hands of the Bureau of Mines, an agency of the Department of the Interior at the time. The bureau also was charged with assisting the minerals industry with research and marketing. This simultaneous relationship as "promoter," on the one hand, and as "enforcer" on the other, added credence to charges that the bureau was "soft on industry" and reluctant to enforce health and safety measures.

In addition, the act gave little enforcement power. Inspectors were required to visit mines at least once a year. Moreover, only if safety and health violations were major, or were not corrected in a reasonable time, could the bureau post an "immediate withdrawal order" to remove all miners until corrections were made.

Adding to the enforcement problems was the general reaction of a large number of miners against government intervention of any kind. Much like the relationship of Tennesee "moonshiners" and "revenuers," the miners of the Coeur d'Alenes resented U.S. and state mine inspectors "checking up on us." No one wanted to lose pay because of a withdrawal order or to get black marks for poor safety. So, often when the bureau notified a union it planned to inspect a mine (notification was required so a union safety representative could be present), the union would tip off management so corrections could be made.

Between 1966 when Congress passed this act and 1970 when it finally went into effect, a major coal mine disaster at Huntington, West Virginia, resulted in the strict Coal Mine Health and Safety Act, also administered by the bureau, which required penalties, public hearings, "stop work" orders, and established very specific standards for enforcement. The public, confused by the two acts, laid blame on the bureau for laxity of enforcement in areas over which it had little control. This, coupled with numerous errors over which it did have control, had resulted in a sharp drop in the bureau's reputation and credibility by the early 1970s.

So, to separate the function of "enforcer" from "promoter" and to generate more strict compliance with the law, assistant secretary for Mineral Resources Hollis M. Dole split the functions of the bureau into "research" and "health and safety," placing a deputy director over each. This was the position in which the Bureau found itself at the time of Sunshine.

I had been Dole's deputy for programs and planning for three years until several months before the disaster, when I assumed a career position in Interior's Office of Communications as the second-ranking information officer. But, because of my knowledge of mineral resource programs and personnel, I was usually called when there was a public affairs problem in that area.

My role with Sunshine began on the evening of the disaster with a phone call at my home from Donald P. Schlick, Bureau of Mines deputy director. He reported that a major disaster was developing and gave details of what had occurred so far. He was sending three top bureau engineers to the scene from Washington, D.C., the first thing Wednesday morning. I telephoned wire services and major newspapers to let them know that a team of experts was on the way from the bureau.

Dole had been charged with the rescue responsibility by Secretary Rogers C. B. Morton. He accepted on the condition that I be assigned as the only government spokesman at the scene and in Washington, D.C., because he believed that the disaster would be a "running story" even after recovery operations were completed. A congressional hearing was certain to follow to establish fault and to recommend new legislation. Thus, it was critical that statements to the media be carefully considered.

The Flight West

So, the next morning I joined Dr. Elburt F. Osborn, bureau director, at Dulles Airport where a chartered Lear Jet waited to fly us west. Bureau reports of Sunshine inspections, copies of the Metal and Nonmetal Health and Safety Act of 1966, implementing regulations, and other data had been delivered to the plane at my request. Dr. Osborn and I needed the six hour flight to become familiar with the mine's record of accidents and with details of bureau responsibilities under the law.

After reviewing the mine's past violations, Dr. Osborn told me that none of them seemingly could have been responsible for the fire. Even the electrical violations found were not major enough to have caused this type of disaster. Besides, all of the violations had been corrected to the satisfaction of the bureau in March.

We also planned the media strategy. I would distribute copies of the inspection reports. These would be explained by Dr. Osborn. He would announce that the department would conduct public hearings into the cause of the disaster but emphasize that, under the law, we could only assist the mine management with the rescue effort, not be responsible for it. After an initial press conference, Dr. Osborn, at my request, would be available to the media while I retained responsibility for public statements. A bureau mining engineer, James Winston, would be assigned to assist me with technical briefings for the media.

A helicopter from the 42nd Air Rescue Recovery Squadron, Fairchild Air Force Base, was waiting at the Spokane airport to fly us to Kellogg. Secretary Morton met us at the Kellogg airport. He had flown from Los Angeles a few hours before to express President Nixon's concern and commitment to help. We drove together up the winding road through Big Creek Canyon for a briefing at the Sunshine office.

Cars of sightseers and rescuers lined the narrow road winding from Interstate 90 to the cluster of mine buildings near the upper reaches of the canyon. Several hundred men and women had gathered. Television vans, cars, trucks, and people jammed the parking lot. A crowd stood near the mine entrance.

Inside, vice president and general manager Marvin Chase introduced his staff and then turned the briefing over to the head of the rescue operations, Gordon Miner, of neighboring Heckla Mining Company. As in most disasters, control of rescue operations was turned over to engineers from a neighboring mine, to obtain outside expertise, to get additional workers, and to permit the stricken mine's management to focus on the needs of the victims' families.

Miner told us nine bodies had been recovered and about 100 men were still trapped. He drew a rough diagram showing how air was being supplied to the mine through a four foot bore hole, known as Number 12 Shaft. Chase then introduced Lem Jones, corporate relations counsel, as the person who would handle media contacts for the company. He would be advised by the corporate attorney.

Outside, Secretary Morton announced to the media that he had instructed the bureau to make every person and piece of equipment available to help as needed. He pointed out that the rescue responsibility belonged to the company but that he would make sure the entire federal government supported the effort. He then introduced Dr. Osborn.

Osborn said that this was the worst disaster since 1917 when 163 men were killed in a Montana copper mine. He pledged that public hearings would be held once the rescue was completed and then discussed the mine's previous inspections by the bureau. Responding to a question, Dr. Osborn said that federal regulations do not require fire drills and that new regulations probably would result from the disaster.

Role of Law and Regulations

Secretary Morton then introduced me as the department's spokesman. He again sympathized with the grieving families and departed for the airport. I telephoned Dole to let him know details of the day. He was irate over Osborn's announcement that new regulations could be expected. This, he believed, immediately put us on the defensive. Tighter regulations had never been issued, he said, because of the present law's vagueness. Legislation, not regulations, probably would be required. Now, we would be in the position of attempting to explain to an emotional media and Congress why we had not published tighter regulations before this, and that the primary fault lay in the legislation passed earlier.

Dole emphasized three times that I would be the only person talking with the media in the future. He also vetoed Dr. Osborn's plan to return to Washington the next day. About 30 reporters, including those from most of the national media, showed up for my 8 A.M. Thursday conference. I made the following points:

> Although copies of the mine inspections had not yet been reproduced, the original reports were available for media perusal after the conference.
> Inspections had been conducted three times since the regulations were published in 1970. Details of the violations were given along with the concluding report that all violations were corrected by March, 1972.
> Three men had been killed by accidents since 1969, and the company seemed at fault in each case.
> A survey of toxic fumes was conducted in 1966.

I was asked if this was a "bad mine" and responded that it probably was slightly better in safety than many others. When asked if previous violations could have caused the fire, I referred to Dr. Osborn's previous statement and said that I believed none of the violations could have caused the disaster. Several reporters complained that security police dictated where they could go and that no area had been designated where they could write or phone their offices.

I met with Lem Jones, an affable veteran of many political and journalistic wars. He was an independent public relations counselor to the Sunshine Mine Corporation and desperately wanted me to be fully responsible for releasing all information about the disaster, thereby minimizing the company's involvement. I agreed—except Chase would be responsible for giving accounts of deaths and of actions taken by his rescue teams.

Jones agreed to establish one of the mine buildings as a press office and to dedicate several phone lines to them. He joined media representatives and me for a tour of the area to establish "off limits" areas for the media, thereby affording families of miners some modicum of privacy—a plan which reporters supported.

More media arrived during the day. *Newsweek, Time, National Observer, Chicago Tribune, Life, Atlantic Monthly, Deseret News, Oregonian,* AP, UPI, Reuters, NBC, ABC, CBS, BBC, and scores of regional publications and stations checked in. A call from Jack Rigg, special assistant to Dole, alerted me that a story had run Wednesday in the *New York Times* saying that the mine had failed to correct safety hazards found by inspectors. Apparently, contrary to instructions, a zealous information officer in the bureau headquarters released inspection reports but omitted the final inspection report that showed violations had been corrected. The article also listed inaccurate figures about the company's accident rate and quoted anonymous inspectors as labeling the mine "a bad one." Rigg gave me the actual statistic that, in keeping with our previous statements, indicated Sunshine had been slightly above average on safety.

My noon conference was lively. Other papers had seen the *Times* story. Their questions bore in on the candor of our previous comments. I announced the statistics for this mining region, compared them to the rest of the United States and to the Sunshine mine. I referred reporters again to the complete inspection reports that now had been reproduced and were available. I also announced that the first team of investigators had arrived. Six attorneys would take depositions from witnesses in three community locations. Finally, I made formal announcement of the ground rules for covering the disaster and for use of the press office.

After the conference I met with Irwin P. Underweiser, president and board chairman of Sunshine. He and his board of directors had been meeting in the Sunshine office when the disaster occurred. Based in New York City, Underweiser had been concerned most of his life with balance sheets, not engineering diagrams. However, he quickly responded with whatever was asked of him by his rescue team and government officials—and wisely delegated rescue efforts to his staff.

Since none of the reporters had been in a mine, I asked that tours be conducted for them in neighboring mines so that they could understand how mines functioned. A visit to the nearby Bunker Hill mine was set but cancelled when only one reporter showed.

Influence of Local News Coverage

I checked the Thursday morning *Spokane Spokesman Review* and afternoon *Spokane Chronicle* to see how our press conferences were being covered. This was particularly important because out-of-state media often use the local media as a guide for their own coverage. Also, the local media are relied upon exclusively for information by rescue workers and families.

The *Chronicle* piece, headed "No Mine Dangers Seen," quoted me as saying that none of several inspections in the past two years had indicated any potential fire hazard. That was not fully accurate, and the article failed to quote inspection reports themselves which did show electrical problems but none serious enough in that mine to cause this type of fire. This slightly distorted, indirect quote, I felt, probably would do little harm, so I kept quiet. I was wrong, as proven later.

Thursday evening Chase announced that eight more victims had been found, bringing the total dead to 32. This type of short, morbid announcement became standard for almost every conference for the next week.

On Friday, a Ralph Nader organization consultant came to the mine site to conduct his own investigation. He brought copies of a privately published, low-circulation newspaper called *Coal Patrol*, which accused Dole's entire staff of ethical and legal violations in their nonenforcement of the Coal Mine Health and Safety Act. We were lumped together as "The motley crew of ex-businessmen, former lobbyists and public relations flacks and Republican political hacks who run the Interior Department. . . ." I was credited with writing "puff pieces for Morton and making sure Nixon's name appeared in news releases the mandatory number of times." My current assignments included one to "make the Nixon mine health-safety record look better than it is." Several reporters showed me their copies of *Coal Patrol* but used none of its material. Nonetheless, our credibility suffered as a result of the Nader Raider visit.

Ralph Nader himself spoke in Spokane and accused the bureau of being industry-oriented. I replied that the advisory group which develops enforcement standards consisted of equal representation of union, state, and federal officials. All of their proposals, I said, "were published for a 30-day comment period during which anyone could make suggestions . . . including Mr. Nader, who never had availed himself of the opportunity."

Friday evening, with the death count at 35, fumes pushed rescue crews' efforts back again. I announced then that the bureau was constructing a "torpedo-like" rescue vehicle that could be lowered 1100 feet down No. 12 shaft from the 3700-foot level to the 4800-foot level.

"It's a longshot," I reported, "and we might never use it because the borehole is only four feet wide. The rescuers could be killed if rocks fall or if the capsule gets stuck. Further, if it gets stuck, air would be blocked from entering the area of the mine where people might be surviving."

I took reporters and photographers to the maintenance shack where a bureau crew was welding together the 15-foot long contraption. We illustrated how two men would enter the torpedo, one on the other's shoulders, and then be lowered into the depths. All reporters were extremely skeptical except one from Reuters news agency who said, "If anyone gets out, it will be through some wild plan such as this."

The situation deteriorated Friday night. A telephone was lowered down the No. 12 borehole. A light on it flashed off and on. It rang and rang . . . no response. Three separate coordinated rescue attempts were taking place but each was bogging down. Carbon monoxide fumes were leaking through the mine's shaft and tunnels faster than bulkheads could be erected to seal off leaks. Special equipment was flown in from as far away as Europe. A powerful extra fan was installed, yet fumes continued to circulate, thwarting all rescue attempts.

Friday night I lay on the floor in a Sunshine office, trying to doze and yet remain available. I had not been able to sleep since Tuesday but, then, neither had anyone else. Winston, the bureau engineer who had been assigned to help me, was ready for the Saturday morning conference. He had never faced the media before but agreed to try. He used a comprehensive plan of the mine as a backdrop on the wall behind him to explain the rescue status.

As soon as he began to trace rescue efforts to date, he was hit with a barrage of "Why did you" and "Why didn't you" questions. One reporter was particularly aggressive.

"What newspaper are you from?" Winston finally shot back.

"The *Deseret News*. Why?"

"Christ, I'm in luck," Winston smiled. "With all those tough questions, I thought you were at least from *Time* magazine!" Laughing reporters began to accept the Helm/Winston briefings.

During several lengthy telephone conversations with Dole, I had expressed fear that the bureau was not asserting itself fully in the rescue. Their advice, I believed, was not being heeded by mine officials. If anyone was to be saved, I told Dole that it must be quickly and through the rescue capsule. Dole should directly and forcefully inject himself by telling Sunshine people that the capsule would be used. If they refused, I recommended that the bureau order the withdrawal of all rescue teams and assume full responsibility for the rescue itself.

That would be a tough move . . . but Dole responded. Preparations took place to make the capsule a priority rescue vehicle if no further progress was made on Sunday. Meanwhile, the bureau cut the telephone line and instead inserted a small Westinghouse television camera down the borehole which could shoot accurate videotape in almost total darkness. This would determine whether the capsule's descent would be obstructed.

Rescue Capsules Arrive

The bureau located two other capsules in the Atomic Energy Commission Nevada Proving Grounds. These were shipped to Kellogg for use instead of our improvised one. The capsules arrived on a trailer truck Sunday morning, right at the time I was holding an outside press conference.

"Come on, Helm. Knock off this 'Mission Impossible' crap!" one reporter exclaimed. "Yeah," another said. "And how do you like his timing on the use of props?"

Rain came down steadily through Sunday. Families and friends drifted away. Reporters talked about leaving. There seemed to be no hope left.

To make matters worse, Chase announced that actually 58 people still were missing instead of 50. The mine had not kept an accurate count by name of people underground. In violation of Bureau of Mines regulations, no procedures were followed to log workers in, pinpoint where they would be, and log them back out. The revised count of missing was based on comments by rescued workers and relatives.

Also on Sunday the United Steel Workers District 38 called for a congressional investigation. As rescue attempts faltered, the principal participants jockeyed not to be blamed for the disaster. Dole and I decided that the best way to handle the union attack was to respond without antagonism. My statement posted on the media bulletin board replied: "Our effort has been directed entirely toward the recovery of the men. We have been taking depositions but the depositions have been secondary and we feel that we can always go back to these if we need additional information. The Steelworkers can be assured that we will give it everything we can."

Sunday afternoon the educational trip to a nearby mine took place for reporters. A handful showed up.

Monday's papers reflected Sunday's lack of progress. An article in the *Chronicle* explored Lem Jones's colorful background; Winston's definitions of mine terms were used; a feature discussed the help of a 14-member contingent from the 321st Engineering Battalion U.S. Army Reserve, of Wallace, Idaho; the union story played fairly; and photos showed the AEC capsule. But the most damaging piece was an Associated Press interview with the mine president:

> Irwin Underweiser, president of the Sunshine Mine, said his company's insurance should prevent any losses to the mine while it is closed by the US Bureau of Mines.
>
> He added that while the silver mine is closed, it almost inevitably will cause a rise in the price of silver.
>
> Consequently, Underweiser said, when the mine begins operating again, the higher price of silver "possibly could enable the mine to wind up with a profit despite the closure!"

The media understood what Underweiser intended to convey but reacted fiercely against a company that was concerned whether it "made a buck" from the disaster.

A local headline reported "Power Fails, Mine Rescue Plans Stall." It was apparent that the desperate Bureau of Mines "Mission Impossible" had become the only hope. After consulting with Dole, who had maintained contact with Osborn and mine officials, I produced Dr. Osborn to discuss Bureau plans at Monday morning's press conference. He described in detail how a 7'3" AEC capsule bearing a two-man crew would be lowered 1100 feet into the borehole from the 3700-foot level.

Rescue Plans Developed

While "Mission Impossible" was under way, all other rescue efforts would be stopped to prevent any drain on electricity or oxygen. Halting other attempts would all but eliminate hope for survivors if the bureau failed. Time had run out.

Sensing that the climactic moment had arrived that Monday, the media gathered in the press office, awaiting word of what was taking place, then paced out to the entrance of the mine where television cameras were set up focusing on the silent crowd. The bureau photographer, Eugene Rapp, was assigned a post at the 3500-foot rescue station.

We placed a tape recorder at the station so that the telephone conversation between men in the capsule and the station crew leaders would be recorded. We would play tapes for the media if anything noteworthy was recorded.

At 6:30 P.M. the first ten-person crew entered the mine. Shortly before 9 P.M. bureau inspectors Wayne Kanack and Donald K. Morris started down. For two hours they struggled in 100 degree heat, scaling loose rocks from the sides of the borehole through open portions of the capsule. They progressed less than 150 feet.

Another team took over. By 3 A.M. Tuesday only 450 feet had been penetrated. A new 12-men crew came in. The *Spokesman Review*'s headline Tuesday, May 9, one week after the disaster hit, read "Rescue Team Fails 1st Try," which had been the case up to midnight, the newspaper's deadline.

However, after midnight conditions improved. At a depth of 580 feet, rock along the side of the hole became more stable and no longer protruded into the opening. We waited. The early morning rain came down in torrents.

Winston ran into the press office about 8:00 A.M. Tuesday. The bottom had been reached and he had a tape recording of a conversation between J. D. Pitts and

Keith Collins and the 3700-foot rescue station crew. We fumbled with our tape recorder. Radio and television microphones were layed on the table. The dozen reporters hovered nearby.

"Lower . . . lower . . . lower. We're down! We're on the bottom!"

"What do you see?"

"A skipjack. A mucker. That's all. There's nothing else. . . ."

"Shout. Try to raise someone."

"Helloooo . . . helloooo."

Silence.

The haunting "helloooo" was heard around the world over BBC and the American networks. But it had not reached the missing miners.

Pitts and Collins returned to the 3700-foot level. The next team, Levy Brake and Robert Riley, was lowered. They explored without success until 1:15 P.M. Tuesday. As soon as they were on the surface, we brought them to the press office.

Riley explained the crew turned west at a split in the tunnel. They discovered some equipment and two boreholes loaded with dynamite charges, indicating men had been working in that area. They took the other tunnel east for 1500 feet before becoming exhausted and returning to the capsule.

Brake's hand, wrapped in a bloody bandage, shook as he tried to light a cigarette. He had been cut by falling rocks as the capsule descended into the borehole. He told of another discovery:

"As we were getting ready to leave, we found the telephone. Its line had been cut when we lowered the TV camera. There was a set of footprints around the phone. They came from the tunnel we had not entered. Apparently, someone found the phone . . . too late."

By this time another team was on the bottom of the mine, tracing the footprints, banging on pipes, calling out. At 5:50 P.M., Tuesday, May 9, Winston announced: "We have an unconfirmed report of two miners alive."

He and I had just left a meeting with Osborn and Chase. We had decided that, since Chase had the responsibility of breaking all of the bad news, he would announce the good news, even though it was a bureau effort. We brought him to the conference room after Winston had alerted the media.

Two Survivors Found

"This is good news and I'm happy to report it," Chase said in his brief statement. Then, he related how the team of Kananck, Morris (both working their second shift in 24 hours), Frank Delimba, and Sonny Becker (who was from Sunshine) had found trapped miners Ron Flory and Tom Wilkinson at 5:45 P.M. Chase then added that seven more bodies had been found near the two survivors. These were the owners of the lunch pails that had helped sustain Wilkinson and Flory during their long ordeal. He could give few additional details except that the men would be examined at the 3700-foot station by Dr. Ernest E. Gnaedinger of Wallace, Idaho, before coming to the surface.

At 7 P.M. Flory was hoisted up in the capsule. At 7:45 Wilkinson joined him. There, at the 3700-foot level, they rested and swigged soft drinks before heading for the surface. Gene Rapp's photo from 3700 down was sensational! A UPI photographer processed the film in his darkroom and gave copies to all the media. Showing Wilkinson and Flory, arm in arm, looking toward heaven, the photo appeared in almost all newspapers and magazines—with a UPI photo credit line.

Three hundred people—friends and relatives of miners who had been trapped for a week deep beneath the surface and rescue workers and reporters—crowded in behind the cameras in front of the mine entrance. We waited in a tense silence to see Tom Wilkinson and Ron Flory return to the world of the living—the only miners found alive from the time deadly smoke was discovered filling the Sunshine mine a week before.

Across Big Creek Canyon, the Bitteroot Mountains grew more black with the night. Yet the circle of light cast by the TV crews—and the hope we felt with the discovery of two survivors—drew us closely together in our quiet vigil. The silence was broken by a small wiry miner.

"After all they been through, they're not gonna be rolled out. They're gonna walk out. They're miners!"

Something moved from within the partially illuminated Jewell shaft.

"Here they come!" someone shouted. Murmurs ran through the crowd. The families of the two miners moved to the entranceway. Reporters and photographers pushed closer, ready to record the first words and actions. I didn't try to keep them out of the restricted area. This was everyone's moment.

Wilkinson and Flory, accompanied by a dozen Bureau of Mines and Sunshine rescuers, finally emerged. They paused—unshaven, dirty, smiling—then started toward the crowd. Frances Wilkinson and Myrna Flory reached for and embraced their husbands. The couples were hurried toward two waiting ambulances for a six-mile trip to the West Shoshone County Hospital. Only as the ambulance pulled away did the small crowd break into applause.

The television lights were cut and the scene went black. As *The Christian Science Monitor* editorialized several days later: "It was one of those small miracles that happen when reason and logic crush expectation and hope seems blind." The miracle had occurred because 28 rescue workers had risked their lives in what reporters had glibly called "Mission Impossible," after the popular television series.

Rescue Efforts Combine

To make sure that rescue efforts continued, Dole accompanied by his assistant, Toby Welo, and bureau Deputy Director Schlick, flew to Kellogg Tuesday night. Dole aggressively prodded the rescue operation to make a rapid, coordinated last effort in case anyone in the mine remained alive.

Dole and Osborn returned to Washington, D.C., Wednesday leaving Schlick to direct the bureau crew. The mood of the rescue effort turned dark again. On Thursday afternoon, while walking across the parking lot, I noticed several men in uniform loudly exchanging words with a UPI photographer, Max Gutierrez. I stepped between the photographer and Lieutenant Meredith D. Haynes, commander of the contingent of reserves from the 321st Engineering Battalion, grabbing their coats to hold them apart.

"I was just doing my job . . . taking pictures. He interfered. This is an approved area," Gutierrez blurted out.

"These are my friends. I'm not about to let him stick his camera in their faces," Haynes shot back.

"You're off base, Lieutenant," I said. "Photographers and reporters have been cleared to use this area by the Sunshine mine and the federal government. When you put on that uniform, you can forget your personal opinions. They're subordinate to your duty."

As Gutierrez walked away, Staff Sergeant Gary J. Hoffman of the 321st snarled, "That Jap bastard had better be careful or he'll end up face down in the creek!"

I beckoned Deputy Sheriff Robert Curtis and repeated the story.

"Look to these reservists first if anything happens to the press," I said. The deputy agreed. The lieutenant and sergeant apologized.

A *Portland Oregonian* photographer shot a picture of me between Haynes and Gutierrez that ran May 19 with a story about the dispute when Gutierrez filed a discrimination complaint against the lieutenant.

Nineteen More Bodies Found

An hour after the Haynes-Gutierrez confrontation Chase came to the press office.

"I regret to inform you that 19 more bodies have been found. Seven men are still unaccounted for."

He left.

Two hours later I carried the final message.

"This is our last announcement. Seven more bodies have just been found. Mr. Chase is breaking the news to their relatives now. Of the 93 men trapped May 2 in the Sunshine mine, only two are alive. These are Tom Wilkinson and Ron Flory, who were saved by the Bureau of Mines."

As Dole predicted, public and legislative interest in the disaster continued. There were congressional hearings and new legislation, and in Kellogg, Idaho, the Department of the Interior held public hearings. A comprehensive and lengthy report eventually was published showing why the fire turned into disaster. But no definite conclusion was reached as to why the fire started.

Atlantic Monthly, whose reporter was there throughout most of the rescue efforts, published the "definitive" piece in December, 1972. It was entitled "Yes, Sir, This Has Certainly Been Considered a Safe Mine." The press release touting the article ranked Secretary Morton and me as equally guilty of "attempting to make the Bureau look good when disaster struck. . . ." Specifically, the author charged that I had attempted to hide the fact that explosives and electrical equipment had been found in the mine during previous inspections.

I was designated as "Morton's chief image-maker and troubleshooter" whose efforts inspired such news stories as one headlined "No Mine Dangers Seen" (the *Spokane Chronicle* article which I had failed to correct in the first days of the disaster). I telephoned the newspaper quoted, told them about the *Atlantic* story, and recalled that all inspection reports that had been given to the media at the scene, including the *Spokane Chronicle* and *Atlantic Monthly*. It was their omission, as much as mine, if nothing had been reported about electrical equipment. I then answered questions about the balance of the article.

The next month I was selected to become assistant secretary of health, education, and welfare for public affairs.

CHAPTER 25

Siege of the BIA Building: Centralizing the Function

Robert A. Kelly

Government public information practitioners, because they are not normally involved in the policy-making sphere, frequently lack the fundamental awareness and understanding of a given situation to either provide public affairs counsel to decision-makers or even respond adequately to media queries regarding public policy, particularly during crisis. However, a number of procedural remedies for many communication problems experienced during a crisis are seen in the case of the American Indian occupation of the Bureau of Indian Affairs Building (BIA) in 1972.

One should also note, though, the broader issues associated with the confusion of loyalty and purpose on the part of the public affairs professional which are raised in this account and best expressed in the form of a series of questions: Who is the "client" of an agency public affairs professional? Does this differ for the political appointee as opposed to the career public affairs person? Where does the public affairs professional draw the line on advocating any one position? Does government public affairs really help to resolve the conflicting demands of the public and its myriad of special interests, the bureaucratic organization, and the political administration, or does it merely serve to widen the gaps by replacing substance with form? And, depending upon the answers to these questions, what is, or should be, the role of public affairs?

The job of informing the public sometimes appears to the information officer in the midst of a public crisis as a 12-alarm fire raging out of control, certain to consume him in the very flames he is trying to fight. Looking back, one could well view the information process at the U.S. Department of the Interior in Washington, D.C., during those seven days which preceded the November, 1972, presidential election through precisely this metaphor—a fire out of control.

In reality, of course, what we saw during that week was the United States government—musclebound with its broad range of communications resources—unable to deal effectively with a massive invasion of the capital by angry constituents, unable to gain what it perceived as a balanced view of breaking events in either print or broadcast media throughout a desperate and protracted crisis.

As an eyewitness to what became a seige, I can report that the Native Americans who visited Washington in the fall of 1972 could have found no better way to dramatize their plight than exactly the way they did! Look at the events as they unfolded.

Filled with bitterness at American society for 200 years of callous unresponsiveness to Indian needs and deeply dissatisfied with the federal government's current Indian policies, a Trail of Broken Treaties Caravan converged upon the nation's Capitol carrying hundreds of determined Indians representing tribes from across the land. The initial targets of this pent-up emotion were the U.S. Department of the Interior and its adjacent Bureau of Indian Affairs headquarters building.

Their political target: a national administration driving for the finish-line in what was perceived in the White House as a hotly contested presidential election.

Deluge of Questions

Interior's Office of Communications became the focal point for both incoming public and media inquiries—but not for long. Events were breaking too fast as the caravan neared the capital, and Interior was deluged with questions: How big is the delegation? Are they armed? What is their stated goal? Is there a responsible leader? What is their agenda? What is our agenda? What is the White House's position going to be if things get bad? And, worst of all, how will this play in Peoria or Window Rock on election day?

At first, it seemed prudent to try to centralize our official responses so that the department and the bureau, as well as the administration, could address the growing number of media queries, and the rapidly changing scene, in an orderly and consistent manner. Gradually, however, the situation began to take on the appearance of an infantry assault on an enemy position, complete with all the communications problems associated with combat action—inaccurate reports, conflicting reports, no reports! But before we knew it, the situation had so escalated that the Indians had taken over the BIA building.

Meanwhile, across the street, back in the office of communications—from whence we were emanating no more than 25 percent of the outgoing official statements—we closed the door, sat down, and asked the basic question: "What the hell is going on?" Our basic goal, we told ourselves—and that of *any* federal public information operation—was, and is, to inform the public, answer the media's inquiries in a responsive and timely manner, and do all possible to keep an accurate stream of facts flowing outward. But we also asked ourselves how is the communicator to defend the government's position when some of the points made by the current "adversary" are, in fact, valid?

I remember thinking one evening, as I scanned three different and conflicting responses we (the White House, Interior, the bureau) had given to a single media inquiry, "God forbid that we should let down the president in this moment of disorganized travail." As I recall, I verbalized that little tidbit to my hardy band of Schedule C's (appointees) after our cadre of GS–15 PIOs (career) had returned to the barricades, which, at that moment, were shaped like telephones. In all, our communications team involved at least 20 print and broadcast specialists assigned to service media inquiries. Some manned incoming telephone calls, others worked with on-the-scene reporters, and certain writers prepared a steady flow of written reports and responses.

Despite these resources, the naked fact was that we were being out-performed by our Indian brothers in the one arena where we were supposed to be the pros—media relations. Not only were we being unresponsive due to the government speaking with many tongues, but we also were unable to stay abreast of events as they broke inside or outside the besieged bureau building, hour by hour.

However, let us give credit where credit is due. The Indians were well-organized and, like any activist group schooled in how to attract public attention, played the media—and the administration's political fears—like a Stradivarius violin. Typical of their performance—and I mean like a movie theater with 5:00, 7:00, 9:00, and 11:00 p.m. shows—I learned of impromptu news conferences by siege leaders on the steps of the BIA ("Someone get over there!")—timed for the evening newscasts and complete with denunciations, gory case studies of government malfeasance, and repeated demands for justice.

After each performance, the flood of media inquiries would begin at Interior's Office of Communications, and we would try to respond gradually, more guardedly, and more prone to investigate what other responses might have been issued from elsewhere in the administration. This job was made much more difficult by television crews who staked out the usual impromptu news conference site outside the BIA building front entrance, while the interviewer visited our communications office seeking a new angle or an inside tip about impending government action. Newspapers sent reporters to the U.S. Park Police headquarters, the BIA building, Interior, and other security agencies to build their story. Radio tape recorders were available for *anyone* willing to comment—all too often that meant the Indians, not us.

We sought guidance from the office of the secretary which, of course, was proper and required, and the then-exiled Bureau of Indian Affairs management. We then checked this data against both ours and that of the office of Assistant Secretary Loesch. Finally, we queried the White House's Domestic Council Indian specialist to see if we were tracking not only with events as they were breaking, but in concert with administration policy as it evolved—at least in my view—on a minute by minute basis.

What we found, of course, was that the media had already called the Domestic Council or the office of the assistant secretary, and (if we had been smart enough in that particular case to delay our response) the media had received only their answer. One should remember that media covering the event regularly sought and received three distinctly different kinds of responses: (1) political from the White House (i.e., "The latest demand has been studied and may be accommodated."); (2) official government responses from Interior, the lead "on-the-ground" agency (i.e., "The latest demand is under study and is not likely to be accommodated."); and (3) responses from the Indian leadership who controlled the BIA building (i.e., "The White House has met our demands").

Too Much, Too Fast

Our plaintive cries for coordination went unheeded, and, in retrospect, I can understand why—too much happening, too fast, and too many possibly quotable sources available to the enterprising reporter, especially one who knows that the higher he or she goes for reaction, the more authoritative and desirable the response. Who could blame them?

A persistent rumor—one we dealt with perhaps five or six times a day—concerned reports that "The government had decided to go in with force and solve the problem." Each time, we checked *all* sources, and each time we issued denials, as did the White House and the various police agencies involved. Of course, each such report served to inflame the issue and provide the Indian occupiers with still another opportunity to list the dire consequences that would result from any such rash action—and to repeat their demands.

Were *we* able to change the situation? Or officially comment in the Office of Communications on which version of a given response was the latest or the more accurate? Could *we* respond to the political thrusts of the Indians who guaranteed that each new charge would be routed by the media *direct* to the White House, which was obsessed with the impact these events might have on the national election?

No! We couldn't, we didn't, and the Indians won the media battle hands down!

Did they win the battle for public opinion? Did they win major concessions on the Hill?

No, for the lack of a coordinated government effort to deal effectively with the issue due to the conflicting interests within government itself and the Indians' own destruction of federal property which also was carried hour by hour on national television severely damaged their cause.

Had two procedural changes been instituted, however, the information flow could have been better managed to, at least, keep conflict and misunderstanding at a minimum. First, the White House and the office of the secretary should have reached firm and immediate agreement as to where the information fire control center would be: The White House? Interior's Office of Communications? Another location less associated with the issues involved, such as the D.C. police mobile van? Second, a White House Domestic Council representative, an Interior communications specialist, a Bureau PIO, and representatives from both the secretary's and assistant secretary's office should have been directly assigned to the fire control center communications office or, at least, *instantly* reachable by telephone from the center.

If these two management decisions had been reached early in the siege, *we* would have had the only game in town with respect to administration-government response to the flow of media inquiries in reaction to Indian pronouncements from the occupied building. We also could have released our originating statements in a more orderly and timely manner.

I believe a tightly controlled information procedure would have resulted in more balanced news reports hour by hour, event by event and, thus, would have provided the public with a more accurate view of the government's careful and responsible reaction to the week-long crisis, something the administration certainly wanted at that delicate moment. By fracturing our response capability, we instead contributed to the public perception of government as unresponsive and insensitive to Indian aspirations.

The lesson? When you are responsible for handling information flow during an emergency drawing wide media attention, make certain your function is centralized with 24-hour, top priority contacts at all of the policy-making, response-producing, or "leak-potential" offices involved in the breaking news event. Without this, even the most capable public information operation cannot accommodate the public's right to know or its organization's communications objectives.

PROGRAMS AND PRACTICES

How is the role of public information actually played out in the various components of the executive, legislative, and judicial branches of government? As we said at the outset, the American government does not speak with one voice. Each part of government handles the task in its own way. And this section of this book takes a specific look at a variety of different agencies which provide a good example of the whole.

We start with the executive branch (White House), legislative (Congress), and judicial (Supreme Court). Although we deal here with the federal government, these three branches operate in similar ways at all levels. Presidents, governors, and mayors have similar responsibilities and often approach their public information problems in similar ways. The same is true of Congress, state legislatures, and local councils. The judiciary, too, operates in similar ways, whether at the Supreme Court level, or the various federal, state, and local court levels.

The White House is truly the place where the spotlight of publicity focuses most intensely. In spite of the theory of the balance of powers, the president of the United States is the most powerful public official, almost entirely because he can command the attention of the mass media. He can communicate with the nation, almost at will. He cannot force the media through legal means to carry his messages, but he can exploit the predilections and patterns of news media more readily than any other individual in the world. So his communication responsibilities are awesome.

Walter Wurfel explores these problems and prospects of presidential press relations in the first chapter of this section. He is now vice president for corporate communications of the Gannett Company, Inc., the country's largest newspaper chain. Before joining Gannett, he was deputy press secretary during most of the administration of President Jimmy Carter. A graduate of the Columbia University graduate school of journalism, he has worked for newspapers, radio, television, and magazines (including *Newsweek*), and was formerly editor of the Straus Editors Report on the mass media. He has also worked as an administrator for the State Department and as a press secretary in the Senate.

In order to compensate for the publicity powers of the president, Congress has had to revolutionize its communications apparatus, mainly through electronics. John W. Eddinger explains this in the second chapter here. He is communications director for Senator Charles McC. Mathias, Jr. (D-Md). A former journalist with the *Baltimore Evening Sun* and the *Washington Star*, he has also served as administrative assistant and press secretary to the mayor of Baltimore. He holds an M.A. from Johns Hopkins University and teaches parttime for the University of Maryland.

The smallest branch of government, the judicial, also has the smallest information operation. Until recently, the courts did little or nothing to communicate with the public. But that is changing, and Barrett McGurn, public information officer for the Supreme Court of the United States, shows how the court's information efforts are growing. He has held that position since 1973. Before that, he spent seven years as a press officer for the State Department, working in Rome, Vietnam, and Washington. For more than three decades, he was a reporter and bureau chief for the New York *Herald Tribune*, serving in Rome, Paris, and Moscow, in addition to New York and many foreign assignments. He graduated from Fordham University, and his alma mater honored him with an honorary doctor of literature degree.

At the State Department, traditional attitudes toward public information are also changing. William D. Blair, Jr., deputy assistant secretary for public affairs, shows how diplomacy can no longer be conducted completely behind closed doors because public attitudes about foreign affairs have changed. Blair, a former foreign correspondent for the *Baltimore Sun* and *Newsweek*, has been in his present position since 1970 and was a press secretary for State from 1962 to 1970. He is a graduate of Princeton University.

Of all the public information operations in government, perhaps none was more complicated than those at the old Department of Health, Education, and Welfare. The new department, Health and Human Services, has inherited most of HEW's old infrastructure. A portrait of HHS's public affairs provides perhaps the best over-all picture of the complexities, politically and technically, of government's efforts to communicate with its multitudinous constituencies. Lewis M. Helm is well equipped to provide that description, since he was assistant secretary for public affairs of HEW from 1973 to 1976. A former newspaper reporter and association executive, he has served in political and governmental public relations roles, including assistant to the secretary of the Department of the Interior and deputy assistant secretary for mineral resources at Interior. Currently Helm is president of Capital Counselors, Inc., a Washington public affairs firm. He holds an M.S. from American University.

The Department of Agriculture represents the newest reorganization of the public relations function in government. Edie Fraser and Wes Pedersen discuss the new organization and show how it could be adopted elsewhere in government as well. Ms. Fraser is president of Fraser/Associates, a Washington public affairs consulting firm. A graduate of Duke University, she has worked in Africa for the Peace Corps, in consumer affairs for HEW, and in public relations for the Carl Byoir Associates and as principal of Fraser/Ruder & Finn. Pedersen was a city editor and columnist before joining the government as an editor for the State Department in 1950. He subsequently joined the U.S. Information Agency (now the International Communication Agency), rising to the job of Chief of the Office of Special Projects before leaving government service for private public affairs counseling in 1979. He received a "Communicator of the Year" award from the National Association of Government Communicators in 1978. He also served as president of that group in 1979. He is now Director of Communications for the Public Affairs Council.

Most agencies of the government have special constituencies, specific publics with which they must relate. The business community is a very important public for government, especially for the Department of Commerce. And Ernest Lotito explains how his department handles that relationship. He is director of public affairs for Commerce. He was formerly director of public affairs for the Corporation for Public Broadcasting, and director of communications for Vice President Walter Mondale when he was senator and for former Senator Joseph Tydings. A former reporter for the *Washington Post*, Lotito is also a weekly newspaper publisher in southern Maryland. He graduated from the Columbia University graduate school of journalism and is a coeditor of *The Political Image Merchants*.

The Interior Department, on the other hand, best exemplifies the agency that takes a traditional approach to public information. Anne Runyan explores this and concludes that, while this approach may not have been innovative in the communications sense, it has produced a number of notable information products and programs.

Finally, the Department of Defense provides an example of a systematic organization that must provide public relations work on a world-wide basis. As Edie Fraser and Wes Pedersen pointed out, it is the only government agency that maintains a fulltime school for information officers.

A well-conceived communication plan, which designs modern systems to inform the people while building components to insure the openness of government and its responsiveness to the needs and interests of its citizens, will in the end make government better, satisfy citizen needs, and improve all of society.

CHAPTER 26

The White House: Center Stage for Government

Walter Wurfel

In the middle of the night, Washington time, Uganda dictator Idi Amin ordered all Americans in his country to meet with him in Kampala. It was the latest step in the harrassment by Amin of Americans living in Uganda.

At 5:45 A.M. in New York, an NBC newsman preparing the first newscast of that morning's "Today Show" called the White House. He asked for the duty spokesman. Three miles away in suburban Virginia, the direct line from the Army Signal Corps switchboard in the Executive Office Building rang, awakening one of the seven spokespersons on the staff of press secretary Jody Powell.

"What's the White House reaction to the Uganda situation," the newsman asked. The spokesman knew nothing about the news development. By experience he knew it would be useless to phone the National Security Council duty officer or Powell for any guidance at that hour. Any public statement would surely await the conclusion of national security adviser Zbigniew Brzezinski's daily 7:30 A.M. briefing of the president.

The White House spokesman asked the newsman to read the wire story from Kampala over the phone.

"I don't have any details," the spokesman responded when he was finished. "I'm sure there won't be any White House comment for hours, at least, but you can be sure that this development will be the subject of close study and intense discussion by officials this morning." He went back to sleep.

An hour and 15 minutes later the first newscast of the "Today Show" featured the news from Uganda, concluding with "The White House said Amin's action would be the subject of immediate attention this morning."

"The White House said . . ." From international crises to the president's jogging habits, it's the byword for the ultimate government authority. From formal presidential press conferences to informal daily press briefings to the mumblings of a half-asleep press aide, what "the White House said" flashes around the world, always news and, more often than not, the front-page variety.

News organizations devote large amounts of money and staff resources to covering the White House. More than 1600 reporters and broadcast technicians have White House press credentials. Some 3000 others who occasionally attend briefings and news events are on a master list for access on an as-needed basis. On any given day, 20 to 100 journalists attend the press secretary's briefing and 100 or more others will seek information over the telephone.

Presidents and their staffs have encouraged this blanket coverage. It has increased their ability to rally public support, to mobilize public pressure on congress, and to pursue public diplomacy. The minus side of this attention is that when things go badly for the president and his policies, there is a large press corps on hand to report that, too.

A casualty of this total coverage is the privacy of the president and his family. When Jimmy Carter and his family rafted down Idaho's Salmon River in 1978,

Powell warned the news media there would be no news events to report. Coverage was restricted to general filming of the start, midpoint, and end of the trip, with a small pool of reporters following the president's raft at some distance. Yet the coverage was heavy, and after the trip's conclusion *U.S. News & World Report* called it a publicity extravaganza.

Ironically it was Richard Nixon, an antagonist of the media, who did the most to improve the working conditions of reporters covering the White House. His press secretary, Ron Ziegler, refined and improved the logistical support for journalists accompanying the president on his travels. During Nixon's first term the FDR swimming pool between the executive mansion and the west wing office area of the White House was decked over to make a large briefing and working area for reporters.

The tradeoff—and perhaps the whole purpose for this generosity—was the separation of reporters from official visitors. Before the move, reporters and visitors to the president and his aides shared the same lobby. Afterwards, the visitors and reporters were separated. Correspondents wishing to question visitors to the president had to wait outside in hope of catching the visitors entering or leaving the lobby—a practice that prevails today.

There are a number of ways that the White House and reporters exchange information. Some of these are highly ritualized, some are almost haphazard. Each serves its own purpose.

Briefings by the press secretary provide a steady stream of announcements, some important, others of little consequence, but all directed toward enhancing the president's image of decisiveness, action, and leadership. Because form often is substance in Washington, the portrayal of this image in fact contributes to the reality.

Regular televised news conferences, restored by Gerald Ford after little use during the Watergate years, let the president speak directly to a television audience of millions. The format favors the president; if a questioner becomes hostile, the public sympathizes with the president. Dan Rather of CBS News learned that during a tart exchange with Nixon during a presidential news conference in Houston after the Watergate scandal erupted. Rather drew criticism from across the nation for being disrespectful to the chief executive.

Background briefings by the press secretary in his office provide the opportunity to explain delicate matters to White House beat reporters without actually putting the White House on the record. These sessions are generally called with little notice and are used to shape the flow of the news from the White House or to give a more detailed view of presidential decision-making on a particular issue than is usually put on the record. Seldom are more than 20 correspondents invited to take part. This eliminates those who cover the White House infrequently and those who, through their past actions, are deemed by the press secretary (and frequently also by the beat correspondents) to be more interested in confrontation than reporting. It also improves the probability that the briefer's ground rules on attribution or quotation will be observed.

Written statements and texts issued by the press office range from the president's daily schedule to texts of presidential speeches and background on major policy announcements. Sometimes the timing and content of these handouts can be used to White House advantage. On several occasions when Carter was to make a prime-time television speech, Powell would provide two or three brief excerpts from the text just in time for use on the early evening network news programs. These selected quotes told at least a major part of the president's message—and to a much larger audience than would tune in later for the real thing. In fairness to

Powell, it should be noted that the final text of a Carter speech to be delivered at 9 P.M. would often not be completed until 7 or 8 P.M.

Since Franklin Roosevelt's first term presidents have spoken directly to the public through radio and, later, TV. Roosevelt explained the details of the New Deal. Nixon spoke to middle America; even at campaign time he found radio flexible and inexpensive compared with national network television. Carter revived the fireside chat format on television and added the radio call-in show.

When Carter conducted his second radio call-in in October 1979, Topic A in Washington and in the national news media was whether Senator Edward Kennedy would challenge him for the 1980 Democratic presidential nomination. The citizens outside Washington didn't once ask about Kennedy or 1980 politics during the two-hour program. They were more interested in energy, inflation, defense, the Strategic Arms Limitation Treaty, and the budget. In contrast, during Carter's nationally televised news conference earlier the same month, Washington journalists used more than a third of the time to explore the policy differences between Carter and Kennedy, although neither was yet a declared candidate. One reporter expounded at such length on a Kennedy criticism of Carter that the president jokingly asked whether the reporter was making a speech on Kennedy's behalf.

Presidents and the journalists who cover them like to escape Washington for visits to what author Ben Wattenberg called "The Real America." For the television correspondent in particular, this travel affords a chance to obtain good action footage of the president outside the White House. Carter frequently capitalized on this by holding town meetings in places like Yazoo City, Mississippi. Here, as in the radio call-in shows, the citizens asked about inflation, jobs, defense, and the problems of big government—not national politics or the in-fighting of the Washington bureaucracy. There were few tough questions, almost no follow-ups, and there was usually at least one "question" that was more a statement of praise for the president.

The national correspondents couldn't write these meetings off as nonnews. Theater they were, but the fresh and newsworthy elements were the local citizens and their reaction to a presidential visit.

After a slow start, Carter increased the number of news conferences held in cities and towns outside Washington—even overseas. He initiated regular sessions with non-Washington journalists, and he resumed the customary practice of social "stroking" of major columnists and bureau chiefs at small dinners in the executive mansion. Like presidents Kennedy, Johnson, Nixon, and Ford, Carter—again after a slow start—made extensive use of individual interviews with favored reporters or with the networks, wire services, newsmagazines, and major newspapers. Such exclusives almost invariably got better "play" than their news content warranted.

Attention to news media outside Washington has taken on added importance since Nixon set up the Office of Communications under Herb Klein in 1969. Under Carter an Office of Media Liaison, part of the press office, was assigned the special task of communicating with editors, editorial writers, columnists, commentators, and reporters of newspapers and broadcast stations around the country.

Media Liaison set up interviews and editorial board meetings for travelling high-level administration officials. It conducted briefings in Washington for out-of-town journalists and for reporters for specialized publications in Washington who ordinarily would have been ignored by the White House. This office also gathered together information on all aspects of administration legislative proposals and policy innovations—from airline deregulation to western water policy—

and provided briefing papers for the same non-Washington audience of journalists. The briefing papers expounded the administration viewpoint but they also gave editorialists the detailed background information that was often not available to them through their regular news channels.

Based on the successful experience of political campaigns and several cabinet departments, Media Liaison, in 1978, began providing audio reports on major news events involving the president and his department chiefs. Radio stations called a toll-free number and obtained brief taped excerpts from the speeches or public comments of these officials. These reports were identified as being from the White House press office. Depending on the flow of the news, from 200 to 500 stations called for these reports each day.

In addition, at about the same time, the press office began to arrange for local television stations to do a limited number of videotaped interviews with White House and agency officials in Washington. This format enabled local reporters to ask questions by telephone while the answer of the Washington official was videotaped, then shipped by airplane to the interviewing station for use on its next newscast. Some television news directors did not allow their staffs to participate, but most had no problem, because the interviews were unrehearsed and unedited, and because they provided a dimension to the local news program that was often unavailable otherwise.

These ventures into broadcasting by the White House press office first drew fire from the writing press and from beat reporters who felt the aim was to bypass them in order to reach less knowledgable local reporters. Some freelance radio and television reporters complained that the White House was threatening their livelihood. The issue of bypassing Washington correspondents to reach journalists in the "boonies," as the Washington hands often call them, has risen regularly since Vice President Spiro Agnew attacked the media in 1969 and 1970. White House correspondents don't really like it when a president holds a news conference outside Washington and makes a special effort to accept the questions of regional reporters, as Carter did. Nor did they like the Carter innovation of twice-monthly, half-hour interviews in Washington with small groups of non-Washington editors.

The usual complaint by White House regulars is that the questions from these journalists are "softballs" the president can hit out of the park, and that only the tough probing of sophisticated Washington correspondents can force a president to divulge all, particularly when the topic is one that the president and his administration have not mastered. There is some merit to the capital journalists' contention that only they know enough obscure details of any given situation to foil a president who so wishes to evade a question. These reporters do seem to forget, however, that some of the editors who take part in these non-Washington presidential interviews are former Washington correspondents themselves and are no patsies.

Nor are the Washington regulars immune from asking irrelevant or softball questions. For example, Godfrey Sperling, Washington bureau chief of the *Christian Science Monitor*, regularly asks questions in presidential press conferences that are so congenial one might have expected such a question from a supporter or presidential staffer rather than a reporter. A close reading of the transcripts shows that the non-Washington editors have done their share of probing questioning. A comparison of the Washington televised press conferences of 1977 and 1978 with Carter's meetings with non-Washington editors over the same time period provides no clear evidence that either category of journalist was superior to the other in tenacity or thoroughness of questioning. In fact, the out-of-town journalists did by far the better job of exploring Carter's philosophy on many aspects of his presidency. The transcripts from these interviews regularly provided front-page news the day following their release.

The press office response to all the criticisms of its reaching out to non-Washington journalists is that they help bridge the seemingly ever-widening gap of understanding between the government in Washington and the nation's citizens. If adding new channels of communication helps build that bridge, then both the president and the public are served.

To the extent that reporters (regulars or outsiders) at televised news conferences have become actors in a news-drama, their ability to pry out unpleasant or embarrassing news from a reluctant president has suffered. Even when limited follow-up questions are allowed, as they have been in recent years, it is possible for a president to give a lengthy and nonspecific answer and then call on another reporter. Because all participants know the news conference will be cut off at approximately 30 minutes to accommodate the networks' schedules, they feel pressed to cover a number of topics instead of following one until it is exhausted. The competing demands of different news organizations also tend to assure that each reporter will ask the question that he or she came prepared to ask, rather than follow-up another reporter's fruitful line of questioning left unsatisfied by the president's answers.

Since the early 1960s, reporters assigned to the White House have complained that presidents call on favorite reporters and avoid those who ask barbed questions. Those working for smaller news organizations and those who cover the White House infrequently have complained that the president calls only on the well-known correspondents from major national news organizations. This unhappiness grew so during the first Nixon administration that a group of reporters met at the Washington Hotel, a block from the White House, to discuss alternative formats. They also met, informally, with the press secretary. In this case, and every other since, the search for improvement foundered on two shoals: the competition between print and television and among news organizations, none of which was willing to be frozen out of the chance to ask a question by the draw of a straw; and the suspicion that any change might give the White House a new opportunity to manage or manipulate the news.

Despite these problems, the televised news conference remains a major method of presidential contact with the news media. News conferences at the White House make efficient use of the president's time. He doesn't have to travel and, if he holds news conferences frequently, he needs a minimum of preparation. The format is at once high-risk and reasonably safe. The risk comes from the possibility that a president will make a major mistake of fact or of judgment for all the world to see. Carter's continued strong statements for Bert Lance prior to Lance's resignation were construed by many in the media to be damaging to the president's fulfillment of his campaign theme "why not the best." The safety of being able to dodge difficult questions, knowing that time and the competition among reporters are on the president's side, has already been discussed. A president can also affect the outcome of a news conference by its timing—delaying a few days until some particular political or policy problem is resolved, or calling a news conference quickly to capitalize on some news event favorable to him.

The whole nation may be able to tune in a news conference, but the press secretary's much more routine meetings with reporters provide the day-in, day-out flow of news from the White House. The briefings let the White House call special attention to matters it wants to emphasize. Because these are often items of less-than-universal concern to reporters, they might pass unnoticed otherwise. The press secretary's announcement of them makes it more risky to ignore them, because of competitive pressures among the reporters. The briefings are also a prime forum for the press secretary to issue political comment, seldom identified as such, on congressional handling of a pet administration bill, or to reply (frequently obliquely) to a presidential critic whose comments have struck home, but will not be dignified by a presidential response.

The White House can fine-tune its responses to critics to achieve the desired impact. The ultimate weapon is a direct response by the president, but that grants a certain credibility to the critic, and that is something the White House seldom desires. The next level of response would be by a senior White House aide or by a cabinet member. A key ally in Congress can respond on the president's behalf without directly involving the administration in the debate. Governors, mayors and nongovernmental officials can also stand up for the president without involving him or putting the stature of his office on the line.

The White House press secretary can issue responses in the president's name, but he cannot shed the label of officialdom. He is expected to be political, however, so his responses may carry less weight than those of a union president or a major business leader—an "outside" authority—who speaks in favor of the president's position.

Washington regulars can read a great deal of significance into how a president reacts to a particular criticism, as indexed by who reacts; whether the response is obviously prepared or seems to be spontaneous; and by how quickly the reaction comes. Sometimes these factors are almost as important as the actual substance of the statement itself. Whether the press secretary is reacting or adopting an active stance in his briefing, the mood can swing wildly from one day to the next, depending upon the flow of the news and the humor and effectiveness of the briefer.

Under some situations the press secretary may not feel able to fully answer reporters' questions—as, for instance, during the Lance case. Before the OMB director resigned under fire for his private banking practices, his situation was under investigation by federal agencies. For the White House to comment on the investigations could have been construed as interference. For the White House not to comment on developments—the course frequently taken by Powell—was viewed by some in the media as a show of favoritism to a Georgian who was a close friend of the president.

Other examples of situations where the press briefer may feel it necessary to be partially unresponsive to reporters are sensitive labor mediations involving the White House, and equally sensitive foreign policy or national defense matters. Reporters are under intense competitive pressure when such situations are in the news to come up with a new development each news cycle. The briefer's restraint frustrates this, and the journalists complain loudly. The press secretary, on the other hand, may believe that the public's best interest is in a swift conclusion of the situation and that is best furthered by keeping mum, at least temporarily. Later a full disclosure can immediately follow the resolution of the problem.

Obviously, in this situation the duties and responsibilities of the presidential spokesman and the news media clash. Some hard-line reporters say there is never a justification to withhold any information. If the issue is one where there is suspicion of White House wrongdoing or a coverup of illegal action the mood can become explosive. The ability of a confident, generally respected and humorous presidential press secretary to "jolly" his way out of a sticky situation is not enough to save the White House from strong media criticism. Whenever this situation arises, the best reporters start to search out the answers from other sources, in the White House and elsewhere in Washington.

There is a fundamental duality to the role of the White House press secretary. He is a government official paid by the taxpayers and is responsible for supplying information to the public. On the other hand, he is a political appointee answerable only to the president, and the president views the spokesman's job to be that of putting the most favorable light on his administration. Therefore, when the president is in trouble his press secretary may be doubly so. The spokesman cannot be untruthful if he expects to survive long in the job, but he must draw the line at providing chapter and verse about everything that went wrong at the White House that day.

Adding to his difficulty is the peculiar situation of the White House beat reporters for some large news organizations. Some of these restrain their White House reporters from following up story leads elsewhere in town. If the White House is uncommunicative, therefore, these reporters must give up the initiative to colleagues in the same organization who are assigned to another Washington beat where the story can be followed.

The most fortunate reporters are those whose editors encourage them to leave the White House briefing room and range across the city, following the story wherever it may develop. The need for this flexibility is frequent and inevitable; at times the White House will dry up as a news source on an administration story. That tends to happen with all institutions when they are under attack. Such a reaction may not be wise in the long run; it is not the most responsible action for the press secretary in his role as a public official; but it will happen.

Although the press secretary's briefings serve an important purpose, they do not fulfill the information exchange needs of either the White House regulars or the president's staff. No correspondent working on an exclusive story or a nonspot news story is likely to ask his or her questions during the briefing and in front of a roomful of competitors. Nor is the press secretary eager in the briefing to get into the sensitive aspects that he can share on a background or not-for-attribution basis only with a handful of trusted reporters. Thus, the briefing is but a starting point, however entertaining, for the press office and enterprising correspondents in the day's information exchange.

For the correspondents, there are private conversations with the press secretary, his deputies, and assistants; interviews with other White House staff; and, for the most enterprising, checks with other sources of information on the story, whether in Washington or elsewhere. In these private conversations leaks are sprung, tips handed out, and documents provided.

Even a one-to-one conversation between a spokesman and a journalist can result in misunderstanding, particularly if one of the parties thinks the other has stepped outside the area of acceptable practice. One such situation occurred before Bert Lance resigned. Powell was the one who stepped into hot water by using the time-hallowed Washington technique of the "hot tip." He used it, however, when the stakes were too high and at a time when his involvement as a defender of Lance was too visible to allow him the luxury of quiet, behind-the-scenes tipstering.

Senator Charles Percy of Illinois had particularly irritated the White House by recommending Lance's departure. Acting on reports from two acquaintances he considered reliable, Powell leaked to several reporters some information he suggested they check out. Powell's apparent aim was to question Percy's own record and thereby to undermine his effectiveness as a critic of Lance. The tip was that Percy had improperly used a corporate airplane for political purposes and had not fully reimbursed a bank for office space provided during his 1972 senate campaign.

At least two Washington bureau chiefs for major papers received Powell's tip and did nothing after their checks failed to substantiate it. However, Loye Miller, chief of the Chicago *Sun-Times* bureau, reported in his newspaper Powell's action and the bureau's inability to find independent corroboration of the assertions. Miller's story made it clear he felt Powell had mounted an attack on Percy.

Powell was furious, saying he had clearly set a not-for-attribution ground rule in his initial conversation with Miller. Miller disputed that. The result was an embarrassment for the White House, an apology by Powell to Percy, and a debate among Miller's fellow journalists as to whether he had done the right thing.

The information source—whether he or she works in the press office or not—may cooperate with a reporter for one or more reasons beyond political skullduggery or simple helpfulness. The reporter may be known to favor the president and his policies; he may work for a large news organization that will play a story bigger if it is an exclusive; he may represent a newspaper or broadcast station in the district or state of a particular member of Congress (or other political leader or officeholder) to whom the White House wants to send a message through the media; or the reporter may be an expert on a particular topic important to the source.

Sometimes a reporter may be known as a confidant of some particular official or lobbyist in Washington. The whole purpose of the source may be to communicate, indirectly, with that third person; the writing or airing of a news story may be completely irrelevant. News sources in the White House and elsewhere in Washington also can benefit from the reverse of that news flow; they glean bits of information from reporters who interview them.

It is not just to impart news or gain favorable coverage by correspondents and columnists that presidents and cabinet members socialize with them. The correspondents are the honeybees of Washington policy development—flitting from policy-maker to policy-maker, pollinating ideas. In this role, senior newspersons in Washington may get tugged over the line that separates reporting the news and making it. The temptation is strong, especially for correspondents who have seen presidents and cabinet members come and go, who gain perspectives valuable to the incoming administration, and who may need the same ego gratification that politicians and entertainers need. The daily or weekly "fix" of the syndicated byline, the front-page story in an influential paper, the evening news commentary or the magazine piece may no longer be enough for the jaded or aging correspondent.

Being asked for advice by a top White House aide or a cabinet member is the new gratification—and not all bad, either. These correspondents do have knowledge to impart on the ways of Washington and the policy-formation process. That knowledge is particularly valuable to new officials who come to Washington without having first served in Congress or a previous administration. But the advice is not always given with grace, or when asked for. More than a few newcomers to executive branch policy jobs have been subjected to unsolicited lectures from senior journalists who came to interview but stayed to sermonize.

An abundance of caution may embolden a White House source to talk to reporters more openly on an individual basis than in groups. If the source says too much inadvertently or reveals too many unpleasant details of internal policy disputes, the president or other aides may be angered. The individual interview (outside the office and away from the popular lunching places, if the topic is really sensitive) gives the source a kind of insulation from criticism if things go wrong. He may have to live with his conscience, but that is less damaging to the career than to incur the wrath of the president.

Ego also motivates some sources. A young campaign aide appointed to a mid-level White House job in a new administration may be awed by the place and the people. The rush of winning the election is still there. The aide never thought he'd get to Washington so fast, especially to work in the White House. Now, Joe

Byline, the powerful nationally respected reporter, seeks him out for some facts. If the new aide doesn't stop to think, he could provide a goldmine of information unavailable from sources more cautious, sophisticated and experienced. What Joe Byline knows he has to watch, however, is that the new aide's information may have some gaps, his interpretation of what he knows may therefore be faulty and, worst of all, he may not have the self-confidence to admit to the reporter where his knowledge runs out.

Although accuracy is the press spokesperson's most essential quality, good timing comes in a close second. Timing was part of the problem in Powell's troubles, described earlier, with his hot tip on Senator Percy during the Bert Lance affair. Even inadvertent bad timing can cause trouble that no amount of explaining can erase. One of those situations occurred during the first year of the Carter administration and related to a salary increase for senior White House aides.

Congress had voted to increase salaries of top government officials at the rank of assistant secretary and above. The government-wide increase was to go into effect soon after the inauguration. It was up to the president to decide whether his staff would be included. There was internal debate on the White House senior staff over what to recommend to Carter. Other matters took precedence, so the date for the increase came and went without a presidential decision. Two months later, the White House decision was announced: presidential aides at the higher ranks would get part of the raise. Their new pay levels would, in every case, be $1500 below their counterparts at the same level elsewhere in the federal government.

Had this happened automatically and concurrently with the other increases there would have been little or no mention in the press, and what mention there was might have been positive. But the delay and the subsequent announcement by Powell of the raise for White House senior aides made news. It was treated by the press as a separate increase for Carter aides, and commentators and editorialists judged it to be inconsistent with Carter's attempts to trim the role of the White House staff and deimperialize the presidency.

It is often asserted that the White House press office can manipulate some of the news media coverage of the president. Some examples of the possibilities have been touched on in this chapter—the release of advance speech text excerpts, the shifting of news conference times, private dinners in the White House. However, no amount of effort on the part of the White House can override the journalist's own judgment, and that judgment almost always reigns supreme. Every president and his aides become increasingly aware of this—and attuned to what they see as the foibles of the media—as his term goes by. Often they wonder if reporters can comprehend any motivation, any presidential statement in any context but the political.

An example of the media's fascination with political angles occurred in April 1978 when Carter spoke in Washington to the annual convention of the American Society of Newspaper Editors. He chose the occasion to make what he and his staff considered to be a major speech on the economy. He announced an administration effort to fight inflation and named Robert Strauss as his chief inflation fighter. Following the speech, the president answered a few questions from editors. It was a time when Carter's rating in the polls had first dipped from its post-inaugural high. The consensus of Washington pundits was that he might be a one-term president. This led one editor to ask whether Carter intended to seek a second term. The president responded that he wasn't sure; he hadn't thought about it yet.

That evening the "CBS Evening News" led with a piece saying that Carter had used the occasion of his ASNE appearance to drop the "bombshell" that he might not seek reelection. There followed a brief comment and analysis speculating on why Carter chose this particular moment, so early in his term, to raise the issue. The anti-inflation speech and appointment of Strauss rated one sentence. The White House was dumbfounded. Why would it be news—or even worth mentioning—that a president only 15 months into a four-year term hadn't thought about reelection?

Thus, despite constant contact between the media and the aides around a pres-ident, there persists not only the attitude of healthy skepticism and cynicism, but also occasional surprise on the part of each group about how little the other actually comprehends. Embattled White House spokespersons sometimes can't understand that dogged persistence by reporters does not necessarily represent hostility toward them or their boss. Reporters, on the other hand, sometimes appear to grab for the conspiracy theory as an explanation for the cause of White House miscues, where sheer lack of coordination or planning is often the culprit. And, White House officials are likely to ascribe malice or bias as the cause of errors that distort the meaning of key stories, when often these occasional occur-rences are the result of carelessness, laziness, or ignorance on the part of the reporter or editor.

The very separation and apartness so essential to the independent pursuit by each—reporter and White House aide—of his main role has as its price a possibly inevitable understanding gap. Only the diligence and integrity of both can keep that gap to manageable proportions. Sometimes both groups try to do too much. The White House press secretary tries to tie together everything the president and his administration do into a comprehensive theme. All too often the pieces don't fit together so neatly, and they certainly don't follow all that closely the ideal tapestry of promises woven during the last campaign. Reporters see that the "emperor" has on BVDs.

On the other hand, correspondents competing for a spot on the evening news or play above the newspaper's fold on page one—and honestly striving to explain the "big picture"—frequently construct a whole story out of half the facts. The public forgets tomorrow, but the unhappy White House aides may fume for days. These suspicions are probably an eternal part of the scene. The roles of spokes-man and reporter do conflict, and no amount of camaraderie during the cam-paign or during the salad days of a presidency can obliterate that fact.

CHAPTER 27

Congress: Toward an Electronic Revolution

John W. Eddinger

Congressional press relations, for good or for ill, have moved sharply in recent years from one-man seat-of-the-pants operations into the high-technology era of video display terminals, information retrieval, automation, computerization, and high-speed word and data processing rivaling anything devised by corporate America. House and Senate press offices, which not too long ago existed solely to serve and service reporters, have become sophisticated information terminals far beyond the press handouts and editorial jaw-boning of the Lyndon Johnson-Sam Rayburn school of press relations. Today's Capitol Hill press aide is likely to be a "communications director" with a salary and support system to match his or her counterpart in private sector public affairs. Moreover, today's congressional communications specialist is likely to have one or more graduate degrees, a background in reporting or mass communications, and in some instances a part-time faculty position at a school of journalism. In short, congressional press relations has made the quantum leap during the past decade into the burgeoning field of mass communications.

There are as many kinds of press operations on Capitol Hill as there are members of Congress. Each is different. Each operates in its own style, which closely parallels the style, interests, and ambitions of the senator or representative it serves. The system, which has evolved, as mass communications itself has evolved in American life throughout the 1970s, is not without its champions and its critics. The common denominator which defines this major new element in the minds of members of Congress in its most lofty representation, is the necessity, indeed the mandate in a popular democracy, to educate the public and to mobilize the consent of the governed behind public policy issues. Whether or not this ideal is truly served, is in large measure left up to the personal ideals and comportment in office of individual members of Congress. As in all institutions, meeting this ideal may or may not always be lived up to.

Press critics such as Ben H. Bagdikian, national correspondent of the *Columbia Journalism Review*, have strongly criticized the system as a misalliance between American journalists and Congress, both of whom need each other to survive. In an incisive article, in the January/February 1974 issue of the *Columbia Journalism Review*, Bagdikian concludes "a responsive and daily accountable Congress has . . . gone largely unwatched in any way significant for local voters. Most members still do not have to answer pertinent questions for the voters back home, and most continue to propagandize their constituents at the constituents' expense with the cooperation of the local news media. . . ."

Bagdikian's criticism is aimed specifically at the system of congressional press relations that this chapter will seek to explain. It is justifiable criticism which has its roots in the American system of representative government. Its tensions stretch across the pages of history since the conflicting concepts of government advanced by Thomas Jefferson and Alexander Hamilton began to take shape in the decade following the ratification of the Constitution.

Jefferson believed a cantankerous and unruly press was better than a weak and controlled press as the fledgling democracy began unfolding. Earlier he had written:

> The people are the only censors of their governors; and even their errors will tend to keep these to the true principles of their institution. To punish these errors too severely would be to suppress the only safeguard of the public liberty. The way to prevent these interpositions of the people is to give them full information of their affairs through the channel of the public papers, and to contrive that those papers should penetrate the whole mass of the people. The basis of our government being the opinion of the people, the very first object should be to keep that right; and were it left to me to decide whether we should have a government without newspapers or newspapers without a government, I should not hesitate for a moment to prefer the latter.

Hamilton's theory of centralist (Federalist) government rejected Jefferson's position outright and paved the way for the harsh Alien and Sedition laws adopted in 1798 to among other things control press criticism of government actions. In The Federalist (No. 84) Hamilton wrote:

> What signifies a declaration that 'the liberty of the press shall be inviolably preserved'? What is the liberty of the press? Who can give it any definition which would not leave the utmost latitude for evasion? I hold it to be impracticable; and from this, I infer, that its security whatever fine declarations may be inserted in any constitution respecting it, must altogether depend on public opinion, and on the general spirit of the people and of the government.

Hamilton's unyielding position led to the framing of the First Amendment devised by advocates of press freedom, which provides that, "Congress shall make no law respecting an establishment of religion, or prohibiting the free exercise thereof; or abridging the freedom of speech, or of the press. . . ." During the term of John Adams, the first Federalist president, the Sedition Act was invoked to suppress criticism of the government by partisan pamphleteers. The act made it a crime, punishable by up to two years imprisonment and $2000 in fines, to speak, write, or publish any "false, scandalous and malicious" writing against the government or its high officials. The act expired March 3, 1801, as Thomas Jefferson took office as the country's third president.

Throughout American history, the tension between a rigorous, searching press and a strong government has not relaxed. As recently as 1971, with the unauthorized publication of the Pentagon Papers by the *New York Times*, this longstanding adversarial relationship flared anew. Although the main adversaries are the press and the executive branch, Congress has also been deeply involved and continues to be today. Unless congressional "press relations" are understood within the wider context of full communications between Congress and the public, however limited and self-serving that concept may be, a true picture of the way Congress communicates will not emerge.

Much of the legislative authority for the development of today's sophisticated system of congressional communications rests on the time-honored device of the "franking privilege," governing congressional mail. Congress established the "frank" or the right to send out free mail over the signature of the sender in 1775. In its most recent updating of the franking privilege (Section 3210 (a) (3) (A) of Title 39 U.S. Code as enacted by Public Law 93–191 of December 18, 1973), Congress authorized the franking of all mail matter "regarding programs, decisions and other related matters of public concern or public service. . . ." Inherent in this statement is the essential concept of two-way communication between senators and representatives and their constituents. It is only a short step from there to employing today's sophisticated tools of mass communication to achieve that goal.

If one accepts the premise that a democracy cannot function without the consent of the governed, then the men and women elected to carry out the wishes of the American people, must be free to communicate with them in the widest possible way.

Title 39 of the U.S. Code fixes that principle in these words:

> It is the intent of Congress that such official business, activities and duties cover all matters which pertain to the legislative process or to any congressional representative functions generally, or to the functioning, working or operating of Congress and the performance of official duties in connection therewith, and shall include but not be limited to, the conveying of information to the public, and the requesting of the views of the public, or the views and information of other authority of government, as a guide or means of assistance in the performance of those functions.

This section of the law governing the use of the mailing frank by Congress sets forth both the communications materials which may be mailed under the frank—newsletters, news releases, audio and video tapes, federal publications, photographs, internal and external correspondence, computerized mailings, questionnaires, and so on—and the penalties for violations.

Levels of Congressional Communications

National

Many but not all, congressional communications offices operate fulltime at the national, state, and local levels maintaining vigorous press relations programs aimed at each. Only a handful of senators and representatives avoid contact with the press. Most members of the U.S. Senate have access to the national communications media on a regular basis. Their committee assignments place them astride the major issues confronting the United States, and the views and comments of individual senators, regardless of party or ideological stripe, are sought after by reporters and commentators to bring depth and perspective to their stories.

The Senate is a smaller body than the 435-member House of Representatives and as a result is much easier to cover by the major national news organizations. Moreover, the Senate tends to narrow the focus of the prime issues facing the country. Coverage of both the Senate and the House takes a wide variety of approaches depending upon the interests and assignments of individual reporters and commentators. But most news coverage focuses on the power centers of both houses: the leadership, committee and subcommittee chairmen, members who distinguish themselves as experts on specific national subjects (defense, diplomacy, energy, taxes, etc.), members who are able to mobilize consent or dissent, members who hold leadership positions on the ideological spectrum, and some like Senator John C. Stennis of Mississippi and Warren G. Magnuson of Washington by their seniority.

The senators and representatives who fall into these categories are, for the most part, the consistent congressional newsmakers. They are the Byrds, the Bakers, the Kennedys, the Javitses, and the Jacksons of the Senate, and the O'Neill's, the Reusses, the Ullmans, the Udalls, and the Rhodeses of the House. Most are accessible and quotable. A story containing a quote by members of this group contains the ring of authority and adds a dimension of balance and perspective to a story.

They are the men and women who provide the grist of daily coverage of Congress. Their comments and opinions are sought after and they are the individuals who appear on the nation's major television news interview programs. Their bylines appear over op-ed articles in the *New York Times* and on the pages of influential journals and publications. They are the "congressional sources" cited in insider stories and frequently supply the tips and background information that appears in analytical or enterprise reporting from Capitol Hill. There is a natural affinity between the press and these individuals. Both are in the news business; one makes it, the other reports it.

Press secretaries to these members of the House and Senate generally develop excellent working relationships with members of the national press corps serving in Washington. Many are themselves former members of that press corps or are experienced journalists who know precisely what a reporter or columnist is seeking in terms of information, and help to provide it. They are hired for their knowledge and expertise, and many earn salaries ranging from the upper thirties to near the maximum. They are considered to be indispensable advisers on the issues and the politics facing the members they serve, particularly at the state and local levels, but at the national level as well. In addition to press secretaries who serve individual members of Congress, a few of the major congressional committees maintain full-time spokesmen who handle press relations on issues before their committees and subcommittees. Usually, however, the press secretary to the committee chairman serves in the dual capacity as personal and committee spokesman.

Much of the interplay between the press and Congress at the national levels of coverage takes place informally and behind the scenes in background or off-the-record interviews or telephone conservations. Because much of what is reported in Washington focuses upon interpretation and analysis, members of Congress are sought after to provide leads, inside information, and appraisals of the internal politics governing an issue or legislative initiative. That is not to say that members do not make news, issue news releases, or hold press conferences. They do, and they do frequently.

But because the national correspondents of the Associated Press, United Press International, the *New York Times, Time, Newsweek,* the *Washington Post,* the *Wall Street Journal,* and so forth, represent publications which maintain Washington bureaus staffed by reporters and commentators who specialize in various areas of government and political affairs and whose knowledge of issues runs deep, analysis and interpretation of complex issues and legislative-political subtleties, the "how" and "why" aspects of today's news have replaced the official pronouncements of senators or representatives which contain little of news value. Washington-based reporters and commentators are not simply interested in reporting the who, what, when, and where of developing news. They want the background and motivations that went into the introduction of legislation or the thinking of the administration and how it will play in Congress. To do this they need authoritative and independent sources of information which will provide the insight and perspective which will enable them to explain a complex issue to the public.

Many critics believe the result of this information trading process is the development of an incestuous partnership in the dispensing of national news. Only a few enterprising and determined individuals such as I. F. Stone have been able to produce outstanding investigative journalism in Washington without relying on the anonymous congressional source. Even the muckraking columnist Jack Anderson has conceded that many of his early inside news stories were based upon tips provided by the late Senator Joseph R. McCarthy, as McCarthy began his move across the pages of U.S. history in the late forties and early fifties.

There is no specific congressional mandate which provides a senator or representative with the necessity to communicate nationally. But it has been the nature of the federal system with its three independent branches that has created the need for an informed national electorate. Many key House and Senate press offices are sufficiently versatile to handle, as well as to capitalize upon, national media coverage.

Moreover, it is at this level that senators and representatives act as their own press spokesmen, and several have consistently gained the attention of the national press corps by developing what might be termed gimmicks (e.g., Senator William Proxmire's annual Golden Fleece Award or concocting bets on the outcome of the Super Bowl or World Series) or through major national investigations—both legitimate and questionable—(Pearl Harbor, Watergate, communist subversion, the Cosa Nostra, etc.). Some are staged more for political opportunism than legislative enlightenment. Political legacies have been established and broken on the investigative rock.

State and Local

It is at the state and local levels that congressional press relations and mass communications have been elevated to high virtuosity. And it is these levels that have brought congressional communications prolonged and persistent criticism. There is a point in American government at which the highest and most inspired form of public service dissolves into the political sphere. This happens every two years for members of the House of Representatives and every six years for Senators. It was true of Lyndon Johnson and Richard Nixon, John F. Kennedy and Warren G. Harding, Sam Rayburn and Gerald Ford, Wilbur Mills and Morris Udall. It is as regular as clockwork for all 535 members of Congress.

The question is simple: When does public service or electoral office become politics? The answer is not as simple, and it is in attempting to come to grips with the answer which has evoked sustained criticism of congressional communications. Cynics see it as a tool for self-perpetuation. In fact, the power of incumbency and the ability to dominate local news in one's state or district has been likened to about $50,000 worth of free advertising and publicity. Others see it as a dilemma inherent in our representative system of government, which can be resolved by total federal funding of congressional political campaigns. The question continues to be debated. Under the present system all congressional mass communications must cease 60 days before a primary or general election.

Senators and representatives who concentrate on national affairs and pay scant attention to their constituents and to communicating with the folks back home frequently find themselves losing the political base needed to return them to office. This is much more pronounced today than a few short years ago as the level of public education is on the rise and as a majority of Americans fail to vote. Regardless of how distinguished and able a nationally recognized member of Congress may be, few will be reelected without sustained and informed two-way communication with constituents.

Members of Congress communicate with their constituents in a wide variety of ways through a wide variety of media. Not all congressional offices, however, are covered by reporters from their home states or districts. As a result, senators and representatives have taken the initiative by communicating directly and frequently with their constituents through the daily and weekly newspapers, radio and television stations, and the specialized publications in their states and districts. Communicating through local newspapers and radio and TV stations on issues of interest to constituents not only keeps a senator's or representative's name in the news, but creates a strong bond with local editors, columnists, writers, reporters and broadcast personnel.

The senator or representative who provides accurate and exclusive information to the news media of his or her state or district becomes a vital news source whose office is consulted frequently, and on some newspapers is a regular newsbeat. Congressional press aides understand the importance of this symbiotic relationship, and in many cases, promote it vigorously. They initiate news stories of interest in the state or district by a telephone call from Washington. Good congressional news stories are given considerable play by the local press, and in some instances full credit for the information is given to the senator or representative by name, and is backed up by authoritative quotes from the member.

The news stories are many and varied, ranging from inside assessments of how the state's congressional delegation will vote on an important state or local issue to routine announcements about government grants and projects affecting facilities and employment. Announcing the location of a multimillion dollar synthetic fuel plant or flood control dam in an economically depressed region will be a page-one news story and will lead the local radio and TV news. It will also lend itself to commentary and feature treatment and visits from the senator or representative as the project progresses. The member of Congress will probably be asked to turn over the first spade of earth as construction begins or to deliver the dedicatory address when it is completed. If the member is especially loved by the local folks, his or her name may appear on the project posthumously. Well-written news releases which deal with an issue or activity factually and without self-congratulatory rhetoric receive high newsplay in local media.

Releases, news tips, information conveyed directly to local columnists, editorial writers, and specialty reporters become the currency of the communications transaction, assuring reporters of exclusive information and members of Congress prominent mention in the story. Television and radio stations seeking an exclusive local angle on a national or international news story seek out their senators and representatives for definitive statements from Washington. Members of Congress use the facilities of the House and Senate radio and television studios to provide state and local broadcasters with timely radio and television actualities, which are carried on the evening or hourly news. Many members write weekly news and opinion columns which are carried by the smaller newspapers of a state or congressional district. These items are usually prepared, packaged, and precisely targeted by the member's press department.

A typical week's activities in the busy press office of a senior U.S. senator means three or four major press releases issued for national, state, and local distribution, a weekly newspaper column for 25 weeklies in the state, a 5-minute radio broadcast for 30 local radio stations on SALT II or the Soviet invasion of Afghanistan or subcommittee testimony on marijuana decriminalization, a possible network TV or radio interview, an appearance on a local radio talk show explaining a major piece of legislation and taking phone calls from listeners, or an op-ed page article in the *New York Times*.

The Tools of Communications

The News Release

In order to carry out their individual roles as communicators, members of Congress employ a wide array of communications tools. Perhaps the most basic of all is the ubiquitous news release. Each day the House and Senate press galleries are flooded with releases as the 535 members of Congress vie to catch the attention of the Capitol Hill press corps. But unless a release contains straightforward factual information related to a significant legislative activity, investigation, or oversight initiative, or represents the comments and views of the leadership of Congress or its committees and subcommittees, or contains exceptionally controversial dissenting views, it will receive no more than perfunctory attention in the press galleries.

Targeted to specific reporters or publications, well-written releases containing timely and relevant information will be regarded with respect, and on some publications will be carried verbatim. As one veteran national reporter observed, "It's not going to hurt you nationally if you don't do press releases. But it can help." Major metropolitan dailies frequently use a senator's or representative's release as the basis for a comprehensive story, giving the member full credit for the information (or misinformation, if that is the case), and smaller or specialty publications carry the entire text of the release if it is relevant to their readers' interest.

The Newsletter

Another staple of congressional communication is the member's quarterly newsletter to constituents. Each member of Congress is given an annual budget of paper, which may be used for official business. Most members communicate directly with constituents on their activities by means of their newsletter. Newsletters vary widely in both quality and character of the information imparted. They range from cracker-barrel folksiness giving constituents information about government services and facilities available in the district, to the examination of serious national issues confronting the country, such as energy, inflation, and military preparedness.

Through the acquisition of direct mail lists, voter registration tapes (without party identification) or by using other professionally developed direct mail techniques, a senator or representative can not only reach most of the people of the state or district with a newsletter, but can target and tailor specific information to groups and organizations (veterans, labor, small business, teachers, public officials, religious leaders, etc.) both nationally and locally. Tied to an effective direct mail program, the newsletter issued by a senator or representative can reach a circulation level beyond that of the state or district's leading newspapers.

It is a powerful tool of public information. Well-documented, factual newsletters evoke strong responses by readers. One U.S. senator's newsletter discussing the problem of inflation reached all of the households of registered voters in his state and prompted the greatest response since he initiated the newsletter a decade before.

Congressional Record Reprints

A timely or relevant speech made on the Senate or House floor, a position paper of interest to a group or organization, a senator or representative's views on a controversial issue placed in the *Congressional Record* can be reprinted and mailed over the member's mailing frank to individuals or to members of organizations through specifically targeted mailings. Computerized mailing systems tied to the franking privilege have given members of Congress an extraordinary new tool and an unprecedented means of communicating directly with constituents. Moreover, such a system circumvents the necessity of depending upon the news media to reflect a member's views and opinions on issues.

The system has come under fire as representing an insidious form of government-subsidized propaganda. Few critics, however, credit Americans with the discernment and knowledge to recognize whether or not they are being given propaganda or facts. As poll after poll indicates, the American public understands precisely and emphatically when it is being fooled. No member of Congress could last in office more than a term or two if the information he or she is providing to constituents is false or frivolous.

The Press Conference

The judicious use of press conferences by members of the House and Senate to provide information both at the national and local levels can produce high quality public information. The give-and-take of the press conference format usually produces accurate information conveyed through the media to constituents, as presidential press conferences have long shown.

Attracting the Washington press corps to a House or Senate press conference requires a topic of national interest, particularly one that has been in the news (e.g., nuclear waste and toxic substance control), new and significant information on any major subject, major remedial or controversial legislation (e.g., the Hyde Amendment limiting federal payment for abortions), or strong dissent from generally accepted views and opinions of matters pending before Congress (e.g., arguments aimed at defeating the SALT II arms limitation treaty).

There are many other subjects which will attract national coverage of a member's press conference (e.g., candidacy for national office or reelection, presidential declarations or endorsements, even a member's retirement and the reasons for it). Press conferences which produce substantive information earn the respect and interest of the press, and usually result in positive coverage for a member who is well prepared.

Press conferences fall flat when:

- No substantive news results.
- Members make self-congratulatory or self-serving statements and observations.
- The issues discussed are irrelevant and nonnewsworthy.
- The press is preoccupied with more significant national news items, which conflict with a member's timing, or the president's or other members' press conference generates more interesting news.
- There are no visual materials to interest network television crews.
- Numerous other activities of greater news value intervene or World War III is declared at the White House.

Held sparingly when a member of Congress has a newsworthy presentation to make, the press conference, particularly during congressional recesses, can result in wide coverage of issues or a member's activities. The essential elements of successful press conferences are:

- A subject of national interest.
- Sufficient preparation by all participants.
- Timeliness of the information.
- Notification of the time, place, and subject matter of the press conference through the wire services' Daybook (UPI) and Calendar (AP) logs of daily congressional activities. This practice alone elevates a member's press conference from the mundane to the important and alerts news decision-makers at all levels.
- Expert supporting information provided by staff and/or specialists along with charts, graphs, maps, and other visual materials for television coverage.

House and Senate Radio and Television Studios

Both houses of Congress maintain sophisticated and professionally staffed facilities for communicating with constituents by means of radio and television. Many members use these facilities weekly. Some conduct regularly scheduled TV and radio programs on national affairs and vital issues, which are broadcast by media outlets in the states and districts. Some smaller local TV and radio stations not only carry the full programs as part of their responsibility to provide public service air time, but newsrooms edit segments of a member's radio or videotape for their news reports.

Senators and representatives from states far removed from the nation's capital record weekly programs for media centers throughout their respective areas. The programs are wide in scope, ranging from interviews with newsmakers or high government officials conducted by members to question-and-answer programs which address national, regional, or local issues. Such activity adds fuel to the argument that incumbent senators and representatives are virtually undefeatable, because the media has been coopted by the Washington mystique, then make the further gift of free air time.

Radio Actualities

Because radio news has become both insatiable and omnipresent in our society, the statements, views, and comments of members of Congress add authority and "actuality" to national or local news broadcasts. Many members oblige their local radio news managers by their willingness to be constantly available for commentary. A telephone call from Washington to Station KOKO, the local 50,000-watt station which reaches a statewide audience, commenting on the president's state of the union speech will be done live, then tape-recorded and carried on every news broadcast throughout the day.

By using a telephone linked to an automated tape system, senators or representatives can communicate with every news station in their states or districts simply by recording a message of up to five minutes and informing the state AP and UPI radio wires, which connect most radio newsrooms. The state radio wires oblige with an advisory to news editors, which describes the message and gives the telephone number at which it can be reached. All a local newscaster must do is call the number and record the message on his studio tape. These so-called "beeper" reports have become another congressional communications standby. Most offices are equipped with the automatic machinery for communicating telephone messages quickly and inexpensively.

Direct Mail

As noted previously, congressional constituent communications have moved swiftly and massively into direct mail programs which rival catalog merchandising activities. As a result, members of Congress are now able to provide a steady flow of information to general and targeted readers. They include newsletters and floor statements, copies of House and Senate bills targeted to specific audiences, specialized mailings to publications (newspapers, magazines, house organs, corporate and organizational newsletters, etc.) at all levels, and automated responses to constituent mail. Busy congressional offices receive hundreds of thousands of pieces of mail each year from constituents on issues of varying importance.

To handle this mountain of communication, the Senate and House have automated their mail-handling systems by means of high-speed word-processing equipment which can spew out thousands of responses a day to constituent mail. Questionnaires and opinion polls add yet another dimension to effective congressional communications. The results of polls and questionnaires can determine the way a Senator or Representative may vote on an issue. Many members of Congress believe automation has brought American government as close as possible to the Jeffersonian ideal of maximum public participation in the affairs of the nation.

Miscellaneous

Through video display terminals (VDTs) with instant access to the United Press International, national, regional and state news files (wires), senators and representatives can comment on news developments as they unfold. By using a keyboard command system, a congressional press aide can punch up UPI's daily news budget, inform the member of the most important stories, and prepare an immediate comment or statement which can then be telephoned to the local radio station and incorporated into the news story itself. Or he can quickly check the way UPI handled the member's speech to the American Bar Association in San Francisco, which he had telecopied as an advance news story two days previously. Wide Area Telephone Service (WATS) lines linked to high-speed telecopying equipment can put a member's press release in the hands of local and regional news editors within minutes.

The same VDT unit also provides immediate access through the LEGIS and SCORPIO computer programs of the Library of Congress to the vast pool of information stored in the library's computer system. Electronic information retrieval and storage eliminates the need for bulky space-consuming files, providing congressional communications offices with precisely indexed materials and information at the press of a computer button.

The electronic revolution has begun to provide Congress with the most extraordinary ability to communicate since the first Continental Congress met in 1774. As this revolution continues in the years ahead, centralized information systems and instantaneous communication will take new directions with ingenious applications. The question evey member of Congress must ask is: Will this vast new technology be used in the public interest as Jefferson's proposition demands, or will it be abused to promote one's self-interest or political survival?

Congress has been sensitive to this question, and has placed strict limitations with criminal penalties for abuse on its use for political purposes prior to primary and general elections. But, as all members of Congress who use the system are fully aware, it adds significantly to an incumbent's advantage over potential opponents. As long as no clear division in American political life remains between a member's public or political statements (theoretically all statements are political in the best sense of that term), there will be a constant uneasiness on the part of the public about the questions of abuse and propaganda.

The answers are not easy and will not be soon forthcoming.

CHAPTER 28

The Supreme Court: Information with Justice

Barrett McGurn

In many respects the work of the Supreme Court of the United States is the most public of all the activities of government. Five thousand cases come to the Supreme Court each year. One thousand or so of these call for rulings which, on occasion, can be made by a single justice. Four thousand, however, seek much more, a full-scale courtroom hearing by the nine justices followed by a precedent-creating decision on the merits. Of these 4000, about half are "paid cases," disputes whose contestants have been so convinced of the importance of the issues that they are willing to shoulder the often significant expenses involved in bringing their contest before the justices for a settlement. The greater share of the Court's most important decisions each year come from this bloc of 2000 "paid cases." What is significant in the area of public information is that every brief brought to the Court by lawyers in these paid cases is provided to the news media at the moment the brief reaches the Court. Unless there is some reason for urgent bench action, many a newsman thus may see the incoming brief before each justice has had occasion to examine it.

Each "paid case" litigant is required by Court rule to submit each presentation in printed booklet form. Forty copies of each document are required. Each justice, of course, receives a set, but, in addition, three sets go to the public information officer for immediate distribution to the news media. The Associated Press assigns a full-time resident correspondent who covers the Court 40 or more hours a week throughout the year—through the October-to-June active term of the Court and also through recess periods. The United Press International goes AP one better, assigning two full-time reporters. Each of these wires gets one full set of the paid briefs from the public information officer, keeping them on file for a year or so and finally turning them back to the information officer for distribution among law libraries across the country. The third set remains on open shelves in the office of the public information director, available for consultation by all other news personnel and also by the general public.

The other 2000 incoming cases arrive "in forma pauperis," meaning that the litigant—often a penniless convict—declares himself impoverished and unable to pay the usual Court costs. These cases may arrive in a single typewritten copy. The clerk of the Court photocopies such petitions for each of the justices. Often no issue of national importance or of constitutional concern is raised in the IFP petitions but there are exceptions. The Miranda case, as one example, provoked a Supreme Court hearing and a landmark decision about the rights of suspects taken into police custody. When the justices choose a pauper case for oral argument the Court, at is own expense, prints up the usual 40 copies and the public information office gets its customary three sets. Otherwise, any news person interested in a pauper case is free to examine the incoming single copy at the clerk's file room. Thus the news media have access to the full documentation on all 4000 incoming cases of each year.

The same is true of an additional 1000 cases which arrive at the Court each year, seeking some sort of judicial help such as a suspension of the effect of rulings in courts below. One justice rather than nine may be able to handle these. The public information officer watches this additional flow, flagging items of apparent news interest to the attention of the Court press corps. On their own the reporters get tips from lawyers. The Court information officer responds promptly to inquiries provoked by such tips. Thus by one route or another the media are informed of the status of all 5000 cases before the Court in any year.

The nine justices have two main tasks in the handling of the 4000 annual requests for courtroom hearings. The first to go through the 4000 selecting 150 or so for oral argument in the courtroom and for subsequent precedent-setting decision on the merits. Some 95 percent are winnowed out during this process; what the final court below decided remains in effect. The second task is to hear the 150 oral arguments of the term and to write the opinions which become foundation elements for national justice. In turning away so many cases there is no suggestion that they lack merit of sorts. It is merely the experience of the Court that 150 cases decided on the merits seem to be the maximum the Court can manage in a year. These average out to one every two calendar days, although the effort is even more concentrated. All hearings and decisions occur within the nine-month active term. Recess periods, such as the summer months, often go in good part to reading the unending flow of incoming cases in preparation for future decisions on how to handle each of them.

Three days a month from October through June the justices publish an orders list. Much of it lists the cases the justices have agreed to hear and the many they must necessarily turn away. The chief justice at the first moment of a Court week announces the release of the list. Within a minute or two the clerk, sitting at the end of the bench, repeats the chief justice's statement into an open telephone. An assistant in the clerk's office phones the public information officer on the floor below the courtroom. The latter, ready with 70 sets of the orders list, turns them right side up and makes an instant distribution to several dozen waiting news personnel. Thus another link is provided in the Court information chain; reporters who have studied incoming cases have immediate information on what the Court has decided to do with regard to 100 or 200 of these applications.

The final link is the handling of oral arguments and the release of the Court judgments on argued cases. All debates before the justices are public business to which the public are welcome as spectators. There are no closed hearings. Often, however, such as in a case like "the United States versus Nixon, President of the United States," there are far more claimants of seats than the relatively small courtroom can accommodate. Even with extra chairs moved into far corners, fewer than 500 persons can enter the courtroom at one time. Litigants and their friends, members of the Congress and Senate, and the never-neglected walk-in public all make powerful claims for space in the courtroom, but the news media are never overlooked. The public information officer has 35 good seats at his disposal to meet media needs at each hearing and, when something such as a Nixon case comes along, he is able to expand his part of the courtroom to accommodate as many as 90 members of news agencies, newspapers, news magazines, radio and TV stations, book writers, and, occasionally, members of Washington's foreign correspondent colony.

Weeks, even months, can elapse between the time of oral argument and the moment of decision. Inside their chambers the justices with the help of two to four young law clerks research the law, study constitutional implications, and draft their opinions. Each justice is free to supplement the Court's own action, the majority's decision, with a concerning or dissenting opinion. Drafts of these documents can go through as many as 15 writings, all of this done in private without public scrutiny. At the moment of decision, however, the same process is followed as in the case of the orders list. The chief justice announces that a decision has been reached and, within two minutes, 30 or 40 news personnel have copies in the office of the public information director. Few words are minced in the decisions as the Court states its decision and as dissenters, with equal vigor, place their opposing views on the public record.

The Court provides help of many kinds in addition to access to all petitions and to all hearings and instant distribution of orders and the texts of opinions. The public information officer has a four-room suite including two workrooms for reporters with assigned cubicles or desk spaces for the agencies that cover the Court most assiduously: AP, UPI, the *Washington Post*, the *Washington Star*, the *Wall Street Journal*, Reuters, the *New York Times*, the *Los Angeles Times*, the *Baltimore Sun*. There are typewriters, free local phone calls, and a ten-cent-a-page duplication machine for copying briefs and other documents. A small library of essential reference works includes the bound volumes of all supreme Court decisions back to 1940. Where there is need, reporters are introduced to the Court's closed library of 250,000 volumes for additional information.

For the radio newscasters there are a row of insulated booths on the ground floor just under the courtroom. These were used originally by the writing press when fewer reporters covered the Court. Opinions at that time were distributed in the courtroom and dropped through chutes to the news booth on the floor below. Occasionally a chute would clog causing panic for the news wire man waiting in the cubicle below. With a score or more additional agencies now covering the Court the chute system became obsolete and the broadcasters inherited the small area.

The orders list which is issued at 10 A.M. when the justices go to the bench at the beginning of a week is a nightmare for an unprepared newsman. It is taciturn and it may list 150 cases or, once a year at the end of the summer recess, as many as 1000 cases. To the uninitiated the listing is inscrutable: "The Court will not hear cases 79–280, Marcinkus v. Jones." The orders list is the fruit of a closed conference justices have had during the previous week, usually on Friday. It would be impossible for the most diligent reporter to read up on all 4000 outstanding cases preparing to send off bulletins instantly on whichever ones the justices chose to place on that particular orders list, so the Court tells newsmen which 150 or so cases are on the justices' Friday agenda. Most of these cases can be expected to show up on the Monday orders list. Reporters are asked not to write news stories on the basis of the conference list, not to say "case so and so is reaching the moment of truth." Routinely reporters respect this confidence. In exchange an impossible job is made more manageable, although reading and summarizing 150 cases is still an immense chore. The conference list goes in pieces to the newsmen as much as six weeks in advance.

Chief Justice Warren E. Burger has provided many modifications of Court information practices making the news personnel's assignment less onerous. For 100 years, until the time of Chief Justice Earl Warren, the immediate Burger predecessor, the Supreme Court had what was called "Decision Mondays." That meant that all orders and all opinions to be released in any week would be distributed as the first order of business when the justices went to the bench on the first day. This caused an immense news glut. Reporters still covering the Court in the early 1980s recalled with horror one day when a complete fat volume of the United States Reports (the collection of Court decisions) was issued at one time. There was an orders list plus 17 opinions. Five of the 17 were landmark decisions. One radio reporter lamented later:

"I had a two-minute spot coming up in forty minutes. On one of those land-mark cases I was unable to provide a complete sentence by itself. I had to handle it in a subordinate clause!"

Chief Justice Burger arranged to meet with a few of the Court's press corps once a year for what he called a "wages, hours and working conditions" session. What he meant was that the meetings could not turn into an impermissable press conference on Court decisions, past or future. With a smile the chief justice pointed out that "wages", too, were nothing about which he could help. "Working conditions" became the center of each annual discussion.

Reporters pointed out that an orders list is a big and awkward story by itself. The fact that a case will not be heard may strike a layman as a nonstory, but to a news person it may be worth even a column; it means that that case, perhaps a famous one, has reached the end of the road and that the decision of the court below—perhaps a significant jail sentence—becomes final. In addition just deciphering the orders list is a good day's work even for a well-prepared reporter.

Earl Warren had begun shifting a few decisions to the Court's second day of a week on the bench. Chief Justice Burger went further. Henceforth, he said, all things being equal, Mondays would be left to orders alone, Tuesday and Wednesdays would be used for opinions, and no day would see more than eight opinions. Thus newsmen had three days in which to do a job previously jammed into one.

Reporters pointed out a second problem. The bound volumes of Court opinions include a useful two- or three-page summary of the facts of the case, the action of the two previous courts, and a breakdown of the Supreme Court's own reasoning and decision. For a news wire, eager to get off a bulletin, such a summary clearly is just as helpful as it is to a lawyer who later researches the law. The trouble, however, was that the Supreme Court, in its desire to protect the confidentiality of its decisions prior to the moment of public release, had never allowed the Court's reporter of decisions to see the opinions until the moment the chief justice made them public. The reporter of decisions supervises preparation of the bound volumes, many of which appear only a year or so after the Court's action. The summaries or "headnotes" were written at a leisurely pace during that year and, of course, were of no help to newsmen. The lack of headnotes on the opinions at the moment of release was discussed by one anguished news agency reporter. She said:

"I got off a fast bulletin on one Opinion and, with all the rest there was to cover, I didn't get a chance to read it through until six hours later. I was horrified to find a footnote which totally reversed what I thought the Court had done!"

Chief Justice Burger changed the old rule. Now the reporter of decisions gets the opinions a few days before release and, often under tight time pressures, gets his headnote into the opinion at the moment of issuance. For afternoon newspaper reporters, wire people, and network correspondents, the change clearly has been a godsend.

The Code of Judicial Conduct for United States Judges "condemns the taking of photographs in the courtroom or its environs" during all but a few ceremonial judicial proceedings, and applies the same restriction to radio-TV coverage. The code is promulgated by the Judicial Conference of the United States and applies to all federal courts other than the Supreme Court. While the Supreme Court is free to adopt its own differing code it does in fact act in a spirit in conformity with what the Judicial Conference has decreed. No TV, still photography, or newsman tape recordings are permitted during Supreme Court oral arguments. Until recent years even sketching by artists was limited sharply. Now the public information officer arranges for unobtrusive clear-vision sketching positions for all interested news artists, as many as a half dozen at a time.

These are the many facilities the Supreme Court provides for the informing of the public. There are a few things the Court does not provide. One of these is on-the-record press conferences explaining Court decisions, or even not-for-attribution backgrounders for the same purpose. The decisions of the Court are carefully worded; the drafting process sometimes takes months. The decisions establish legal precedents. Lawyers and other judges scan the decisions word by word. They must speak for themselves. There cannot be an authoritative explanation of what the language of the decision fails itself to express. This involves problems for reporters seeking to understand the breadth and thrust of some rulings.

To fill this gap, law professors of the United States, as a public service, prepare 1500-word analyses of all cases accepted for oral argument. The Court accepts no responsibility for the professor-author's interpretation of the significance of each case but, lacking anything official from the Court, reporters have found these professional studies greatly helpful. (The professors call these studies "previews").

The one other area of information which the Court does not provide concerns the institution's innermost workings while judicial decisions are made. Five days each month during the active term, the nine justices meet in their private conference room to discuss which of the 4000 cases to hear, and which 200-or-so to decide on the merits. The justices assemble alone. No secretaries, law clerks, messengers, or other staff members attend them. Conversational exchanges are candid and, often, impromptu. Sometimes justices reverse themselves as they hear the comments of their fellows. Long experience has suggested to the justices that the privacy of these exchanges provides the best means for forming the collective opinion which may later provide new legal precedent. When orders are issued and decisions released, the core of what has transpired in the closed conference is published, often in great detail as defenders of the court decision collide in print with eloquent dissenters.

The cause of ample public information is served, no litigants or speculators receive unfair or improper advantage through leaks and, most important, the justices have had the modicum of confidentiality which they find essential to the correct discharge of the decision-making responsibility.

CHAPTER 29

State Department: Communication with Diplomacy

William D. Blair, Jr.

The Need

·Six years after the Arab oil embargo, according to a Roper poll, a majority of Americans believed that "There never was any real oil shortage. . . ." Five debate-filled months after the signing of the SALT II Treaty on strategic nuclear weapons, a majority of Americans knew too little about the treaty to identify the two countries which signed it. More than a decade after negotiations began for a new Panama Canal treaty, a majority of Americans were unable to attribute ownership of the canal either to Panama or to the U.S., and at the height of the debate on the new treaties, a majority of Americans questioned told pollsters that they were paying little or no attention to the issue.

Opinion survey findings such as these suggest one of the factors which give the public information task of the State Department its particular character. Historically, most Americans, most of the time, have not paid as much attention to their foreign relations as to domestic concerns.

While there are certainly exceptions to this rule (our united outrage at the Iranian seizure of our embassy and its personnel in Tehran is one example), the public in general has usually been willing to leave even the most important foreign policy questions, like the SALT II and Panama Canal treaties, to the small minorities who feel strongly about them—feelings which may or may not always be based on a careful weighing of the national interest.

Undoubtedly contributing to this relative unconcern over time is the preparation we Americans give our young people, in school and college, for understanding and dealing with the world community which will shape their lives. By any standard, the international and intercultural dimension in our educational system is a weak one. According to various authorities, not more than 10 percent of American undergraduates on graduation have taken courses containing non-Western materials; only about 2 percent of curricular time in our high schools is devoted to such studies, and many high schools have no courses at all which deal in any way with world affairs or non-Western culture. Language study is in serious decline on the campus and has all but disappeared in high school and earlier; only 15 percent of our high school students, for example, now study a foreign language for even one year, and very few go farther.

A presidential commission set up to study the problem reported in November, 1979, that "Our schools [are graduating] a large majority of students whose knowledge and vision stops at the American shoreline, whose approach to international affairs is provincial, and whose heads have been filled with astonishing misinformation." For the nation as a whole, the commission concluded, this results in "dangerously inadequate understanding of world affairs."

There are other special factors which affect the public information responsibility of the State Department. One is the fact that federal government information activity is conducted today in a different climate of opinion than in earlier decades. The finding of a Public Agenda Foundation study that popular trust in government plummeted from 75 percent to 33 percent between 1964 and 1976 (a finding broadly supported by other surveys) summarizes the change. While this has touched all of government, the national security agencies, because of their association with the Vietnamese war and other unpopular issues, have been, with the presidency, particularly targeted. Reestablishing greater confidence and trust is important not only to the morale and performance of government employees, but to the life expectancy of our political system. Awareness of this need has to be ever-present in the thinking of State Department information officers today—and of their colleagues and superiors.

Another special factor is the fact that some of the information in the possession of the Department of State is temporarily "classified" and withheld from the public, most often for one of two reasons: either it was given to us by a foreign government on the understanding that we would keep it confidential until it was no longer sensitive; or its release would damage U.S. security interests in other countries—by exposing our plans or negotiating positions prematurely, by gratuitously offending other governments, or in other ways.

While only a fraction of the total State Department record is classified (currently fewer than 25 percent of the documents being entered into our central files, and many of these only in part), failure to protect this fraction for an adequate period would drastically reduce our sources of information abroad, alienate our allies, undermine our negotiators, and ensure the failure of other American diplomatic efforts around the world. It is this need to protect *some* information temporarily which often prevents total disclosure at a given moment, and thereby makes the State Department "sound like the State Department." All of these considerations lead to the same conclusion, which is the basic operating principle for State Department public information efforts today: the only acceptable policy is one of maximum openness with the public, consistent with the clearly demonstrable needs of national security.

To raise the level of public attention to, and understanding of, the critical foreign policy issues, the department must work aggressively to make the essential facts on these issues more widely known. To build respect for the classification system so as to provide effective protection for information which genuinely requires it, in the national interest, we must classify as little as possible and for as brief a time as possible.

Above all, to contribute to the restoration of confidence in our political institutions and in the democratic process, we must demonstrate by our responsiveness to the popular demand for information our recognition that the public business we are conducting is indeed the public's, not our own. If these are not the traditional attitudes of diplomacy—and indeed they are not—it is nevertheless true that they are more and more being recognized and adopted by our American diplomatic professionals today as indispensable to mustering the public support without which no American foreign policy can be sustained.

Response to Demand

The channel through which the public's desire to know is presented most forcefully and continuously to the State Department is the insistent daily pressure from news media. Any event anywhere in the world which seems to impinge in one way or another on American interests is likely to produce an instantaneous barrage of inquiries to the department. Today, such events occur several times a day.

To respond as positively as possible to this demand, the State Department has developed the institution known as the "noon briefing," conducted by the spokesman of the Department. The noon briefing, which actually often begins at noon (a compromise between morning and evening newspaper interests), takes place at least five days per week, and on six or seven days if the news warrants. Attended regularly by at least 50 reporters, and in times of crisis by as many as 150, these news conferences have been open since the early days of the Carter administration to electronic as well as copy-paper coverage. The spokesman retains the right to go off the record, or more commonly to speak "on background" (not for attribution), and thereby for a particular response to turn off the cameras and tape recorders.

Preparing for the noon briefing occupies a good part of the day, not only for the spokesman, but for his subordinates in the Office of Press Relations, and for the so-called "public affairs advisers"—information officers specializing in the subject matter of a particular bureau (e.g., the Bureau of European Affairs, the Bureau of Economic and Business Affairs). Long before official office hours begin at 8:45 A.M., press officers will have digested the major east coast newspapers and the network morning newscasts and produced a news "budget"—a list of the current stories likely to inspire questions at the day's briefing. The spokesman will have discussed them with his staff and also, normally around 8:00 A.M., with the secretary of state. Questions will have been farmed out to the different bureaus of the department through the public affairs adviser in each bureau.

By mid-morning, the proposed answers—sometimes merely factual, sometimes involving a statement of U.S. policy and/or anticipated government action—are beginning to reach the spokesman. As the noon hour approaches, a cluster of press officers and PAAs is forming in his office to explain and supplement the "guidance" material and, if necessary, to phone urgently back to the desks concerned in search of a more responsive answer. Normally within a few minutes after noon, virtually always within an hour, the spokesman will be at the podium in the briefing room, before a large outline map of the world, to open with any announcements, and then to take questions until the senior wire service reporter present decides they have been at it long enough. In times of major news stories, this may be as much as an hour later.

Important as it is in conveying facts and foreign policy to the public—only the much less frequent news conferences of the president and secretary of state are more important—the noon briefing is by no means the only means by which the State Department facilitates news coverage of its work. Unlike many if not most of the foreign offices of the world, the department makes working space available behind its carefully guarded doors to any and all accredited news correspondents, foreign and domestic, assigned to regular coverage of the agency (*Pravda* and *Tass* not excluded), and even hands the newly arriving correspondent a department telephone book with a detailed organization chart showing exactly who is in charge of every country desk or other office, with his or her room number and phone number—information which in many closed societies would be considered state secrets. Correspondents are free to roam the corridors, telephone to any office, and talk to whomever can find the time to talk with them. (Interviews with the secretary and his principal deputies, of course, require prearrangement and are not unlimited in number, but they are not infrequent either.) The result is clear: No other foreign office in the world produces such an extensive outpouring of news and comment on the news.

Few public inquiries arrive more urgently or dramatically than the 2:00 A.M. wire-service telephone call which awakens the press office duty officer at home with rumors of revolution in a distant land. Still, the public has no hesitation in putting its questions directly, as thousands of phone calls and anywhere from 100,000 to a half-million letters and telegrams a year forcefully attest. To the telephone caller seeking information from a bureaucracy, nothing is more frustrating or infuriating than to be referred seemingly endlessly from one office to another, only to find at each stop that this office too is incapable of answering the question. Many callers give up, after several unsuccessful tries. In an effort to minimize its own misdeeds of this kind, the State Department offers a Public Information Service (PIS), telephone number (202) 632–6575, which promises, and delivers, one-stop service. If the small staff of this service cannot give the answer immediately, its members will take the name and telephone number of the caller, hang up, seek the answer through as long a chain of frustrating references around the department as necessary, and either call the inquirer back with the desired information, or make sure that the appropriate expert calls him or her back—usually the same day, often within the hour. No pass-the-buck referrals are allowed.

On one recent occasion, the PIS was able to solve a problem for a caller from a telephone booth at Boston's international airport, who had arrived there with his family for an overseas flight, only to find that not all members of the family had proper passports. The ruin of the family vacation loomed an hour away at the time of his call. Before he got off the line (many PIS phone calls on another line later), the problem had been resolved, and the family made the plane on time.

Many callers seek neither information nor service so much as an opportunity to express their views on an issue, and an assurance that those views will be considered by a competent official. This too the PIS provides, by offering a hearing by knowledgeable State Department officers, and by reporting to the desks concerned the views of callers who so request, or even of callers who do not request it but whose comments are of special interest. At the time of writing, the service is receiving more than 1000 calls a month.

The task of responding to the bulk of the mail which arrives daily in search of information from the department is similarly centralized, for efficiency and economy. While letters requiring an individual response by a particular person will naturally receive it, the larger part of the mail is impersonal and repetitive in character, and numbers of inquiries can be answered with the same or similar responses.

A small Communications Management Division performs this task, by analyzing the mail referred to it, consulting the other parts of the department and preparing responses to the different questions, feeding those responses into a computer, and instructing the computer to produce a reply incorporating the correct combination of responses to meet the needs of each correspondent. The result, in most cases, is an informative and individual letter of reply to each incoming telegram or letter. Before computer help was available, many thousands of communications had to be answered, usually somewhat inadequately, by printed form letters or postcards, or not at all, to keep within our limitations of funds and staff.

Obviously the full explanation of complex issues, and of policy concerning them, often requires greater length than is convenient in correspondence. To meet this need for information in greater depth, the State Department like most agencies conducts a publications program. Ours is not elaborate. Its elements are:

- in simple, looseleaf notebook-sized format for easy reference, the full texts of speeches, congressional testimony and other public statements of policy on current issues by the president, the secretary of state and other senior officials, and the texts of official documents and reports on those issues;
- *GIST* papers: single-sheet, thumbnail summaries of the facts and the policy on particular current issues;

- *Background Notes on the Countries of the World*: unclassified country papers, periodically updated, with maps and basic statistics, again in looseleaf notebook-size format (because of their extreme popularity—millions of copies have been sold—these are available only by purchase individually or by subscription from the Superintendent of Documents, Government Printing Office, Washington, D.C. 20402);
- the *Department of State Bulletin*, the official monthly record of U.S. foreign policy, in a magazine format ($18 for an annual subscription from the superintendent of documents); and
- occasional special-purpose publications.

When appropriate, these publications are used in partial response to particular inquiries. In addition, the department maintains mailing lists totaling around 50,000 persons who have asked in writing to receive our publications in one or more specified subject categories, and new publications other than the *Background Notes* and the *Bulletin* are distributed accordingly.

Another public information need which we try to meet is the continuing demand for first-hand, face-to-face discussion of the international issues with State Department officers. This takes the form of numerous requests for briefings at the department in Washington, or for participation by department officers as speakers at meetings across the country, from groups interested in one or another aspect of foreign affairs. This kind of personal contact with private citizens in different parts of the country is especially valuable to an agency whose line positions are largely staffed by foreign service officers—career diplomats who spend at least half their working lives abroad, and who particularly need while home to get up to date on the interests and concerns of their countrymen. For this reason, as well as for the information they can impart, we try to get as many of them as possible, of all ranks, out of Washington and around the country.[1]

To stretch limited resources as far as they will go, we normally ask organizations requesting a speaker to pay his or her travel expenses (fees are not allowed), but we make exceptions for worthwhile groups which could not afford the cost. For officers other than the secretary of state, whose public statements, with the president's, are the primary national vehicle for announcing foreign policy, we try to avoid formal speeches, and ask sponsoring organizations to allow the State Department visitor to spend most of his or her time in open discussion with the members of the host group. We also try to see that our officers make maximum use of their time in communities outside of Washington by talking with newspaper editorial boards, appearing on radio and television discussion programs, calling on leaders of local organizations concerned with policy issues, and so forth.

Last year (FY-79), several hundred different representatives of the department took a total of nearly 1500 such working trips to other parts of the country.

No serious group, from a high school class on up, is denied a briefing at its request in the department. If openness is the first rule of our public information effort, the second is "More people out, more people in." We want more of our officers to spend more time out and around the country, and we want to attract more private American citizens with knowledge and experience of foreign affairs into our offices in Washington, for exchanges of ideas and information with us.

To increase these contacts, we conduct an annual series of a dozen or more so-called "seminars," each a two- to five-day program bringing together a small group from academia, the media, business, labor, or other occupations around the country with host officers and policy-makers of the department, for frank, off-the-record discussion of critical issues. In collaboration with interested private organizations, we also conduct national and regional conferences each year, in Washington and other cities, on one or more areas of foreign policy.

Perhaps the most basic demand for information which the American people make on the State Department is for access to the department's records—even though requests for such access tend to come primarily from a small number of specialists. Since some of those records, as noted above, are classified, the goal of providing as much access as possible requires special efforts on our part: to declassify and publish the essential record systematically and as early as possible in a series of documentary volumes, *Foreign Relations of the United States*; to open the full record as early as possible to the public at the National Archives; and to review individual records for possible declassification and/or release in response to requests under the Freedom of Information Act, the Privacy Act, and Executive Order 12065 on national security information.

The *Foreign Relations* series is unique in the world. Currently being published at 26–29 years after the event—in 1980, in other words, we are publishing volumes dealing with the years 1951–1954—it reprints about 10,000 pages per year of the most important official documentation relating to the development and conduct of U.S. foreign policy. It is compiled and edited under strict guidelines of accuracy and objectivity, and is highly respected by scholars and other foreign affairs professionals both for its historical integrity and for its indispensability as a reference and finding aid.

While publication 26–29 years after the event may seem glacially slow to the layman, in the context of diplomatic records it is lightning fast. Most countries of the world open or publish their foreign relations records only highly selectively, if at all. No other government publishes as promptly as the United States does, and none publishes so comprehensively.

In preparing the *Foreign Relations* volumes, State Department historians first compile a large selection of the records, not only of the State Department, but also of the National Security Council, the Defense Department, the Central Intelligence Agency, and other foreign affairs agencies, to include all the important foreign policy decisions. This rough compilation is then submitted to appropriate authority in each agency for review for declassification as necessary. If declassification is denied in too many cases, so that too few unclassified or declassified documents are available to describe and explain the key decisions, publication of the volume is delayed until adequate declassification can be obtained.

On the basis of this review of a large sample of the records, under a recently reorganized system, a new departmental Declassification Center prepares guidelines for the review and declassification of the total State Department record for the period in question. The full block of files of that period can then be transferred physically to the National Archives for permanent retention and early opening to the public. The archives in turn will screen those files, page by page, under the department's guidelines; refer back for detailed scrutiny at the department any files or documents requiring further examination; and set aside certain documents for continued protection to the extent required by the department and authorized by law and executive order. In practice, this means that most State Department files now are open to the public through 1949; we expect to begin opening the files for 1950–1954 during 1980.

Under President Carter's executive order 12065, which took effect on December 1, 1978, the agencies dealing with classified information were given 10 years from that date to get down to a 20-year deadline for review and declassification of most classified information. The principal exception affecting State Department records is for information supplied by foreign governments on the understanding that it will be kept in confidence; declassification review of information in this category, when necessary, may be deferred to 30 years. We are working to meet the general 20-year requirement in less than the allotted decade.

A third method of providing access to department records is in response to individual requests for information under the Freedom of Information and Privacy Acts and the mandatory declassification review provisions of E.O. 12065. As all agencies are subject to these legal requirements, only two points concerning State Department compliance seem worth noting here. First, the department has established a strongly positive record of response to these requests, with the great bulk of the material requested (approximately 90 percent) being released immediately or on appeal. Second, in an effort to speed up our handling of such requests, we have recently centralized the review of materials requsted, so that the function is now performed by a single office established for this purpose—the new declassification center—rather than by desk officers primarily concerned with other business in all the bureaus of the department.

Special Needs

The programs discussed above attempt to respond directly to the expressed needs of the public for information from the State Department about our foreign relations. These programs absorb most of the public information resources of the department. However, the department has other public information needs of its own.

Foremost among these needs is an informed and analytical awareness of American public opinion on the major foreign policy issues. As already noted, this is one of the principal reasons for sending our personnel to different parts of the country: to listen, as well as to speak. But this is a fragmentary and subjective kind of opinion research.

To provide more objective information, a small staff of public-opinion specialists in the department monitors polls conducted by opinion-survey organizations around the country. Combining data from diverse sources, the staff makes its own analyses of public opinion on current issues. Reviews of newspaper editorial comment by the same office, and the reports of our public correspondence and telephone inquiry services, provide corroboration of some of the attitudes reported.

Interpreting the evidence, the public opinion analysts report to the secretary of state and his senior subordinates on opinion trends and popular perceptions and misconceptions of foreign policy. (Example: During the debate on the Panama Canal treaties, the analysts found that a good deal of the opposition to the treaties was based on fears for the security of the canal after the American presence had been reduced or removed. The point which was not popularly appreciated was the fact that the *avoidable* threat to the canal in this missile era was internal, not external. The internal threat would diminish to the extent that the Panamanians regarded the canal as their own.) Such reporting can contribute significantly both to the policy-making process and to the effort to inform the public.

A second important need from the department standpoint is the ability to mount a public information program independent of public demand—that is, on subjects which government finds vital, but to which the public is relatively indifferent. The twin cases of energy (to the public, the "noncrisis") and SALT II, surely the most important issue of the decade for national survival, but a mystery too arcane to tackle, to most of the electorate, are cases in point. While there was, and is, at this writing, great national need for more understanding of these two subjects, public pressure on the government for information about them has been conspicuously light. Given the importance of the subject matter, for the department to limit its information efforts on these issues to the low level of public requests would be irresponsible.

To ensure that a portion of our scarce resources is reserved for such purposes, the State Department in recent years has assessed its public information priorities systematically. At least once a year, more often if necessary, the policy planning and public affairs staffs of the department prepare a short list of the issues which in their judgment will require special public information efforts in the months ahead. Keeping the list realistically short, in view of limited staff and funds, can be a bureaucratic struggle. Eventually, a recommended list is forwarded to the secretary of state for his personal review and possible amendment. (The list in effect at this writing includes both energy and SALT, among the others.)

Once the list is approved, a Public Affairs Bureau planning officer works with the Public affairs advisers of the other bureaus concerned to plan a concerted public information effort on each priority subject. Such an effort may include particularly careful analysis of the available public opinion data on these subjects; an attempt to identify the nongovernmental groups around the country which are actually or potentially most interested in them, and to reach these groups through the ongoing speaking, briefing, seminar and conference programs; and publication of any new printed materials needed. Special conferences or other meetings of organization representatives and community leaders may be arranged in Washington or other cities to attract more attention to these issues.

A third departmental need, related to both of the first two, is more contact and communication with groups which have not traditionally been part of the active foreign affairs constituency. This includes some ethnic minorities, such as the black and Hispanic Americans; farmers, and to some extent labor unions; and many newer interest groups such as women's rights organizations and other human rights advocates (although some older women's groups, like the influential League of Women Voters, have concerned themselves with foreign policy for many years). The days when the audience for foreign policy was limited primarily to the United Nations associations and world affairs councils are long gone, but it has taken time to build working relationships between the State Department and the more recent participants in the public policy forum. Much of our outreach today is aimed at correcting this shortfall—an effort in which the secretary of state and his deputies have taken personal part, through meetings with leaders of the groups involved.

A final special objective of our information activity is to help bring about an enlargement of the international dimension in American education, for the reasons suggested at the beginning of this chapter. While education is not the function of the State Department, we obviously have to be concerned about what the presidential commission on Foreign Language and International Studies recently called "the widening gap" between our national security needs "and the American competence to understand and deal successfully with other peoples in a world in flux."

Accordingly, we look for opportunities to call the problem to the attention of a wider public, through the comments of our senior officials. We lend encouragement and support to the public and private organizations which are trying to deal directly with the problem. Senior State Department officers, for example, have participated in a continuing effort by the National Council on Philanthropy to enlarge the meager share of American corporate and foundation financial support being allocated to public education about foreign affairs. From time to time we prepare information materials designed at least partly to assist and stimulate classroom and adult education programs in world affairs. A popular example of these efforts is the four-part historical film series produced by the department in recent years to trace the evolution of U.S. foreign policy from the Revolution through the war in Vietnam. The films have been widely used at schools and colleges and in continuing education activities across the country.

In the foregoing summary of public information programs, there is no mention of institutional publicity, and this is an accurate reflection of the fact. The department does publish an occasional pamphlet about the Foreign Service to support recruitment. And every few years a basic publication describing the organization and functions of the department is published or revised. Apart from these minimal responses to the public's often rather hazy notions of what the State Department and Foreign Service actually do, we have preferred to put our information resources into discussion of the issues, and to leave it to the public to draw its own conclusions about the institution and its personnel from the quality of that discussion and from their substantive performance.

We make that choice despite our awareness that diplomatic services and foreign offices, like prophets, are not apt to be overly honored in their own countries. So long as state departments and foreign services remain the principal channels through which the national interests of other countries are factored into the policy process of their own country, they will always be a little suspect to many of their countrymen. Institutional publicity could do little to alter this. In the predictable future, the only "solution" for this public relations problem is a reasonably thick skin, and a clear eye on what matters: not the popularity of the institution, but the effectiveness of our national foreign policy.

Organization and Cost

Responsibility for the information programs of the Department of State lies principally, though not exclusively, with the assistant secretary for public affairs, and with the Bureau of Public Affairs which he or she heads. For several years until recently, the assistant secretary served as department spokesman as well—an innovation in the Carter administration. (At other times, the press spokesman has been either a senior subordinate of the assistant secretary for public affairs or a member of the personal staff of the secretary. Under the latter arrangement, which Secretary Muskie re-instituted on succeeding Secretary Vance this year (1980), the spokesman is organizationally separate from the Public Affairs Bureau.)

The bureau administers five program offices:

- an Office of Press Relations (round-the-clock information services to the news media);
- an Office of Public Communication (public inquiries and mail, publications, films; also staff support for the appeals review boards, chaired by the assistant secretary, which decide on appeals of denials of requests for access to records under the FOI and Privacy Acts and E.O. 12065);
- an Office of Public Programs (speaking trips, briefings, seminars, conferences);
- an Office of the Historian (*Foreign Relations*, ad hoc policy-related historical research, assistance to outside researchers), and
- an Office of Plans and Opinion Analysis (public opinion analysis; surveys of editorial comment in the press; public affairs planning).

For all functions, including administrative services, the bureau is presently authorized 137 positions and about $5.4 million a year, of which more than $3.3 million represents payroll costs.

The Public Affairs Bureau and its programs receive a good deal of help from the information officers assigned to the other bureaus and major offices of the department—the so-called public affairs advisers and their staffs. A part of the work of the PAAs is directed toward foreign publics, rather than toward Americans. However, they add about 40 positions, and a payroll cost of around $800,000 to the department's information resources.

Finally, primary responsibility for access to the department's records and for their systematic declassification, in accordance with the FOI and Privacy Acts and executive order, is assigned to the Bureau of Administration. In that bureau, the task is divided between the Foreign Affairs Document and Reference Center, or central files, and the new Declassification Center, which reviews documents requested with a view to release. (As indicated above, appeals against denials of access by the Declassification Center are decided by appeals review boards chaired by the assistant secretary for public affairs.) The Declassification Center also reviews a large sample of the more important documents from each year's files, as a basis for preparing guidelines for the declassification of the total record at the National Archives. All together, the equivalent of about 75 full-time positions (most of the records reviewers are recently retired foreign service officers working part-time), and about $2.6 million, mostly for salaries, are allocated to these functions.

In sum, the Department of State allocates over-all approximately 255 positions or the equivalent, and $8.8 million to public information, broadly defined. The substantial costs of public access to records and their review and declassification, included in this total, would be omitted from many compilations, as representing primarily records management rather than public information. On the other hand, these figures do not include the cost of the time of other noninformation personnel who contribute as sometime speakers and writers and in other indispensable ways to information programs. By any measure, the total cost is a miniscule share (by this calculation, less than half of one percent) of the $1.9 billion total State Department budget.

Notes

1. Similarly dual purposes are served by two other department activities: the diplomats in residence program, under which about six senior foreign service officers annually spend an academic year teaching at different universities and colleges around the United States; and the special domestic assignments (Pearson Amendment) program, congressionally inspired, under which a limited number of mid-level officers each year, currently 20, are assigned to work in state and local governments and other nonfederal, nonprofit organizations away from the capital city. While officers participating in both programs can and often do contribute to public information projects where they are assigned, the prime purpose of these activities is professional development.

CHAPTER 30

HHS: A Public Affairs Conglomerate

Lewis M. Helm

The Department of Health and Human Services, formerly the Department of Health, Education, and Welfare, is a governmental conglomerate that spends more on its programs than any other single entity in the world. Likewise, within the federal establishment, its public affairs apparatus is second only to the the U.S. International Communications Agency in the cost of services and products, and it outpaces the net gross billings of even the world's largest public relations agency.[1]

The official "Government Manual," which contains the mission statements of government agencies, describes the department in this way:

> The Department of Health and Human Services is the Cabinet level department of the Federal executive branch most concerned with people and most involved with the Nation's human concerns. In one way or another—whether it is mailing out social security checks or making health services more widely available—HHS touches the lives of more Americans than any other Federal agency. It is literally a department of people serving people, from new-born infants to our most elderly citizens.

From the time HEW was created on April 11, 1953, it was on the vanguard of highly visible programs that have had a massive impact on the public. Many of these programs have stirred emotion and controversy. Welfare, school desegregation, women's rights, busing, aid for the elderly and handicapped, drugs, diseases, education . . . all have seen extended public debates before and during legislation; then, even as programs are being administered, discussion often has intensified as the public reacts to the new social legislation and the bureaucracy's method of implementing it.

Because of this continuing debate about its activities, the department has undergone massive and frequent redirection of programs and structures following national elections. Likewise, the department's public affairs apparatus, supporting highly visible programs, has been affected by both the style and substance of leadership changes, frequently undergoing its own major redirection. However, public affairs efforts have consistently been ranked high for creativity, competence, and effectiveness in communicating with the department's publics. In fact, the department has often provided new techniques which the White House and other departments have adapted to their own programs.

HEW's Structure and Programs

To understand the depth and scope of its public affairs efforts, it is necessary to review the department's structure and programs. The department has four principal operating components (POCs), each containing a variety of major agencies. In addition, the secretary of health and human services is assisted by an under secretary (his chief deputy), general counsel, inspector general, and five staff assistant secretaries in the areas of public affairs, legislation, planning and evaluation, personnel administration, and management and budget.

The department also has government's most extensive regional network with offices in ten federal regional centers—Boston, New York City, Philadelphia, Atlanta, Chicago, Dallas, Kansas City, Denver, San Francisco, and Seattle. These offices represent the department in relations with state and local government officials and handle program activities in those areas.

Most of the department's major agencies, coordinated by the POCs, have regional offices in addition to their headquarters in the Washington, D.C., area. Their regional outlets generally report directly to their major agency in Washington with only a loose relationship with the secretary's principal regional official and an even more general relationship to regional public affairs offices.

While still within HEW, the Education Division, created in 1972 and headed by an assistant secretary, ranked as perhaps the least responsive to departmental guidance. While the Office of Education was under nominal control of the assistant secretary for education, many of its programs had both authorization and appropriations passed directly to them by Congress, specifically excluding the secretary of HEW's supervisory authority. In this way Congress kept influence over financial aid passed back to congressional districts. Thus, in the reorganization, greater control and responsibility for education programs is placed with a cabinet-level secretary and staff.

The Department of Education has high budget item programs including ones directed toward elementary and secondary education, occupational and adult education, education for the handicapped, postsecondary education, Indian education, and student financial assistance. The National Institute of Education also was under the assistant secretary's aegis and since has been transferred to the new education department. Created to provide leadership in the conduct of scientific inquiry into the educational process, it attempts to obtain dependable knowledge about educational quality and to improve the educational process.

The Office of Human Development (HDS), a POC headed by an assistant secretary remains in HHS and administers a broad range of social and rehabilitative services designed to deal with problems of groups such as the elderly, children of low income families, mentally or physically handicapped, runaway youth, and native Americans. Its subordinate agencies are the Administration for Children, Youth, and Families; Administration on Aging; Administration for Public Services; Administration for Native Americans; and the Rehabilitation Services Administration.

The Public Health Service, reporting to an assistant secretary for health, is among government's oldest organizations. It was created July 16, 1798, and has seen numerous new mandates through the years. While still considered as a "commissioned" service with a rank structure similar to that of the army, navy, air force, marines, coast guard and merchant marines, Public Health's activities are divided into six very major operating agencies.

The Alcohol, Drug Abuse, and Mental Health Administration (ADAMHA) provides research and leadership to reduce and eliminate health problems caused by the abuse of alcohol and drugs. The Center for Disease Control (CDC) is responsible for the prevention and control of diseases and other preventable conditions in the country. The Food and Drug Administration (FDA) directs activities toward protecting the health against impure and unsafe foods, drugs, and cosmetics. The Health Resources Administration (HRA) addresses the problem of coordinating and developing the nation's health manpower resources in an effort to strengthen state and local health capabilities. The Health Services Administration (HSA) addresses federal support of health delivery systems nationwide. The National Institutes of Health (NIH) supports innovative biomedical research into the causes, prevention, and cure of most of the known diseases through its institutes specifically directed toward various diseases.

Another POC is the Health Care Financing Administration, created in 1977 to oversee the Medicare and Medicaid programs. It is headed by an administrator of assistant secretary rank. The Social Security Administration, headed by a commissioner of assistant secretary rank, administers the national contributory social insurance program which has become the biggest trust fund in the world. Two separate offices report directly to the secretary. They are the Office for Civil Rights and the Office of Child Support Enforcement established in 1977 to enforce support obligations of parents. The executive secretariat, a mini-bureaucracy of considerable size, coordinates the massive flow of correspondence, decision papers, and other documents related to the operation of the department.

The Changing Role of Public Affairs

Because of the size and complexity of the department, it is most difficult for the office of the assistant secretary for public affairs to screen the issues and then select those with which to become involved as an integral, meaningful part of the decision-making and communications process. Then, too, there is a continuing resistance to public affairs "input." Normally, each separate governmental entity develops its own élan. Support evolves from groups benefitting from agency programs and also from members of Congress who, themselves believe in the benefits of particular programs or who have vocal constituents who do. This causes what some students of government call "the iron triangle"—bureaucracy, Congress, and clientele working together to perpetuate and increase government funding for an activity. Influence that cannot be controlled within the "triangle" can become suspect and often resisted even though the efforts might be totally supportive. The National High Blood Pressure Education Program described in Chapter 18 is, arguably, an example of an iron triangle composed of private sector health interests, NIH heart specialists, and key congressmen and staffs.

Also, the assistant secretary for public affairs is a presidential appointee, responsible for the *political* as well as programmatic interests of the president and the secretary.[2] Therefore, that office's participation in programs reflects a degree of partisanship. Again, because partisanship is alien to the continuation and progress of the programs, the "iron triangle" may resist a probing incursion by the assistant secretary for public affairs.

The most highly publicized attempt by an administration to cut programs came during the 1973 "Battle of the Budget" by the Nixon White House. All public affairs heads of executive branch agencies were instructed by the White House Office of Communications to develop "horror stories" about some agency programs which the administration hoped to eliminate or reduce. This direction did not always meet with approval of department heads who felt it was too heavy-handed and ill-conceived. With this conflict it became difficult for public affairs programs to be managed at the departmental level. Deep suspicion of motives prevented a close working relationship with agencies.

Also, although in theory the secretary of health and human services controls the department's budget through the assistant secretary for management and budget, in truth, the agencies themselves decide how most of the funds will be spent. They usually are influenced strongly by the wishes of the secretary (who along with the Office of Management and Budget submits the departmental/agency budgets to Congress), but administration of approved budgets rests with the agency head.

Further, there is insufficient time and workforce at the secretarial level to plan and administer public affairs programs in support of more than 300 separate activities. Only spot-checks of activities are possible to determine whether they are legal and cost efficient. However, when programs are of presidential interest the assistant secretary for public affairs' office assumes responsibility for communications and strategy.

One such activity, for example, was the development of regulations for the Title IX Amendments to the Education Act. Under the aegis of the Office for Civil Rights and supported by the general counsel's office, a series of public forums between June 24 and August 2, 1974, was developed by the assistant secretary for public affairs as a vehicle to publicize the issue and to receive public comment.

The department was responsible for adopting regulations to implement a vaguely worded, short law Congress had passed barring use of federal funds by educational institutions which discriminated against women. By its vagueness in the legislation, Congress had managed to pass the controversy about tough decisions to the then Department of Health, Education, and Welfare. The women's movement at that time was gaining momentum in its fight against sex discrimination and very vocally supported strong regulations. However, the ramifications of effect of the law on existing practices in athletics, research, supporting college organizations, and other programs throughout public and private educational institutions was widely feared by academia, organized athletics and by conservative legislators. Consequently, regardless of whether the then-secretary of HEW, Caspar W. Weinberger, resolved to issue strong or mild regulations, vituperations were certain to follow.

Therefore, the public affairs plan, in addition to obtaining comment, was created to balance adverse reaction with positive reaction to the department's fairness in the wide solicitation of comments. Public affairs staff members worked for four months in developing the forums and following up on the comments. In each of 12 cities a civil rights and legal team used a wide range of media outlets to air the issue. Then, affected interest groups and individuals testified at public hearings before the HEW team. These comments, along with the media coverage, were synthesized, analyzed, and passed along to the secretary for his consideration. All told, more than 3500 people attended the hearings and asked 600 questions. The media briefings were covered by 71 newspapers and wire services, 41 radio stations, and 38 television stations. Through this process, the department was finally able to announce a set of regulations. The effort was praised by Senator Jacob Javits as a successful example of participatory government. Media representatives as well as affected groups reacted favorably to the process.

Because of the necessity to pick and choose how the limited resources within the office of the assistant secretary for public affairs might be used successfully, each HEW secretary has redirected the public affairs focus to suit his own management style. Consequently, the size and missions of the office have varied widely over the last decade. This state of affairs, hardly unique to HEW, was underscored by the aforementioned January, 1979, General Accounting Office audit of public affairs activities within the department. Drawing upon the major finding that all agencies within the federal government lack uniform definitions of public affairs and consistent public affairs campaign planning, GAO specifically recommended that the department "develop procedures to ensure that criteria . . . be adequately and consistently applied to . . . public affairs activities and campaigns." The report went on to suggest the proper criteria for "developing public information campaigns." Despite the problems with consistency, however, there are a number of activities and relationships that have remained fairly constant throughout changes in administrations and directions at HEW.

The Office of Public Affairs

The Office of Public Affairs is the focal point of all departmental public affairs activity. It consists of five divisions—news, freedom of information, regional and outreach, audio-visual, and editorial and publications management.

The News Division directs and coordinates all releases to the press and broadcast media, regardless of whether they are agency or departmental releases. In addition, the News Division arranges for news conferences, briefings and media interviews.

The Freedom of Information Division is responsible for implementing Freedom of Information Act (FOIA) regulations and other regulations related to the Federal Advisory Committee Act and Government in the Sunshine Act. The Privacy Act is administered separately by other offices of HEW. This was done to preclude one office from wielding such strong influence in such an important area. Each agency public affairs office is the contact for Freedom of Information requests. The appellate process is handled by the assistant secretary for public affairs. This is unique in government since almost all other departments use the general counsel as the FOIA denial authority.

The Regional and Outreach Division coordinates public affairs assistance in the ten regional offices, as well as coordinating trips and briefings for the secretary and White House staff members.

The Audio-visual Division reviews and approves agency audiovisual products and exhibits, requiring preapproval of films and television tapes before production is started or outside contracts signed.

The Editorial and Publications Management Division reviews more than 1000 HEW publications a year. The division requires that agencies submit for approval a plan for publications outlining the need, cost, and mode(s) of distribution. In addition, the division prepares speeches, statements, articles, and related material for the secretary and top officials. It edits congressional testimony, prepares a departmental publication, and publishes the daily "Green Sheets," a summary of news about the department.

The Office of Public Affairs also provides the secretary with the management capability to evaluate and direct public affairs plans, expenditures, and personnel of the department's components. The following outlines most of the relationships of the office to other department elements:

1. To the secretary
   a. Provides public affairs counsel
   b. Provides public affairs comment on all major policy decisions
   c. Coordinates the secretary's speaking, travel, and media activities
   d. Writes speeches and other statements
2. To other assistant secretaries
   a. Provides public affairs counsel
   b. Concurs in the selection of top public affairs staff members
   c. Participates in developing program policy
   d. Gives public affairs input on planning
3. To agencies
   a. Reviews and approves the structure of public affairs organizations
   b. Reviews and approves annual public affairs plans and budgets
   c. Concurs in professional appointments of public affairs personnel
   d. Evaluates continuing and special public affairs activities
   e. Approves all news releases
   f. Provides public affairs policy direction
   g. Reviews and approves all outside contracts for public affairs
   h. Reviews and approves all audio-visual projects

    i. Reviews and approves all publications
    j. Approves all denials of FOIA requests
    k. Develops departmental regulations pertaining to FOIA
    l. Coordinates agency public affairs activities in implementing departmental programs
4. To regional offices
    a. Provides policy guidance
    b. Reviews and approves public affairs plans
    c. Approves staffing procedures
    d. Concurs in selection of key public affairs personnel
    e. Coordinates multiregional public affairs activities
    f. Provides liaison with key HEW elements
    g. Directs regional public affairs activities in support of White House and secretarial initiatives
5. To the White House
    a. Makes recommendations for Advertising Council projects
    b. Represents the department in the development of multidepartmental public affairs policies and programs
    c. Furnishes briefings for executive office travel in the field
    d. Provides public affairs support for presidential trips

Public affairs can be a control device in addition to a communications tool. The flow of information from program offices often is the first indication of wide public interest in or of problems with activities. Also, it is an entry point where the secretary can inject himself into the "iron triangle" to influence the evolution of program activities. Therefore, management- (as opposed to program-) oriented secretaries work closely with the assistant secretary for public affairs to monitor and control public affairs.

For example, because of his background as director of management and budget, former secretary Weinberger was interested in all tools through which the department could be made more responsive to efforts to decrease the growth in spending. Also, during Weinberger's first year as HEW secretary, the Nixon administration was fighting its famous "Battle of the Budget" against growth in federal spending. Consequently, we presented to the secretary an option paper to obtain direction during his tenure in office. The paper sought clarifications of how the secretary wished to direct public affairs actions.

Among the major decisions obtained were: a restructuring of the Public Affairs Office to focus on the decrease of public affairs products, budgets, and personnel; participation by public affairs in all major program and policy decisions; coordination of other presidential appointees' public affairs activities; the drastic reduction in the size of the department's public affairs apparatus; and reduction in the number of publications and films it issued.

Public Affairs Reorganization

As a result of the decision paper, the secretary issued a departmental public affairs reorganization plan on September 4, 1973, which included five major points:

1. Public affairs purpose would be "solely to keep the public informed about HEW programs and services and the decisions we make that affect them."
2. There would be no "self-serving, promotionally-oriented material" issued by the department.
3. HEW officials would be accessible to the media as a prime responsibility of office.
4. Public affairs would concentrate on communications through mass media.
5. The assistant secretary for public affairs would have far greater control over all aspects of the department's public affairs activities.

The Weinberger decision resulted in far more centralization of operations than was ever made before. Previously, the Office of Public Affairs had been concerned primarily with media relations and with an early effort to assess potential audiences for departmental messages as evidenced by its old organizational chart and public affairs job descriptions. Weinberger placed the major focus on Freedom of Information, the availability of program directors to the media, and control of materials released by agencies.

During the brief tenure of Secretary David Mathews (1975–1976), the public affairs focus was limited to his immediate media coverage with no concern about institutional public affairs. More recently, Secretary Joseph Califano, through Assistant Secretary Eileen Shanahan, focused heavily on media relations while reinstituting a strong control over departmental public affairs as shown by his public affairs organizational plan. As of this writing, Secretary Patricia Harris has not yet established clear public affairs policies through her assistant secretary for public affairs, William Wise.

The Weinberger Approach

With a high degree of public affairs centralization, agencies have less latitude to release material that attempts to promote programs. There is reluctance by the agency to make a direct public appeal for additional funding for activities through the media, films, releases, and interviews if prior approval must be obtained from the Office of Public Affairs. Consequently, with tight controls there is a tendency to "leak" memoranda and to give "background" interviews with selected favorable media. Secretary Weinberger balanced this tendency by obtaining a summary of all news appearing in wire stories, the *New York Times*, the *Washington Post*, the *Washington Star*, the *Wall Street Journal*, and news magazines every morning by 7:30 A.M. The summary, circulated throughout the department, was thoroughly discussed at daily staff meetings with his assistant secretaries and immediate staff. Unauthorized statements and those which disagreed with the departmental position were rehashed in detail during the sessions and instructions were given on how to handle the news inquiry in the future. This form of secretarial direction led to fewer "unofficial" news stories.[3]

While maintaining tight scrutiny of public statements, Weinberger attempted to increase media accessibility to top officials, as shown by his Title IX public hearings. To aid in this effort the Office of Public Affairs created "media days," day-long media seminars held in key cities throughout the country. At each seminar, half a dozen department-level officials (usually agency heads, assistant secretaries, and the secretary himself) would present current issues and then answer media questions. More than 700 reporters attended 12 sessions during the first year. They asked 1260 questions about a variety of interests.

In this way HEW successfully carried detailed information about programs directly to regional media. This eliminated reliance on the Washington bureaus of media which, during 1973 and 1974, were committed to covering the Watergate story. *Public Relations News* cited HEW's efforts as an effective attempt to "build public confidence" during a time when faith in government was being rapidly eroded. The *Boston Evening Globe* called for more frequent media seminars and declared that the "entire operation reflects great credit" on the department.

However, not all efforts to publicize issues generate favorable media response, as shown by HEW's attempt to inform the public about its proposed "Comprehensive Health Insurance Program" (CHIP) in 1974. The program to guarantee health coverage to all persons was a major administration initiative. A supporting public affairs plan was developed to generate maximum discussion of its features and to receive public comments about its merits and shortcomings, much as in the case of Title IX regulations.

A meeting was called for regional public affairs and health officials to brief them and to make plans to develop a series of public forums. Several trips were made to key parts of the country to continue the discussions with HEW personnel. Because the plan was highly controversial, and similar plans remain so today, someone within HEW leaked a misleading story to reporters about HEW's attempts to "sell" CHIP. A *Washington Star* article implied that the department had violated the antilobbying law.

Two senators, in a letter to the comptroller general, expressed fear that "this public information activity (may) become a front for a major propaganda and lobbying effort (in defiance of the public's) right to be fully and objectively informed regarding the alternative proposals for National Health Insurance." However, the Office of Public Affairs had first obtained a written opinion from the HEW general counsel that its public information efforts would not constitute lobbying. Further, each person involved had been instructed not to advocate the administration's position. Instead, they would tell the public about all of the plans being considered by the Congress. Thus, no misuse of public funds could be legitimately charged.

Directing HEW public affairs at the time, I believed that by publicizing all plans, the less known Comprehensive Health Insurance Plan would have more of an opportunity to be recognized as worthy of passage. Further, during this entire period, it had become all but impossible to obtain coverage of program activities through the Washington-based media because of its full focus on Watergate events.

However, to be successful in planning and implementing department-wide public affairs activities, it is essential to maintain a high level of talent in regional and agency public affairs staffs. Therefore, HEW has periodically audited the activities of its subordinate public affairs offices. Copies of the audits have been returned to the responsible office head as well as the public affairs chief. In the case of regional public affairs offices, a comprehensive matrix was developed so that the offices could be compared for effectiveness. Summaries of the audits were given to the secretary. Each auditing process resulted in modifications in the HEW public affairs procedures and generated new communications techniques.

Nevertheless, public affairs is a staff function, and it is the secretary of a department or head of an agency who sets the tone of all public affairs activities. Secretarial direction for public affairs is essential if it is to be effective. Just as Secretary Weinberger was asked for guidance in establishing his public affairs priorities, so was his successor, David Mathews.

The Mathews Philosophy

Before the effective date of Weinberger's resignation from HEW on August 7, 1975, a complete activities summary of the Office of Public Affairs was developed for Mathews. It explained the interrelationships of the department's communications structure and presented areas in which he might wish some form of personal involvement. A recommended schedule suggested how he might learn about departmental programs while maintaining a high visibility immediately upon assuming office. The plan was sent for consideration to his assistant at the University of Alabama, as Mathews had requested. A series of brief talks before HEW regional employees in key media centers, personal interviews with select reporters, some "soft news" television show appearances, and visits to interesting HEW projects outside of Washington, D.C., were recommended. Mathews, however, during his year in office sought minimum involvement in HEW's daily operation and eschewed any key role in its public affairs.

Centralized control over the appointments of top public affairs personnel and assistant secretary approval for outside public affairs contracts and audio-visual-broadcast material ceased to be enforced by Mathews. Instead, agencies were usually permitted to make final public affairs decisions without concurrence of the assistant secretary for public affairs.

Mathews did develop a committee of speechwriters to "brainstorm" concepts and develop think pieces which he could incorporate into his own generally broad philosophic speeches. Interviews and regular luncheon sessions with reporters, instituted under Weinberger, were dropped. As a result, HEW began to disappear as a major news beat as the media looked elsewhere in the Ford administration for stories.

At one point, Secretary Mathews's executive assistant sent an editorial entitled "Has HEW Gone Bananas?" from the *New Orleans Times Picayune* to the assistant secretary for public affairs saying that this type of editorial was "killing the department" and asking what public affairs was doing about it.

As assistant secretary, I responded:

> The only effective way to prevent recurrence of this type of editorial and uninformed articles is by successfully conveying accurate information as of the time the program is announced. The best way to assure accurate coverage of programs is through the words of the Secretary as HEW's chief spokesman. Lesser officials rarely receive comparable coverage.
>
> To date the Secretary has not emphasized specific issues and programs through interviews, speeches and media seminars which we previously conducted throughout the country. Therefore, the odds have increased substantially that this type of editorial will appear. In fact, we're lucky they have not been more frequent.
>
> I would suggest that he begin to become far more specific in his comments on programs as the remedy and that we refrain from generalizations and overall philosophies. Further, we should have far greater access for the media to the Secretary while they still are somewhat interested.
>
> A letter to the editor so late after the editorial will do little good, in my opinion, but if you want one prepared for either his signature or mine, please let me know.

In effect, Mathews never used the public affairs apparatus of the department either as a management tool or as a means to generate an understanding of policies and programs.

The Califano Approach

However, a new direction again was taken beginning in January, 1977. Using some of the Weinberger management tools to regulate public affairs, Joseph A. Califano, Jr., restored the Office of Public Affairs as the primary vehicle to project the department's programs and policies. Assistant Secretary for Public Affairs Eileen Shanahan emphasized public accessibility to HEW officials and documents and instituted strong centralized controls over the use of all forms of communication, including the Office of Education's educational television contributions. She also generated continuing, extensive coverage of HEW positions by using Califano as the focal point of departmental issues. This personalized approach to issues led to his early departure from the cabinet in July, 1979, when he was fired by President Carter along with four others.

Public Affairs Turnover

Califano's sudden departure as secretary and the arrival of his successor, Patricia Harris, amid considerable national publicity, emphasized again that the public affairs plans for government departments and agencies change as rapidly as the personalities in the top office. The average tenure for an assistant secretary government-wide has been 20 months. However, the turnover of public affairs heads has been even more rapid, with negative results. When a changed image is desired for a department, the assistant secretary for public affairs most frequently is removed. Likewise, when secretaries leave, as in the case of Califano, the public affairs head generally leaves also to be replaced by the incoming secretary's spokesperson.

A most highly regarded reporter for the *Washington Post*, Suzanna McBee had been selected by Califano and nominated by the White House to become assistant secretary for public affairs after Eileen Shanahan resigned to return to journalism. The Califano firing occurred one week before McBee's Senate confirmation hearing. Harris immediately announced that she would bring her public affairs assistant, Bill M. Wise, with her from the Department of Housing and Urban Development. McBee withdrew her nomination after officially serving for three months as only a consultant.

Likewise, I served for 33 months as assistant secretary until March, 1976. My departure was triggered by the exchange of memos about Secretary Mathews's availability to the media and by his opposition to the appointment of a person lacking public affairs experience as head of public affairs for the office of Education.

An acting assistant secretary was named for six months until a successor was confirmed by the Senate in October, 1976. She filled the position for only three months. Although Shana Gordon attempted to remain with the new administration, she was dismissed with other Ford appointees. Thus, during a six-year period beginning in June, 1973, six persons filled the top public affairs position at HEW—three for less than half a year.

This continuing turnover at the top of the department's public affairs structure decreased the ability of HEW to project an accurate understanding of its programs and the issues it addresses. The top media advisor, often lacking an understanding of even the most major programs, much less the smaller ones, frequently was forced to address "technique" rather than substance, preoccupied with conveying an image as opposed to dealing with the nature and content of department programs. Only during the tenure of Shanahan and myself was there an opportunity to play a role in program and issue development based on a personal knowledge of needs and objectives.

This turnover of top public affairs people lends credence to the belief that public affairs people have no role in "substantive" matters. In fact, throughout the government, public affairs people often are instructed to confine their roles to the preparation of release material based on data obtained from "the substantive people." In recent years the department has had continuing problems in generating program coverage in sufficient depth to develop an understanding among both the potential beneficiaries and the taxpayers. Coverage of human-related programs has frequently been the result of philosophical controversy or a clash in personalities, not the result of in-depth reporting.

Most public affairs experts believe that to inform the public, the media or "gatekeepers" to the public must first be informed. Unfortunately, the decreasing financial resources of media have resulted in smaller editorial staffs covering governmental activities, especially nonsensational program areas such as research and education. Regardless of the reasons, however, rational governmental decisions can be made only through public understanding of the facts—and the Department of Health, Education, and Welfare and its successors, the Departments of Health and Human Services and Education, are losing ground in their efforts to communicate with the people they serve.

Notes

1. Associated Press wire #123 (HEW Cuts), July 24, 1973, by John Stowell, quoted Secretary Caspar W. Weinberger as estimating that the department spent $175 million during that fiscal year for public affairs-related activities. No estimate has been made since. Department of Defense estimates are somewhat lower for that department but do not include research time for publications which was included in the HEW estimate. The 1979 fiscal year budget for the International Communications Agency authorized $418 million for that agency. Gross net billings for 1978 for Hill and Knowlton, the world's largest public relations agency, was $22,558,248, according to "O'Dwyer's Public Relations Profiles." The largest advertising agency, J. Walter Thompson, had 1978 billings of $1.48 billion, according to *The Wall Street Journal*, June 28, 1979. Only the 30 positions in the new Department of Education were transferred in the reorganization with 95 percent of the HEW personnel remaining in place.
2. Only the Departments of Defense, State, Treasury, Agriculture, HHS, and now Education have assistant secretaries for public affairs. Other agencies have appointees at lower grades which do not require Senate confirmation.
3. "The Green Sheets," as HEW called the daily news summary, were published by the Office of Public Affairs. One information officer who edited "The Green Sheets" took great delight in placing articles on the front page which were unfavorable to an assistant secretary with whom he had unhappy professional experiences. As a result of this placement that assistant secretary seemed to be in trouble consistently throughout his tenure at HEW.

CHAPTER 31

Department of Agriculture: A Structural Model

Edie Fraser and Wes Pedersen

Early in 1980, the Department of Agriculture completed a sweeping reorganization of its Office of Governmental and Public Affairs. It concentrates on functional "centers" rather than administrative divisions, a fact not brought out by the chart. More important, public affairs and external liaison have been combined under a USDA Assistant Secretary for Governmental and Public Affairs.

Agriculture, which *U.S. News & World Report* has called one of "the most publicity-minded" of all federal agencies, has a staff of nearly 1,200 information specialists around the country and has had a budget for them of more than $40 million, $25 million of which goes for printing. Although it is considering a Public Affairs Manual, it has not yet produced any written materials explaining its new Public Affairs structure. The size of the staff notwithstanding, it is the closest example of a new, "model" Public Affairs structural concept. The basic concepts could be adapted by any federal public affairs department.

Agriculture's Office of Governmental and Public Affairs is clearly identified as an agency of the Secretary's Office, and thus has prestige within the Department.

Prestige is important in that it encourages interdepartmental cooperation. It also increases the involvement of non-public affairs executives, which renders public affairs programs more productive.

Functions

The Office of Governmental and Public Affairs at Agriculture is charged with "maintaining the flow of information and providing the liaison between USDA and the Congress, mass communications media, state and local governments and the public at large." USDA "also directs and coordinates information with the various agencies and has final review of all informational materials involving departmental policy." In addition, it provides "assistance and facilities in the production of motion pictures, still photography (including a Central Photo Library), and design materials."

Structure

The Office is headed by the assistant secretary for governmental and public affairs. The administration of the three major segments of the Office is conducted by a Director of Public Affairs, a Director of Congressional Affairs and a Director of Intergovernmental Affairs. Public Affairs is by far the largest operation, with more than 190 people assigned to it. There are up to 20 persons assigned to each of the other two major units. Again, it is the structural concept here that is most important, not the size of the staffs.

Under a Special Reports Division, other liaison/external relations activities are positioned. There is a Director of Hispanic Information, a Director of Consumer Information, a Director of International Information, a Director of Rural Information and other key liaison posts.

An additional 994 persons serve in public affairs roles in the Department's 10 agencies and five regional offices (though the latter were not yet apart of OGPA's responsibilities at the time this was written).

Under the Assistant Director for News are the News Center and the Media Liaison Center. Under a second Assistant Director are the Publications Center and Special Programs Center. The Assistant Director for Broadcasting and Film supervises the Film Center and the Radio and Television Center, while the Assistant Director for Graphic Arts is in charge of the Design Center, the Photography Center and the Printing Center.

There is an overlapping of certain functions, but the Office of Governmental and Public Affairs is working to rectify the situation. Still, the responsibilities of each Center are far better organized than those in most federal agencies.

The News Center prepares key news releases, speeches, feature articles, issues briefing papers, and congressional testimony, as required, but its primary responsibility is the review, evaluation and approval of such materials produced by the Department's agencies. The Media Liaison Center works with the media in general, supplementing the efforts of the agencies' staffs. It is, however, placing increasing emphasis on reaching special media audiences, such as Hispanic and black newspapers, magazines, radio and TV. For example, it prepares radio and TV news tapes in Spanish for Hispanic stations, and is expanding its efforts for black radio and TV stations. Other stations include a woman's magazine liaison office, which works with such publications as *Family Circle, Woman's Day,* and *Redbook,* seeking to interest the editors in consumer-oriented stories. In addition, a liaison officer works with TV talk shows. He reaches the producers of such shows and suggests guests they can use from the Department. The Publications Center is primarily a critical-eye operation, overseeing all Departmental publications. It reviews an average of 1,200 titles a year including books, magazines, brochures, technical reports, bulletins, etc. The Department now publishes numerous magazines, but intends to reduce the total. It edits a few publications of its own, chiefly the Departmental employee newsletter. The Special Progams Center handles special projects for the Department. It is called upon to organize and develop special slide shows, TV spots, etc., as needed. The Film Center produces perhaps a half-dozen 30-minute training films for the agencies each year. It also does regular videotapes. It works with external producers to assist them when the opportunity arises. The Radio and TV Center works closely with the News and Media Liaison Centers. It operates four "newslines" which radio and TV shows can call at their own expense. Each newsline offers specific subject-area news spots for taping by the calling stations. Each tape will include up to five stories, with a ten-second pause between each report. An additional 30 radio spots are taped each week, for regular distribution to 3,000 stations.

The Center produces a half-hour general farm interest TV show each week. Up to 300 copies are then sent to TV stations around the country, regardless of the network affiliation. These tapes are frequently "bicycled"—passed from one station to another. One TV spot of 1 to 2½ minutes' duration is taped a week. Eighty duplicates are made for "bicycling" among cooperating stations. The production of films and TV tapes is under the supervision of the Center. The Radio and TV Center also works in liaison with broadcasters, "filling the gaps the News people do not handle." Moreover, the Center does a weekly written report to brief radio/TV farm directors. The Design Center was pulled together some time ago from the Department's various agencies. The staff performs all design functions for the Department, using contractors if necessary. The Photography Center handles all still photo assignments, in color and black and white. It maintains a Central Photo Library, from which the agencies and the media obtain file photos. The Printing Center supervises all Departmental printing requirements, working closely with GPO.

How does the Department handle clearance and distribution of news releases? Each agency prepares its own release. This is cleared within the agency, then sent to the News Center (the equivalent of the "Managing Editor's" desk). If it is satisfactory, it then goes to the Assistant Secretary whose office has responsibility for whatever is discussed in the release. If it is not acceptable, the News Center Director instructs the agency to rewrite the text, or the Center does the rewrite itself. When necessary, the release will be cleared by the Under Secretary or the Secretary. Any release containing the name of the Secretary is automatically sent to his office for clearance there.

The distribution of news releases is immediate upon completion of clearance. The AP, UPI, Reuters and Commodity News Service bureaus in the Department receive copies of each release as soon as clearance has been obtained. Copies then go to all other correspondents assigned to the Department and to a daily distribution of 300 organizations and individuals, including the national press, the Washington media, the Washington bureaus, the trade press, private organizations, and Congressmen who have asked for the materials on a continuing basis. The National Farm Broadcasters Association and the National Association of Broadcasters are called whenever an important release is issued. When an item is of interest to a member of Congress, his office will be called by Congressional Liaison.

Each agency within the Department also maintains its own news release mailing list, but seeks to avoid distribution duplicating that of the Office of Governmental and Public Affairs.

The Office insists that everyone on a public affairs mailing list is there because he or she has requested to be. There is, as we were told by the Office, no haphazard distribution. The mailing lists are continually updated. Actually, the mailing lists are limited chiefly to news releases, and to radio and TV tape distribution. Since publications are targeted to subscribers, the Government Printing Office handles publication subscription lists.

Although the Department does not maintain an "800" line for radio and TV stations calling in to tape newscasts and spots on-line, it has an "800" number for the nation's farmers. They can call daily for a minute of current information on commodities, a service mandated by Congress. However, over 50 radio stations have found the taped information extremely useful, and they take regular advantage of the free number.

But, the Office of Governmental and Public Affairs emphasizes, "We get more calls from the stations on our non-"800" numbers. If a broadcaster wants something, we've found that he's willing to pay for the call." Incidentally, the Office obtains cooperation from the media by the personal approach, whenever possible, and total honesty at all times.

Five Regional Information Offices

The Department's regional information offices are linked to the Department by telecopier as well as telephone. They are not, however, under the jurisdiction of the Office of Governmental and Public Affairs. They are administered instead by the Agricultural Marketing Service, which set them up years ago. They work under that Service plus, the Animal and Plan Health Inspection Service and the Office of Transportation. However, the Secretary of Agriculture has stated that the regional information offices shall come under the purview of the Office of Governmental and Public Affairs, a natural move since the regional offices now release national announcements as well as regional and local information; in addition, they handle requests for information from organized groups and the public at large for the five agencies and handle significant information assignments for the Office of the Secretary and the Office of Governmental and Public Affairs.

To keep all hands in the Department's public affairs/information operations up to date on developments in their counterpart offices throughout the Department and in the field, Agriculture produces a weekly newsletter. It discusses policies, programs, offerings and personnel in the Department. It includes word about information developments in the State Departments of Agriculture and the Land-Grant Universities. It has the "personal touch," and it is widely acclaimed in the Department as a fine, fast way of keeping information personnel current on matters affecting them and their programs.

CHAPTER 32

Commerce Department: Business as a Special Public

Ernest A. Lotito

In a public speech more than a decade ago, Roger Blough, then chairman of the U.S. Steel Corporation said, "Clearly we shall be in a sorry shape if our nation is divided into two hostile camps, with government and enterprise arraigned against each other. So, I should like to hope that we can create an additional group of revolutionaries—in both business and government—who can innovate ways of cooperation where only conflict grew before." Coming from a man who had a confrontation with President Kennedy over the question of national interest in an increase of steel prices, Blough's statement represented a major shift by a senior corporation official in the corporate approach to government relations and citizenship.

The 100 percent antagonistic and belligerent attitude of business toward government and vice versa has been replaced today with a mixture of hostility, disagreement, conciliation, and partnership. The steel chief's utterance expressed a synthesis of the philosophy now articulated and carried out in the public affairs offices of both government and industry. It holds that finding a compact between business and government is a large order, but the order must be filled. Too often government and business have been adversaries, each failing to realize the other's contributions to the national well-being. Yet the pursuit of common goals demands that we draw upon the resources of both government and industry.

Government and business relations involve a two-way public relations-public affairs process. For example, as counsellor to the secretary and director of public affairs at the Department of Commerce, I have jurisdiction over departmental agencies with public affairs units that work directly with the public relations offices of major corporations. In fact, on many issues the public affairs offices of government and business have worked jointly.

Furthermore, demands for business's participation in government social programs, coupled with business's continued concern about further government intervention and regulation of economic matters, will, I believe, accelerate the public affairs trends toward accommodation on both sides in the 1980s. Actually, the interaction of business and government in almost all areas affecting the public interest has been increasing for many years. Employment and unemployment are economic. They are also social, as are the psychological factors in automation. Exploitation of the consumer is a legal matter. It also gets into matters of moral and ethical responsibility.

The overriding problem business and government share is attaining productive results while each preserves the independence of its own prerogatives, with neither taking on excessive power over the other, or over the public. Carlton Spitzer, a counselor who has served both government and business, puts the value of collaboration this way:

> It follows that each can serve best by serving together. Government can help business by
> reducing bureaucratic red tape, coordinating related and overlapping programs, and

offering specific ideas. . . . Business can help the government by offering realistic plans and proposals that respond to general needs as well as company goals.

For government's part there is the need for the maze of government to be explained, interpreted, and clarified. People have only a small amount of time and attention to give to their government. Today's citizens, particularly business people, need a system of communications that will give them the same voice and understanding that their forefathers acquired in the town meeting.

By the same token, today's government administrators need the face-to-face relationship that their predecessors of years ago had. The administrators dare not lose the common touch. The bureaucrats must guard themselves against isolation and insulation from the people whose lives they so profoundly affect. This is an age-old problem, but one greatly magnified by the accelerating changes of the Age of Technology. If, we believe an informed citizenry is the foundation of democracy, then public affairs is one of the most critical functions of government. Without it, the job of ferreting out the massive amounts of information it makes available would be an impossible task for the media and the millions of business people and ordinary citizens that require it in their daily lives.

Public affairs in government is to help tell the people the facts so they can make the enlightened decisions that ensure the survival and success of our democratic system. If they are lied to, they will make the wrong choices—and pretty soon, they won't be allowed to choose for themselves at all. Somebody else will usurp that function.

But information put out by business is also critically important if we are to maintain a competitive enterprise system. Without it, consumers would be unable to make intelligent choices in the marketplace. And business spends some $35 billion annually to inform them about products through advertising. The $93 million the government is said to spend on public information hardly compares; but admittedly practically all its information is carried free in the form of news story. As for some ideas of the size of the government information job, let me cite the example I know best, the task of Commerce, which, incidentally, is one of the small agencies of government.

It is the special responsibility of the Department of Commerce in the federal government to communicate with the business community in hundreds of areas. For example, the department's Bureau of Economic Analysis provides the big picture of the economy. Through its work, the government issues the data on such things as the Gross National Product, corporate profits, personal income, the balance of payments, and the composite index of leading economic indicators. The department also provides the little pieces, and through analysis and interpretation, shows how they relate to the big picture. Through the National Economic Accounts the government is able to provide breakdowns by regions, sectors, and industries.

These data make headlines constantly, and there is not a policy-maker in business or government that does not follow every little squiggle on the chart which the figures provide. And if we in public affairs make a major error of substance in our press releases, the reaction could be anything from people dancing in the streets to people jumping out of windows. And not just in this country, but in capitals around the world. In addition, Commerce, under its broad congressional mandate to foster the nation's commerce, has a key role in economic development policies.

The department's Economic Development Administration is responsible for some of these policies. The Economic Development Administration conducts research programs into the causes and effects of lagging economic growth, and helps to recommend methods of investing public resources to sustain job development. For example, public affairs efforts were a key element in helping to communicate to business, especially minority firms, the potential for contract work under the EDA $4 billion counter-cyclical program in 1977. The total American economy benefited.

The department's Minority Business Development Agency plays an active role in helping to upgrade the quality of life and work in our cities, and to advance minority business enterprise in the nation. The agency's public affairs office helps to ensure that the public as well as special interest business groups interrelate with government officials. In fact, minority business development activities demand a true partnership with private industry in order to ensure that minorities—blacks, Hispanics, Indians, Asian Americans, Aleuts, and others—develop business expertise necessary to help them join the mainstream of the American economy.

The National Oceanic and Atmospheric Administration serves as a leader in a national effort to improve our understanding and uses of the earth's physical environment and its oceanic life. This activity is carried out through a mass of public information programs. One of this agency's most important programs is the National Weather Service. This service provides weather forecasts to the general public, and issues warnings against tornadoes, hurricanes, floods, and other weather hazards. It also develops and furnishes specialized services which support the needs of agriculture, aviation, maritime, space and military operations. Through various public affairs projects, the Weather Service works with business to lessen the negative impact of weather hazards on the economy.

The Patent and Trademark Office, which plays such a key role in invention and innovation, has been processing new record highs in patents, while reducing the average pendency time of patent applications. Its public information programs emphasize the need for a revival of the spirit of Yankee inventiveness and ingenuity, which are foundation stones of the American standard of living. The office has given special priority to the processing of applications for patents which may aid in conserving energy and curbing environmental abuses.

The Maritime Administration is responsible for developing and maintaining a U.S. flag merchant marine capable of meeting the country's waterborne foreign domestic shipping requirements. Through its public affairs unit, the Maritime Administration informs business of its financial assistance programs for industry. These programs include such direct aids as construction differential subsidy and operating differential subsidy, as well as in indirect forms such as ship mortgage insurance and tax deferred capital construction funds. The Maritime Administration also writes war-risk insurance and oversees the federal government's cargo preference program. All of these efforts and others must be explained to business and the public, for it is critical that they be understood if they are to help to achieve balanced growth during the years.

Most government agencies have an established system of field offices that provide the public with services and information without having to come to Washington. And these offices function as a public affairs tool for many large agencies. The Commerce Department's 43 district offices, located in industrial and commercial centers throughout the United States, provide information and counseling to the business community. Working directly with business firms across the country, district offices promote economic growth by encouraging U.S. firms to seek and expand domestic and overseas markets for their products.

In 1978, district office trade specialists answered more than one million business queries on a wide variety of subjects including exporting, census statistics, and scientific and technical information. To assist the ever-growing program, more than 900 chambers of commerce, boards of trade, and similar business groups in 50 states and Puerto Rico have volunteered their services as "Commerce Department Associate Offices." Each works closely with its nearest district office to inform local businesses of opportunities in domestic and industrial trade.

While carrying government programs to business, district offices, in turn, give business a voice in government. This results from trade specialists relaying local business needs and problems to headquarters, where these "grassroots" findings are put to practical use in formulating departmental and administration programs and policies. In another related public affairs activity, district offices coordinate a series of one-day procurement conferences which are sponsored by members of Congress and coproduced by the department and various other agencies. These conferences bring business representatives together with procurement specialists, who explain how to sell to federal, state, and local government. Seminars are held on "How to Prepare a Bid" and "Export Opportunities."

As I mentioned earlier, business is an important special interest group for DOC and other agencies. In recognition of the difficulty in finding available help within the government, DOC created the Office of the Ombudsman. The office maintains close relationships with other federal agencies providing ready access to current information on a wide variety of subjects. The staff can ferret out information or find the proper official or the right program in the bewildering array of federal policies and activities carried on to foster commerce and economic development.

The public affairs offices in most government agencies—federal, state, or local—operate as service units. The public affairs office coordinates activities to provide high-ranking officials as speakers and guests at business gatherings such as annual meetings, seminars, and national conferences. An invitation to government officials to speak before such gatherings is an opportunity for the government unit to reiterate an administration policy or to clarify government positions and statements that may not be fully understood. Similarly, the event may be considered as an opening for government to request support from business on a particular issue, or as an occasion to develop contacts with the nation's leading business people.

Public affairs offices also help arrange meetings with high level government officials for business people. For example, business groups frequently request the Department of Commerce public affairs units to arrange briefings for them on certain pressing issues such as international trade, tariff regulation, export and import quotas, trade with China, product liability insurance, and industrial innovation. Though meetings such as these, government officials are able to answer questions directly for business people, rather than using the press as a conduit.

No agency of government—including the White House itself—can manage news, nor does it wish to in our open society. Therefore, government public affairs offices have a responsibility to inform and to preserve a code of reliability, accuracy, and candor. And the business community is fortunate to have available to it a specialized press. Each day pages of the nation's leading newspapers cater to business people in articles that sometimes make use of the technical and often specific economic jargon. There are also weekly and monthly publications that provide in-depth coverage of government activities and business issues. National television and radio networks have begun specialized business coverage. These news organizations come to government to get much of their information.

Government public affairs offices must oblige this special interest. Interviews with and briefings by major government officials are provided to reporters, editors, and writers of the business press. It is also common for cabinet-level officers and other top government officials to write articles for the business press.

In addition, public affairs offices also find it helpful to ask people in business to help explain government's policies and goals to the citizen-voter, or to help carry out a specific governmental responsibility. For example, the Department of Commerce Public Affairs Office has enlisted the support of the business community to help educate the public about the importance of the decennial census. The business community makes extensive use of the census data in its marketing process, planning and development of new business centers, and so on.

But some segments of the public are reluctant to provide information to the Census Bureau for a variety of reasons. To overcome some of the obstacles of educating the public on the importance of this decennial activity, business groups provide public service announcements on television and radio and in the print media. Business associations have allowed the census messages to be stamped on envelopes customers use for paying their bills; similar messages have been provided on grocery bags, on posters inside business establishments, and on car stickers given to customers by business.

But for more years than one would like to mention, government has been trying to sell the business community on the idea of corporate social responsibility. During the administration of Juanita Kreps as secretary of commerce, the public affairs office, as did other agencies of the department, worked the business community on the subject. It is recognized today that both government and the corporate communities have a responsibility to the public. A corporation's constituents and the government's constituents possess an escape valve for grievances. And, they are not at all shy about using this valve—the U.S. Congress.

Consequently, government through its relations with the business community has a responsibility to get this message across: social responsibility is no longer a matter of voluntarily deciding to do what is moral or ethical. The only choice corporations have today is a choice between acting responsibly of their own free will, and doing so because the Congress tells them they must and sets down—section and subsection—exactly how it is to be done.

What is needed is recognition of the fact that between government, business, and the public, there is a triangular community interest. We have already established that it is in the business community's interests to shape its behavior to prevailing public values; it is more efficient to do so than not to do so. We have established too that government is the high-cost alternative through which public values are imposed on corporations that do not accurately perceive these values.

Obviously, it would be much more efficient if a larger proportion of government's energies could be devoted to acquainting corporations with public expectation so they could accommodate them voluntarily, and a small proportion to administering regulations. We would get better results because corporations would remain free to be innovative in addressing public needs, and these results would come at lower cost because corporations would not have to incur and pass on to the consumer the cost of all the unforseen side effects which seem inevitably to accompany mandated solutions. A continuing dialogue between government and business will improve the quality of public policies as they impact on businesses.

During my tenure at Commerce, the administration has faced difficult policy choices on anti-inflation policies, regulatory reform, the Arab boycott, international trade, and many other issues. We have needed the advice and constructive criticism of the business community before we made final decisions that affected all Americans. The chief goal of our public affairs effort has been to provide a means for exchanging views between business and government. To my way of thinking, that is a role for public affairs that provides an invaluable service for the nation and all the American people.

CHAPTER 33

Interior Department: A Traditional Approach

Anne S. Runyan

The U.S. Department of Interior, as a medium-sized, rather old, and thus traditional government institution, provides an excellent example of the status quo in government public information. Although its problems are somewhat unique, its public affairs modus operandi can be extrapolated government-wide. The Interior Department is one of the most decentralized cabinet departments. Over the years it has increasingly embraced a large number of conflicting programs and missions—dam building and protection of fish and wildlife; mining and national parks; historic preservation and urban mass recreation. Indeed, the titles of its nine different bureaus attest to this constant duality of purpose: National Park Service, U.S. Fish and Wildlife Service, Bureau of Land Management, Water and Power Resources Service (formerly Bureau of Reclamation), Office of Surface Mining, U.S. Geological Survey, Bureau of Mines, Bureau of Indian Affairs, and Heritage Conservation and Recreation Service.

As its role has expanded, so too have its programs, personnel, and problems. Increasing pressures have been brought from industry, environmentalists, and the general public to address the highly salient issues of energy, pollution, endangered wildlife, and mine safety over which Interior has growing responsibility. However, when issues become too intense, the pattern has been for such programs to be transferred from Interior to another department or to be established as separate, independent agencies (a pattern which is only now surfacing for the former Department of Health, Education, and Welfare). Examples of this during the 1970s include elements of the Department of Energy, Environmental Protection Agency, Council for Environmental Quality, Mine Enforcement and Safety Administration, Bureau of Commercial Fish, and the coastal zone management programs. In short, Interior is affectionately known in government as the "mother of new departments."

Nor is Interior free from political pressures. Changes in administrations invariably bring changes in priorities and programs. It is in this constantly changing and somewhat disruptive environment (which is by no means unique in government) that Interior's Office of Public Affairs (OPA) must operate. The OPA is headed by a director who also serves as an assistant to the secretary of Interior. In 1979, the office had a staff of 20, including 12 professionals, and an operating budget of $826,200. Half of the rest of Interior's approximately 200 public affairs professionals are assigned to the Washington offices of the different offices and bureaus. The other half work in the regional and field offices.

With the majority of Interior's personnel scattered across the country working on Indian reservations, hydroelectric power projects, wildlife refuges, national parks, or mining projects, in the words of Harmon Kallman, deputy director of OPA, "any serious effort to impose a highly centralized public affairs system on this diverse and diffused department would more likely backfire than succeed.

The solution has been something approaching local autonomy as long as a spokesman for the department stays within broad policy guidelines."

Thus, Interior employees, particularly those in remote local offices, are permitted to comment to the media if they confine their comments to the facts, but when they begin to wander into the area of policy speculation, OPA clearance is required. However, by departmental regulation, advance clearance from OPA must be obtained for all news releases, films, slide programs, and publications (with the exception of scientific-technical publications and short, factual park brochures) before their release.

The OPA is divided into four program specialty areas, each headed by a senior public affairs staff person assigned to work with offices and bureaus involved in that program area. Each of the nine major bureaus maintains a Washington public affairs office and six of these have regional public affairs offices. Materials developed in the bureaus are cleared by OPA after the scrutiny of the assistant secretary responsible for the program. OPA is also the ultimate authority when it comes to all public affairs personnel decisions. In an attempt to simplify these organizational relationships, Kallman offers the following illustration:

> To understand how it works, imagine an information officer for the National Park Service assigned to its Western Regional Office in San Francisco. His immediate boss is his Regional Director, who supervises all NPS activities in a number of Western states. But he also reports to the NPS' Chief of Public Affairs in Washington, who reports not only to the Director of NPS, but to the Director of OPA as well. That is the chain of command. In effect each information officer has a responsibility to two bosses—one with whom he lives every day, and one in Washington. The primary loyalty is to the bureau, and 95 percent of the work is done for the bureau. If conflicts arise, however, they are resolved in favor of the bigger muscle and the stronger will. If things aren't unusually topsy-turvy at the time, that means the OPA director. But direct confrontations are really very rare.

Each bureau also maintains its own freedom of information officer, designated to administer the Freedom of Information Act. If material is denied and appealed, the appeals officer is the assistant secretary for policy, budget, and administration with counsel from OPA and the solicitor's office.

At Interior, as in other government departments, the effectiveness of the public affairs activity depends to a major degree on the relationship between the OPA director and the secretary. But also, as in the case of all government departments, a change in administration often leaves a new secretary and a new set of programmatic goals in its wake which public affairs must scramble to support. In such a diffuse and diverse department as Interior, subjected to a myriad of pressures, priorities can and do shift dramatically.

Kallman describes the shifting posture of Interior public affairs this way:

> Whenever there is a change of Administration, public affairs immediately becomes 100 percent reactive. It's impossible to make long-range plans. The direction of the department's major programs always goes into limbo. We can only try to respond to media queries. After this initial period, the longer the Interior Secretary and Public Affairs Director remain in office, the more opportunity we have to plan for the next month, the next year.

Fortunately, in recent years, the secretary has increasingly brought the director of OPA in on major decisions and strategy sessions as a trusted adviser. In turn, the director has also insisted that each bureau maintain detailed public affairs plans for "critical issues" to the department. Each of these plans must include an "outreach" effort to communicate with various publics affected by the issue it addresses.

An example where Interior public affairs might solicit opinions from various publics to reach, if not a consensus, then, at least an understanding, is in the designation of wilderness areas, which has resulted in continuing controversy among preservationists, land developers, and farmers. In such cases, public affairs must make detailed plans on which audiences to reach and by what methods to obtain maximum and balanced "input" on the issue as it did for the Bureau of Land Management "Wilderness Management Program" in 1978.

In addition, Interior public affairs planning, even in crisis situations, must encompass general awareness campaigns to gain broad acceptance of programs and policies. One notable "awareness" effort was "Johnny Horizon," born during the 1960s to the Bureau of Land Management as the personification of clean lands and promoted to a department-wide effort in the early 1970s. Although in April, 1976, "Johnny" met his demise at the hands of another "clean lands" advocate, "Woodsey the Owl," from the Department of Agriculture, the national campaign, a joint project of the public and private sectors, remains one of the few major examples of public affairs planning at Interior.

The major part of Interior's public affairs activity consists of responding to media queries. This orientation does win the praise of the media. Washington Researchers, after polling reporters in 1977, ranked Interior as the most responsive government entity in Washington, D.C. In 1978, although dropping several notches over-all, Interior still outpaced all other departments in terms of responsiveness.

CHAPTER 34

Department of Defense: A World-Wide Operation

Edie Fraser and Wes Pedersen

No government public relations program has been more widely criticized over the years than has the program of the Department of Defense. Senators have written sarcastic books about it (*The Pentagon Propaganda Machine*, by Senator J. W. Fulbright, New York: Liveright, 1970). Networks have produced bitter documentaries (CBS's "The Selling of the Pentagon"). The news magazines have published countless features, often with a critical tone.

Yet no other government public relations program operates across such a wide front, and none other has the problem of continually providing training for a constantly shifting staff. Indeed, of all government departments, the Department of Defense maintains the only regular school for public information. It must provide training to staff the function at military bases throughout the world and ships that ply the seven seas.

Each branch of the military service has its own public affairs organization. Since each is quite similar, we will focus only on one of those—the Air Force—in addition to examining the overall Department of Defense program.

The Public Affairs Office of the Department of Defense supervises the public affairs programs of the Departments of the Army, Navy, and Air Force, in addition to the information operations of unified and specified commands. The public affairs budgets are enormous, with emphasis on large recruiting contracts to advertising agencies.

Defense public affairs has no manual which incorporates planning objectives, relying instead on a series of guidance documents and directives as well as a plans staff. This situation necessitates much searching of files on occasion.

The Office of Public Affairs identifies its operations, and those of DOD's many elements, as "responsive"—that is, reactive rather than proactive. This is understandable. DOD simply does not have to stimulate interest in, and concern with, its programs. The influentials on Capitol Hill and in the media exercise ample initiative in giving voice to DOD projects (and in requesting information about them).

The fact that Defense does not "market" its programs, as do other Departments, is reflected in the memorandum of "Principles of Public Information" issued by Secretary Harold Brown on June 22, 1977, and still a basic document. (The marketing which does occur supports military recruitment.)

The memorandum declares, in part:

> President Carter has pledged a new openness in government. The President's commitment to candid communication with the American people is firmly rooted in the conviction that, given the facts, they will make wise decisions.
>
> In its activities, abroad as well as at home, the Department of Defense will seek at all times to fulfill the letter and spirit of the President's pledge. In the discharge of their duties, officials will be mindful of that responsibility.
>
> It will be the Department's basic policy to make available timely, accurate information about plans, budgets and activities so that the public, the Congress, the press, radio and

television may assess and understand Defense programs. Requests for information, from organizations and private citizens, will be answered responsively and as rapidly as possible. Coordination with other Departments and Agencies will be accomplished, when necessary, without undue delay.

Responsibilities

DOD's Public Affairs Office runs a large operation. At the head is the Assistant Secretary of Defense for Public Affairs. His assistants number nearly 300 with civilian employees outnumbering the military. Of the total, 174 work in the Office of Public Affairs, with the remaining 123 attached to the Office as members of the unique American Forces Information Service.

Aside from the Armed Forces Information Services, best known for its world-spanning radio and TV network for the military, the Office of Public Affairs is organized into five Directorates.

The Assistant Secretary of Defense for Public Affairs serves as the principal staff assistant to the Secretary of Defense for public and internal information and community relations matters. He is responsible for carrying out an integrated Department of Defense public affairs program that provides the American people with maximum information about the Department of Defense, consistent with the requirements of national security; and undertakes activities contributing to good relations between the Department of Defense and all of the public, at home and abroad; in overseas areas these activities are carried out in collaboration with the Department of State and the International Communication Agency.

An American Forces information program includes internal information materials and resources used in support of the Department's internal information effort and provides news and information for military, Department of Defense civilian, reserve and national guard personnel and their dependents and for retired military personnel and their spouses.

In addition, the Assistant Secretary directs and controls the Defense Audiovisual Agency, which provides centrally-managed production, acquisition, distribution, and depository support and services for selected audiovisual products for use by all Department components.

Structure

Most of the operational activities of the Assistant Secretary's office are carried out by the staffs of six directors, all of whom are under the direct supervision of the Assistant Secretary.

Functions of Directorates

The Directorate for Defense Information is responsible for providing the American public with the maximum amount of information about the Department of Defense.

The Directors serve as the focal point for the release of Department of Defense information that is of national or international interest. They are the point of liaison with national and international print and electronic news media at the seat of government; and they are the point of contact on public information activities for other Department of Defense components, including the military services and the unified and specified commands.

These functions are carried out through *The News Division* which is responsible for contacts with national and international news media on matters of immediate news value. The staff responds to media inquiries; issues news releases, fact sheets, speech texts, statements of Department officials, and related informational materials; gives public affairs guidance to and maintains liaison with the military departments, organization of the Joint Chiefs of Staff, unified and specified commands, and other agencies of the Department of Defense. It enunciates public information policies and procedures and provides support to news media representatives—including arranging for travel by military aircraft when such travel is related to a news-gathering assignment.

The Audiovisual Division establishes and carries out policies covering the preparation and distribution of audiovisual materials to the public. The Division serves as the source of military-oriented audiovisual information of national interest, and it is the point of coordination between the military services and radio and television networks and outlets, film producers, and photo news agencies and publications.

The Plans Staff reviews public affairs plans submitted by unified and specified commands for development of public affairs guidance and plans supporting military operations and activities. It represents the Assistant Secretary at meetings of boards, working groups, and planning committees concerned with the development of policies and procedures for and the implementation of programs and initiative of the Department of Defense. It coordinates long- and mid-range public affairs plans to submitted to the Directorate, and undertakes detailed public affairs planning covering Department activities of sensitive nature.

THE DIRECTORATE FOR COMMUNITY RELATIONS establishes and implements policies covering armed forces participation in public events and similar activities and monitors compliance by components of the Department of Defense; and plans, coordinates, supervises, and evaluates armed forces community relations activities.

These functions are carried out through the Programs Division, which formulates policies and procedures to be followed by Department of Defense commands and agencies in connection with tours, conferences, seminars, exhibits, musical and ceremonial support for public events and other activities in the public domain. The National Organizations Division serves as the point of contact for liaison with national organizations and associations—except for groups oriented toward a single military service. The Division disseminates information to organizations expressing an interest in defense matters and, upon request, arranges for briefings and orientation sessions. The Public Activities Division sets and carries out policies governing speaking engagements and public appearances by military and civilian officials of the Department. It publishes daily, weekly, and monthly listings of scheduled speaking engagements. This Division also formulates policies for and controls the scheduling of military aerial demonstration teams.

THE DIRECTORATE FOR FREEDOM OF INFORMATION AND SECURITY REVIEW is responsible for security clearance of Department of Defense information and material intended for public disclosure; concurrent review of such material for conflict with established policy; security review of information and testimony presented at Congressional hearings. It is also responsible for administering the Freedom of Information and Mandatory Declassification Review Programs and preparing or arranging for responses to the public's requests under the Freedom of Information Act, the Federal Privacy Act, and Executive Order 12065. These functions are carried out through the Program Management Division, which provides for centralized administration, security, correspondence control, records management, clerical support, and research and analysis. The

Division also prepares the annual Freedom of Information Report for submission to the Congress; maintains a public reading room as required by the Freedom of Information Act; maintains a *research center*, reference library, and repository of security and policy guidance on which major security review decisions are based. It maintains an automated data base that stores texts of public statements by key Department officials and data on requests processed under the Freedom of Information Acts and Executive Order 12065.

THE DIRECTORATE FOR AUDIOVISUAL MANAGEMENT POLICY implements audiovisual policies and provides overall policy guidance, management objectives, and standardized procedures for audiovisual activities of the Department of Defense. It recommends elimination, consolidation, or centralization of AV facilities as warranted. It also maintains a management information system to provide information on AV products in preparation; an integrated index or catalogue of AV products as available; data for inclusion in annual reports on DOD AV activities and facilities; and support for AV product-booking and depository operations. It furnishes AV management reports for use within the Department and to meet requirements of the Office of Management and Budget and the Congress. It directs and monitors a program for standardizing AV equipment and formats. As executive agent for the Office of Management and Budget, it operates the Federal Audiovisual Contract Management Office in support of all federal agencies. And it monitors and guides the operations of the Defense Audiovisual Agency.

THE DIRECTORATE FOR MANAGEMENT is responsible for correspondence control, personnel administration, and administrative and logistical support services for the Office of the Assistant Secretary and its elements. It prepares and issues procedural guidance in the areas of administration and logistical support. It assembles the annual budget requests for the office and monitors expenditures. It records incoming correspondence and staff papers and assigns them for action by appropriate elements of the office. It reviews all outgoing correspondence, coordination actions, and staff papers and makes revisions as necessary. And it supervises the operations of the Public Correspondence Branch, which prepares responses to a wide variety and high volume of inquiries from the public.

THE AMERICAN FORCES INFORMATION SERVICE provides internal information support for the armed forces and carries out the Armed Forces Information Program. It also provides policy guidance for armed forces newspapers, Department of Defense periodical publications, and American Forces Radio and Television. It reviews, monitors, coordinates, and evaluates the activities of the military departments and the Unified and Specified Commands in the area of internal information.

Hard news, news analysis, public affairs and information features, sportscasts, and special live programs are relayed from the statewide commercial radio and TV networks and news services. A weekly radio package (86 program hours) is sent to 450 AFRT radio outlets. A weekly television package (62½ program hours) is sent to 195 AFRT TV outlets.

The American Forces Press and Publications Service publishes a wide range of printed material in a variety of formats for the information and entertainment of members of the Armed Forces and their dependents.

Training for the Information Program

Facilities are available to provide training in various aspects of the information program. The Defense Information School, operated by the Department of Defense, is a joint service facility which offers training in a wide spectrum of the communicative arts to qualified officers and enlisted personnel. The school is located at Ft. Benjamin Harrison, Indiana, and offers eight courses ranging from 2 to 10 weeks. Courses include: journalism, radio-television broadcasting, advanced information techniques, newspaper editing, and public affairs seminars. The school provides training in all aspects of mass communications. Students receive instruction from four academic departments: Applied Journalism offers instruction in basic and advanced news-writing, photo-journalism, newspaper editing, makeup and news-gathering techniques. International Relations and Government provides the students with intensive training in American local, state and Federal government; foreign affairs; and area studies of strategic areas of the world. Radio-Television offers the student training in the skills necessary to be a radio and television broadcaster. Public Affairs explains the environment in which the graduate will work by teaching him the policy considerations surrounding his responsibilities. Case studies of past information and public relations problems are used extensively. The Department also teaches media relations and prepares the graduate for his responsibilities in the area of personal communications. Students are trained in the techniques necessary for effective speaking and in the construction and use of audiovisual aids to accompany oral presentation.

The Air Force

The Office of Public Affairs of the Air Force, like other offices under the jurisdiction of the Office of Public Affairs of the Department of Defense, is (unlike the latter) headed by a high-ranking military officer. As with all Defense establishment public affairs operations, its communications programs are primarily responsive.

Under its charter, the Office of Public Affairs, "under the direction of the Secretary of the Air Force and the general supervision of the Under Secretary, and consistent with policies established by the Office of the Secretary of Defense, is assigned the authority and responsibility" to conduct the operations of the Air Force Information Program; plan, direct, and supervise internal and external information activities; develop and supervise programs designed to maintain effective Air Force-community relations; maintain liaison with counterpart information offices of the Secretary of Defense, Army, Navy, and other governmental and industrial organizations; and perform security review and clearance of official information proposed for release through any medium of information under Freedom of Information Act and the Privacy Act of 1974.

The Director of Public Affairs is responsible to the Secretary of the Air Force for planning, promulgating and supervising the Air Force program. He is also responsible for providing advice and counsel on information matters to the Secretary of the Air Force, the Chief of Staff and the Air Staff. Conduct of the information program in the field is a command responsibility at all levels.

Each commander is responsible for the effectiveness of his information program. In most cases he is assisted by an information officer who is a member of his staff. He is under orders to participate in many facets of the program such as briefing personnel on pertinent matters and topics of interest and concern to them and representing the Air Force in civic functions and activities.

The Air Force public affairs program was established to increase the degree of understanding and knowledge the American public possesses concerning Air Force missions and requirements. Says the Air Force manual: "Recognition of public interests and attitudes is essential, since the role of aerospace power in our national defense structure eventually must be resolved by the citizens of the

United States. It is axiomatic that public understanding cannot be achieved if proper understanding is not present within the Air Force. Therefore, an initial step in formulating a program to carry out the primary objective must be to develop our personnel resources. Each individual in the Air Force, military and civilian, must be thoroughly familiar with the roles and missions of the Air Force, and become a source of reliable and factual information for all the publics with whom he comes into contact."

Included under the Office of Public Affairs are the following:

The Community Relations Divison includes a speakers' branch, the arts and museum branch, the special events branch, and the bands branch. The objective of this program is to integrate the Air Force into community life, both at home and abroad, through effective two-way communication and action at all levels of Air Force command.

The Media Relations Division handles public inquiries as well as media relations, and includes a pictorial broadcast branch.

The Office for Plans and Resources is responsible for planning and programming the use of information resources to obtain public and internal understanding of Air Force objectives.

SECTION VI
APPENDIXES

Freedom of Information Act

The Freedom of Information Act as Amended in 1974 by Public Law 93–502

§ 552.   Public information; agency rules, opinions, orders, records, and proceedings

(a) Each agency shall make available to the public information as follows:

(1) Each agency shall separately state and currently publish in the Federal Register for the guidance of the public—

(A) descriptions of its central and field organization and the established places at which, the employees (and in the case of a uniformed service, the members) from whom, and the methods whereby, the public may obtain information, make submittals or requests, or obtain decisions;

(B) statements of the general course and method by which its functions are channeled and determined, including the nature and requirements of all formal and informal procedures available;

(C) rules of procedure, descriptions of forms available or the place at which forms may be obtained, and instructions as to the scope and contents of all papers, reports, or examinations;

(D) substantive rules of general applicability adopted as authorized by law, and statements of general policy or interpretations of general applicability formulated and adopted by the agency; and

(E) each amendment, revision, or repeal of the foregoing.

Except to the extent that a person has actual and timely notice of the terms thereof, a person may not in any manner be required to resort to, or be adversely affected by, a matter required to be published in the Federal Register and not so published. For the purpose of this paragraph, matter reasonably available to the class of persons affected thereby is deemed published in the Federal Register when incorporated by reference therein with the approval of the Director of the Federal Register.

(2) Each agency, in accordance with published rules, shall make available for public inspection and copying—

(A) final opinions, including concurring and dissenting opinions, as well as orders, made in the adjudication of cases;

(B) those statements of policy and interpretations which have been adopted by the agency and are not published in the Federal Register; and

(C) administrative staff manuals and instructions to staff that affect a member of the public; unless the materials are promptly published and copies offered for sale. To the extent required to prevent a clearly unwarranted invasion of personal privacy, an agency may delete identifying details when it makes available or publishes an opinion, statement of policy, interpretation, or staff manual or instruction. However, in each case the justification for the deletion shall be explained fully in writing. Each agency shall also maintain and make available for public inspection and copying current indexes providing identifying information for the public as to any matter issued, adopted, or promulgated after July 4, 1967, and required by this paragraph to be made available or published. Each agency shall promptly publish, quarterly or more frequently, and distribute (by sale or otherwise) copies of each index or supplements thereto unless it determines by order published in the Federal Register that the publication would be unnecessary and impracticable, in which case the agency shall nonetheless provide copies of such index on request at a cost not to exceed the direct cost of duplication. A final order, opinion, statement of policy, interpretation, or staff manual or instruction that affects a member of the public may be relied on, used, or cited as precedent by an agency against a party other than an agency only if—

(i) it has been indexed and either made available or published as provided by this paragraph; or

(ii) the party has actual and timely notice of the terms thereof.

(3) Except with respect to the records made available under paragraphs (1) and (2) of this subsection, each agency, upon any request for records which (A) reasonably describes such records and (B) is made in accordance with published rules stating the time, place, fees (if any), and procedures to be followed, shall make the records promptly available to any person.

(4) (A) In order to carry out the provisions of this section, each agency shall promulgate regulations, pursuant to notice and receipt of public comment, specifying a uniform schedule of fees applicable to all constituent units of such agency. Such fees shall be limited to reasonable standard charges for document search and duplication and provide for recovery of only the direct costs of such search and duplication. Documents shall be furnished without charge or at a reduced charge where the agency determines that waiver or reduction of the fee is in the public interest because furnishing the information can be considered as primarily benefiting the general public.

(B) On complaint, the district court of the United States in the district in which the complainant resides, or has his principal place of business, or in which the agency records are situated, or in the District of Columbia, has jurisdiction to enjoin the agency from withholding agency records and to order the production of any agency records improperly withheld from the complainant. In such a case the court shall determine the matter de novo, and may examine the contents of such agency records in camera to determine whether such records or any part thereof shall be withheld under any of the exemptions set forth in subsection (b) of this section, and the burden is on the agency to sustain its action.

(C) Notwithstanding any other provision of law, the defendant shall serve an answer or otherwise plead to any complaint made under this subsection within thirty days after service upon the defendant of the pleading in which such complaint is made, unless the court otherwise directs for good cause shown.

(D) Except as to cases the court considers of greater importance, proceedings before the district court, as authorized by this subsection, and appeals therefrom, take precedence on the docket over all cases and shall be assigned for hearing and trial or for argument at the earliest practicable date and expedited in every way.

(E) The court may assess against the United States reasonable attorney fees and other litigation costs reasonably incurred in any case under this section in which the complainant has substantially prevailed.

(F) Whenever the court orders the production of any agency records improperly withheld from the complainant and assesses against the United States reasonable attorney fees and other litigation costs, and the court additionally issues a written finding that the circumstances surrounding the withholding raise questions whether agency personnel acted arbitrarily or capriciously with respect to the withholding, the Civil Service Commission shall promptly initiate a proceeding to determine whether disciplinary action is warranted against the officer or employee who was primarily responsible for the withholding. The Commission, after investigation and consideration of the evidence submitted, shall submit its findings and recommendations to the administrative authority of the agency concerned and shall send copies of the findings and recommendations to the officer or employee or his representative. The administrative authority shall take the corrective action that the Commission recommends.

(G) In the event of noncompliance with the order of the court, the district court may punish for contempt the responsible employee, and in the case of a uniformed service, the responsible member.

(5) Each agency having more than one member shall maintain and make available for public inspection a record of the final votes of each member in every agency proceeding.

(6) (A) Each agency, upon any request for records made under paragraph (1), (2), or (3) of this subsection, shall—

(i) determine within ten days (excepting Saturdays, Sundays, and legal public holidays) after the receipt of any such request whether to comply with such request and shall immediately notify the person making such request of such determination and the reasons therefor, and of the right of such person to appeal to the head of the agency any adverse determination; and

(ii) make a determination with respect to any appeal within twenty days (excepting Saturdays, Sundays, and legal public holidays) after the receipt of such appeal. If on appeal the denial of the request for records is in whole or in part upheld, the agency shall notify the person making such request of the provisions for judicial review of that determination under paragraph (4) of this subsection.

(B) In unusual circumstances as specified in this subparagraph, the time limits prescribed in either clause (i) or clause (ii) of subparagraph (A) may be extended by written notice to the person making such request setting forth the reasons for such extension and the date on which a determination is expected to be dispatched. No such notice shall specify a date that would result in an extension for more than ten working days. As used in this subparagraph, "unusual circumstances" means, but only to the extent reasonably necessary to the proper processing of the particular request—

(i) the need to search for and collect the requested records from field facilities or other establishments that are separate from the office processing the request;

(ii) the need to search for, collect, and appropriately examine a voluminous amount of separate and distinct records which are demanded in a single request; or

(iii) the need for consultation, which shall be conducted with all practicable speed, with another agency having a substantial interest in the determination of the request or among two or more components of the agency having substantial subject-matter interest therein.

(C) Any person making a request to any agency for records under paragraph (1), (2), or (3) of this subsection shall be deemed to have exhausted his administrative remedies with respect to such request if the agency fails to comply with the applicable time limit provisions of this paragraph. If the Government can show exceptional circumstances exist and that the agency is exercising due diligence in responding to the request, the court may retain jurisdiction and allow the agency additional time to complete its review of the records. Upon any determination by an agency to comply with a request for records, the records shall be made promptly available to such person making such request. Any notification of denial of any request for records under this subsection shall set forth the names and titles or positions of each person responsible for the denial of such request.

(b) This section does not apply to matters that are—

(1) (A) specifically authorized under criteria established by an Executive order to be kept secret in the interest of national defense or foreign policy and (B) are in fact properly classified pursuant to such Executive order:

(2) related solely to the internal personnel rules and practices of an agency;

(3) specifically exempted from disclosure by statute;

(4) trade secrets and commercial or financial information obtained from a person and privileged or confidential;

(5) inter-agency or intra-agency memorandums or letters which would not be available by law to a party other than an agency in litigation with the agency;

(6) personnel and medical files and similar files the disclosure of which would constitute a clearly unwarranted invasion of personal privacy;

(7) investigatory records compiled for law enforcement purposes, but only to the extent that the production of such records would (A) interfere with enforcement proceedings, (B) deprive a person of a right to a fair trial or an impartial adjudication, (C) constitute an unwarranted invasion of personal privacy, (D) disclose the identity of a confidential source and, in the case of a record compiled by a criminal law enforcement authority in the course of a criminal investigation, or by an agency conducting a lawful national security intelligence investigation, or confidential information furnished only by the confidential source. (E) disclose investigative techniques and procedures, or (F) endanger the life or physical safety of law enforcement personnel;

(8) contained in or related to examination, operating, or condition reports prepared by, on behalf of, or for the use of an agency responsible for the regulation or supervision of financial institutions; or

(9) geological and geophysical information and data, including maps, concerning wells.

Any reasonably segregable portion of a record shall be provided to any person requestioning such record after deletion of the portions which are exempt under this subsection.

(c) This section does not authorize withholding of information or limit the availability of records to the public, except as specifically stated in this section. This section is not authority to withhold information from Congress.

(d) On or before March 1 of each calendar year, each agency shall submit a report covering the preceding calendar year to the Speaker of the House of Representatives and President of the Senate for referral to the appropriate committees of the Congress. The report shall include—

(1) the number of determinations made by such agency not to comply with requests for records made to such agency under subsection (a) and the reasons for each such determination;

(2) the number of appeals made by persons under subsection (a) (6), the result of such appeals, and the reason for the action upon each appeal that results in a denial of information;

(3) the names and titles or positions of each person responsible for the denial of records requested under this section, and the number of instances of participation for each;

(4) the results of each proceeding conducted pursuant to subsection (a) (4) (F), including a report of the disciplinary action taken against the officer or employee who was primarily responsible for improperly withholding records or an explanation of why disciplinary action was not taken;

(5) a copy of every rule made by such agency regarding this section;

(6) a copy of the fee schedule and the total amount of fees collected by the agency for making records available under this section; and

(7) such other information as indicates efforts to administer fully this section.

The Attorney General shall submit an annual report on or before March 1 of each calendar year which shall include for the prior calendar year a listing of the number of cases arising under this section, the exemption involved in each case, the disposition of such case, and the cost, fees, and penalties assessed under subsections (a) (4) (E), (F), and (G). Such report shall also include a description of the efforts undertaken by the Department of Justice to encourage agency compliance with this section.

(e) For purposes of this section, the term "agency" as defined in section 551(1) of this title includes any executive department, military department, Government corporation, Government controlled corporation, or other establishment in the executive branch of the Government (including the Executive Office of the President), or any indepedent regulatory agency.

Federal Advisory Committee Act

Public Law 92–463
92nd Congress, H. R. 4383
October 6, 1972

An Act

To authorize the establishment of a system governing the creation and operation of advisory committees in the executive branch of the Federal Government and for other purposes.

Be it enacted by the Senate and House of Representatives of the United States of America in Congress assembled, That this Act may be cited as the "Federal Advisory Committee Act".

Federal Advisory
Committee Act.

FINDINGS AND PURPOSES

SEC. 2. (a) The Congress finds that there are numerous committees, boards, commissions, councils, and similar groups which have been established to advise officers and agencies in the executive branch of the Federal Government and that they are frequently a useful and beneficial means of furnishing expert advice, ideas, and diverse opinions to the Federal Government.

(b) The Congress further finds and declares that—

(1) the need for many existing advisory committees has not been adequately reviewed;

(2) new advisory committees should be established only when they are determined to be essential and their number should be kept to the minimum necessary;

(3) advisory committees should be terminated when they are no longer carrying out the purposes for which they were established;

(4) standards and uniform procedures should govern the establishment, operation, administration, and duration of advisory committees;

(5) the Congress and the public should be kept informed with respect to the number, purpose, membership, activities, and cost of advisory committees; and

(6) the function of advisory committees should be advisory only, and that all matters under their consideration should be determined, in accordance with law, by the official, agency, or officer involved.

DEFINITIONS

SEC. 3. For the purpose of this Act—

(1) The term "Director" means the Director of the Office of Management and Budget.

(2) The term "advisory committee" means any committee, board, commission, council, conference, panel, task force, or other similar group, or any subcommittee or other subgroup thereof (hereafter in this paragraph referred to as "committee"), which is—

(A) established by statute or reorganization plan, or

(B) established or utilized by the President, or

(C) established or utilized by one or more agencies,

in the interest of obtaining advice or recommendations for the President or one or more agencies or officers of the Federal Government, except that such term excludes (i) the Advisory Commission on Intergovernmental Relations, (ii) the Commission on Government Procurement, and (iii) any committee which is composed wholly of full-time officers or employees of the Federal Government.

(3) The term "agency" has the same meaning as in section 551 (1) of title 5, United States Code.

(4) The term "Presidential advisory committee" means an advisory committee which advises the President.

APPLICABILITY

SEC. 4. (a) The provisions of this Act or of any rule, order, or regulation promulgated under this Act shall apply to each advisory committee except to the extent that any Act of Congress establishing any such advisory committee specifically provides otherwise.

Restrictions. (b) Nothing in this Act shall be construed to apply to any advisory committee established or utilized by—

(1) the Central Intelligence Agency; or

(2) the Federal Reserve System.

(c) Nothing in this Act shall be construed to apply to any local civic group whose primary function is that of rendering a public service with respect to a Federal program, or any State or local committee, council, board, commission, or similar group established to advise or make recommendations to State or local officials or agencies.

RESPONSIBILITIES OF CONGRESSIONAL COMMITTEES

Review. SEC. 5. (a) In the exercise of its legislative review function, each standing committee of the Senate and the House of Representatives shall make a continuing review of the activities of each advisory committee under its jurisdiction to determine whether such advisory committee should be abolished or merged with any other advisory committee, whether the responsibilities of such advisory committee should be revised, and whether such advisory committee performs a necessary function not already being performed. Each such standing committee shall take appropriate action to obtain the enactment of legislation necessary to carry out the purpose of this subsection.

Guidelines. (b) In considering legislation establishing, or authorizing the establishment of any advisory committee, each standing committee of the Senate and of the House of Representatives shall determine, and report such determination to the Senate or the House of Representatives, as the case may be, whether the functions of the proposed advisory committee are being or could be performed by one or more agencies or by an advisory committee already in existence, or by enlarging the mandate of an existing advisory committee. Any such legislation shall—

(1) contain a clearly defined purpose for the advisory committee;

(2) require the membership of the advisory committee to be fairly balanced in terms of the points of view represented and the functions to be performed by the advisory committee;

(3) contain appropriate provisions to assure that the advice and recommendations of the advisory committee will not be inappropriately influenced by the appointing authority or by any special interest, but will instead be the result of the advisory committee's independent judgment;

(4) contain provisions dealing with authorization of appropriations, the date for submission of reports (if any), the duration of the advisory committee, and the publication of reports and other materials, to the extent that the standing committee determines the provisions of section 10 of this Act to be inadequate; and

(5) contain provisions which will assure that the advisory committee will have adequate staff (either supplied by an agency or employed by it), will be provided adequate quarters, and will have funds available to meet its other necessary expenses.

(c) To the extent they are applicable, the guidelines set out in subsection (b) of this section shall be followed by the President, agency heads, or other Federal officials in creating an advisory committee.

RESPONSIBILITIES OF THE PRESIDENT

SEC. 6. (a) The President may delegate responsibility for evaluating and taking action, where appropriate, with respect to all public recommendations made to him by Presidential advisory committees.

Report to Congress. (b) Within one year after a Presidential advisory committee has submitted a public report to the President, the President or his delegate shall make a report to the

Congress stating either his proposals for action or his reasons for inaction, with respect to the recommendations contained in the public report.

(c) The President shall, not later than March 31 of each calendar year (after the year in which this Act is enacted), make an annual report to the Congress on the activities, status, and changes in the composition of advisory committees in existence during the preceding calendar year. The report shall contain the name of every advisory committee, the date of and authority for its creation, its termination date or the date it is to make a report, its functions, a reference to the reports it has submitted, a statement of whether it is an ad hoc or continuing body, the dates of its meetings, the names and occupations of its current members, and the total estimated annual cost to the United States to fund, service, supply, and maintain such committee. Such report shall include a list of those advisory committees abolished by the President, and in the case of advisory committees established by statute, a list of those advisory committees which the President recommends be abolished together with his reasons therefor. The President shall exclude from this report any information which, in his judgment, should be withheld for reasons of national security, and he shall include in such report a statement that such information is excluded.

Annual report to Congress.

Exclusion.

RESPONSIBILITIES OF THE DIRECTOR,
OFFICE OF MANAGEMENT AND BUDGET

Sec. 7. (a) The Director shall establish and maintain within the Office of Management and Budget a Committee Management Secretariat, which shall be responsible for all matters relating to advisory committees.

Committee Management Secretariat. Establishment.

(b) The Director shall, immediately after the enactment of this Act, institute a comprehensive review of the activities and responsibilities of each advisory committee to determine—

Review.

    (1) whether such committee is carrying out its purpose;

    (2) whether, consistent with the provisions of applicable statutes, the responsibilities assigned to it should be revised;

    (3) whether it should be merged with other advisory committees; or

    (4) whether it should be abolished.

The Director may from time to time request such information as he deems necessary to carry out his functions under this subsection. Upon the completion of the Director's review he shall make recommendations to the President and to either the agency head or the Congress with respect to action he believes should be taken. Thereafter, the Director shall carry out a similar review annually. Agency heads shall cooperate with the Director in making the reviews required by this subsection.

Recommendations to President and Congress.

Agency cooperation.

(c) The Director shall prescribe administrative guidelines and management controls applicable to advisory committees, and, to the maximum extent feasible, provide advice, assistance, and guidance to advisory committees to improve their performance. In carrying out his functions under this subsection, the Director shall consider the recommendations of each agency head with respect to means of improving the performance of advisory committees whose duties are related to such agency.

Performance guidelines.

(d) (1) The Director, after study and consultation with the Civil Service Commission, shall establish guidelines with respect to uniform fair rates of pay for comparable services of members, staffs, and consultants of advisory committees in a manner which gives appropriate recognition to the responsibilities and qualifications required and other relevant factors. Such regulations shall provide that—

Uniform pay guidelines.

    (A) no member of any advisory committee or of the staff of any advisory committee shall receive compensation at a rate in excess of the rate specified for GS–18 of the General Schedule under section 5332 of title 5, United States Code; and

    (B) Such members, while engaged in the performance of their duties away from their homes or regular places of business, may be allowed travel expenses, including per diem in lieu of subsistence, as authorized by section 5703 of title 5, United States Code, for persons employed intermittently in the Government service.

Travel expenses.

80 Stat. 499; 83 Stat. 190.

    (2) Nothing in this subsection shall prevent—

    (A) an individual who (without regard to his service with an advisory committee) is a full-time employee of the United States, or

(B) an individual who immediately before his service with an advisory committee was such an employee.

from receiving compensation at the rate at which he otherwise would be compensated (or was compensated) as a full-time employee of the United States.

Expense recommendations.

(e) The Director shall include in budget recommendations a summary of the amounts he deems necessary for the expenses of advisory committees, including the expenses for publication of reports where appropriate.

RESPONSIBILITIES OF AGENCY HEADS

SEC. 8. (a) Each agency head shall establish uniform administrative guidelines and management controls for advisory committees established by that agency, which shall be consistent with directives of the Director under section 7 and section 10. Each agency shall maintain systematic information on the nature, functions, and operations of each advisory committee within its jurisdiction.

Advisory Committee Management Control Officer, designation.

(b) The head of each agency which has an advisory committee shall designate an Advisory Committee Management Officer who shall—

(1) exercise control and supervision over the establishment, procedures, and accomplishments of advisory committees established by that agency;

(2) assemble and maintain the reports, records, and other papers of any such committee during its existence; and

81 Stat. 54.

(3) carry out, on behalf of that agency, the provisions of section 552 of title 5, United States Code, with respect to such reports, records, and other papers.

ESTABLISHMENT AND PURPOSE OF ADVISORY COMMITTEES

SEC. 9. (a) No advisory committee shall be established unless such establishment is—

(1) specifically authorized by statute or by the President: or

Publication in Federal Register.

(2) determined as a matter of formal record, by the head of the agency involved after consultation with the Director, with timely notice published in the Federal Register, to be in the public interest in connection with the performance of duties imposed on that agency by law.

(b) Unless otherwise specifically provided by statute or Presidential directive, advisory committees shall be utilized solely for advisory functions. Determinations of action to be taken and policy to be expressed with respect to matters upon which an advisory committee reports or makes recommendations shall be made solely by the President or an officer of the Federal Government.

Charter, filing.

(c) No advisory committee shall meet or take any action until an advisory committee charter has been filed with (1) the Director, in the case of Presidential advisory committees, or (2) with the head of the agency to whom any advisory committee reports and with the standing committees of the Senate and of the House of Representatives having legislative jurisdiction of such agency. Such charter shall

Contents.

contain the following information:

(A) the committee's official designation;

(B) the committee's objectives and the scope of its activity;

(C) the period of time necessary for the committee to carry out its purposes;

(D) the agency or official to whom the committee reports;

(E) the agency responsible for providing the necessary support for the committee;

(F) a description of the duties for which the committee is responsible, and, if such duties are not solely advisory, a specification of the authority for sucn functions;

(G) the estimated annual operating costs in dollars and man-years for such committee;

(H) the estimated number and frequency of committee meetings;

(I) the committee's termination date, if less than two years from the date of the committee's establishment; and

(J) the date the charter is filed.

Copy.

A copy of any such charter shall also be furnished to the Library of Congress.

ADVISORY COMMITTEE PROCEDURES

SEC. 10. (a) (1) Each advisory committee meeting shall be open to the public.

Meetings.

(2) Except when the President determines otherwise for reasons of national

security, timely notice of each such meeting shall be published in the Federal Register, and the Director shall prescribe regulations to provide for other types of public notice to insure that all interested persons are notified of such meeting prior thereto.

(3) Interested persons shall be permitted to attend, appear before, or file statements with any advisory committee, subject to such reasonable rules or regulations as the Director may prescribe.

(b) Subject to section 552 of title 5, United States Code, the records, reports, transcripts, minutes, appendixes, working papers, drafts, studies, agenda, or other documents which were made available to or prepared for or by each advisory committee shall be available for public inspection and copying at a single location in the offices of the advisory committee or the agency to which the advisory committee reports until the advisory committee ceases to exist.

(c) Detailed minutes of each meeting of each advisory committee shall be kept and shall contain a record of the persons present, a complete and accurate description of matters discussed and conclusions reached, and copies of all reports received, issued, or approved by the advisory committee. The accuracy of all minutes shall be certified to by the chairman of the advisory committee.

(d) Subsections (a) (1) and (a) (3) of this section shall not apply to any advisory committee meeting which the President, or the head of the agency to which the advisory committee reports, determines is concerned with matters listed in section 552 (b) of title 5, United States Code. Any such determination shall be in writing and shall contain the reasons for such determination. If such a determination is made, the advisory committee shall issue a report at least annually setting forth a summary of its activities and such related matters as would be informative to the public consistent with the policy of section 552 (b) of title 5, United States Code.

(e) There shall be designated an officer or employee of the Federal Government to chair or attend each meeting of each advisory committee. The officer or employee so designated is authorized, whenever he determines it to be in the public interest, to adjourn any such meeting. No advisory committee shall conduct any meeting in the absence of that officer or employee.

(f) Advisory committees shall not hold any meetings except at the call of, or with the advance approval of, a designated officer or employee of the Federal Government, and in the case of advisory committees (other than Presidential advisory committees), with an agenda approved by such officer or employee.

AVAILABILITY OF TRANSCRIPTS

SEC. 11. (a) Except where prohibited by contractual agreements entered into prior to the effective date of this Act, agencies and advisory committees shall make available to any person, at actual cost of duplication, copies of transcripts of agency proceedings or advisory committee meetings.

(b) As used in this section "agency proceeding" means any proceeding as defined in section 551 (12) of title 5, United States Code.

FISCAL AND ADMINISTRATIVE PROVISIONS

SEC. 12. (a) Each agency shall keep records as will fully disclose the disposition of any funds which may be at the disposal of its advisory committees and the nature and extent of their activities. The General Services Administration, or such other agency as the President may designate, shall maintain financial records with respect to Presidential advisory committees. The Comptroller General of the United States, or any of his authorized representatives, shall have access, for the purpose of audit and examination, to any such records.

(b) Each agency shall be responsible for providing support services for each advisory committee established by or reporting to it unless the establishing authority provides otherwise. Where any such advisory committee reports to more than one agency, only one agency shall be responsible for support services at any one time. In the case of Presidential advisory committees, such services may be provided by the General Services Administration.

RESPONSIBILITIES OF LIBRARY OF CONGRESS

SEC. 13. Subject to section 552 of title 5, United States Code, the Director shall provide for the filing with the Library of Congress of at least eight copies of each report made by every advisory committee and, where appropriate, background

Depository.

papers prepared by consultants. The Librarian of Congress shall establish a depository for such reports and papers where they shall be available to public inspection and use.

TERMINATION OF ADVISORY COMMITTEES

SEC. 14. (a) (1) Each advisory committee which is in existence on the effective date of this Act shall terminate not later than the expiration of the two-year period following such effective date unless—

(A) in the case of an advisory committee established by the President or an officer of the Federal Government, such advisory committee is renewed by the President or that officer by appropriate action prior to the expiration of such two-year period; or

(B) in the case of an advisory committee established by an Act of Congress, its duration is otherwise provided for by law.

(2) Each advisory committee established after such effective date shall terminate not later than the expiration of the two-year period beginning on the date of its establishment unless—

(A) in the case of an advisory committee established by the President or an officer of the Federal Government such advisory committee is renewed by the President or such officer by appropriate action prior to the end of such period; or

(B) in the case of an advisory committee established by an Act of Congress, its duration is otherwise provided for by law.

Renewal.

(b) (1) Upon the renewal of any advisory committee, such advisory committee shall file a charter in accordance with section 9 (c).

(2) Any advisory committee established by an Act of Congress shall file a charter in accordance with such section upon the expiration of each successive two-year period following the date of enactment of the Act establishing such advisory committee.

(3) No advisory committee required under this subsection to file a charter shall take any action (other than preparation and filing of such charter) prior to the date on which such charter is filed.

Continuation.

(c) Any advisory committee which is renewed by the President or any officer of the Federal Government may be continued only for successive two-year periods by appropriate action taken by the President or such officer prior to the date on which such advisory committee would otherwise terminate.

EFFECTIVE DATE

SEC. 15. Except as provided in section 7 (b), this Act shall become effective upon the expiration of ninety days following the date of enactment.
Approved October 6, 1972.

LEGISLATIVE HISTORY:
HOUSE REPORTS: No. 92-1017 (Comm. on Government Operations) and
No. 92-1403 (Comm. of Conference).
SENATE REPORT: No. 92-1098 accompanying S. 3529 (Comm. on Government
Operations).
CONGRESSIONAL RECORD, Vol. 118 (1972):
May 9, considered and passed House,
Sept. 12, considered and passed Senate, amended, in lieu of S. 3529.
Sept. 19, Senate agreed to conference report.
Sept. 20, House agreed to conference report.

The Privacy Act

Public Law 93-579:
The Privacy Act of 1974

Be it enacted by the Senate and House of Representatives of the United States of America in Congress assembled, That this Act may be cited as the "Privacy Act of 1974."

Sec. 2.

(a) The Congress finds that—
   (1) the privacy of an individual is directly affected by the collection, maintenance, use, and dissemination of personal information by Federal agencies;
   (2) the increasing use of computers and sophisticated information technology, while essential to the efficient operations of the Government, has greatly magnified the harm to individual privacy that can occur from any collection, maintenance, use, or dissemination of personal information:
   (3) the opportunities for an individual to secure employment, insurance, and credit, and his right to due process, and other legal protections are endangered by the misuse of certain information systems;
   (4) the right to privacy is a personal and fundamental right protected by the Constitution of the United States; and
   (5) in order to protect the privacy of individuals identified in information systems maintained by Federal agencies, it is necessary and proper for the Congress to regulate the collection, maintenance, use, and dissemination of information by such agencies.
(b) The purpose of this Act is to provide certain safeguards for an individual against an invasion of personal privacy by requiring Federal agencies, except as otherwise provided by law, to—
   (1) permit an individual to determine what records pertaining to him are collected, maintained, used, or disseminated by such agencies;
   (2) permit an individual to prevent records pertaining to him obtained by such agencies for a particular purpose from being used or made available for another purpose without his consent;
   (3) permit an individual to gain access to information pertaining to him in Federal agency records, to have a copy made of all or any portion thereof, and to correct or amend such records;
   (4) collect, maintain, use, or disseminate any record of identifiable personal information in a manner that assures that such action is for a necessary and lawful purpose, that the information is current and accurate for its intended use, and that adequate safeguards are provided to prevent misuse of such information;
   (5) permit exemptions from the requirements with respect to records provided in this Act only in those cases where there is an important public policy need for such exemption as has been determined by specific statutory authority; and
   (6) be subject to civil suit for any damages which occur as a result of willful or intentional action which violates any individual's rights under this Act.

Sec. 3

Title 5, United States Code, is amended by adding after section 552 the following new section:

"552a. Records maintained on individuals

"(a) DEFINITIONS.—For purposes of this section—
   "(1) the term 'agency' means agency as defined in section 552(e) of this title;
   "(2) the term 'individual' means a citizen of the United States or an alien lawfully admitted for permanent residence;
   "(3) the term 'maintain' includes maintain, collect, use, or disseminate;
   "(4) the term 'record' means any item, collection, or grouping of information about an individual that is maintained by an agency, including, but not limited to, his education, financial transactions, medical history, and criminal or employment history and that contains his

name, or the identifying number, symbol, or other identifying particular assigned to the individual, such as a finger or voice print or a photograph;

"(5)   the term 'system of records' means a group of any records under the control of any agency from which information is retrieved by the name of the individual or by some identifying number, symbol, or other identifying particular assigned to the individual;

"(6)   the term 'statistical record' means a record in a system of records maintained for statistical research or reporting purposes only and not used in whole or in part in making any determination about an identifiable individual, except as provided by section 8 of title 13; and

"(7)   the term 'routine use' means, with respect to the disclosure of a record, the use of such record for a purpose which is compatible with the purpose for which it was collected.

"(b)   CONDITIONS OF DISCLOSURE.—No agency shall disclose any record which is contained in a system of records by any means of communication to any person, or to another agency, except pursuant to a written request by, or with the prior consent of, the individual to whom the record pertains, unless disclosure of the record would be—

"(1)   to those officers and employees of the agency which maintains the record who have a need for the record in the performance of their duties;

"(2)   required under section 552 of this title;

"(3)   for a routine use as defined in subsection (a)(7) of this section and described under subsection (e)(4)(D) of this section;

"(4)   to the Bureau of the Census for purposes of planning or carrying out a census of survey or related activity pursuant to the provisions of title 13;

"(5)   to a recipient who has provided the agency with advance adequate written assurance that the record will be used solely as a statistical research or reporting record, and the record is to be transferred in a form that is not individually identifiable;

"(6)   to the National Archives of the United States as a record which has sufficient historical or other value to warrant its continued preservation by the United States Government, or for evaluation by the Administrator of General Services or his designee to determine whether the record has such value;

"(7)   to another agency or to an instrumentality of any governmental jurisdiction within or under the control of the United States for a civil or criminal law enforcement activity if the activity is authorized by law, and if the head of the agency or instrumentality has made a written request to the agency which maintains the record specifying the particular portion desired and the law enforcement activity for which the record is sought;

"(8)   to a person pursuant to a showing of compelling circumstances affecting the health or safety of an individual if upon such disclosure notification is transmitted to the last known address of such individual;

"(9)   to either House of Congress, or, to the extent of matter within its jurisdiction, any committee or subcommittee thereof, any joint committee of Congress or subcommittee of any such joint committee;

"(10)   to the Comptroller General, or any of his authorized representatives, in the course of the performance of the duties of the General Accounting Office; or

"(11)   pursuant to the order of a court of competent jurisdiction.

"(c)   ACCOUNTING OF CERTAIN DISCLOSURES.—Each agency, with respect to each system of records under its control, shall—

"(1)   except for disclosures made under subsections (b)(1) or (b)(2) of this section, keep an accurate accounting of—

"(A)   the date, nature, and purpose of each disclosure of a record to any person or to another agency made under subsection (b) of this section; and

"(B)   the name and address of the person or agency to whom the disclosure is made;

"(2)   retain the accounting made under paragraph (1) of this subsection for at least five years or the life of the record, whichever is longer, after the disclosure for which the accounting is made;

"(3)   except for disclosures made under subsection (b)(7) of this section, make the accounting made under paragraph (1) of this subsection available to the individual named in the record at his request; and

"(4)   inform any person or other agency about any correction or notation of dispute made by the agency in accordance with subsection (d) of this section of any record that has been disclosed to the person or agency if an accounting of the disclosure was made.

"(d)   ACCESS TO RECORDS.—Each agency that maintains a system of records shall—

"(1)   upon request by any individual to gain access to his record or to any information pertaining to him which is contained in the system, permit him and upon his request, a person of his own choosing to accompany him, to review the record and have a copy made of all or any portion thereof in a form comprehensible to him, except that the agency may require the individual to furnish a written statement authorizing discussion of that individual's record in the accompanying person's presence;

"(2) permit the individual to request amendment of a record pertaining to him and—

"(A) not later than 10 days (excluding Saturdays, Sundays, and legal public holidays) after the date of receipt of such request, acknowledge in writing such receipt; and

"(B) promptly, either—

"(i) make any correction of any portion thereof which the individual believes is not accurate, relevant, timely, or complete; or

"(ii) inform the individual of its refusal to amend the record in accordance with his request, the reason for the refusal, the procedures established by the agency for the individual to request a review of that refusal by the head of the agency or an officer designated by the head of the agency, and the name and business address of that official;

"(3) permit the individual who disagrees with the refusal of the agency to amend his record to request a review of such refusal, and not later than 30 days (excluding Saturdays, Sundays, and legal public holidays) from the date on which the individual requests such review, complete such review and make a final determination unless, for good cause shown, the head of the agency extends such 30-day period; and if, after his review, the reviewing official also refuses to amend the record in accordance with the request, permit the individual to file with the agency a concise statement setting forth the reasons for his disagreement with the refusal of the agency, and notify the individual of the provisions for judicial review of the reviewing official's determination under subsection (g)(1)(A) of this section;

"(4) in any disclosure, containing information about which the individual has filed a statement of disagreement, occurring after the filing of the statement under paragraph (3) of this subsection, clearly note any portion of the record which is disputed and provide copies of the statement, and if the agency deems it appropriate, copies of a concise statement of the reasons of the agency for not making the amendments requested, to persons or other agencies to whom the disputed record has been disclosed; and

"(5) nothing in this section shall allow an individual access to any information compiled in reasonable anticipation of a civil action or proceeding.

"(e) AGENCY REQUIREMENTS.—Each agency that maintains a system of records shall—

"(1) maintain in its records only such information about an individual as is relevant and necessary to accomplish a purpose of the agency required to be accomplished by statute or by executive order of the President;

"(2) collect information to the greatest extent practicable directly from the subject individual when the information may result in adverse determinations about an individual's rights, benefits, and privileges under Federal programs;

"(3) inform each individual whom it asks to supply information, on the form which it uses to collect the information or on a separate form that can be retained by the individual—

"(A) the authority (whether granted by statute, or by executive order of the President) which authorizes the solicitation of the information and whether disclosure of such information is mandatory or voluntary;

"(B) the principal purpose or purposes for which the information is intended to be used;

"(C) the routine uses which may be made of the information, as published pursuant to paragraph (4)(D) of this subsection; and

"(D) the effects on him, if any, of not providing all or any part of the requested information;

"(4) subject to the provisions of paragraph (11) of this subsection, publish in the *Federal Register* at least annually a notice of the existence and character of the system of records, which notice shall include—

"(A) the name and location of the system;

"(B) the categories of individuals on whom records are maintained in the system;

"(C) the categories of records maintained in the system;

"(D) each routine use of the records contained in the system, including the categories of users and the purpose of such use;

"(E) the policies and practices of the agency regarding storage, retrievability, access controls, retention, and disposal of the records;

"(F) the title and business address of the agency official who is responsible for the system of records;

"(G) the agency procedures whereby an individual can be notified at his request if the system of records contains a record pertaining to him;

"(H) the agency procedures whereby an individual can be notified at his request how he can gain access to any record pertaining to him contained in the system of records, and how he can contest its content; and

"(I)   the categories of sources of records in the system;

"(5)   maintain all records which are used by the agency in making any determination about any individual with such accuracy, relevance, timeliness, and completeness as is reasonably necessary to assure fairness to the individual in the determination;

"(6)   prior to disseminating any record about an individual to any person other than an agency, unless the dissemination is made pursuant to subsection (b)(2) of this section, make reasonable efforts to assure that such records are accurate, complete, timely, and relevant for agency purposes;

"(7)   maintain no record describing how any individual exercises rights guaranteed by the First Amendment unless expressly authorized by statute or by the individual about whom the record is maintained or unless pertinent to and within the scope of an authorized law enforcement activity;

"(8)   make reasonable efforts to serve notice on an individual when any record on such individual is made available to any person under compulsory legal process when such process becomes a matter of public record;

"(9)   establish rules of conduct for persons involved in the design, development, operation, or maintenance of any system of records, or in maintaining any record, and instruct each such person with respect to such rules and the requirements of this section, including any other rules and procedures adopted pursuant to this section and the penalties for noncompliance;

"(10)   establish appropriate administrative, technical, and physical safeguards to insure the security and confidentiality of records and to protect against any anticipated threats or hazards to their security or integrity which could result in substantial harm, embarrassment, inconvenience, or unfairness to any individual on whom information is maintained; and

"(11)   at least 30 days prior to publication of information under paragraph (4)(D) of this subsection, publish in the *Federal Register* notice of any new use or intended use of the information in the system, and provide an opportunity for interested persons to submit written data, views, or arguments to the agency.

"(f)   AGENCY RULES.—In order to carry out the provisions of this section, each agency that maintains a system of records shall promulgate rules, in accordance with the requirements (including general notice) of section 553 of this title, which shall—

"(1)   establish procedures whereby an individual can be notified in response to his request if any system of records named by the individual contains a record pertaining to him;

"(2)   define reasonable times, places, and requirements for identifying an individual who requests his record or information pertaining to him before the agency shall make the record or information available to the individual;

"(3)   establish procedures for the disclosure to an individual upon his request of his record or information pertaining to him, including special procedure, if deemed necessary, for the disclosure to an individual of medical records, including psychological records, pertaining to him;

"(4)   establish procedures for reviewing a request from an individual concerning the amendment of any record or information pertaining to the individual, for making a determination on the request, for an appeal within the agency of an initial adverse agency determination, and for whatever additional means may be necessary for each individual to be able to exercise fully his rights under this section; and

"(5)   establish fees to be charged, if any, to any individual for making copies of his record, excluding the cost of any search for and review of the record.

The Office of the Federal Register shall annually compile and publish the rules promulgated under this subsection and agency notices published under subsection (e)(4) of this section in a form available to the public at low cost.

"(g)   —

"(1)   CIVIL REMEDIES.—Whenever any agency

"(A)   makes a determination under subsection (d)(3) of this section not to amend an individual's record in accordance with his request, or fails to make such review in conformity with that subsection;

"(B)   refuses to comply with an individual request under subsection (d)(1) of this section;

"(C)   fails to maintain any record concerning any individual with such accuracy, relevance, timeliness, and completeness as is necessary to assure fairness in any determination relating to the qualifications, character, rights, or opportunities of, or benefits to the individual that may be made on the basis of such record, and consequently a determination is made which is adverse to the individual; or

"(D)   fails to comply with any other provision of this section, or any rule promulgated thereunder, in such a way as to have an adverse effect on an individual, the individual may bring a civil action against the agency, and the district courts of the United States shall have jurisdiction in the matters under the provisions of this subsection.

"(2) —

"(A) In any suit brought under the provisions of subsection (g)(1)(A) of this section, the court may order the agency to amend the individual's record in accordance with his request or in such other way as the court may direct. In such a case the court shall determine the matter *de novo*.

"(B) The court may assess against the United States reasonable attorney fees and other litigation costs reasonably incurred in any case under this paragraph in which the complainant has substantially prevailed.

"(3) —

"(A) In any suit brought under the provisions of subsection (g)(1)(B) of this section, the court may enjoin the agency from withholding the records and order the production to the complainant of any agency records improperly withheld from him. In such a case the court shall determine the matter *de novo*, and may examine the contents of any agency records *in camera* to determine whether the records or any portion thereof may be withheld under any of the exemptions set forth in subsection (k) of this section, and the burden is on the agency to sustain its action.

"(B) The court may assess against the United States reasonable attorney fees and other litigation costs reasonably incurred in any case under this paragraph in which the complainant has substantially prevailed.

"(4) In any suit brought under the provisions of subsection (g)(1)(C) or (D) of this section in which the court determines that the agency acted in a manner which was intentional or willful, the United States shall be liable to the individual in an amount equal to the sum of—

"(A) actual damages sustained by the individual as a result of the refusal or failure, but in no case shall a person entitled to recovery receive less than the sum of $1,000; and

"(B) the costs of the action together with reasonable attorney fees as determined by the court.

"(5) An action to enforce any liability created under this section may be brought in the district court of the United States in the district in which the complainant resides, or has his principal place of business, or in which the agency records are situated, or in the District of Columbia, without regard to the amount in controversy, within two years from the date on which the cause of action arises, except that where any agency has materially and willfully misrepresented any information required under this section to be disclosed to an individual and the information so misrepresented is material to establishment of liability of the agency to the individual under this section, the action may br brought at any time within two years after discovery by the individual of the misrepresentation. Nothing in this section shall be construed to authorize any civil action by reason of any injury sustained as the result of a disclosure of a record prior to the effective date of this section.

"(h) RIGHTS OF LEGAL GUARDIANS.—For the purposes of this section, the parent of any minor, or the legal guardian of any individual who has been declared to be incompetent due to physical or mental incapacity or age by a court of competent jurisdiction, may act on behalf of the individual.

"(i) —

"(1) CRIMINAL PENALTIES.—Any officer or employee of an agency, who by virtue of his employment or official position, has possession of, or access to, agency records which contain individually identifiable information the disclosure of which is prohibited by this section or by rules or regulations established thereunder, and who knowing that disclosure of the specific material is so prohibited, willfully discloses the material in any manner to any person or agency not entitled to receive it, shall be guilty of a misdemeanor and fined not more than $5,000.

"(2) Any officer or employee of any agency who willfully maintains a system of records without meeting the notice requirements of subsection (e)(4) of this section shall be guilty of a misdemeanor and fined not more than $5,000.

"(3) Any person who knowingly and willfully requests or obtains any record concerning an individual from an agency under false pretenses shall be guilty of a misdemeanor and fined not more than $5,000.

"(j) GENERAL EXEMPTIONS.—The head of any agency may promulgate rules, in accordance with the requirements (including general notice) of sections 553(b)(1), (2), and (3), (c), and (e) of this title, to exempt any system of records within the agency from any part of this section except subsections (b), (c)(1) and (2), (e)(4)(A) through (F), (e)(6), (7), (9), (10), and (11), and (i) if the system of records is—

"(1) maintained by the Central Intelligence Agency; or

"(2) maintained by an agency or component thereof which performs as its principal function any activity pertaining to the enforcement of criminal laws, including police efforts to prevent, control, or reduce crime or to apprehend criminals, and the activities of prosecutors, courts, correctional, probation, pardon, or parole authorities, and which consists of (A) information compiled for the purpose of identifying individual criminal offenders and alleged offenders and consisting only of identifying data and notations of arrests, the nature and disposition of criminal charges, sentencing, confinement, release, and parole and probation status; (B) information compiled for the purpose of a criminal investigation, including reports of informants and investigators, and associated with an identifiable individual; or (C) reports identifiable to an individual compiled at any stage of the process of enforcement of criminal laws from arrest or indictment through release from supervision.

At the time rules are adopted under this subsection, the agency shall include in the statement required under section 553(c) of this title, the reasons why the system of records is to be exempted from a provision of this section.

"(k) SPECIFIC EXEMPTIONS.—The head of any agency may promulgate rules, in accordance with the requirements (including general notice) of sections 553(b)(1), (2), and (3), (c), and (e) of this title, to exempt any system of records within the agency from subsections (c)(3), (d), (e)(1), (e)(4)(G), (H), and (I) and (f) of this section if the system of records is—

"(1) subject to the provisions of section 552(b)(1) of this title;

"(2) investigatory material compiled for law enforcement purposes, other than material within the scope of subsection (j)(2) of this section: *Provided, however,* That if any individual is denied any right, privilege, or benefit that he would otherwise be entitled by Federal Law, or for which he would otherwise be eligible, as a result of the maintenance of such material, such material shall be provided to such individual, except to the extent that the disclosure of such material would reveal the identity of a source who furnished information to the Government under an express promise that the identity of the source would be held in confidence, or, prior to the effective date of this section, under an implied promise that the identity of the source would be held in confidence;

"(3) maintained in connection with providing protective services to the President of the United States or other individuals pursuant to Section 3056 of title 18;

"(4) required by statute to be maintained and used solely as statistical records;

"(5) investigatory material compiled solely for the purpose of determining suitability, eligibility, or qualifications for Federal civilian employment, military service, Federal contracts, or access to classified information, but only to the extent that the disclosure of such material would reveal the identity of a source who furnished information to the Government under an express promise that the identity of the source would be held in confidence, or, prior to the effective date of this section, under an implied promise that the identity of the source would be held in confidence;

"(6) testing or examination material used solely to determine individual qualifications for appointment or promotion in the Federal service the disclosure of which would compromise the objectivity or fairness of the testing or examination process; or

"(7) evaluation material used to determine potential for promotion in the armed services, but only to the extent that the disclosure of such material would reveal the identity of a source who furnished information to the Government under an express promise that the identity of the source would be held in confidence, or, prior to the effective date of this section, under an implied promise that the identity of the source would be held in confidence.

At the time rules are adopted under this subsection, the agency shall include in the statement required under section 553(c) of this title, the reasons why the system of records to be exempted from a provision of this section.

"(l) ARCHIVAL RECORDS.—

"(1) Each agency record which is accepted by the Administrator of General Services for storage, processing, and servicing in accordance with section 3103 of title 44 shall, for the purposes of this section, be considered to be maintained by the agency which deposited the record and shall be subject to the provisions of this section. The Administrator of General Services shall not disclose the record except to the agency which maintains the record, or under rules established by that agency which are not inconsistent with the provisions of this section.

"(2) Each agency record pertaining to an identifiable individual which was transferred to the National Archives of the United States as a record which has sufficient historical or other value to warrant its continued preservation by the United States Government, prior to the effective date of this section, shall, for the purposes of this section, be considered to be maintained by the National Archives and shall not be subject to the provisions of this section, except that a statement generally describing such records (modeled after the requirements relating to records subject to subsections (e)(4)(A) through (G) of this section) shall be published in the *Federal Register*.

"(3)   Each agency record pertaining to an identifiable individual which is transferred to the National Archives of the United States as a record which has sufficient historical or other value to warrant its continued preservation by the United States Government, on or after the effective date of this section, shall, for the purposes of this section, be considered to be maintained by the National Archives and shall be exempt from the requirements of this section except subsections (e)(4)(A) through (G) and (e)(9) of this section.

"(m)   GOVERNMENT CONTRACTORS.—When an agency provides by a contract for the operation by or on behalf of the agency of a system of records to accomplish an agency function, the agency shall, consistent with its authority, cause the requirements of this section to be applied to such system. For purposes of subsection (i) of this section any such contractor and any employee of such contractor, if such contract is agreed to on or after the effective date of this section, shall be considered to be an employee of an agency.

"(n)   MAILING LISTS.—An individual's name and address may not be sold or rented by an agency unless such action is specifically authorized by law. This provision shall not be construed to require the withholding of names and addresses otherwise permitted to be made public.

"(o)   REPORT ON NEW SYSTEMS.—Each agency shall provide adequate advance notice to Congress and the Office of Management and Budget of any proposal to establish or alter any system of records in order to permit an evaluation of the probable or potential effect of such proposal on the privacy and other personal or property rights of individuals or the disclosure of information relating to such individuals, and its effect on the preservation of the constitutional principles of federalism and separation of powers.

"(p)   ANNUAL REPORT.—The President shall submit to the Speaker of the House and the President of the Senate, by June 30 of each calendar year, a consolidated report, separately listing for each Federal agency the number of records contained in any system of records which were exempted from the application of this section under the provisions of subsections (j) and (k) of this section during the preceding calendar year, and the reasons for the exemptions, and such other information as indicates efforts to administer fully this section.

"(q)   EFFECT OF OTHER LAWS.—No agency shall rely on any exemption contained in section 552 of this title to withhold from an individual any record which is otherwise accessible to such individual under the provisions of this section."

Sec. 4.

The Chapter analysis of chapter 5 of title 5, United States Code, is amended by inserting:

   "552a. Records about individuals."

   immediately below:

   "552. Public information; agency rules, opinions, orders, and proceedings.".

[Section 5 of the Privacy Act established a Privacy Protection Study Commission for a period of two years. Its term has now expired. Among other things, the Commission was charged with the responsibility of assessing the effectiveness of privacy protections throughout the society. In July 1977, it issued a report entitled "Personal Privacy in an Information Society" which proposed a series of recommendations directed toward safeguarding personal privacy in both the public and private sector. This report can be obtained from the Superintendent of Documents, Government Printing Office, Washington, D.C. 20420 for a charge of $5.]

Sec. 6.

The Office of Management and Budget shall—

(1)   develop guidelines and regulations for the use of agencies in implementing the provisions of section 552a of title 5, United States Code, as added by section 3 of this Act; and

(2)   provide continuing assistance to and oversight of the implementation of the provisions of such section by agencies.

Sec. 7.

(a)   —

(1)   It shall be unlawful for any Federal, State or local government agency to deny to any individual any right, benefit, or privilege provided by law because of such individual's refusal to disclose his social security account number.

(2)   The provisions of paragraph (1) of this subsection shall not apply with respect to—
   (A) any disclosure which is required by Federal statute, or
   (B) the disclosure of a social security number to any Federal, State, or local agency maintaining a system of records in existence and operating before January 1, 1975, if such disclosure was required under statute or regulation adopted prior to such date to verify the identity of an individual.

(b)   Any Federal, State, or local government agency which requests an individual to disclose his social security number to any Federal, State, or local agency maintaining a system of records in existence and operating before January 1, 1975, if such disclosure was required under statute or regulation adopted prior to such date to verify the identity of an individual.

(c)   Any Federal, State, or local government agency which requests an individual to disclose his social security account number shall inform that individual whether that disclosure is mandatory or voluntary, by what statutory or other authority such number is solicited, and what uses will be made of it.

Sec. 8.

The provisions of this Act shall be effective on and after the date of enactment, except that the amendments made by section 3 and 4 shall become effective 270 days following the day on which this Act is enacted.

Sec. 9.

There is authorized to be appropriated to carry out the provisions of section 5 of this Act for fiscal years 1975, 1976, 1977 the sum of $1,500,000, except that not more than $750,000 may be expended during any such fiscal year.

Approved December 31, 1974

Open Meetings Act

Public Law 94-409
94th Congress, S. 5
September 13, 1976

An Act

To provide that meetings of Government agencies shall be open to the public, and for other purposes.

Be it enacted by the Senate and House of Representatives of the United States of America in Congress assembled, That this Act may be cited as the "Government in the Sunshine Act".

Government in the Sunshine Act. 5 USC 552b note.
5 USC 552b note.

DECLARATION OF POLICY

SEC. 2. It is hereby declared to be the policy of the United States that the public is entitled to the fullest practicable information regarding the decisionmaking processes of the Federal Government. It is the purpose of this Act to provide the public with such information while protecting the rights of individuals and the ability of the Government to carry out its responsibilities.

OPEN MEETINGS

SEC. 3. (a) Title 5, United States Code, is amended by adding after section 552a the following new section:

"552b. Open meetings

"(a) For purposes of this section—

"(1) the term 'agency' means any agency, as defined in section 552(e) of this title, headed by a collegial body composed of two or more individual members, a majority of whom are appointed to such position by the President with the advice and consent of the Senate, and any subdivision thereof authorized to act on behalf of the agency;

"(2) the term 'meeting' means the deliberations of at least the number of individual agency members required to take action on behalf of the agency where such deliberations determine or result in the joint conduct or disposition of official agency business, but does not include deliberations required or permitted by subsection (d) or (e); and

"(3) the term 'member' means an individual who belongs to a collegial body heading an agency.

"(b) Members shall not jointly conduct or dispose of agency business other than in accordance with this section. Except as provided in subsection (c), every portion of every meeting of an agency shall be open to public observation.

"(c) Except in a case where the agency finds that the public interest requires otherwise, the second sentence of subsection (b) shall not apply to any portion of an agency meeting, and the requirements of subsections (d) and (e) shall not apply to any information pertaining to such meeting otherwise required by this section to be disclosed to the public, where the agency properly determines that such portion or portions of its meeting or the disclosure of such information is likely to—

"(1) disclose matters that are (A) specifically authorized under criteria established by an Executive order to be kept secret in the interests of national defense or foreign policy and (B) in fact properly classified pursuant to such Executive order;

"(2) relate solely to the internal personnel rules and practices of an agency;

"(3) disclose matters specifically exempted from disclosure by statute (other

5 USC 552b.
Definitions.

5 USC 552.

5 USC 552.

than section 552 of this title), provided that such statute (A) requires that the matters be withheld from the public in such a manner as to leave no discretion on the issue, or (B) establishes particular criteria for withholding or refers to particular types of matters to be withheld;

"(4) disclose trade secrets and commercial or financial information obtained from a person and privileged or confidential;

"(5) involve accusing any person of a crime, or formally censuring any person;

"(6) disclose information of a personal nature where disclosure would constitute a clearly unwarranted invasion of personal privacy;

"(7) disclose investigatory records compiled for law enforcement purposes, or information which if written would be contained in such records, but only to the extent that the production of such records or information would (A) interfere with enforcement proceedings, (B) deprive a person of a right to a fair trial or an impartial adjudication, (C) constitute an unwarranted invasion of personal privacy, (D) disclose the identity of a confidential source and, in the case of a record compiled by a criminal law enforcement authority in the course of a criminal investigation, or by an agency conducting a lawful national security intelligence investigation, confidential information furnished only by the confidential source, (E) disclose investigative techniques and procedures, or (F) endanger the life or physical safety of law enforcement personnel;

"(8) disclose information contained in or related to examination, operating, or condition reports prepared by, on behalf of, or for the use of an agency responsible for the regulation or supervision of financial institutions;

"(9) disclose information the premature disclosure of which would—

"(A) in the case of an agency which regulates currencies, securities, commodities, or financial institutions, be likely to (i) lead to significant financial speculation in currencies, securities, or commodities, or (ii) significantly endanger the stability of any financial institution; or

"(B) in the case of any agency, be likely to significantly frustrate implementation of a proposed agency action.

except that subparagraph (B) shall not apply in any instance where the agency has already disclosed to the public the content or nature of its proposed action, or where the agency is required by law to make such disclosure on its own initiative prior to taking final agency action on such proposal; or

"(10) specifically concern the agency's issuance of a subpena, or the agency's participation in a civil action or proceeding, an action in a foreign court or international tribunal, or an arbitration, or the initiation, conduct, or disposition by the agency of a particular case of formal agency adjudication pursuant to the procedures in section 554 of this title or otherwise involving a determination on the record after opportunity for a hearing.

5 USC 554.

Recorded voting.

"(d) (1) Action under subsection (c) shall be taken only when a majority of the entire membership of the agency (as defined in subsection (a) (1)) votes to take such action. A separate vote of the agency members shall be taken with respect to each agency meeting a portion or portions of which are proposed to be closed to the public pursuant to subsection (c), or with respect to any information which is proposed to be withheld under subsection (c). A single vote may be taken with respect to a series of meetings, a portion or portions of which are proposed to be closed to the public, or with respect to any information concerning such series of meetings, so long as each meeting in such series involves the same particular matters and is scheduled to be held no more than thirty days after the initial meeting in such series. The vote of each agency member participating in such vote shall be recorded and no proxies shall be allowed.

"(2) Whenever any person whose interests may be directly affected by a portion of a meeting requests that the agency close such portion to the public for any of the reasons referred to in paragraph (5), (6), or (7) of subsection (c), the agency, upon request of any one of its members, shall vote by recorded vote whether to close such meeting.

Copies, availability.

"(3) Within one day of any vote taken pursuant to paragraph (1) or (2), the agency shall make publicly available a written copy of such vote reflecting the vote of each member on the question. If a portion of a meeting is to be closed to the public, the agency shall, within one day of the vote taken pursuant to paragraph (1) or (2) of this subsection, make publicly available a full written explanation of its action closing the portion together with a list of all persons expected to attend the meeting and their affiliation.

"(4) Any agency, a majority of whose meetings may properly be closed to the public pursuant to paragraph (4), (8), (9) (A), or (10) of subsection (c), or any combination thereof, may provide by regulation for the closing of such meetings or portions thereof in the event that a majority of the members of the agency votes by recorded vote at the beginning of such meeting, or portion thereof, to close the exempt portion or portions of the meeting, and a copy of such vote, reflecting the vote of each member on the question, is made available to the public. The provisions of paragraphs (1), (2), and (3) of this subsection and subsection (e) shall not apply to any portion of a meeting to which such regulations apply: *Provided*, That the agency shall, except to the extent that such information is exempt from disclosure under the provisions of subsection (c), provide the public with public announcement of the time, place, and subject matter of the meeting and of each portion thereof at the earliest practicable time.

Meeting closure, regulation.

Public announcement.

"(e) (1) In the case of each meeting, the agency shall make public announcement, at least one week before the meeting, of the time, place, and subject matter of the meeting, whether it is to be open or closed to the public, and the name and phone number of the official designated by the agency to respond to requests for information about the meeting. Such announcement shall be made unless a majority of the members of the agency determines by a recorded vote that agency business requires that such meeting be called at an earlier date, in which case the agency shall make public announcement of the time, place, and subject matter of such meeting, and whether open or closed to the public, at the earliest practicable time.

Scheduling, public announcement.

"(2) The time or place of a meeting may be changed following the public announcement required by paragraph (1) only if the agency publicly announces such change at the earliest practicable time. The subject matter of a meeting, or the determination of the agency to open or close a meeting, or portion of a meeting, to the public, may be changed following the public announcement required by this subsection only if (A) a majority of the entire membership of the agency determines by a recorded vote that agency business so requires and that no earlier announcement of the change was possible, and (B) the agency publicly announces such change and the vote of each member upon such change at the earliest practicable time.

Scheduling changes, public announcement.

"(3) Immediately following each public announcement required by this subsection, notice of the time, place, and subject matter of a meeting, whether the meeting is open or closed, any change in one of the preceding, and the name and phone number of the official designated by the agency to respond to requests for information about the meeting, shall also be submitted for publication in the Federal Register.

Scheduling notice, publication in Federal Register.

"(f) (1) For every meeting closed pursuant to paragraphs (1) through (10) of subsection (c), the General Counsel or chief legal officer of the agency shall publicly certify that, in his or her opinion, the meeting may be closed to the public and shall state each relevant exemptive provision. A copy of such certification, together with a statement from the presiding officer of the meeting setting forth the time and place of the meeting, and the persons present, shall be retained by the agency. The agency shall maintain a complete transcript or electronic recording adequate to record fully the proceedings of each meeting, or portion of a meeting, closed to the public, except that in the case of a meeting, or portion of a meeting, closed to the public pursuant to paragraph (8), (9) (A), or (10) of subsection (c), the agency shall maintain either such a transcript or recording, or a set of minutes. Such minutes shall fully and clearly describe all matters discussed and shall provide a full and accurate summary of any actions taken, and the reasons therefor, including a description of each of the views expressed on any item and the record of any rollcall vote (reflecting the vote of each member on the question). All documents considered in connection with any action shall be identified in such minutes.

Closed meetings, certification.

Transcripts, recordings or minutes.

"(2) The agency shall make promptly available to the public, in a place easily accessible to the public, the transcript, electronic recording, or minutes (as required by paragraph (1)) of the discussion of any item on the agenda, or of any item of the testimony of any witness received at the meeting, except for such item or items of such discussion or testimony as the agency determines to contain information which may be withheld under subsection (c). Copies of such transcript, or minutes, or a transcription of such recording disclosing the identity of each speaker, shall be furnished to any person at the actual cost of duplication or transcription. The agency shall maintain a complete verbatim copy of the tran-

Public availability.

Retention.

script, a complete copy of the minutes, or a complete electronic recording of each meeting, or portion of a meeting, closed to the public, for a period of at least two years after such meeting, or until one year after the conclusion of any agency proceeding with respect to which the meeting or portion was held, whichever occurs later.

Regulations. Notice, publication in Federal Register.

Judicial proceeding.

"(g) Each agency subject to the requirements of this section shall, within 180 days after the date of enactment of this section, following consultation with the Office of the Chairman of the Administrative Conference of the United States and published notice in the Federal Register of at least thirty days and opportunity for written comment by any person, promulgate regulations to implement the requirements of subsections (b) through (f) of this section. Any person may bring a proceeding in the United States District Court for the District of Columbia to require an agency to promulgate such regulations if such agency has not promulgated such regulations within the time period specified herein. Subject to any limitations of time provided by law, any person may bring a proceeding in the United States Court of Appeals for the District of Columbia to set aside agency regulations issued pursuant to this subsection that are not in accord with the requirements of subsections (b) through (f) of this section and to require the promulgation of regulations that are in accord with such subsections.

Jurisdication.

Civil actions.

"(h) (1) The district courts of the United States shall have jurisdiction to enforce the requirements of subsections (b) through (f) of this section by declaratory judgment, injunctive relief, or other relief as may be appropriate. Such actions may be brought by any person against an agency prior to, or within sixty days after, the meeting out of which the violation of this section arises, except that if public announcement of such meeting is not initially provided by the agency in accordance with the requirements of this section, such action may be instituted pursuant to this section at any time prior to sixty days after any public announcement of such meeting. Such actions may be brought in the district court of the United States for the district in which the agency meeting is held or in which the agency in question has its headquarters, or in the District Court for the District of Columbia. In such actions a defendant shall serve his answer within thirty days after the service of the complaint. The burden is on the defendant to sustain his action. In deciding such cases the court may examine in camera any portion of the transcript, electronic recording, or minutes of a meeting closed to the public, and

Relief.

may take such additional evidence as it deems necessary. The court, having due regard for orderly administration and the public interest, as well as the interests of the parties, may grant such equitable relief as it deems appropriate, including granting an injunction against future violations of this section or ordering the agency to make available to the public such portion of the transcript, recording, or minutes of a meeting as is not authorized to be withheld under subsection (c) of this section.

Inquiry.

"(2) Any Federal court otherwise authorized by law to review agency action may, at the application of any person properly participating in the proceeding pursuant to other applicable law, inquire into violations by the agency of the requirements of this section and afford such relief as it deems appropriate. Nothing in this section authorizes any Federal court having jurisdiction solely on the basis of paragraph (1) to set aside, enjoin, or invalidate any agency action (other than an action to close a meeting or to withhold information under this section) taken or discussed at any agency meeting out of which the violation of this section arose.

Litigation costs, assessment.

"(i) The court may assess against any party reasonable attorney fees and other litigation costs reasonably incurred by any other party who substantially prevails in any action brought in accordance with the provisions of subsection (g) or (h) of this section, except that costs may be assessed against the plantiff only where the court finds that the suit was initiated by the plantiff primarily for frivolous or dilatory purposes. In the case of assessment of costs against an agency, the costs may be assessed by the court against the United States.

Report to Congress.

"(j) Each agency subject to the requirements of this section shall annually report to Congress regarding its compliance with such requirements, including a tabulation of the total number of agency meetings open to the public, the total number of meetings closed to the public, the reasons for closing such meetings, and a description of any litigation brought against the agency under this section, including any costs assessed against the agency in such litigation (whether or not paid by the agency).

"(k) Nothing herein expands or limits the present rights of any person under section 552 of this title, except that the exemptions set forth in subsection (c) of this section shall govern in the case of any request made pursuant to section 552 to copy or inspect the transcripts, recordings, or minutes described in subsection (f) of this section. The requirements of chapter 33 of title 44, United States Code, shall not apply to the transcripts, recordings, and minutes described in subsection (f) of this section. | 5 USC 552.

44 USC 3301.

"(l) This section does not constitute authority to withhold any information from Congress, and does not authorize the closing of any agency meeting or portion thereof required by any other provision of law to be open.

"(m) Nothing in this section authorizes any agency to withhold from any individual any record, including transcripts, recordings, or minutes required by this section, which is otherwise accessible to such individual under section 552a of this title.".

(b) The chapter analysis of chapter 5 of title 5, United States Code, is amended by inserting:

5 USC 552a.
5 USC prec. 500.

"552b. Open meetings."

immediately below:

"552a. Records about individuals.".

EX PARTE COMMUNICATIONS

Sec 4. (a) Section 557 of title 5, United States Code, is amended by adding at the end thereof the following new subsection:

"(d) (1) In any agency proceeding which is subject to subsection (a) of this section, except to the extent required for the disposition of ex parte matters as authorized by law—

"(A) no interested person outside the agency shall make or knowingly cause to be made to any member of the body comprising the agency, administrative law judge, or other employee who is or may reasonably be expected to be involved in the decisional process of the proceeding, an ex parte communication relevant to the merits of the proceeding;

"(B) no member of the body comprising the agency, administrative law judge, or other employee who is or may reasonably be expected to be involved in the decisional process of the proceeding, shall make or knowingly cause to be made to any interested person outside the agency an ex parte communication relevant to the merits of the proceeding;

"(C) a member of the body comprising the agency, administrative law judge, or other employee who is or may reasonably be expected to be involved in the decisional process of such proceeding who receives, or who makes or knowingly causes to be made, a communication prohibited by this subsection shall place on the public record of the proceeding:

"(i) all such written communications;

"(ii) memoranda stating the substance of all such oral communications; and

"(iii) all written responses, and memoranda stating the substance of all oral responses, to the materials described in clauses (i) and (ii) of this subparagraph;

"(D) upon receipt of a communication knowingly made or knowingly caused to be made by a party in violation of this subsection, the agency, administrative law judge, or other employee presiding at the hearing may, to the extent consistent with the interests of justice and the policy of the underlying statutes, require the party to show cause why his claim or interest in the proceeding should not be dismissed, denied, disregarded, or otherwise adversely affected on account of such violation; and

"(E) the prohibitions of this subsection shall apply beginning at such time as the agency may designate, but in no case shall they begin to apply later than the time at which a proceeding is noticed for hearing unless the person responsible for the communication has knowledge that it will be noticed, in which case the prohibitions shall apply beginning at the time of his acquisition of such knowledge.

Applicability.

"(2) This subsection does not constitute authority to withhold information from Congress.".

(b) Section 551 of title 5, United States Code, is amended—

(1) by striking out "and" at the end of paragraph (12);

(2) by striking out the "act," at the end of paragraph (13) and inserting in lieu thereof "act; and"; and

(3) by adding at the end thereof the following new paragraph:

"(14) 'ex parte communication' means an oral or written communication not on the public record with respect to which reasonable prior notice to all parties is not given, but it shall not include requests for status reports on any matter or proceeding covered by this subchapter.".

"Ex parte communication."

(c) Section 556(d) of title 5, United States Code, is amended by inserting between the third and fourth sentences thereof the following new sentence: "The agency may, to the extent consistent with the interests of justice and the policy of the underlying statutes administered by the agency, consider a violation of section 557(d) of this title sufficient grounds for a decision adverse to a party who has knowingly committed such violation or knowingly caused such violation to occur.".

5 USC 557.

CONFORMING AMENDMENTS

SEC. 5. (a) Section 410(b) (1) of title 39, United States Code, is amended by inserting after "Section 552 (public information)," the words "section 552a (records about individuals), section 552b (open meetings).".

(b) Section 552(b) (3) of title 5, United States Code, is amended to read as follows:

"(3) specifically exempted from disclosure by statute (other than section 552b of this title), provided that such statute (A) requires that the matters be withheld from the public in such a manner as to leave no discretion on the issue, or (B) establishes particular criteria for withholding or refers to particular types of matters to be withheld;".

5 USC app. I.

(c) Subsection (d) of section 10 of the Federal Advisory Committee Act is amended by striking out the first sentence and inserting in lieu thereof the following: "Subsections (a) (1) and (a) (3) of this section shall not apply to any portion of an advisory committee meeting where the President, or the head of the agency to which the advisory committee reports, determines that such portion of such meeting may be closed to the public in accordance with subsection (c) of section 552b of title 5, United States Code.".

EFFECTIVE DATE

5 USC 552b note.

SEC. 6. (a) Except as provided in subsection (b) of this section, the provisions of this Act shall take effect 180 days after the date of its enactment.

(b) Subsection (g) of section 552b of title 5, United States Code, as added by section 3(a) of this Act, shall take effect upon enactment.

Approved September 13, 1976.

LEGISLATIVE HISTORY:

HOUSE REPORTS: No. 94–880, Pt. I and No. 94–880, Pt. 2, accompanying H.R. 11656 (Comm. on Government Operations) and No. 94–1441 (Comm. of Conference).

SENATE REPORTS: No. 94–354 (Comm. on Government Operations), No. 94–381 (Comm. on Rules and Administration) and No. 94-1178 (Comm. of Conference).

CONGRESSIONAL RECORD:

Vol. 121 (1975): Nov. 5, 6, considered and passed Senate.

Vol. 122 (1976): July 28, considered and passed House, amended, in lieu of H.R. 11656.

WEEKLY COMPILATION OF PRESIDENTIAL DOCUMENTS:

Vol. 12, No. 38 (1976): Sept. 13, Presidential statement.

OMB Guidelines on Public Surveys

Office of Management and Budget

Implementation of the Privacy
Act of 1974

Supplementary Guidance

November 21, 1975.

This material is provided to address comments and questions of general interest raised since the release of the Office of Management and Budget's guidelines for implementing section 3 of the Privacy Act of 1974. (FEDERAL REGISTER, Volume 40, Number 132, dated July 9, 1975, pp. 28949–28978.)

Additional supplements will be issued as necessary.

JAMES T. LYNN,
Director.

1. *Definition of System of Records* (5 U.S.C. 552a(a) (5)). On page 28952, third column, after line 27, add:

"Following are several examples of the use of the term 'system of records':

"Telephone directories. Agency telephone directories are typically derived from files (e.g., locator cards) which are, themselves, systems of records. For example, agency personnel records may be used to produce a telephone directory which is distributed to personnel of the agency and may be made available to the public pursuant to 5 U.S.C. 552a(b) (1) and (2), (intra-agency and public disclosure, respectively). In this case the directory could be a disclosure from the system of records and, thus, would not be a separate system. On the other hand, a separate directory system would be a system of records if it contains personal information. A telephone directory, in this context, is a list of names, titles, addresses, telephone numbers, and organizational designations. An agency should not utilize this distinction to avoid the requirements of the Act including the requirement to report the existence of systems of records which it maintains.

"Mailing lists. Whether or not a mailing list is a system of records depends on whether the agency keeps the list as a separate system. Mailing lists derived from records compiled for other purposes (e.g., licensing) would be considered disclosures from that system and would not be systems of records. If the system from which the list is produced is a system of records, the decision on the disclosability of the list would have to be made in terms of subsection (b) (conditions of disclosure) and subsection (n) (the sale or rental of mailing lists). A mailing list may, in some instances, be a stand-alone system (e.g., subscription lists) and could be a system of records subject to the Act if the list is maintained separately by the agency, it consists of records (i.e., contains personal information), and information is retrieved by reference to name or some other identifying particular.

"Libraries. Standard bibliographic materials maintained in agency libraries such as library indexes, Who's Who volumes and similar materials are not considered to be systems of records. This is *not* to suggest that all published material is, by virtue of that fact, not subject to the Act. Collections of newspaper clippings or other published matter about an individual maintained other than in a conventional reference library would normally be a system of records."

2. *Routine Uses—Intra-agency disclosures* (5 U.S.C. 552a(a) (7))

On page 28953, first column, after line 17, add:

"Intra-agency transfer need not be considered routine uses. Earlier versions of House privacy bills, from which the routine use concept derives, permitted agencies to disclose records within the agency to personnel who had a need for such access in the course of their official duties thus permitting intra-agency disclosure without the consent of the individual. The concept of routine use was developed to permit other than intra-agency disclosures after it became apparent that a substantial unnecessary workload would result from having to seek the consent of the subject of a record each time a transfer was made for a purpose '. . . compatible with the purpose for which [the record] was collected' (5 U.S.C. 552a(a) (7)). To deter promiscuous use of this concept, a further provision was added requiring that routine uses be subject to public notice. (5 U.S.C. 552a(e) (11)). It is our view that the concept of routine was devised to cover disclosures other than those to officers or employees who have a need to for the record in the performance of their official duties within the agency.

"It is not necessary, therefore, to include intra-agency transfers in the portion of the system notice covering routine uses (5 U.S.C. 552a(e) (4) (D)) but agencies may, at their option, elect to do so. The portion of the system notice covering storage, retrievability, access controls, retention and disposal (5 U.S.C. 552a(e) (4) (E)) should describe the categories of agency officials who have access to the system."

3. *Consent for access in response to congressional inquiries* (5 U.S.C. 552a(b) (9))

On page 28955, third column, after line 18, add:

To assure that implementation of the Act does not have the unintended effect of denying individuals the benefit of congressional assistance which they request, it is recommended that each agency establish the following as a routine use for all of its systems, consistent with subsections (a) (7) and (e) (11) of the Act:

> Disclosure may be made to a congressional office from the record of an individual in response to an inquiry from the Congressional office made at the request of that individual.

The operation of this routine use will obviate the need for the written consent of the individual in every case where an individual requests assistance of the Member which would entail a disclosure of information pertaining to the individual.

In those cases where the congressional inquiry indicates that the request is being made on behalf of a person other than the individual whose record is to be disclosed, the agency should advise the congressional office that the written consent of the subject of the record is required. The agency should not contact the subject unless the congressional office requests it to do so.

In addition to the routine use, agencies can, of course, respond to many congressional requests for assistance on behalf of individuals without disclosing personal information which would fall within the Privacy Act, e.g., a congressional inquiry concerning a missing Social Security check can be answered by the agency by stating the reason for the delay.

Personal information can be disclosed in response to a congressional inquiry without written consent or operation of a routine use—

If the information would be required to be disclosed under the Freedom of Information Act (Subsection (b) (2));

If the Member requests that the response go directly to the individual to whom the record pertains;

In "compelling circumstances affecting the health or safety of an individual * * *" (Subsection (b) (8)); or

To either House of Congress, or to the extent of matter within its jurisdiction, any committee or subcommittee thereof * * *" (Subsection (b) (9)).

The routine use recommended above and disclosures thereunder are, of course, subject to the 30 day prior notice requirement of the Act (Subsection (e) (11)). In the interim, however, it should be possible to respond to most inquiries by using the provisions cited in the previous paragraph. Furthermore, when the congressional inquiry indicates that the request is being made on the basis of a written request from the individual to whom the record pertains, consent can be inferred even if the constituent letter is not provided to the agency.

"This standard for implied consent does not apply to the other than congressional inquiries."

4. *Describing the purpose in the accounting of disclosures* (Subsection (c) (1))

On page 28956, first column, after line 42, add:

"Agencies which submit inquiries to other agencies in connection with law enforcement or pre-employment investigations (e.g., record checks) are reminded to include the purpose in their record check in order to preclude having record checks returned to them to ascertain the purpose of the check. It is noted that this is necessary whether the inquiry is made pursuant to the subsection (b) (3) or (b) (7) ('routine use' or law enforcement disclosures). At a minimum, the inquiring agency must describe the purpose as either a background or law enforcement check."

5. *Agency procedures for review of appeals of denials of requests to amend a record* (Subsection (d) (3))

On page 28959, second column, after line 39, add:

"This does *not* mean that the officer on appeal must be a justice or judge. Rather, the reviewing official designated by the agency head may be a justice or judge (unlikely in this case) or any other agency official who meets the criteria in 5 U.S.C. 2104a (1), (2), and (3)."

6. *Correcting records released to an individual* (Subsection (e) (6)) ·

On page 28965, second column, after line 6, add:

"While this language requires that agencies make reasonable efforts to assure the accuracy of a record before it is disclosed, when an individual requests access to his or her record, pursuant to subsection (d) (1), above, the record must be disclosed without change or deletion except as permitted by subsections (j) and (k), exemptions. To avoid requiring individuals to file unnecessary requests for amendment, however, the agency should review the record and annotate any material disclosed to indicate that which it intends to amend or delete."

7. *Rights of parents and legal guardians* (Subsection (h))

On page 28970, second column, after line 59, add:

"This is not intended to suggest that minors are precluded from exercising rights on their own behalf. Except as otherwise provided in the Act (e.g., general or specific exemptions) a minor does have the right to access a record pertaining to him or herself. There is no absolute right of a parent to have access to a record about a child absent a court order or consent."

8. *Relationships to the Freedom of Information Act* (Subsection (q))

On page 28978, third column, after the last line, add:

"In some instances under the Privacy Act an agency may (1) exempt a system of records (or a portion thereof) from access by individuals in accordance with the general or specific exemptions (subsection (j) or (k)); or (2) deny a request for access to records compiled in reasonable anticipation of a civil action or proceeding or archival records (subsection (d) (5) or (1)). In a few instances the exemption from disclosure under the Privacy Act may be interpreted to be broader than the Freedom of Information Act (5 U.S.C. 552). In such instances the Privacy Act should not be used to deny access to information about an individual which would otherwise have been *required* to be disclosed to that individual under the Freedom of Information Act.

"Whether a request by an individual for access to his or her record is to be processed under Privacy Act or Freedom of Information Act procedures involves several considerations. For example, while agencies have been encouraged to reply to requests for access under the Privacy Act within ten days wherever practicable, consistent with the Freedom of Information Act (FOIA), the Privacy Act does not establish time limits for responding to requests for access. (See discussion of subsection (d) (1).) The Privacy Act also does not require an administrative appeal on denial of access comparable to that under FOIA although agencies are encouraged to permit individuals to request an administrative review of initial denials of access to avoid, where possible, the need for unnecessary judicial action. It can also be argued that requests filed under the Privacy Act can be expected to be specific as to the system of records to which access is sought whereas agencies are required to respond to an FOIA request only if it 'reasonably describes' the records sought. Further, the Freedom of Information Act permits charging of fees for search as well as the making of copies while the Privacy Act permits charging only for the direct cost of making a copy upon request.

"It is our view that agencies should treat requests by individuals for information pertaining to themselves which specify either the FOIA or the Privacy Act (but not both) under the procedures established pursuant to the Act specified in the request. When the request specifies, and may be processed under, both the FOIA and the Privacy Act, or specifies neither Act, Privacy Act procedures should be employed. The individual should be advised, however, that the agency has elected to use Privacy Act procedures, of the existence and the general effect of the Freedom of Information Act, and of the differences, if any, between the agency's procedures under the two Acts (e.g., fees, time limits, access and appeals).

"The net effect of this approach should be to assure the individuals do not, as a consequence of the Privacy Act, have less access to information pertaining to themselves than they had prior to its enactment."

[FR Doc. 75–32297 Filed 12–3–75; 8:45 am]

GAO Audit of Public Affairs at HEW

Developing Public
Information Campaigns*

I. *Establishing Objectives*
  A. Legitimacy
     Does the organization have the authority to pursue the objectives?
     1. Is the campaign related to the organization's mission? If so, how?
     2. Is the campaign mandated by law?
  B. Specificity
     Are objectives adequately described so that progress toward and achievement of the objectives can be determined?
     1. Are the objectives quantitative?
     2. Are the objectives qualitative?
  C. Relationship with cost and other program objectives.
     1. Have the objectives been developed with adequate knowledge and consideration of program cost and costs associated with the problem?
     2. Have the objectives been developed with adequate knowledge and consideration of other program objectives?
  D. What are the objectives?
     1. Agency recruiting.
     2. To educate and/or modify behavior such as high blood pressure and smoking.
     3. Promotion of government objectives such as pollution control and sale of savings bonds.
     4. To inform or advise such as those eligible for federal assistance.
II. *Planning the Campaign*
  A. Targeting
     1. The more precisely the intended audiences are identified, the better will be the specific messages based on audience knowledge, attitudes and behavior, and media habits. Has the intended audience been adequately determined?
        a. Should the audience be general?
        b. Should the audience be a narrow segment of the population?
        c. Can selected audiences be prioritized?
     2. How was the target audience established?
        a. How was the prevalence of the problem determined?
  B. Timing
     1. What should the lifespan be?
        a. Should the campaign be finite or continuous?
        b. If continuous, at what level of effort?
     2. Have incremental steps or milestones been established?
  C. Budgeting
     1. What is the basis of resource estimates?
        a. Based on budget constraints?
        b. Based on amount of effort needed?
  D. Campaign methods
     1. Is there a strategy developed which specifies a coordinated approach for each segment of the target audience?
     2. Will alternative strategies, concepts, and approaches be presented in the planning stages? If so, how?
     3. What media will be used?
        a. What products will be used for each media?
        b. How has it been determined that the selected media and product will be successful?

---

*As presented in *Difficulties in Evaluating Public Affairs Government-Wide and at the Department of Health, Education, and Welfare*, Report by the Comptroller General of the United States, LCD79–405, January 18, 1979.

    4. What other communication efforts will be used?
       a. Intermediary channels such as community and professional organizations.
       b. Education channels.
    5. Will other interpersonal approaches, such as workshops and seminars, be used?
    6. Have the potential barriers to effectiveness been identified and countermeasures planned?
    7. Is an outside contractor being used to support the campaign? If so, how?
       a. What is the nature and cost of contractor support?
  E. Availability of similar information
    1. Has there been an effort to determine if materials and products are already in existence?
       a. At the National Audio Visual Center?
       b. At the Government Printing Office?
       c. At the Consumer Information Center?
       d. At private organizations?
III. *Monitoring and controlling campaigns*
  A. Is there in-process feedback on the campaign?
  B. Where does control reside?
    1. Public affairs management?
    2. Program management?
IV. *Campaign effectiveness evaluation*
  A. Is there a planned evaluation effort?
    1. What is the nature and extent of the evaluation of goal achievement and adequacy of campaign strategies?
    2. Are any forms of product testing planned?
  B. What are the major external influences and how have they been accounted for?
  C. How is effectiveness evaluation tied into feedback information for campaign control?

Tentative Standards for the Classification and Qualification of Public Affairs Specialists

United States Office of Personnel Management

(This draft of standards for public affairs specialists was revised in 1980 by the Standards Development Center, U.S. Office of Personnel Management. It sets forth the basic classifications and qualifications for public affairs specialists in the U.S. government. This draft was in the process of final approval at the time of publication of this book.)

PUBLIC AFFAIRS SERIES

This series includes positions responsible for communicating with various publics served or affected by Federal agencies. Such positions provide information and educational material concerning agency programs, responsibilities and services to a broad spectrum of individuals and groups. The work also involves obtaining, and analyzing, from interested parties, feedback regarding such information for management consideration in the development of agency programs. Work in this series requires a knowledge of communication methods, principles, techniques and practices, analytical methods and interpersonal relations practices.

This standard supersedes and is to be substituted for the Public Information Series, GS-1081, issued in April 1961.

SERIES COVERAGE

Positions in the Public Affairs Series are primarily concerned with the application of communication knowledges and skills to the establishment and maintenance of meaningful and effective communication channels between Federal agencies and the various publics served or affected by the programs, policies and regulations of those agencies. Such positions work in and support a variety of functional programs. The term functional program refers to the basic objectives of a Federal agency and its operations and activities in achieving them. A functional program may include the entire mission of an agency or any one of many programs administered by the department or agency. Positions in this series require some knowledge of functional programs to carry out the support function of facilitating communication between an agency and its publics on program-related problems and issues.

While the work requires a practical understanding and knowledge of the functional program much of this knowledge is obtained from specialists in functional program areas. This broad functional program knowledge is similar to that found in staff support positions working directly with program managers and specialists. Knowledge about agency functional programs can be acquired through reading agency developed material, interviewing program specialists or reviewing professional or trade publications. The work of this series does not require the depth or breadth of functional program knowledge about the agency's activities that necessitated any previous experience or training in that field. Positions in the Public Affairs Series:

1. develop and disseminate informational and educational materials directly to the general public or specialized target groups and obtain and analyze feedback or input from such sources to provide program management officials with reaction concerning agency programs.

2. provide information of particular value and interest to agency employees including material related to agency programs, policies and information of personal benefit to employees;

3. establish and maintain effective working relationships with representatives of the print and broadcast media and develop and disseminate informational materials to the various publics through the media;

4. organize, plan and direct a public affairs program in a department or agency, or in an organization of a department or agency.

Many positions in the series involve duties in all of these areas. Such positions often are in charge of public affairs programs that, to varying degrees of complexity and scope, require the dissemination of information through the print and broadcast media, communicating with community or specialized groups and provision of information to employees.

Some positions reflect a combination of functions with the specialist either heading up such a program or reporting to a higher-level specialist or management official. Such positions, for example, disseminate information through the various media and analyze input from affected groups or deal with such groups and direct an internal communication program or any combination of such functions.

Other positions include duties restricted to one specific area and employee dealings with specialized groups affected by agency programs or dissemination of information through the print or broadcast media or working exclusively in an internal information program.

EXCLUSIONS

Excluded from this series are positions that primarily:

1. Perform the work essential to an agency's functional programs and require possession of an in-depth knowledge of the program and the processes, methods and principles necessary for the successful performance of the work. Such positions are appropriately assigned to a series where such work is characteristic and program knowledges are required in the qualifications, See, for example, the Home Economics Series, GS-493, Pharmacology Series, GS-405, Environmental Engineering Series GS-819, etc.

2. Write, rewrite, or edit material to be used in several different media. Such positions require skill in adapting style, manner of presentation and format to the requirements of the medium used and needs of the intended audience. Such positions do not require the broad communication knowledges and skills characteristic of the Public Affairs Series, GS-1035. See the Writing and Editing Series, GS-1082.

3. Perform or supervise writing or editing work which requires the application of substantial subject-matter knowledges and the ability to determine the type of presentation best suited to the audiences being addressed. See the Technical Writing and Editing Series, GS-1083.

4. Perform or supervise work involved in communicating information through visual means. These positions require a knowledge of the principles of artistic design and display skill to communicate information through visual materials, and skill to apply these principles to the field of visual communication. See the Visual Information Series, GS-1084.

5. Work with the production of audio-visual materials, requiring skill to plan, organize, and direct the work of writers, actors, set designers, etc., to produce the actions, sounds, or visual effects required for the finished production; or to select and arrange appropriate sequences of action, dialogue, sound effects, visual effects, and music to create an effective finished production. See the Audio-Visual Production Series, GS-1071.

6. Perform editorial support work to prepare manuscripts for publication and verify factual information in such manuscripts. These positions require skill in using reference works to verify information and knowledge of grammar, punctuation, spelling, and good English usage. See the Editorial Assistance series, GS-1087.

7. Advise on, administer, supervise, or perform work in the planning, construction, installation, and operation of exhibits, the preparation of gallery space for exhibits or the restoration or preparation of items to be exhibited. Work requires artistic and technical knowledges and skills and some knowledge of subject-matter concepts conveyed by the exhibits. See the Exhibits Specialist Series, GS-1010.

8. Perform (a) still, motion picture, television, high-speed, aerial, or other similar camera work, or (b) photographic processing work, or (c) a combination of the two. Such positions require, in addition to a knowledge of the equipment, techniques, and processes of photography, either a knowledge about the subject matter to be photographed or artistic skill in taking, processing, printing or retouching prints or both. See the Photography Series, GS-1060.

9. Apply full professional knowledge of the theories, principles, and techniques of education and training in such areas as instruction, guidance counseling, education administration, development or evaluation of curricula, instructional materials and aids, and educational tests and measurements and specialized knowledge of one or more subjects in which the education is given. See the Education and Vocational Training Series, GS-1710.

10. Conduct research in a variety of fields affecting the consumer, requiring basic, academic-type research skills *and* knowledge of a subject matter area such as advertising, industrial food processing and packaging, automotive design and maintenance, etc. Such positions might conduct research in these and similar areas for the possible development of industry or government

standards to protect consumers. See, for example, the Psychology Series, GS-180, Food Technology Series, GS-1382 and Mechanical Engineering Series, GS-830.

11. Represent and advocate a consumer perspective within an agency and participate in the development and review of all agency rules, policies, legislation and programs that impact consumers. In addition to using knowledges and skills characteristic of the Public Affairs Series, these positions also apply substantial knowledge of various subject matter fields. Positions should be analyzed carefully to identify the kind and extent of program knowledges required avoiding a mechanical classification decision based on functional location alone. See the Miscellaneous Administration and Program Series, GS-301.

12. Involve responsibility for administering an agency's Privacy Act and Freedom of Information Act activities. The Privacy Act is concerned with the right of an individual to have withheld from unlimited disclosure, information concerning that person which is contained in a governmental system of records. Under this law, any disclosure of a record about an individual contained in a system of records requires the written consent or request of that individual, unless disclosure of the record falls within a category specified by the law. The Freedom of Information Act deals with the right of the public to have access to information contained in government files except when records fall within any of nine categories of exceptions contained in this act. The administration of these two laws involves a knowledge of the statutes and the case law that has evolved since their enactment. Often, responsibility for this function is located outside the public affairs area and those involved in Freedom of Information Act and Privacy Act matters consult with and rely heavily on the agency's legal counsel on the judicial ramifications of contemplated decisions. This underscores the basic lack of similarity with the Public Affairs Series which requires knowledge in the communication area. See, for example, the Administrative Officer Series, GS-341.

OCCUPATIONAL INFORMATION

Nature of Public Affairs

Many activities engaged in by Federal agencies produce some service or in some way impact a given public. Publics include the general population or a more specialized group such as farmers, women, environmentalists, military personnel, manufacturers, educators, energy producers and so on. In addition, many individuals are simultaneously members of several different publics. For example, a person receiving a social security annuity may also be a supporter of the Smithsonian Institution, a visitor to national parks, cigarette smoker, live close to a military installation, or be in a variety of other specialized groups. Federal agencies, to carry out their missions, communicate with a myriad of publics, in a variety of ways, for many different purposes and in countless settings across the country.

To facilitate their dealings with these publics, Federal agencies establish positions where the primary objective is the establishment of mechanisms for the meaningful interchange of communication between Federal agencies and the various publics served or affected by these agencies. Incumbents of these positions use a variety of communication media, methods and techniques in making known the programs, policies, services and responsibilities of the agencies and obtaining feedback to agency programs from various groups and individuals. This feedback and input serves to guide agency management in developing programs that are more responsive and appropriate in meeting the needs of the publics they serve while still conforming to the legislative and executive mandates establishing the programs.

Structure of Public Affairs Positions

The public affairs function exists throughout the Federal government at all major organizational levels including headquarters, agency, region, command, district and local installation in both domestic and foreign locations and is staffed by public affairs specialists who support a variety of agency program functions such as, defense, regulatory, scientific, arts, education, etc. While the public affairs specialist deals with program specialists and specialized audiences in such areas as, regulation of financial institutions, providing health care to veterans, encouraging fine arts appreciation, international relations, etc., they are not experts in these varied fields. However, through on the job experience they develop a knowledge of the concepts and issues of the subject of agency programs. Although public affairs specialists do acquire a substantial degree of program knowledge, it is their knowledge of the principles, methods, practices and techniques of communication that enables them to facilitate the effective communication between agencies and their various publics.

The diversity of program areas in which public affairs specialists are found and the variety of organizational alignments and structures of the public affairs function among the agencies, produces a wide variability among positions in this series. When viewed from the broader perspective of the primary purpose of the job, positions in this series can be identified with one of the following three categories:

1. Positions that directly inform, familiarize, and obtain feedback from an agency's various publics concerning the programs, policies, services, and regulations. They analyze input from the publics to present feedback to the agency's decision-makers. Such positions are located in functions referred to as public information or education. Characteristic duties include:
   - Arrange and conduct workshops, seminars and other meetings with various organizations to stimulate interest in agency activities and to motivate these groups to conduct similar programs for their membership;
   - Communicate, in person, agency programs and regulations to representatives of local communities, county and State officials to enable them to effectively cope with changes that have a substantial impact on the economic growth and development of their communities;
   - Advise and assist personnel at subordinate echelons and field locations on carrying out community relations activities, furnishing policy guidance, developing directives for policy procedures, and evaluating program effectiveness;
   - Promote and coordinate environmental education in schools throughout a region by developing liaison with officials of schools located near agency so students will use land and water resources under supervision of agency's professional conservation staff;
   - Collect and summarize input from specialized groups or individuals through surveys or group meetings and prepare reports to management on the public's perception of agency programs;
   - Arrange and conduct tour of facility, briefing local, national and international visitors and officials on the function and operation of the organization.

2. Positions that provide information to agency employees concerning programs, staff achievements, awards, and information of personal benefit to employees such as, pay, benefits, retirement, charity appeals, blood drives, etc. Such positions are found in activities known as internal information, internal relations, employee communication or information, command information, etc. Characteristic duties include:
   - Prepare newsletters for distribution to field offices to keep them acquainted with programs at agency headquarters;
   - Direct the facility's internal information program designed for the benefit of the American employees as well as the foreign nationals employed by the organization;
   - Maintain liaison with subordinate organizations' public affairs officers to produce articles, ideas and visuals for use in the headquarters magazine, and to develop recommendations on ways the magazine can better serve the total mission;
   - Brief personnel going overseas as to the customs and conditions in the country of destination;
   - Plan, design and conduct awards and special recognition programs designed to improve employee morale by rewarding outstanding performance and encouraging greater employee productivity;
   - Plan and conduct attitude and opinion surveys among employees to assess worker perception and evaluation of programs, policies, and practices of management and develop recommendations to improve communication;
   - Write and publish in-house newspaper to keep employees informed concerning programs, policies and benefits of personal value to employees.

3. Positions that establish and maintain relationships with representatives of the news media, utilizing methods and techniques of the media, to provide information about agency programs, policies, and services through the print and broadcast media including newspapers, magazines, press releases, fact sheets, radio, television, films, etc. Such operations are referred to as media relations, press relations, etc. Characteristic duties include:
   - Organize and coordinate press, radio and television interviews with staff, and oversee arrangements with media involving organization activities; provide visual and written materials as required;
   - Establish and maintain relations with the national print media, radio and television networks, syndicated columnists, and free lance writers to enlist their cooperation in providing the public with information about benefit programs;
   - Gather information, write, rewrite and edit news releases and other informational materials concerning departmental policies, programs and activities for dissemination to the national news media;

- Advise regional public affairs specialists on most efficient use of print and broadcast media, motion pictures, slide presentations, group meetings, exhibits, etc.;
- Survey mass and specialized media coverage of agency scientific research activities and recommend methods and techniques for disseminating information that will increase public awareness of programs and benefits to the public;
- Plan, initiate, coordinate and review the complete and continuing national radio and television program for the development and dissemination of public service announcements;
- Develop and maintain cooperative working relationships with representatives of foreign print and broadcast media in order to facilitate communication between facility and its foreign national neighbors.

The Communication Process

The communication field is a collection of research findings and writings from a variety of areas including anthropology, mathematics, philosophy, political science, psychology, rhetoric and semantics. Although communication has been conceived and described in a number of different ways, most practitioners agree that the process involves certain common elements. These elements include:

1) sender—an individual who seeks to affect the behavior of another person through communication.

2) message—the content of communication expressed as symbols representing ideas and an intended meaning.

3) medium—the means through which a message is sent.

4) receiver—one for whom a message is intended and who assigns meaning to it.

5) feedback—signals sent back to the sender by receiver which permit the sender to evaluate the effect of the message on the receiver.

The basic principles of communication such as the one just described, namely, that the process of communication exhibits common elements or that human attention is highly selective or that active participation in the process increases the likelihood of inducing changes in the receiver's behavior, all serve as part of the foundation for the development of methods to achieve communication goals or objectives.

The methods of communication represent the ways or rules by which messages are constructed or transmitted to achieve the accurate reception of an intended meaning. For example, to increase the probability that the correct meaning will be apprehended by a receiver, the sender uses a variety of methods to facilitate understanding on the part of the receiver by emphasizing key ideas. Methods of achieving this emphasis are to direct attention to ideas that have been discussed, to announce ideas that will be developed later and to intensify the impact of ideas currently being expressed. The sender may use any one of these methods, combine various aspects of the methods or use all three depending on the nature of the message or the audience.

Techniques are specialized procedures or mechanics used in carrying out methods. For example, to intensify the impact of an idea being presented, a sender, in an oral presentation, uses techniques such as gestures, movements or vocal inflections to emphasize a key idea. In written communication, emphasis may be achieved through such techniques as underscoring, use of examples or quotations or vivid metaphors.

The practices of communication refer to the application of the knowledges, methods and techniques of the field to actual situations. Examples include the delivery of a speech to an audience, conveying information through the presentation of ideas in a seminar or workshop, or writing a feature story for a magazine, a script for a radio interview or a brochure announcing a new program, product or service.

Communication Modes

Public affairs specialists use a variety of communication modes in carrying out their mission to inform agency publics about the programs, policies, services, etc. that are of interest to or affect various groups or individuals. Included are:

Mode	Vehicle
Written	Press release, fact sheet, press kit, written response to press or public inquiry, feature articles, pamphlets, newsletters, magazines
Oral	Television, radio, audio tapes

Visual   Photographs, films, slides, video tapes

Personal   Interviews, briefings, seminars, hearings, tours, awards ceremonies, speeches, workshops, news conferences, discussions.

TITLES

Public Affairs Specialist is the basic title authorized for all positions in this series. Positions which meet or exceed the criteria in the Supervisory Grade-Evaluation Guide for evaluation as a supervisor are titled Supervisory Public Affairs Specialist.

GRADING OF POSITIONS

The grade level criteria contained in this standard are applicable to all non-supervisory positions at grades GS-5 through GS-15 in the Public Affairs Series. Supervisory positions should be evaluated by reference to the Supervisory Grade-Evaluation Guide.

Positions should be evaluated on a factor-by-factor basis, using one or more of the comparable Office of Personnel Management benchmarks or factor level descriptions, or both, for the Public Affairs Series. Only the designated point values may be used. More complete instructions for evaluating positions are contained in the Instructions for the Factor Evaluation System.

This standard includes benchmarks for typical non-supervisory positions GS-9 through GS-14. The absence of a benchmark for positions at any grade from GS-5 to GS-15 does not preclude evaluation of positions at that grade.

GRADE CONVERSION TABLE

Total points on all evaluation factors are converted to GS grades as follows:

Point Range	Grade
855–1100	GS-5
1105–1350	GS-6
1355–1600	GS-7
1605–1850	GS-8
1855–2100	GS-9
2105–2350	GS-10
2355–2750	GS-11
2755–3150	GS-12
3155–3600	GS-13
3605–4050	GS-14
4055–up	GS-15

QUALIFICATIONS REQUIRED

Although there is a wide variability among positions in the Public Affairs Series, there are certain basic qualification requirements applicable to these types of positions. The requirements described below are found at various grade levels throughout the series.

—Written communication skill

- Skill in producing written information so that an intended audience understands the material.
- Skill in producing written information for audiences with different levels of understanding.
- Skill in producing written material to gain acceptance of various points of view by others.
- Skill in producing written material to gain acceptance among audiences with varying levels of comprehension of and resistance to material presented.

—Oral communication skill

- Skill in transmitting information by spoken word so that the intended audience comprehends the presentation.
- Skill in transmitting information by spoken word to audiences with differing levels of comprehension.
- Skill in presenting concepts orally to gain acceptance of a point of view in a structured setting.
- Skill in defending points of view in an unstructured setting.

—Interpersonal relations skill
  • Skill in interacting with others and avoiding offense in dealing with people.
  • Skill in working with people having similar interests to attain mutually positive ends.
  • Skill in establishing and maintaining effective working relationships with people having different interests.
  • Skill in establishing and maintaining effective working relationships with others representing opposing points of view and conflicting interests.

—Analytical skill
  • Skill in interpreting data to arrive at valid conclusions.
  • Skill in gathering, evaluating and interpreting complex data.
  • Skill in drawing appropriate conclusions from varied and complex data including identifying sources of information.
  • Skill in drawing appropriate conclusions from conflicting data including determining what kinds of information are needed and ways of collecting data.

Since the Public Affairs Series covers a broad and varied spectrum of positions some may require specialized knowledges and skills not identified in these qualifications. In appropriate cases, selective factors may be constructed by agencies to indicate those knowledges and skills considered *essential* to produce a list of eligibles qualified to perform the duties of the position satisfactorily. The selective factors for a position should represent the *basic* qualifications for the job and must be demonstrably job-related and reflected in the duties and responsibilities assigned to the position. Selective factors must represent knowledges or skills required of a candidate at the time of entry into a position or those which could not be learned during a reasonable probationary period.

QUALIFICATION STANDARD

Public Affairs Series

Public Affairs Specialist, GS-5/15

DESCRIPTION OF WORK

This series includes positions responsible for communicating with various publics served or affected by Federal agencies. Such positions provide informational and educational material concerning agency programs, responsibilities and services to a broad spectrum of individuals and groups. The work also involves obtaining, and analyzing, from interested parties, feedback regarding such information for management consideration in the development of agency programs. Work in this series requires a knowledge of communication principles, methods, practices and techniques, analytical methods and interpersonal relations practices.

For further information about the nature of work performed by employees in the Public Affairs Series, see the position classification standard. The criteria in the classification standard, and especially the benchmark descriptions, should prove helpful in evaluating the level of experience a candidate has gained outside of the Federal government, or in any other position outside of the General Schedule.

MINIMUM EXPERIENCE REQUIREMENTS

Minimum time requirements have been established for this series. This minimum experience requirement insures that an applicant will have had a period of time to both develop and demonstrate the required knowledges and skills of a position. The requirement also provides the employing agency with minimum assurance that the candidate can perform the work of the position. It further provides each applicant with an equal amount of time to demonstrate possession of the required knowledges and skills.

Minimum requirements for the various grade levels in this series are presented in tabular format as indicated below:

Grade Level	Requirements
GS-5	Table 1
GS-7	Table 1
GS-9	Table 2
GS-11	Table 3
GS-12 and above	Table 4

NOTE: The tables identified above present the requirements for this series in terms of the skills required to perform the work of the level indicated. While the requirements are depicted as skills in four distinct areas, the underlying knowledge to practice the skill is presumed to exist and is inferred, along with the skill, from the examples shown in the tables.

SELECTIVE AND QUALITY RANKING FACTORS

The Public Affairs Series covers a broad and varied spectrum of positions some of which may require specialized knowledges and skills not identified in this standard. In appropriate cases, selective factors may be constructed by agencies to indicate those knowledges and skills considered *essential* to produce a list of eligibles qualified to perform the duties of the position satisfactorily. The selective factors requested for a position should represent the *basic* qualifications for the job and must be demonstrably job-related and reflected in the duties and responsibilities assigned to the position. Selective factors must represent knowledges or skills required of a candidate at the time of entry into a position or those which could not be learned during a reasonable probationary period. Examples of selective factors that may be required in public affairs positions, at any grade level, include a requirement for fluency in Spanish, German, Japanese or other foreign language.

For some positions in this series, especially at the GS-9 and above levels, agencies may request the use of specific quality ranking factors to identify the *better qualified* candidates from a group of persons basically qualified for a position. Properly identified and justifiable quality ranking factors should present a qualifications pattern which would most likely assure superior performance in a position. Quality ranking factors must also be directly related to the duties and responsibilities of the position and shown to be predictive of superior performance. Examples of quality ranking factors may include subject matter program knowledge, experience with a given aspect of the work such as in a particular medium or experience working with a specialized group.

Additional guidance concerning the evaluation and documentation of selective and quality ranking factors is provided in FPM Chapter 332, Subchapter 4 and Appendix B.

PHYSICAL REQUIREMENTS—ALL LEVELS

Applicants must be physically and mentally able to efficiently perform the essential functions of the position without hazard to themselves or others. Depending on the essential duties of a specific position, usable vision, hearing, or speech may be required. However, in most cases, a specific physical condition or impairment will not automatically disqualify an applicant for appointment. The loss or impairment of a specific function may be compensated for by the satisfactory use of a prosthesis or mechanical aid. Reasonable accommodation may also be considered in determining an applicant's ability to perform the duties of a position. Reasonable accommodation may include, but is not limited to: the use of assistive devices, job modification or restructuring, provision of readers and interpreters, or adjusted work schedules.

SUPERVISORY POSITIONS

Use the qualification standard for "Supervisory Positions in General Schedule Occupations" in Part II of handbook X-118 in conjunction with this statement.

BASIS OF RATING

All candidates will be rated on a scale of 100. The basis of rating will be an evaluation of the candidate's experience, education, and training in relation to the duties of the position to be filled. Work or volunteer experience and relevant course work above the minimum required for a particular position at a particular grade level will be considered in ranking qualified applicants based on the relatedness of the work or volunteer experience or courses to the position's required knowledges and skills. Rating will be based on statements in the application form, any supplemental information forms, and any additional evidence received. A written test is not required.

Table 1.   Requirements for GS-5/7.

Applicants for GS-5 positions must meet the requirements of A, B, or C below:

A. Three years of experience in an occupational field where the work required demonstrated possession of the skill necessary to learn and perform the work characteristic of this series.   OR

B. Successful completion of a full 4 year course in an accredited college or university leading to a bachelor's degree in any field.   OR

C. Any equivalent combination of experience and education defined in A and B. In combining education with experience, an academic year of study is considered equivalent to 9 months of experience.

The total creditable experience, education or combination described in A, B or C above *must* indicate possession of the following skills:

Written Communication Skill	Oral Communication Skill	Interpersonal Relations Skill	Analytical Skill
This requires skill in imparting factual information in writing. It involves producing written information so that the intended audience understands the material presented.	This requires skill in conveying information orally. It involves transmitting information by spoken word so that the intended audience understands the presentation.	This requires skill in dealing with people effectively. It includes avoiding offense in interacting with others.	This requires skill in interpreting data to arrive at conclusions.
This skill may be indicated by:	This skill may be indicated by:	This skill may be indicated by:	This skill may be indicated by:
a. work experience that required writing narrative reports;	a. work experience that required oral expression such as handling customer complaints;	a. work experience that required working closely with people such as customer relations representative;	a. work experience that involved any kind of investigative or similar duties that required analysis of data;
b. successful completion of a college course that required a final paper as part of the requirements;	b. successful completion of an undergraduate course in speech or public speaking or similar courses; or	b. successful completion of undergraduate courses such as counseling, contract negotiation or similar courses; or	b. successful completion of an undergraduate course covering techniques for data collection and analysis; or
c. successful completion of an undergraduate course in journalism, radio and television writing or similar courses; or	c. other equivalent demonstration of oral communication skill.	c. other equivalent demonstration of interpersonal relations skill.	c. other equivalent demonstration of analytical skill.
d. other equivalent demonstration of written communication skill.			

Applicants for GS-7 positions must meet the requirements of A, B or C below:

A. One year of satisfactory performance in a GS-5 or equivalent position that is closely related to the position being filled.   OR

B. Superior academic achievement as defined in Part II, Section II of Handbook X-118.   OR

C. One full year of graduate education in a field directly related to the position being filled such as journalism, communication, creative writing or other similarly related areas.

The total creditable experience or education described in A, B or C above *must* indicate possession of all of the skills required for GS-5 above. However, possession of higher levels of these skills will have been more clearly demonstrated by concrete work accomplishments, post-graduate education achievement or unusual scholarship.

Table 2. Requirements for GS-9.

Applicants for GS-9 positions must meet requirements of A or B below:

A. One year of satisfactory performance in a GS-7 or equivalent position that is closely related to the position being filled.

OR

B. Two full academic years of graduate education or completion of all requirements for a master's or equivalent degree in a field directly related to the position being filled such as journalism, creative writing, communication or other similarly related area.

The total creditable experience or education described in A or B above *must* indicate possession of the following skills:

Written Communication Skill	Oral Communication Skill	Interpersonal Relations Skill	Analytical Skill
This requires skill in imparting complex information in writing using a variety of formats. It includes producing written information for audiences with different levels of understanding so that all types of audiences understand the material.	This requires skill in conveying complex information orally using a variety of presentation methods. It includes transmitting information by spoken word to audiences with differing levels of understanding so that all types of audiences understand the material.	This requires skill in working with people having similar interests to attain mutually positive ends in an effective manner. It includes maintaining such relationships and dealing with potentially unpleasant situations in a manner such as not to produce antagonism.	This requires skill in drawing appropriate conclusions from complex information. It includes determining the sources of information, gathering, evaluating and interpreting data to arrive at conclusions.
This skill may be indicated by:	This skill may be indicated by:	This skill may be indicated by:	This skill may be indicated by:
a. work experience that involved various writing assignments using various formats such as news reporter, magazine writer, etc.;	a. work experience requiring considerable oral expression such as personnel recruiting;	a. work experience that required working with others to accomplish a goal such as working as a project team member or caseworker;	a. work experience that required analysis of complex or involved data such as computer systems analysis or management analysis;
b. undergraduate majors in journalism, communication, or related areas;	b. undergraduate major in speech;	b. undergraduate major in counseling or similarly related areas;	b. undergraduate major in physical or social science;
c. graduate courses in journalism, radio and television writing, etc.; or	c. experience on a college debating team; or	c. graduate courses in counseling, social work, arbitration social work, arbitration, or similarly related courses; or	c. graduate course in research design and methodology; or
d. other equivalent demonstration of such written communication skill.	d. other equivalent demonstration of oral communication skill.	d. other equivalent demonstration of interpersonal relations skill.	d. other equivalent demonstration of analytical skill.

Table 3.   Requirements for GS-11

Applicants for GS-11 positions must have at least one year of experience at the GS-9 or equivalent level performing work similar to that of the position being filled. This experience *must* indicate possession of the following skills:

Written Communication Skill	Oral Communication Skill	Interpersonal Relations Skill	Analytical Skill
This requires skill in producing written material to gain acceptance of various points of view by others. It includes the development of stated strategies to present concepts, ideas or positions in a logical and persuasive manner so that audiences with varying levels of understanding accept the material presented.	This requires skill in presenting concepts or positions orally to gain acceptance of a point of view. It includes developing and transmitting concepts, ideas and positions in a logical and persuasive manner, in a structured setting, so that audiences with varying levels of understanding comprehend and accept the views presented.	This requires skill in establishing and maintaining effective working relationships with people having different interests. It includes working with others having different interests and perspectives in attaining a mutually beneficial objective and advocating a position, or point of view despite opposition.	This requires skill in drawing appropriate conclusions from varied and complex data. It includes identifying sources of data useful in problem solving situations, employing information gathering techniques and evaluating, interpreting and synthesizing information to arrive at conclusions and develop basic recommendations.
This skill may be indicated by: work experience involving the writing of materials to convince others to follow a certain course or accept a concept such as in editorial writing; preparing articles, brochures, and the like to persuade people to practice a certain health regimen; or other similarly related experience.	This skill may be indicated by: work experience that involved persuading others to accept certain information as valid which was performed in a formal or clearly structured setting as in classroom teaching or conducting training courses or community organizing activities; or other similarly related experience.	This skill may be indicated by: work experience that involved performing staff consulting duties to a line function such as in position classification; management analysis; quality assurance; or other similarly related experience where the applicant used this skill to convince others of the benefit of the services provided.	This skill may be indicated by: work experience in any of a number of staff positions which required analyzing basic functions and suggesting ways to improve operation such as management analysis; computer systems analysis; or other similarly related experience.

Table 4. Requirements for GS-12 and above.

Applicants for GS-12 positions must have at least one year of experience at the GS-11 or equivalent level performing work similar to that of the position being filled. This experience *must* indicate possession of the following skills:

Written Communication Skill	Oral Communication Skill	Interpersonal Relations Skill	Analytical Skill
This requires skill in creating written materials using many modes to gain acceptance of a point of view. It includes the origination and full development of concepts and strategies or plans for presenting a wide variety of subjects using multi-communication techniques in such a manner so as to gain acceptance among audiences with varying levels of comprehension of and resistance to the material presented.	This requires skill in defending points of view in an unstructured setting. It includes making impromptu presentations to audiences with opposing points of view and to continue to adhere to a position and defend it rationally and effectively.	This requires skill in dealing with people having conflicting interests and points of view. It includes establishing and maintaining effective working relationships with others representing opposing points of view and conflicting interests; achieving moderation of opposing views to produce realistic compromise; or to mediate group differences to arrive at a conclusion acceptable to all.	This requires skill in drawing appropriate conclusions from conflicting data. It includes determining what kinds of information are needed and developing new and specific ways of gathering, collecting and evaluating the data and presenting conclusions and recommendations giving consideration to the various conflicting information and specifying reasons for acceptance or rejection.
This skill may be indicated by: work experience involving the development of multi-media campaigns such as in institutional advertising where the duties included furnishing information about the social or economic values that the institution fosters and the importance of its activities to the nation; or similarly related experience.	This skill may be indicated by: work experience that required developing on the spot presentations to counter a criticism or charge by others in an adversary position such as in positions serving as spokespersons at news conferences for organizations; contract negotiating; or other similarly related experience.	This skill may be indicated by: work experience that involved performing enforcement or compliance duties where violators resisted and strenuously defended their positions and the applicant relied on tact and persuasion to lead persons responsible for noncompliance activities to make efforts to correct the situation; or other similarly related experience.	This skill may be indicated by: work experience in any of the social or physical sciences that involved performing research on a variety of topics; investigating work that required uncovering a large number of conflicting facts and making a judgment as to their validity and drawing conclusions from them; or other similarly related experience.

Selected Bibliography

Ackerly, Robert L., and William J. Spriggs. *Freedom of Information: Course Manual.* Washington: Federal Publications, Inc., 1979.

American Historical Association. *Access to government documents, papers presented to a session of the American Historical Association,* Dec. 1972. Manhattan, Kansas: Military Affairs, 1974.

Anderson, David A., and Brandon C. Janes, eds. *Privacy and public disclosures under the Freedom of Information Act.* Austin, Texas: Tarlton Law Library, University of Texas School of Law, 1976.

Anderson, Jack. *The Anderson Papers.* New York: Ballantine Books, 1974.

Anon., *America's Need to Know.* New York: Magazine Publishers Association, 1973.

Anon., *The First Amendment and the News Media.* Cambridge, Mass.: Roscoe Pound-American Trial Lawyers Foundation, 1973.

Archibald, Samuel J., *The Pollution of Politics.* Washington, D.C.: Public Affairs Press, 1971.

Bagdikian, Ben H. *The Effete Conspiracy and Other Crimes by the Press.* New York: Harper & Row, 1972.

Balk, Alfred. *A Free and Responsive Press* (a background paper on a national news council). New York: Twentieth Century Fund, 1973.

Ball, Howard. *No Pledge of Privacy.* Port Washington, N.Y.: Kennikat Press, 1977.

Barker, Carol M., and Matthew H. Fox. *Classified Files: The Yellowing Pages* (a report on scholars' access to government documents). New York: Twentieth Century Fund, 1972.

Barnds, William J. *The Right to Know, to Withhold, and to Lie.* New York: The Council on Religion and International Affairs, 1969.

Barrett, Marvin. *The Politics of Broadcasting.* New York: Crowell, 1973.

Berdes, George R. *Friendly Adversaries: The Press and Government.* Milwaukee, Wisconsin: Marquette University Press, 1969.

Berg, Richard K., and Stephen H. Klitzman. *An Interpretive Guide to the Government in the Sunshine Act.* Washington: U.S. Government Printing Office, 1978.

Berger, Raoul. *Executive Privilege: A Constitutional Myth.* Cambridge, Mass.: Harvard University Press, 1974.

Bloom, Melvin H. *Public Relations and Presidential Campaigns: A Crisis in Democracy.* New York, Crowell, 1973.

Bok, Sissela. *Lying: Moral Choice in Public and Private Life.* New York, Pantheon Books, 1978.

Breckenridge, Adam Carlyle. *The Executive Privilege: Presidential Control over Information.* Lincoln: University of Nebraska Press, 1974.

Bushkin, Arthur A., and Samuel I. Schaen. *The Privacy Act of 1974: A Reference Manual for Compliance.* McLean, Va.: System Development Corp., 1976.

Chafee, Zecharia, Jr. *Government and Mass Communications* (A Report from the Commission on Freedom of the Press). Chicago: University of Chicago Press, 1947.

Chief Justice Earl Warren Conference on Advocacy in the United States, Cambridge, Mass., 1974. *Privacy in a Free Society: Final Report.* Cambridge, Mass., Rosco Pound-American Trial Lawyers Foundation, 1974.

Chittick, William O. *State Department, Press and Pressure Groups.* New York: Wiley, 1970.

Clark, David G., and Earl R. Hutchinson. *Mass Media and the Law.* New York: Wiley, 1970.

Cohen, Bernard C. *The Press and Foreign Policy.* Princeton, N.J.: Princeton University Press, 1963.

Cox, Arthur Macy. *The Myths of National Security.* Boston: Beacon Press, 1975.

Cross, Harold L. *The People's Right to Know—Legal Access to Public Records and Proceedings.* Morningside Heights, New York: Columbia University Press, 1953.

Crouse, Timothy. *The Boys on the Bus: Riding with the Campaign Press Corps.* New York: Random House, 1973.

Cutlip, Scott, and Allen Center. *Effective Public Relations*, 5th ed. Englewood Cliffs, N.J.: Prentice-Hall, 1978.

Devol, Kenneth S. *Mass Media and the Supreme Court (The Legacy of the Warren Years)*. New York: Hastings House, 1971.

Dorsen, Norman, and Stephen Gillers, eds. *Government Secrecy in America: None of Your Business*. New York: Viking, 1974.

Dunn, Delmer D. *Public Officials and the Press*. Reading, Mass: Addison-Wesley Publishing Company, 1969.

Emery, Walter B. *Broadcasting and Government: Responsibilities and Regulations*. East Lansing: Michigan State University Press, 1971.

Essays on Executive Privilege. Chicago: American Bar Foundation, 1974.

Fixx, James F. *The Mass Media and Politics (The Great Contemporary Issues from the New York Times)*. New York: Arno Press, 1972.

Franck, Thomas M., and Edward Weisband, eds. *Secrecy and Foreign Policy*. New York. Oxford University Press, 1974.

Galnoor, Tizhak, ed. *Government Secrecy in Democracies*. New York: New York University Press, 1977.

Gilbert, Robert E. *Television and Presidential Politics*. N. Quincy, Mass: Christopher Publishing House, 1972.

Gilbert, William H. *Public Relations in Local Government*. Washington, D.C.: International City Management Association, 1975.

Goulding, Phil G. *Confirm or Deny: Informing the People on National Security*. New York: Harper & Row, 1970.

Graebner, Norman A. *The Records of Public Officials*. New York: The American Assembly, Columbia University, 1975.

Guido, Kenneth J., Jr. *The Right of the House Judiciary Committee to All Presidential Documents It Deems Necessary for Its Impeachment Inquiry*. Washington: Common Cause, 1974.

Halperin, Morton H., and Daniel Hoffmann. *Freedom vs. National Security*. New York: Chelsea House Publishers, 1977.

Hamby, Alonzo, and Edward Weldom, eds. *Access to the Papers of Recent Public Figures: The New Harmony Conference*. Bloomington: Organization of American Historians, 1977.

Hess, Stephen. *The Presidential Campaign: The Leadership Selection Process after Watergate*. Washington D.C.: The Brookings Institution, 1974.

Hiebert, Ray Eldon. *The Press in Washington*. New York: Dodd, Mead, 1966.

Hiebert, Ray Eldon, et al. *Political Image Merchants*. Washington, D.C.: Acropolis, 1971, 1975.

Hiebert, Ray Eldon, and Carlton E. Spitzer. *The Voice of Government*. New York: Wiley, 1968.

IPI Survey. *Government Pressures on the Press*. Zurich: International Press Institute, 1955.

IPI Survey. *The Press in Authoritarian Countries*. Zurich: International Press Institute, 1959.

Irvine, Dallas. *The Origin of Defense-Information Markings in the Army and Former War Department*. Washington: National Archives and Records Service, General Services Administration, 1964.

Kail, F. M. *What Washington Said: American Rhetoric and the Vietnam War: 1949–1969*. New York: Harper & Row, 1973.

Kelley, Stanley, Jr. *Professional Public Relations and Political Power*. Baltimore: Johns Hopkins University Press, 1956.

Keogh, James. *President Nixon and the Press*. New York: Funk & Wagnalls, 1972.

Knappman, Edward W. *Government and the Media in Conflict, 1970–74*. New York: Facts on File, 1974.

Kotler, Philip. *Marketing for Non-Profit Organizations*. Englewood Cliffs, N.J.: Prentice-Hall, 1975.

Krasnow, Erwin G., and Lawrence D. Longley. *The Politics of Broadcast Regulations*. New York: St. Martin's Press, 1973.

Ladd, Bruce. *Crisis in Credibility: An Investigation into Secrecy and Deceit in the U.S. Government*. New York: New American Library, 1968.

Lee, John. *Diplomatic Persuaders (New Role of Mass Media in International Relations)*. New York: Wiley, 1968.

Lee, Richard W. *Politics and the Press*. Washington, D.C.: Acropolis Books, 1970.

Levenson, Alan B., and Harvey L. Pitt. *Government Information: Freedom of Information Act, Sunshine Act, Privacy Act*. New York: Practicing Law Institute, 1978.

Marwick, Christine, ed. *Litigation Under the Amended Federal Freedom of Information Act*, 5th ed. Washington: The Center for National Security Studies, 1979.

McGinniss, Joe. *The Selling of the President 1968*. New York: Trident Press, 1969.

Merritt, LeRoy Charles. *The United States Government as Publisher*. Chicago: The University of Chicago Press, 1943.

Mezines, Basil J., Jacob A. Stein, and Jules Gruff. *Administrative Law: Acquisition, Use and Disclosure of Government Information; Freedom of Information, Privacy, Sunshine, and Related Acts*, vol. 2. New York: Matthew Bender & Co., 1977.

Mickelson, Sig. *The Electric Mirror: Politics in an Age of Television*. New York: Dodd, Mead, 1972.

Minor, Dale. *The Information War (How the Government and the Press Manipulate, Censor and Distort the News)*. New York: Hawthorn Books, 1970.

Minow, Newton, John Bartlow Martin, and Lee M. Mitchell. *Presidential Television*. New York: Basic Books, 1973.

Mollenhoff, Clark R. *Washington Cover-Up (How Bureaucratic Secrecy Promotes Corruption and Waste in the Government)*. New York: Doubleday, 1962.

Morehead, Joe. *Introduction to United States Public Documents*. Littleton, Colo.: Libraries Unlimited, 1975.

Mueller, Claus. *The Politics of Communication*. New York: Oxford University Press, 1973.

Nelson, Anna Kasten, ed. *The Records of Federal Officials: A Selection of Materials from the National Study Commission on Records and Documents of Federal Officials*. New York: Garland Publishing, Inc. 1978.

Nimmo, Dan D. *Newsgathering in Washington*. New York: Atherton Press, 1964.

Nimmo, Dan D. *The Political Persuaders (The Techniques of Modern Election Campaigns)*. Englewood Cliffs, N.J.: Prentice-Hall, 1970.

O'Reilly, James T. *Federal Information Disclosure: Procedures, Forms, and the Law*, 2 vols. Colorado Springs, Colo: Shepard's Inc. and New York: McGraw-Hill, 1978.

Orman, John M. *Secrecy, Accountability and Presidential Power: The Case of Gerald R. Ford*. Prepared for delivery at the 1977 annual meeting of the Midwest Political Science Association. The Pick-Congress Hotel, Chicago, Illinois, April 21–23, 1977.

Perry, James M. *The New Politics (The Expanding Technology of Political Manipulation)*. New York: Clarkson N. Potter, 1968.

Perry, James M. *Us & Them: How the Press Covered the 1972 Election*. New York: Clarkson N. Potter, 1973.

Pimlott, J.A.R. *Public Relations and American Democracy*. Princeton, N.J.: Princeton University Press, 1951.

Pollard, James E. *The Presidents and the Press: Truman to Johnson*. Washington, D.C.: Public Affairs Press, 1964.

Reston, James. *The Artillery of the Press*. New York: Harper & Row, 1966.

Revel, Jean-Francois. *Without Marx or Jesus: The New American Revolution Has Begun*. New York: Doubleday, 1970.

Rivers, William. *The Adversaries: Politics and the Press*. Boston: Beacon Press, 1970.

Rivers, William. *The Opinion Makers*. Boston: Beacon Press, 1965.

Rivers, William, and Michael Nyhan. *Aspen Notebook on Government and the Media*. New York: Praeger, 1973.

Roll, Charles W., Jr., and Albert H. Cantril. *Polls: Their Use and Misuse in Politics*. New York: Basic Books, 1972.

Rourke, Francis E. *Secrecy and Publicity: Dilemmas of Democracy*. Baltimore: Johns Hopkins University Press, 1961.

Rubin, Bernard. *Political Television*. Belmont, Ca.: Wadsworth Publishing Company, 1967.

Schiller, Herbert I. *Mass Communications and American Empire*. Boston: Beacon Press, 1971.

Schmeckebier, Laurence F., and Roy B. Eastin. *Government Publications and Their Use*, 2d. rev. ed. Washington: The Brookings Institution, 1969.

Schrag, Peter. *Test of Loyalty*. New York: Simon & Schuster, 1974.

Seymour-Ure, Colin. *The Political Impact of Mass Media*. Beverly Hills, Ca.: Sage Publications, 1974.

Shapiro, Martin, ed. *The Pentagon Papers and the Courts*. San Francisco: Chandler Publishing Company, 1972.

Sherick, L. G. *How to Use the Freedom of Information Act (FOIA)*. New York: Arco Publishing Company, 1978.

Shils, Edward A. *The Torment of Secrecy: The Background and Consequences of American Security Policies*. Glencoe, Ill.: Free Press of Glencoe, 1956.

Siebert, Fred S., Theodore Peterson, and Wilbur Schramm. *Four Theories of the Press*. Urbana: University of Illinois, 1956.

Sigal, Leon. *Reporters and Officials: The Organization and Politics of Newsmaking*. Lexington, Mass.: D.C. Heath, 1973.

Small, William J. *Political Power and the Press*. New York: W.W. Norton, 1972.

Small, William. *To Kill a Messenger: Television News and the Real World*. New York: Hastings House, 1970.

Sofaer, Abraham D. *War, Foreign Affairs, and Constitutional Power*. Cambridge, Mass.: Ballinger Publishing Co., 1976.

Steele, Fritz. *The Open Organizations: The Impact of Secrecy and Disclosure on People and Organizations*. Reading: Addison-Wesley, 1975.

Smith, Robert Ellis. *Privacy: How to Protect What's Left of It*. Garden City, N.Y.: Anchor Press/Doubleday, 1979.

Summers, Robert E. *Federal Information Controls in Peacetime*. New York: The H.W. Wilson Company, 1949.

Thomson, Charles A.H. *Television and Presidential Politics*. Washington, D.C.: The Brookings Institution, 1956.

Twentieth Century Fund Task Force. *Press Freedoms Under Pressure*. New York: Twentieth Century Fund, 1972.

Ungar, Sanford J. *The Papers and the Papers: An Account of the Legal and Political Battle over the Pentagon Papers*. New York, E.P. Dutton, 1972.

Whalen, Charles W., Jr. *Your Right to Know (How the Free Flow of News Depends Upon the Journalist's Right to Protect His Sources)*. New York: Random House, 1973.

Wiggins, James Russell. *Freedom or Secrecy*, rev. ed. New York: Oxford University Press, 1964.

Wise, David. *The Politics of Lying: Government Deception, Secrecy and Power*. New York: Random House, 1973.

Woodward, Robert, and Carl Bernstein. *All the President's Men*. New York: Simon & Schuster, 1974.

Wolfson, Lewis W., and James McCartney. *The Press Cover's Government: The Nixon Years from 1969 to Watergate*. Washington, D.C.: American University, no date.

Index